BALOCHISTAN, THE BRITISH AND THE GREAT GAME

T. A. HEATHCOTE

Balochistan, the British and the Great Game

The Struggle for the Bolan Pass, Gateway to India

HURST & COMPANY, LONDON

First published in the United Kingdom in 2015 by
C. Hurst & Co. (Publishers) Ltd.,
41 Great Russell Street, London, WC1B 3PL
© T. A. Heathcote, 2015
All rights reserved.

Printed in India

Distributed in the United States, Canada and Latin America by
Oxford University Press, 198 Madison Avenue, New York, NY 10016,
United States of America.

A Cataloguing-in-Publication data record for this book is available
from the British Library.

978-1-84904-479-0 *hardback*

This book is printed using paper from registered sustainable
and managed sources.

www.hurstpublishers.com

Potentates such as the Khan of Khelat or the Ameer of Kabul are mere dummies or counters, which would be of no importance to us, were it not for the costly stakes we put on them, in the great game for empire we are now playing with Russia

Private letter from Edward Robert Bulwer Lytton, 2nd Baron Lytton of Knebworth, Viceroy and Governor-General of India, to Major Robert Sandeman, Deputy Commissioner of Dera Ghazi Khan, head of the British Mission to Kalat, Balochistan, 29 September 1876.

Lytton Papers 518/1 (Letters dispatched 1876), India Office Collections, British Library

CONTENTS

PREFACE

At the time of this writing, Balochistan, which means 'the country of the Baloch people', is the name both of the westernmost and largest of the four provinces of the Islamic Republic of Pakistan and, when coupled with Sistan, of the easternmost and poorest of the thirty provinces of the Islamic Republic of Iran. This book is mostly concerned with the history of what is now Pakistani Balochistan, a region forming 43 per cent of that state's land mass and containing most of its mineral resources but only 5 per cent of its population. Covering an area of about 134,000 square miles (comparable with the 138,000 of present-day Germany), it is bounded in the south by the Arabian Sea, in the west by Iran, in the north by the Islamic Republic of Afghanistan, and in the east by the mountains and deserts that separate it from the rest of Pakistan. The Balochistan coastline comprises 75 per cent of Pakistan's entire sea-board and stretches along the Arabian Sea for almost 500 miles, from Cape Monze (Ras Muari) near Karachi in the east, to the Iranian border near the mouth of the Dasht River in the west. Though mostly shallow, this coast has since December 2006 seen the the ancient harbour of Gwadur become, with the aid of the Chinese People's Republic, a deep-water seaport suitable for bulk cargo carriers and, potentially, major warships. The primary strategic highway in Balochistan continues to be that through the Bolan Pass, the historic route between the lower Indus valley and southern Afghanistan. Though from its extremes of climate and terrain Balochistan is of little intrinsic value, its location across a traditional invasion route between Central Asia and the Indian subcontinent has long made it of strategic interest to more powerful neighbouring countries.

That the title 'the gateway to India' is now generally applied not to the Bolan but its northern counterpart, the Khyber, says much for the success of

British frontier policy in the south and its failure in the north. Once Balochistan came under British control, the Bolan was guarded by a strong garrison above the pass, at Quetta, and the neighbouring Baloch tribes were controlled through British subsidies to their chiefs. In the Khyber, on the other hand, the British garrison (the largest in the Empire) was below the pass, at Peshawar. The Pashtun (otherwise termed Pakhtun or Pathan) inhabitants of the surrounding mountain tracts were left to govern themselves, resulting in problems that still continue more than sixty years after the end of the British Raj.

This book is a study of how and why the British achieved control of Balochistan, particularly through their relations with the khanate of Kalat, the largest state of the country. It reveals the impact on Balochistan not only of 'the Great Game', the competition between rival European empires for domination in Central Asia, but also of the local turf wars between rival British frontier officers, each with their own political aims and personal ambitions. It includes accounts of conventional fighting in the built-up areas of Kalat city as well as of cavalry actions against the tribes who preyed on the frontier settlements and robbed the passing caravans. Some passages resemble accounts of activities in the American West at the same period. Others, with tales of tyrannical princes, treacherous ministers, ambitious warlords and disguised travellers, resemble adventures from the *Arabian Nights*.

Balochistan remains an area of interest if only through its position in a politically unstable region. Pakistani rule is currently challenged by Baloch nationalists looking back to the days of an independant Kalat; by Baloch irredentists looking forward to a Greater Balochistan; by Baloch separatists complaining of neglect or exploitation by a state in which Punjabis and Pashtuns are the dominant majorities; and by local Islamic extremists, the Taleban (the plural of *talib*, a disciple or student of religion). At an international level, the idea of Gwadur as a potential naval base is one that concerns several states with interests in the Indian Ocean. Alhough this book is intended primarily for readers interested in the history of British India's far western frontier, it will also prove useful to analysts and commentators should future events bring Balochistan to the attention of a wider audience.

In the transliteration of Indian words and names, I have generally used the 'Hunterian' system, indicating how they are written in the Persi-Arabic alphabet rather than how they are pronounced, and thus making it easier for anyone with a basic knowledge of Urdu (Hindustani) or Farsi (Persian) to find them in dictionaries of these languages. The main exceptions are where modern atlases prefer to show pronunciation, especially where an unvoiced vowel is modified by the proximity of the "h" sound (for example Herat for Harat). Diacritic marks have been omitted as being a distraction to the non-specialist reader, a superfluity to the specialist and an expense to the publisher.

ACKNOWLEDGEMENTS

I take this opportunity of expressing my gratitude to all those who, over many years, have encouraged me in the completion of this work. In particular, I acknowledge the invaluable advice and inspiration given by Dr Malcolm Yapp in his supervision of my PhD thesis at the School of Oriental and African Studies (SOAS) in the University of London, from which much of this book is derived. I also thank my former colleagues in the Royal Military Academy Sandhurst Collection, especially including its first departmental secretary, my friend Marilyn Weekes, who typed the original thesis when we worked together in the Arts Department of the National Army Museum. I am grateful, too, for the continuing support of the ever-helpful staff of the Royal Military Academy Sandhurst Library, headed by Andrew Orgill and his deputy, Jon Pearce, and the kind co-operation of the desk officials at the India Office Collection at the British Library (still the India Office Library and Records in the Foreign and Commonwealth Office when this work was first undertaken), the National Archives (formerly the Public Records Office), the Scottish National Records Office, and the libraries of the University of Cambridge, Christ Church, Oxford, and SOAS. Most of all, I am grateful to my wife, Mary, herself a SOAS historian, for her constant affection and support, and for her skill in proofreading this and all my other historical works.

Map 1

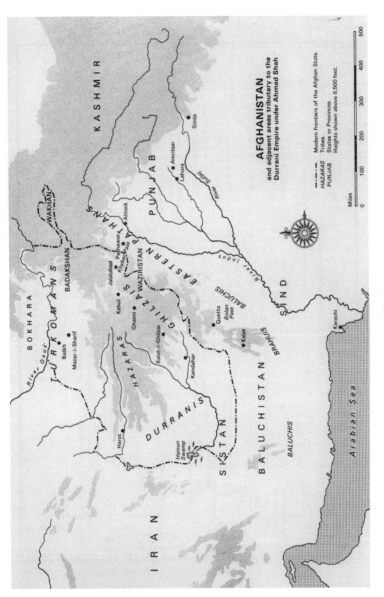

Map 2

Sir Henry Bartle Frere. Commissioner in Sind, 1850-59; Governor of Bombay 1862–1867. Lithograph by Frederick Huth after Sir George Reid.

Brigadier-General John Jacob. Political Superintendent and Commandant, Upper Sind Frontier, 1847–58. Engraving by Thomas Atkinson.

Colonel Sir William Lockyer Merewether. Political Superintendent and Commandant, Upper Sind Frontier. 1858–61; Commissioner in Sind 1867-77. Photograph.

Colonel Sir Robert Groves Sandeman. Deputy Commissioner, Dera Ghazi Khan, Punjab, 1866–77; Agent to the Governor-General for Baluchistan, 1877–93. Photograph.

Mir Khudadad Khan. Khan of Kalat, 1857–93. Photograph.

Kelat city
and citadel
Residence of the
Khan of Kalat Chief of Balochistan.

John Day. 1883.

Kalat City, crowned by the Miri or Khan's palace. Water Colour sketch by John Day, 1883.

The Storming of Kalat, 13 November 1839. Lithograph by W. Taylor after Lieutenant Thomas Wingate, 2nd Foot (The Queen's Royal Regiment). The British advance to the city walls.

The Storming of Kalat, 13 November 1839. Lithograph by W. Taylor after Lieutenant Thomas Wingate, 2nd Foot (The Queen's Royal Regiment). Last Stand of the Khan of Kalat, Mir Mahrab Khan II.

BALUCH CHIEF OF THE JEKRANI TRIBE IN THE BOLAN PASS.

A sardar or chief of the Jakrani tribe, c. 1842. Lithograph by Louis Haghe after James Atkinson.

OFFICER IN FIGHTING ORDER.

1846.

The Scinde Irregular Horse, c. 1849. Undress or Combat Uniform. Engraving after a sketch by Ensign William Sitwell, 31st Bengal Native Infantry.

Sinde Irregular Horse.

The Scinde Irregular Horse, c. 1849. Full Dress Uniform. Aquatint by John Harris the Younger after Henry Martens.

1

BALOCHISTAN BACKGROUND

THE COUNTRY, THE PEOPLE AND THE PRINCES

They say the Lion and the Lizard keep
The Courts where Jamshyd gloried and drank deep:
And Bahram, that great Hunter, the Wild Ass
Stamps o'er his head and cannot break his sleep.

Edward Fitzgerald's *Rubaiyat of Omar Khayyam*, ed 4, xix

The Country

Balochistan lies in the south-eastern part of the Iranian plateau. On the map, what is now the Pakistani province of Balochistan appears as an irregularly-shaped lozenge. Its shorter diagonal measures 475 miles, running north-west from Cape Monze to Koh-i-Malik Shah, where Iran, Pakistan and Afghanistan meet. Its longer diagonal measures 625 miles, running north-east from the coastal junction with Iran to the mountains of Southern Waziristan.[1] The terrain is among the least hospitable in the world, largely comprised of either sandy deserts or boulder-strewn mountains. A low annual rainfall of between 3 and 12 inches, combined with temperatures alternating between intense heat and extreme cold, produces vegetation suitable mostly for rearing sheep and goats in the north-east, or camels and donkeys in the south-west. The few natural watercourses sometimes dry out completely but, in favoured areas, meltwater from the winter snow feeds springs and wells that allow the cultivation of grain and other crops for human consumption and pasture for cattle.

1

Irrigation canals and *karezes* (deep channels, covered to prevent evaporation) can bring water from miles away, but their efficiency depends upon regular clearance, a procedure liable to disruption in times of disorder. Elsewhere, semi-nomadic shepherds move their flocks between traditional grazing grounds, where water rights are as important as land rights.

The few fertile valleys contain towns and villages, usually with mosques, bazars, administrative centres and the fortified residences of local magnates. In watered areas that for any reason are uncultivated, vegetation grows tall enough to become *jangal* (forest or thickets), providing cover for wild animals and potential robbers. Flat desert areas occasionally experience violent sandstorms that bring intense darkness, even at noonday, and also short-lived, intensely hot, *simoom* winds (said locally to be caused by Satan opening the doors of Hell) capable of producing fatal cases of heatstroke in men and beasts alike. After distant rains, as in similar desert regions, dry ravines can suddenly fill with torrential floods that drown unwary travellers in their camps.

A notable example of variation between the desert and the sown is Kachhi, a great triangular plain some 2,000 square miles in extent, stretching northwards from Upper Sind. Away from water, the land is a scorched wilderness. Near water, it is fertile and productive. During the period covered by this book the land revenue was collected as the government's share of the crop, a practice common throughout central and southern Asia. The staple product of Balochistan, wool from its vast flocks of sheep, was not taxed but yielded revenue through transit tolls or customs duties which were levied on all goods passing through the country. Kachhi was especially valuable as a source of such income, for it was the strategically vital and economically lucrative main route for traffic using the Bolan Pass, a defile stretching for over 44 miles and rising from a mere 500 feet above sea level at Dadhar, the northernmost town of Kachhi, to 6,000 feet at Quetta, the first town above the pass.

For safety, merchants and others normally travelled in organized convoys or kafilas (Arabic *qafila*), each headed by professional *qafila-bash* or Master of the Caravan, whose leadership role was much the same as that of the wagon-masters familiar from the early American West. Each kafila was a separate association formed for the duration of the journey, and could alter its route or destination in response to reports of danger ahead or of a better market being found. The district of Shal, above the Bolan Pass, commonly referred to as Quetta (in early transliterations, Kwatta) from the name of its principal town, is cooler than Kachhi on account of its higher altitude. Balochistan's second-most valuable region in terms of land revenue, its strategic importance derives from its command of the approaches to the Bolan. Some 50 miles from Quetta, the much shorter Khojak Pass links Balochistan with southern Afghanistan.[2]

Until modern times the roads leading to the Bolan were mostly suitable only for pack transport, and wheeled vehicles moved only with great difficulty. As elsewhere, benevolent or pious individuals sometimes built *serais*, the equivalent of present-day service stations, where travellers and their animals could rest overnight. Distances were measured in terms of days' marches, according to the difficulty of each stretch. In the driest stretches, kafilas might include extra pack animals to carry food and water for those moving the commercial pay-load, just as modern convoys following the same route can include their own fuel bowsers. A baggage animal or a motor vehicle can only travel a limited distance into a desert area before it has itself consumed all the water, fodder or fuel it can carry. Movement remains effectively confined to routes where such items can be obtained either by local purchase or from pre-stocked depots, which themselves need regular replenishment. Such depots, however, can prove attractive to raiders and need their own protection.

Under Shari'a law, customs duties were chargeable at a rate of two and a half per cent of the value of the goods carried. In practice, transit fees were levied at as high a rate as the traffic would bear, and were a legitimized protection racket, with a few token riders employed by local chiefs to escort each kafila through their territory and show potential robbers that the dues for safe passage had been paid. This was accepted as a form of insurance because, if a kafila was robbed, those who had taken fees for its protection were expected to pay compensation for the goods and animals lost and for personal injuries suffered by the travellers.

The Peoples

The Baloch or Baluchis who give their name to Balochistan are a pastoral, semi-nomadic people of Indo-European origin. According to their own legends, during the regional migration of peoples in the fourteenth and fifteenth centuries they journeyed from lands south-east of the Caspian to seek new pastures in or beyond Sistan. The present-day existence of sizeable Baloch populations in eastern Iran and southern Central Asia lends support to this belief. The dominant community in Balochistan, however, was another group of pastoralists, the Brahuis. These people, though culturally Indo-European, speak a tongue related to the Dravidian languages of southern

India. Various explanations have been advanced to account for this linguistic anomaly, including suggestions of a link with the prehistoric Indus Valley Civilization, traces of which remain throughout Balochistan, but the subject remains controversial.[3]

The Brahui heartland occupies the central area of the country, comprising the hill city of Kalat and the twin provinces of Sarawan and Jhalawan (the Upper and Lower Highlands) to its north and south respectively. To the west of this area, Makran, stretching down to the Arabian Sea littoral, and Kharan, its northern hinterland (both consisting mostly of deserts) were occupied by the incoming Baloch. To the east, between Kachhi on one side and Sind on the other, the impressive but barren ranges of the Suleiman Mountains and their foot-hills also became the home of Baloch tribes, of whom the Marris and Bugtis were among the most warlike.

In the early eighteenth century, the Kalhora princes then ruling Sind granted to a Marri clan, the Talpurs, land-holdings in return for military service. Those who came as mercenaries eventually overthrew their employers and in 1783 the Talpurs took control of Sind for themselves. The country notionally remained a single entity, just as it had been when part of the Mughal Empire, before the Kalhora period, but in practice it became three virtually independent states, whose princes or *amirs* (commanders) remained closely linked by family ties. The amirs granted land-holdings to their Baloch followers, who became the dominant military class of the country at the expense of the ordinary Sindi population and thereby extended still further the Baloch diaspora.

Baloch and Brahuis shared a broadly similar social structure, in which bands of pastoralists, mostly based on kinship groups, were part of clans and tribes often thousands strong. Both peoples generally dressed in much the same way, with the men wearing their hair in long, oiled, ringlets and the women going unveiled. The eastern Baloch called their tribal chiefs *tomandar*, a term made up of the suffix *dar* (literally, the holder of a post or appointment) and the Turkish word for ten thousand, though the title, like all military ranks, was not taken literally. The usual style of a chief was *Sardar* (also transliterated as Sirdar), the Persian word for a political or military leader. British officials tended to regard the tribal sardars as if they were Scottish clan chieftains from the days before the Highland clearances, or English barons from the Wars of the Roses, perceptions owing much to the novels of Sir Walter Scott and the history plays of William Shakespeare that such officers had studied in their schooldays. There were, in fact, important differences between these respective societies, but the sardars of Balochistan certainly resembled medieval European noblemen in their refusal to tolerate any slight on their personal honour or threat to their political power. Sardars were expected to dispense justice in accordance with local custom, advised by those learned in the Holy Law. The settlement of disputes was based on a codified system of compensation paid to the aggrieved parties by those guilty of any offence against property or persons. This did much to prevent the blood-feuds that were a common feature among their Pashtun neighbours, whose code or rule, the *Pashtunwali*, taught that the killing of a male relative or the seduction of a female one was a stain on family honour that could only be wiped out in blood. In Balochistan, feuds could still arise if the due compensation was not paid (especially for a killing), and might continue for years, often between one sardar and another, or against their rulers, with grave consequences for the country as a whole.

Sardars derived their political power from their ability to muster military contingents from their clansmen. The position of sardar was not inherited but awarded by a consensus of tribal elders, generally to the most respected member of the tribe's leading family. Respect was gained and retained by the ability of a sardar to provide for the well-being of his followers, especially by financial means such as paid military employment or the grant of grazing rights or land-holdings. To do this and to fund the feasts and benefactions expected of his social position, a sardar needed significant personal wealth, normally obtained through a combination of income from his own harvests and flocks; periodic exactions on his clansmen; financial rewards from the ruler of the country in return for military or political support; and raids into neighbouring areas. Such practice is regrettably common in many pastoral societies where property consists mostly of mobile livestock.[4]

Military Organization

Like many medieval kingdoms in Europe and Asia, Balochistan was for centuries organized on a system of military tenure. In return for supplying contingents for the ruler when required, great men were granted *jagirs*, liens on the revenue (normally the government's share of the crop) of specified areas. In theory, the ruler was free to assign jagirs to anyone capable of producing the required number of troops. In practice, where society was based on a tribal organization, the *jagirdar* or assignee was usually a local chief who recruited the troops from his own clansmen, for whom such employment was an important source of income. Over time, jagirs tended to become a form of hereditary land-holding and, to British eyes, the collection of revenues by a jagirdar seemed little different from the collection of rents by a great landlord in their own country.

In more developed societies such as those of medieval Europe, Iran and South Asia, the requirement to produce troops was converted to a cash equivalent. This was more convenient both for governments, who obtained ready money with which to hire their own, more reliable, soldiers, and for assignees who had no wish to serve in person. In Balochistan such developments were unwelcome to the sardars, who preferred to raise their own contingents and thereby boost their standing as leaders and employers. If a contingent was mobilised for more than a limited period, responsibility for paying and supplying it passed to the central government. Because of the strain this imposed on their treasuries, impoverished rulers were often reluctant to call out such levies. When they did, campaigns tended to be of restricted duration and be settled by negotiation rather than battlefield victory.

When not needed for husbandry, many Brahui and Baloch migrated southwards for seasonal agricultural employment. As an alternative, most seemed ready enough to exchange honest labour for the more exciting and less arduous occupation of raiding, especially as while doing so they were maintained at their chief's expense. Young men in many societies relish being tested in war and gaining esteem among their fellows by acts of daring. After a successful raid, all received their share of the proceeds and, during it, were free to take any kind of private property. Such raids were not only for the theft of livestock or grain. Men, women and children could be carried off, at best for ransom, at worst for sale in the slave-markets of Herat and Central Asia. Those who suffered most from such depredations were generally the *Jats* or farmers. The free-spirited Baloch and Brahui stockmen generally despised tillers of the soil and underook such work only as a last resort.

Most men owned the traditional weapons of the country, consisting of long spears, daggers, curved Indo-Saracenic swords, small round shields made of tough hide strengthened with metal bosses, and *jezails*, long-barrelled smoothbore matchlock muskets. Men without arms of their own would be equipped by their richer fellows or clan leaders. Those who could afford them wore coats of mail and the conical steel helmets widely used in Oriental warfare. Others relied on the thick folds of their turbans for head-protection. In addition to the tribal levies, who were mustered as the need arose, there were a few professional soldiers or sepoys (*sipahis*). These were employed as household troops or artillerymen but, as regular soldiers were both unproductive and expensive, only the wealthiest chiefs maintained them on a permanent basis. If prolonged conventional operations were envisaged, mercenaries could be hired for the duration of the campaign or until the money to pay them ran out, which was generally the same thing.[5] Logistic support was supplied by local contractors and merchants as part of their usual business activities. *Hakims*, the learned men who formed part of the domestic household of every great chief, acted as surgeons and chaplains. An equally important member of the war-band was the bard (*raizwar*) who raised the morale of combatants by singing of their ancestors' victories and chronicling their own deeds as they occurred. *Loris* (artisans) accompanied the fighting men as armourers, with mobile workshops for the repair of damaged weapons and equipment.[6]

The practice of robber bands preying on peaceful cultivators and travellers was by no means unique to Balochistan. It was, and is, common in any country whose government is too weak to protect those unable to defend themselves. In Balochistan, the problem was greater because the quasi-feudal organization of the country meant that the military resources needed to deter raiding, or to punish raiders and recover stolen property if deterrence failed, were in the hands of the sardars. As a class, they had little incentive to incur the expense of calling up their retainers other than for the protection of their own holdings or to raid those of others. When they did take to the field, they were often as likely to oppose the government as to support it. This combination of endemic armed robbery and constant rebellion against central rule always brought the risk of external intervention. In itself a political backwater, Balochistan was widely perceived by its neighbours as a land of robbers who harried travellers and preyed upon settlements regardless of international borders. When the British became the dominant force in the region, they had to deal not only with the prospect of some other power using Balochistan as a route for the invasion of India but also with the local defence of their frontier districts against Baloch raiders.

The Princes

Kalat, the principal city of the Brahui country, takes its name from a corruption of the Arabic *Qil'a* or fort. Like the English words Chester and Borough, both of which mean much the same thing, Kalat (also transliterated as Khelat, Qalat, Qala, Killa, etc.) is a common element in place-names in a part of the world with many forts, often in conjunction with that of a local ruler or group.

In the early sixteenth century, Kalat city became a seat of local government as part of the Mughal province of Kandahar. A century later, Ahmad Khan, a Brahui prince, came to power in the area extending north-eastwards from Kalat, through Mastung, to Quetta. In return for tribute from local farmers, he provided protection against raiders and became wealthy enough for other Brahui sardars to accept his leadership. In 1666 he declared himself Khan (Lord) of Kalat. His family retained their ancestral name Kambarani (from Kambar, an early Brahui chief), and his dynasty became known as the Ahmadzai, 'the children of Ahmad'. At the head of a Brahui alliance, Ahmad Khan I led a revolt against the waning authority of the Mughals and enlarged his new khanate to include districts inhabited by neighbouring Baloch tribes. He then took the title Khan-i-Baloch, one kept by his heirs and successors until the present day.[7]

In addition to jagirs granted by the khans, the Brahui and Baloch sardars retained ancestral holdings (known as *inam* lands) predating the establishment of the khanate. The most powerful chiefs tended to regard the khan as first among equals rather than an absolute sovereign. This was despite the teachings of orthodox jurists (Brahuis and Balochis alike belonged to the Sunni branch of Islam) that a king is the vice-gerent of God upon earth, and that therefore sharing power is the same as giving God a partner, the sin of polytheism. Since, by this doctrine, legitimate power derives only from God, Sunni law-givers constantly debated the issue of whether, or when, it was lawful to resist a tyrant. In Balochistan, the sardars had little doubt as to the answer and, citing tyranny as their justification, were always ready to oppose the khan when it suited their own interests. When a khan decided disputes between sardars, the losing side frequently challenged his authority by appealing to neighbouring rulers in Sind or Kandahar, both of which had vague residual claims to sovereignty over Balochistan. There was, nevertheless, sufficient common interest between khan and sardars for Kalat to continue as a quasi-independent state, at least while civil wars distracted neighbouring empires from asserting their claims over it. Successive khans, dependant on the sardars' military contingents for their armies, adopted a Machiavellian policy of divide and rule as a way of maintaining their own supremacy.

The khanate's central government was headed by the *wazir* (vizier), whose principal responsibility was the treasury, making him the chief minister. Almost equally influential was the *daroga*, a minister whose title, like constable or marshal, could mean either a high officer of state or a local policeman, but here approximated to Home Secretary or Minister of the Interior. These were supported by a small number of royal officials or *shaghasis*, a term commonly translated as chamberlain, corresponding to senior civil servants. Generally they belonged to the *khanazad* class, high-status slaves belonging to the personal household of the ruler. At the provincial level, the Khan's authority was exercised through his *naibs* (lieutenants or deputies), often minor sardars who could find paid employment for their own clansmen in enforcing local government. The most important part of the naibs' duty was to collect the revenue, often in kind, especially grain, which was then sold to local contractors for cash. In consequence, most centres of local government had their own treasuries and warehouses, attractive targets for malefactors in times of trouble. Customs and transit tolls collected by the naibs were used to fund their own salaries and that of their men, or shared with the sardars who provided escorts for the caravans. Any balance was remitted to the central treasury. It was commonly supposed that naibs supplemented their official income by various unauthorised means, though it was equally common for naibs to complain of being left with insufficient funds. In towns, magisterial powers of arrest, trial and punishment were administered by the *qadi*, an official learned in the Holy Law.

Balochistan and Nadir Shah of Iran

In 1738 the great conqueror Nadir Shah, after restoring Iranian rule over eastern Afghanistan, pursued his Afghan enemies into the Mughal provinces of Ghazni and Kabul. Finding that the Mughals, weakened by civil wars, could offer only limited resistance, he invaded India and, after his victory at Karnal (13 Feb 1739), entered Delhi in triumph. The Mughal emperor Muhammad Shah was forced to cede all the former Mughal territories west of the Indus to Nadir, including Kalat, where successive khans had continued as gatherers of the Baloch lands.[8]

The fourth Khan of Kalat, Mir Abdulla Khan, who ascended the throne in 1714 and became known as the Mountain Hawk (translated more poetically as the Royal Eagle of Kohistan), was a redoubtable warrior and a shrewd politician. In 1740 he accepted Nadir Shah as his new overlord, agreed to produce a contingent of 500 troopers and gave his two sons, Muhabat and Nasir, as hostages. In accordance with the conventions of the time, these princes became part of Nadir Shah's household and fought beside him in battle, including campaigns in north-west India. Nadir Shah awarded Abdulla Khan the hereditary title Beglarbeg (chief of chiefs), corresponding to Governor-General in Western hierarchies.

In 1730 Nur Muhammad Kalhora, the ruler of Upper Sind, forced Abdulla Khan to withdraw his claim on Kachhi and give two daughters in marriage to two of Nur Muhammad Kalhora's sons. Five years later Abdulla Khan attempted to regain the province but was defeated and killed along with some 300 of his men, leaving the throne of Kalat to his son Muhabat Khan. In 1739, when Nadir Shah entered Sind to take possession of the former Mughal lands, Nur Muhammad Kalhora unsuccessfully opposed him and was taken prisoner. Nadir Shah was then persuaded by Abdulla Khan's widow, the Bibi (Lady) Maryam, to deliver Nur Muhammad to her son, Muhabat Khan, to avenge Abdulla Khan's death. Muhabat declared that he would rather have the land for which his father died than the blood of his enemy. At the head of the Kalat contingent, Muhabat Khan had played a part in the capture of Kandahar by Nadir Shah, who now granted him Kachhi as a reward for this service and compensation for the blood of Abdulla Khan. This province thus became part of Kalat state, with large areas being granted in jagir to the Brahui sardars whose contingents had made up the army that fought for it.

Balochistan and Ahmad Shah of Afghanistan

Nadir Shah went on to become one of the greatest rulers in the history of Iran, restoring much of the power and prestige lost during the preceding civil wars and recovering territory from both the Russian and Ottoman Empires. Nevertheless, many of his subjects came to view him as an oppressor, to such an extent that he feared for plots against his life. He had long included Afghans in his army and increasingly came to rely on them, not least because, as members of the Sunni branch of Islam, they could be trusted not to combine against him with the mostly Shia Iranians. In 1747, while waging a campaign against rebels in Kurdistan, he ordered the commander of his household troops, Ahmad Khan, a thirty-five-year-old prince of the Abdali tribe of Pashtuns, to arrest a number of Iranian generals whom he suspected of plotting against him. A spy warned the generals, who then killed Nadir Shah before he could kill them. Ahmad Khan escaped with his men and led them back to their Afghan homeland.

En route to Kandahar, they encountered a kafila carrying much of the loot taken at Delhi eight years earlier. Its escort, drawn from another division of Nadir Shah's trusted Afghan guards, went over to Ahmad Khan, who thus found himself with a trained army and ready money to pay it. By 1748 he was accepted by the majority of Afghans as their king and became Ahmad Shah, taking the title Dur-i-Durran, Pearl of the Pearls, a graceful pun on the Persian words *dauran* (age or epoch) and *durran*, the pearls that he and his followers habitually wore. His tribe, the Abdalis, became the Durranis or 'Pearlies' and his family, the Sadozai (from Sado, the name of their ancestral prince), became the ruling dynasty of the newly-created Afghan kingdom.[9]

Earlier, Ahmad Shah had taken part in Nadir Shah's invasion of India and seen both the wealth of the country and the weakness of its defenders. In 1748, following Nadir's example, he led his army down the Khyber in the first of a series of campaigns against the Mughal Emperor Shah Alam. After successive defeats, Shah Alam was forced to grant Ahmad Shah all the Mughal provinces (including Kalat) previously ceded to Nadir Shah and to give imperial princesses in marriage both to Ahmad himself and his eldest son, Timur Mirza. At its greatest extent, Ahmad Shah's Durrani Empire stretched from the Oxus to the Indus, and from Kashmir to the Arabian Sea. He died in 1773, in the fiftieth year of his life and the twenty-sixth of his reign, one of the greatest Muslim kings of his day.

Towards the end of his reign, Nadir Shah publicly advised Mir Nasir Khan Ahmadzai to depose his half-brother, Muhabat Khan, for misgovernment and restore Kalat to the prosperity it had enjoyed under their father, the heroic Abdulla Khan. Mir Nasir Khan had fought alongside Nadir Shah in his Indian campaigns and impressed him by his energy and good judgement. Before Mir Nasir Khan could act on this advice, Nadir Shah was murdered by his generals, but later that same year, Muhabat Khan was also stabbed to death in his own citadel, either by his palace guards or by Mir Nasir Khan in person. A less colorful version of events is that Nasir Khan remained outside until his step-brother was murdered in a palace coup and then rode in as the long-awaited deliverer from Muhabat Khan's tyranny.

Nasir Khan, while recognizing Ahmad Shah Durrani as king of Afghanistan, considered that any external authority over Kalat had died with Nadir Shah. After ten years in power, at a time when Ahmad Shah was occupied in campaigns elsewhere, he formally declared his independence. The Durrani governor of Kandahar led a force to re-establish Ahmad Shah's authority, but Nasir called out his tribal contingents and defeated the Durranis near Mastung, about 70 miles north of Kalat. Ahmad Shah arrived in person at the head of a stronger force and, after another battle, Nasir Khan retreated to his prepared defences at Kalat. Ahmad Shah followed him and laid siege to the city. Three attempts on the walls failed and Nasir Khan personally aimed a gun at Ahmad Shah's tent, where the ball hit the prayer carpet on which Ahmad Shah had just finished his devotions.

With other demands on his time and army, Ahmad Shah complimented his opponent on his skill as a gun-layer and raised the siege in return for Nasir Khan's accepting the same terms that had been in force under Nadir Shah. Ahmad Shah's only concession was that the contingent of 500 troopers would not be required to serve in a civil war. A daughter of Hajji Khan (son of the late Muhabat Khan) was given in marriage to Ahmad Shah, who then returned to Kandahar with his new wife, accompanied by Hajji Khan, her brother Bahram Khan, and Hajji Khan's mother, a princess who never forgave Nasir Khan for the murder of her husband and the usurpation of the throne she considered as rightfully belonging to her son. This arrangement was agreeable to both Ahmad Shah, who thus had in his camp a constant reminder to Nasir Khan that there was a rival claimant to the throne of Kalat, and to Nasir Khan himself, as it removed that claimant from Kalat territory.

Balochistan under Nasir Khan the Great of Kalat

Nasir Khan lived up to his agreement and fought beside Ahmad Shah in the overwhelming defeat of the Marathas by the Afghans at Panipat (12 January 1761). In 1769, at the head of 3,000 troopers, he served under Ahmad Shah's son, Timur Mirza, against an Iranian attempt to take the city of Herat in western Afghanistan. For his services, he was rewarded with the jagirs of Shal (Quetta) and Harrand, on the south-west edge of the Punjab. To his existing domains of Kachhi, Sarawan and Jhalawan, he added the Baloch hill tracts between Kachhi and Harrand on his eastern border, and the deserts of Makran, Kech, Panjgur and Kharan in the west. Las Bela, on the coast between Karachi and Makran, was left under its own chief, the Jam, in return for his paying tribute and accepting Nasir Khan as overlord.

Under Nasir Khan's rule, the state of Kalat reached its greatest extent, including Karachi and neighbouring parts of Sind. In the far west, in 1783, he granted asylum to Sultan Said, the exiled ruler of Oman, and assigned him the port of Gwadar, at that time a mere roadstead surrounded by date groves and deserts. Sultan Said undertook to suppress raids by the neighbouring Baloch tribes and to resist any Iranian incursions, an obligation that he continued to honour when he regained the throne of Oman a decade later. Gwadar would continue under Omani rule until 1955, when it was purchased by Pakistan with the proviso that Oman could still recruit soldiers from among the Baloch.

Nasir Khan's achievements in domestic matters matched those of his foreign policy. He organized Sarawan and Jhalawan into two separate provinces, appointing a leading sardar at the head of each and giving them places in his *darbar* (council) on his right and left sides respectively. He repaired and strengthened the defences of Kalat city, planted orchards and gardens at his own expense and encouraged artisans and merchants to settle there. The safety of kafilas passing through the Bolan and Kachhi was secured by regular cash payments to the local sardars. He gained a reputation for being courageous in battle, indifferent to personal adornment, generous (though not with gifts of money, which he said encouraged idleness), just, merciful, and true to his word. He became popular with his subjects and was the only Khan of Kalat to be known as 'The Great'. In later reigns, when there were disputes about how the country should be governed, all sides referred to the situation in his time as the rightful state of affairs, in much the same way that Englishmen relied on Magna Carta, though in both instances few knew what this actually had been. He died at an advanced age in June 1794, leaving five daughters and three sons, of whom the youngest, Mir Mahmud, then aged seven, succeeded him as khan.[10]

The Collapse of the Durrani Empire

In Afghanistan, Ahmad Shah was succeeded by his son Timur, Nasir Khan's old comrade-in-arms. Timur Shah died (probably from poison) a year before Nasir Khan. Most of his twenty-three sons gathered at Kabul to choose a successor. There, Zaman Mirza, Timur Shah's fifth son by his first wife, imprisoned them until they agreed to recognize him as Zaman Shah. One of the two brothers who had not gone to Kabul, Mahmud Mirza, went instead to Herat, where he defied Zaman Shah and ruled as Mahmud Shah. Zaman Shah established control over the rest of the Durrani kingdom, including Balochistan, Sind and Peshawar.

Seeking to make himself less dependent on the contingents of the Afghan tribal sardars, Zaman Shah attempted to form a standing army paid from central revenues. This alienated all those who saw the new national army as a threat to themselves, especially as their jagirs, no longer needed for their original purpose, would be resumed in order to fund it. In 1801 a group of leading sardars plotted to depose him in favour of his brother, Shuja-ul-Mulk. The plot failed and the conspirators were executed in Zaman's presence. Among those killed was Painda Khan, head of the Barakzai ('children of Barak') family of Durranis. Painda Khan's son, Fatah Khan, was given asylum by Mahmud Shah at Herat and persuaded him to lead the Barakzais in revolt. Zaman Shah was defeated, captured and blinded (thus disqualifying him, under orthodox Islamic law, from kingship) and imprisoned at Kabul, where his brother Mahmud Shah then took the throne. Soon afterwards, in 1802, Mahmud Shah was deposed in favour of Shah Shuja-ul-Mulk by another set of conspirators and fled to Herat.

Neither Mahmud Shah nor Fatah Khan accepted Shah Shuja-ul-Mulk's claim to the Durrani throne. During 1809 Mahmud Shah returned from Herat and again seized Kabul. Shah Shuja-ul-Mulk continued the war from Peshawur and Mahmud Shah gathered more troops against him, though Mahmud Khan of Kalat refused the call on the grounds that he was not obliged to serve in a civil war. In 1810 Mahmud Shah captured Peshawar and travelled on to Rawalpindi to meet his new neighbour, Maharaja Ranjit Singh.

This Sikh prince, once viceroy of the western Punjab under Zaman Shah, had turned his former charge into the independent kingdom of Lahore, a state whose boundaries he steadily increased. In July 1813 Shah Shuja-ul-Mulk, who had taken refuge in Ranjit Singh's camp, handed over the Koh-i-Nur diamond (taken from the Mughals by Ahmad Shah Durrani) in return for a promise of aid in regaining his throne. The gem was added to Ranjit's treasury but no troops were provided and in 1816 Shah Shuja-ul-Mulk fled across the Satlej to the British-protected state of Ludhiana. The British gave him asylum and funds, partly in recognition of his having agreed, when in power, to oppose any European army attempting to invade India through Afghanistan, and partly to secure his gratitude should he at any future time recover his kingdom.

By 1818, after years of feuding between Sadozais and Barakzais, and between brothers inside each family, the empire created by Ahmad Shah had fallen apart. Kalat and Sind were for all practical purposes independent. Mahmud Shah still ruled in Herat but the rest of Afghanistan had fallen to the Barakzai brothers, Dost Muhammad in Kabul and Ghazni, Kohan Dil Khan and Rahim Dil Khan in Kandahar, and Sultan Muhammad Khan in Peshawar. In 1818, hoping to take advantage of quarrels between the Barakzais, Shah Shuja-ul-Mulk gathered a new army and, with Ranjit Singh's co-operation, marched against Peshawar. At the same time, Mahmud Shah reached the outskirts of Kabul before retreating back to Herat. Shah Shuja-ul-Mulk briefly occupied parts of Upper Sind and the province of Peshawar, but was defeated by the Barakzais and by 1822 was again a British pensioner in Ludhiana.

Balochistan under Mahmud Khan of Kalat

Meanwhile, in Kalat, a similar series of feuds had led to a similar result, the loss of outlying provinces and a weakening of the centre. Even while Nasir Khan the Great still lived, the Muhabatzai pretender Hajji Khan and his son Bahram Khan attempted to take the throne of Kalat, only to be defeated in battle and return to Kandahar. On Nasir Khan's death, they launched another rebellion with the aid of sardars sympathetic to their cause and captured the citadel of Kalat. Mahmud Khan's ministers appealed to Zaman Shah and gathered their forces against the insurgents. The chief sardar of Jhalawan, Khoda Baksh, who had promised support both to Hajji Khan and to Mahmud Khan, led his men to join Mahmud. When reproached for duplicity, he said that he had given (sworn by) the Koran to Hajji, but his beard (a greater oath still) to Mahmud. Hajji Khan was defeated and taken back as a state prisoner to Kandahar, where he later died. Bahram Khan was granted Kachhi in return for accepting Mahmud Khan as ruler of the rest of Kalat.

With the revenues of Kachhi at his disposal, Bahram Khan then raised an army from the Baloch in Sind, and demanded that he should become khan for the duration of his lifetime, with the young Mahmud Khan as his designated successor. Mahmud Khan's party again appealed to Zaman Shah, but Bahram Khan rejected his mediation. This led to a war of succession at the end of which Bahram was wounded and defeated. He fled south to Sind but Mir Ghulam Ali Talpur, the amir of Hyderabad, was unwilling to offend Zaman Shah and refused him asylum. Bahram Khan and his two sons then turned north-east, hoping to find refuge with Nawab Sadiq Muhammad Khan II, ruler of Bahawalpur, but eventually became Mahmud Khan's prisoners at Kalat, where Bahram Khan died in captivity.

Bahram Khan's cause was taken up by Mahmud Khan's half-sister. In 1801 she arranged a marriage between Bahram Khan's only daughter and Mir Ghulam Ali Talpur, in return for the latter's promise of help in deposing Mahmud Khan and restoring the Muhabatzai line. After the betrothal ceremony, Mir Ghulam Ali declared he had no intention of interfering in the internal affairs of Kalat. This did nothing to mollify Mahmud Khan, who took the alliance of a Brahui princess to a member of the Talpur family (whom he regarded as no more than a set of usurping Baloch mercenaries) as a personal insult. Unable to prevent the marriage without provoking a war with the Talpurs, he had to content himself with sending word to Zaman Shah that he would seek revenge later. He found that Zaman Shah, facing defeat and deposition by his brother Mahmud Shah, was no longer in a position to intervene.

After the final defeat of Bahram Khan, the governorship of Kachhi was given to Mir Mustafa Khan, one of Mahmud Khan's two older half-brothers. He maintained a force of 800 regular Afghan troopers, paid out of his own revenues and therefore independent of the tribal sardars, and conducted a series of punitive expeditions against raiders from the Baloch hills. Heavy fines were imposed on their tribes and any robbers taken alive were impaled as a warning to others. To stamp out the system of Hindu travellers paying Muslims for safe passage, he fined any Hindu who paid protection money and executed any Muslim who took it. When he passed along a road, he would throw down rolls of cloth on the ground and expect them to be left untouched until his return, as evidence that his authority was respected.

Mir Mustafa Khan achieved a rare period of security for cultivators and kafilas and was praised for the conventional virtues of bravery in combat, justice in government and open-handedness to his friends and supporters. He was rumoured to have made an agreement with Nawab Sadiq Muhammad Khan II of Bahawalpur to partition Sind between them. All Sind west of the Indus, including Karachi (recovered by the amirs of Sind during Kalat's wars of succession) was to be taken by Kalat and the remainder by Bahawalpur on the east side. He certainly forced the Talpurs to agree that they would hand back to Kalat the revenues of Karachi but died before he could implement his greater plans.

Mir Mustafa Khan was killed as he returned from a hunting party that he had joined in preference to attending the funeral of the mother of his half-brother Rahim Khan. Incensed by this insult, Rahim Khan ambushed, shot and wounded Mir Mustafa Khan, who lived up to his reputation for valour by calling out "O Rahim, do not destroy me from a distance; if thou art a man, close with me and fight hand-to-hand".[11] In the ensuing struggle Mir Mustafa Khan was killed, after which Rahim Khan fled to Sind, where he gathered a force and took possession of Harrand, defying his other half-brother, Mahmud Khan, and rejecting an offer of pardon. In November 1812, possibly with a view to making his peace with Mahmud Khan, he entered Kachhi with an escort of fifty men and approached the town of Gandava, despite warnings that the sister of the late Mir Mustafa Khan (his own half-sister) was there, planning to avenge her brother's death. Rahim Khan declared that he scorned to turn aside for fear of a woman, but the lady persuaded a local sardar, Qadir Baksh, to call out his men in Mahmud Khan's name. A fight then took place in which Rahim Khan and most of his followers were killed.

Mahmud Khan ruled in Kalat for some thirty-five years. Distracted by family feuds and lacking an appetite for war, he accepted the recapture of

Karachi by the amirs of Sind, the re-assertion of independence by the Jam of Las Bela and the refusal by the sardars of Makran and Kharan to pay their due tribute. In his eastern provinces, following the death of Mir Mustafa Khan, the Baloch tribes resumed their raiding. Harrand, left virtually undefended, was so thoroughly pillaged that cultivation was abandoned, the irrigation canals silted up and most of the population fled. In 1819 it was occupied by Ranjit Singh, who initially granted it to Nawab Sadiq Muhammad Khan II of Baha-walpur but in 1830 transferred it to the neighbouring province of Multan, part of his own kingdom of Lahore. The loss of Harrand to Multan was included among the accusations of treachery levied against Daud Muhammad Ghilzai, the unpopular wazir of Mahmud Khan's successor, Mahrab Khan II. Later, as part of the Punjab district of Dera Ghazi Khan, it would greatly complicate British involvement in Kalat affairs.

Mahmud Khan died in 1831, still only in his early forties in a country where men rarely die of natural causes until reaching twice that age. Some said his demise was due to over-indulgence in wine-drinking, a sin to which his late half-brother, the heroic Mir Mustafa Khan, was also known to have been prone. Others attributed it to his excessive gallantry towards a troop of danc-ing girls whom he had imported from Sind, to the neglect of his government, his wives, and his own health. It was rumoured in the bazar that he had been poisoned by one of the neglected wives although, in Balochistan, conspiracy theories of this kind were normal when any great man died other than in battle. It was certainly the case that Mahmud Khan was succeeded by his son, Mir Mahrab, whose mother was the suspected poisoner. By then, the khanate extended over little more than Kalat city, the two original Brahui provinces of Sarawan and Jhalawan, and the plain of Kachhi.

Balochistan under Mahrab Khan II of Kalat

With all the energy of a new ruler, Mahrab Khan II decided to re-assert his authority over the tribal sardars and recover the khanate's lost lands. He began by dismissing his late father's wazir and replacing him by a Ghilzai Pashtun, Daud Muhammad. This act in itself offended many sardars, as the wazirship had previously been hereditary within the same noble Tajik family and succes-sive khans had always gained the agreement of the sardars, if only as a matter of practical politics, whenever a new wazir was appointed. Nevertheless, the reign started well, with control being restored over Makran and action taken against raiders elsewhere. Mahrab Khan II's succession was then disputed by

Ahmad Yar Khan Muhabatzai, a son of the late Bahram Khan, in a series of risings supported by various Brahui and Baloch sardars. Ahmad Yar Khan was defeated on each occasion, being pardoned the first three times and finally taken as a prisoner to Kalat, where he died, or was killed on the advice of Wazir Daud Khan. It was said that the wazir also wished to eliminate Shah Nawaz Khan and Mir Fatah Khan, Ahmad Yar's two sons who had been captured with him, but that Mahrab Khan II forbade it. However, some two dozen other Brahui chiefs and notables lost their lives in these rebellions, thereby creating blood feuds between their families and Mahrab Khan II.

A coalition of rebel sardars gathered their men and marched to Kalat, where they elected a new khan, the Akhund (a religious leader) Muhammad Sadiq. The city was held for Mahrab Khan II by the daroga, Ghul Muhammad, but Mahrab Khan II himself was surrounded in his camp outside the walls. It was then agreed that the rebels would allow Mahrab Khan II to re-enter the city by one gate while Daroga Ghul Muhammad allowed the Akhund's wives and children to leave by another. As soon as this was done, the daroga ordered the citadel's guns to open fire on the rebel camp, causing the dissidents to flee in confusion.[12]

Mahrab Khan II managed to re-establish his authority over most of the country, though from time to time various sardars fought against each other and against him, occasionally appealing for support to Rahim Dil Khan, the Barakzai ruler of Kandahar. In 1832 Shah Nawaz Khan and his brother Mir Fatah escaped from Kalat and, aided by the Sarawans, took control of Kachhi. The Magsis, a Baloch tribe occupying the south-eastern part of Kachhi, gave their support to Mahrab Khan II and the Muhabatzais were defeated. Shah Nawaz Khan found asylum in Kandahar while Mir Fatah fled to Sind. Mahrab Khan II's increasingly unpopular wazir, Daud Muhammad, long suspected of treachery, was then murdered (possibly with Mahrab Khan II's assent) by Naib Mulla Hasan, a son of the previous wazir for whose death many held Daud Muhammad responsible. Naib Mulla Hasan was appointed wazir in Daud Muhammad's place but continued to hold a grudge against Mahrab Khan II for having dismissed (and possibly murdered) his father. Akhund Muhammad Sadiq was forgiven for his rebellion and given a place in the Khan's council.

No sooner had Mahrab Khan II dealt with Shah Nawaz Khan than Shah Shuja-ul-Mulk entered Kalat in yet another attempt to recover his own throne. Maharaja Ranjit Singh offered to support Shah Shuja-ul-Mulk by invading Afghanistan through the Khyber Pass in return for the cession of

Peshawar. Shah Shuja-ul-Mulk, not actually being in possession of this province (it was at this time under Barakzai rule), was happy to agree and planned to lead an army of his own into southern Afghanistan via Sind, Kachhi and the Bolan. The British governor-general in India, Lord William Bentinck, from whom Shah Shuja-ul-Mulk also sought help, declared that British policy was not to intervene in the affairs of neighbouring states and urged him not to start another war. When it became clear that Shah Shuja-ul-Mulk would disregard this advice, Bentinck gave him a substantial advance of his annual pension, thus allowing him to march from Ludhiana in January 1833 and reach Shikarpur, in Upper Sind, with an army of mercenaries.

Shah Shuja-ul-Mulk was at first welcomed by the amirs of Sind, who were becoming increasingly alarmed at the interest being shown in their country by both the British and Ranjit Singh. Accepting Shah Shuja-ul-Mulk (who claimed Sind as part of Ahmad Shah's Durrani empire), they reasoned, would strengthen them against these rival powers. They soon found that, with an army to maintain, he expected more than nominal subjection. After an armed clash at Rohri on 1 January 1834, the amirs agreed to pay their arrears of tribute and supply a contingent for his army. In return, he abandoned all his claims over their country, an agreement sworn to by all parties and recorded in two Korans given to the amirs.

Shah Shuja-ul-Mulk then entered the dominions of Mahrab Khan II, who gave orders that he should be treated with respect and co-operation. He reached Kandahar and held the city for a few months until Dost Muhammad came to support the Barakzai cause. Deserted by his mercenaries, Shah Shuja-ul-Mulk fled westwards to Herat where, five years earlier, his nephew Kamran Shah had succeeded Mahmud Shah as ruler. As a dynastic rival, he was given asylum but no other support, so that he then journeyed southwards through the deserts of Sistan. Rahim Dil Khan Barakzai, having regained Kandahar, went in pursuit. Shah Shuja-ul-Mulk reached Kalat, where Mahrab Khan II sheltered him and, in accordance with the local convention that a guest must be protected at all costs, refused to give him up to the pursuing Barakzais. Rahim Dil Khan's brother, Kohan Dil Khan, wished to attack the city but Rahim Dil Khan declared that Mahrab Khan II had shown himself to be a man of honour and praised his conduct. As a compromise, the Barakzais called off the pursuit and Mahrab Khan II obliged Shah Shuja-ul-Mulk to return through Sind to Ludhiana, where he once again became a pensioner of the British. Reporting these proceedings to London in March 1835, Bentinck commended Mahrab Khan II for displaying the generosity and hospitality for which, he said, the Baloch nation was renowned.

Dost Muhammad, to mark his victory over Shah Shuja-ul-Mulk, took the title Amir. In the east, Ranjit Singh captured Peshawur, of which he claimed he was now the legitimate ruler in accordance with Shah Shuja-ul-Mulk's grant. In April 1837 Amir Dost Muhammad sent troops under his eldest son and best general, Muhammad Akbar Khan, to recover the city, the former Durrani summer capital. At the end of that month they attacked Jamrud, guarding the lower end of the Khyber. Ranjit Singh's field army was defeated but Jamrud fort held out and, after a few days, Akbar Khan withdrew to Jalalabad on the Afghan side of the pass. British interest in Shah Shuja-ul-Mulk's former dominions continued. There was increasing concern among British statesmen that Russia or, more probably, Iran under Russian pressure, had designs on the lands north-west of the Indus. Beyond Balochistan, the Great Game was already under way.

2

THE OPENING OF THE GREAT GAME

BRITISH INDIA, RUSSIA, IRAN AND AFGHANISTAN, 1798–1838

... sad stories of the death of kings:
How some have been deposed, some slain in war,
Some poisoned by their wives, some sleeping kill'd
All murder'd: for within the hollow crown
That rounds the mortal temples of a king
Keeps Death his court and there the antick sits,
Scoffing his state and grinning at his pomp;

King Richard, Richard II, *Act III, scene ii.*

For the British, the natural route to India was by sea. As long as the Royal Navy dominated the Indian Ocean, British cargoes and troops could come and go freely. The overland route through Central Asia, on the other hand, was one that no battleship could protect. Even if British policy-makers knew little of the early Aryan invasions of India, their classical education had taught them about the campaigns of Alexander the Great, including his descent into the Indus valley and his return along the Makran coast.

In 1800 the Russian Emperor Paul I, previously a British ally in the war against Revolutionary France, reversed his policy and agreed to Napoleon Bonaparte's plan for a joint expedition against British India. This scheme came to nothing when Paul was assassinated (some said by British secret agents) in March 1801. The new tsar (emperor), Alexander I, rejoined the war, but becoming impatient at British delays in opening a promised second front, made his own peace with Napoleon, by this time Emperor of the French, at the treaty of Tilsit (25 June 1807). The two emperors proclaimed their hatred of the English and planned to drive the Ottoman Turks from Europe and open the way to India. By the end of 1810, however, Alexander's enthusiasm for his French allies had waned and he re-opened his ports to British shipping. Napoleon's consequent invasion of Russia in June 1812 meant that Russians and Britons were once again comrades in arms, with Alexander I becoming the darling of the Western liberal establishment. After Napoleon's final defeat in 1815, British public opinion changed much as it would after the defeat of Germany in 1945. Russia was no longer seen as the brave ally who had liberated Europe from a hated dictator but a threat to British interests.

The Government of British India

Until 1857 British India was ruled through what in modern times would be called a quango, the East India Company, whose dividends were regulated by Parliament and whose stock corresponded to investments in government bonds. It was headed in London by a Court of Directors, whose twenty-four members were elected by the Company's stockholders, the Court of Proprietors. In practice, directorships were normally filled by co-option from those with experience of high office in the Company's service and were retained for long periods. Directors advanced in seniority at each annual election until they became Deputy Chairman and finally Chairman. The two 'Chairs' formed the Secret Committee, which dealt directly with the Board of Control for the Affairs of India. This body, a department of State established by Pitt's India Act of 1784, was headed by a Cabinet minister, the President of the Board of Control, who saw all important letters arriving from India and ensured that all important despatches sent to India conformed to government policy.[1]

British territories in India were divided into three largely autonomous governments or Presidencies (each headed by a Governor and President in Council) originally formed as coastal trading agencies. At first widely separated from each other, it was not until 1774 that the Presidencies of Madras and Bombay were subordinated in the conduct of foreign policy to that of Bengal (though keeping the right to correspond with the authorities in London and to implement British policy towards states in their respective areas of influence). The former Governor of Bengal then became Governor-General (though his title was not changed to 'of India' until 1853) and his officials formed the Government of India. Governor-Generals and Governors were nominated by the Cabinet but the Directors, whose servants they then temporarily became, had the right to recall them. Most were minor British politicians with no Indian experience. To make up for this, they were required to govern with the aid of a Council whose members, like themselves, were appointed for a term of five years, and whose majority agreement was normally necessary in all policy decisions. The majority of Councillors were civilians (civil servants and others). Only one at a time needed to be an old soldier of the Company's service to make up for the lack of specific regional military experience among the commanders-in-chief of each of the Company's three Armies (Bengal, Madras and Bombay), who were predominantly drawn from the British Army.

Though most of the troops were servants of the East India Company (after 1858, the Crown in India), a proportion always belonged to the British Army, serving in India for a limited period and charged to Indian revenues, with their numbers decided by the British government. The greater part of the Company's troops were Indian sepoys, led by British officers and trained in the same way as the British Army, with their uniforms, (red coats for the infantry and blue for the artillery), modelled on British patterns. From a distance, only the Company's Light Cavalry, who wore French grey rather than the dark blue of British light dragoons, could be distinguished from their British counterparts. The Company's few European regiments, recruited from the United Kingdom, were virtually identical in appearance to those of the British Army.

Each Presidency retained its own separate civil, military, judicial and medical services, and conducted relations with neighbouring states through their respective Political (i.e. Diplomatic) Services, whose members were drawn from their military as well as civil services. Indeed, in periods when the Company's dominions expanded more rapidly than civil servants could be recruited, it was only through the use of army officers that diplomacy, or even ordinary administration, could be carried on. Many officers joined the Indian Armies with little intention of soldiering as a career, but with the ambition of transferring as soon as possible to political or civil posts, with their associated prestige, pay and allowances. Political officers, civil or military, were ranked in a hierarchy of agencies and residencies, paid according to the size and importance of the states to which they were accredited. Princes and chiefs who ruled in accordance with their advice could be sure of continued British support in the form of influence, money and troops. Those who rejected it might find

23

themselves replaced by rivals more willing to implement British policy. Like diplomats everywhere, 'Politicals' included intelligence-gathering as an essential part of their duties.

Early British relations with Iran

At the end of the eighteenth century, when French diplomats arrived in Iran to negotiate for the proposed overland invasion of India, the British sent their own representatives to counter them. The newly-crowned Fatah Ali Shah agreed to oppose the passage of French troops through Iran, in return for British friendship against Zaman Shah of Afghanistan, whom it was feared would welcome French assistance to recover territories recently lost in the Punjab. In 1798 the East India Company appointed Harford Jones, one of its most talented orientalists, as Resident at Baghdad. Though this city was in Ottoman, not Iranian, territory, it was on the usual route between Western Europe and the Iranian capital at Tehran. Jones considered his area of responsibility to also include British relations with Iran and wrote to Jonathan Duncan, the Governor of Bombay, warning that to encourage Fatah Ali Shah to move against Zaman Shah ran the risk of stirring up a religious war between the Shi'a Iranians and the Sunni Afghans. He thought that Zaman Shah was more likely to be irritated than intimidated by a British-inspired threat from Iran and suggested that a diplomatic mission to Kabul might achieve better results. Duncan replied that he had made such a suggestion to Zaman Shah but, having received no answer, thought it best to refer the whole question to London. In the event, Fatah Ali Shah did threaten Herat (by then held not by Zaman Shah but by his brother and rival, Mahmud Shah) and Zaman Shah did withdraw from the Punjab, though in both cases for reasons unconnected with the British.[2]

The reference to London was pre-empted by the Marquis Wellesley (previously Earl of Mornington), who had become Governor-General in April 1798. He decided to send an embassy to Iran led by Captain John Malcolm of the Madras Army, an experienced political officer and a fluent speaker of Persian, who had been noted for his part in establishing the new British administration of Mysore (annexed by Wellesley after the defeat of Tipu Sultan in 1799). Malcolm's instructions were to establish an alliance against the French Democrats (at this time a term of disapproval) and to revive trading contacts between Iran and British India. Early in 1801 Fatah Ali Shah agreed to allow the East India Company's subjects to trade in his dominions and forbade the French from setting up any establishments on Iranian coasts or islands. The

British undertook to aid Fatah Ali Shah if he were attacked by the French and in return he promised to attack Zaman Shah if the latter invaded British India. These agreements were almost immediately overtaken by events. Zaman Shah was deposed by his brother Mahmud Shah and Russian troops occupied the kingdom of Georgia, despite long-standing Iranian claims to this part of the Caucasus. In 1804, when the Russians moved south to occupy Erivan, Fatah Ali Shah invoked the treaty he had made with Malcolm but the British refused to help, claiming that they were bound to act only against a French invasion.

As a consequence, British influence in Tehran declined, and French influence revived. In May 1807, at the treaty of Finkenstein, Iranian diplomats secured an undertaking from Napoleon that he would force the Russians to hand over the disputed Georgian lands if Fatah Ali Shah declared war on the British and gave free passage to a French army. An alliance was drafted between Napoleon, Fatah Ali Shah and Shah Shuja-ul-Mulk, who in 1803 had taken Mahmud Shah's throne at Kabul. All British subjects were to be expelled from Iran, while French advisors would be sent to train the Iranian army and establish modern cannon factories. As a result, some Iranian regular units were formed under French officers and the artillery, which had previously been completely outmatched by that of the Russians, was dramatically improved. Before the new army had a chance to prove itself against its Russian opponents, the Treaty of Tilsit made France and Russia allies once again. With nothing remaining of the Finkenstein accords apart from a treaty of friendship with Shah Shuja-ul-Mulk (of little value, since Herat remained independent under Mahmud Shah), Fatah Ali Shah accepted fresh British overtures.

Early British contacts with Sind

At the same time, the British sought to re-establish relations with the Talpur amirs of Sind. The East India Company had maintained a trading station at Tatta, at the mouth of the Indus, in both the seventeenth and eighteenth centuries, but this had eventually been closed. In 1799 the Bombay Government set up a new commercial agency there, partly in connection with Wellesley's measures to counter a French approach to India, and partly to gather intelligence about Zaman Shah of Afghanistan, who had re-asserted Durrani authority over Sind. Zaman Shah became suspicious of British motives and in 1801 ordered the ruler of Hyderabad (Lower Sind), Mir Fatah Ali Khan, to close the agency and expel its staff.

By 1808 both Zaman Shah and Mir Fatah Ali Khan had left the political scene and the amirs of Sind, with Durrani control receding, were willing to accept a British envoy. Captain Seton of the Bombay Army was received at Hyderabad and concluded a treaty promising the amirs protection against Iran. As this exceeded the instructions he had been given by the then Governor-General, Lord Minto, he was recalled and a new mission dispatched, headed by Nicholas Hankey Smith, an experienced political belonging to the Bombay Civil Service. A new treaty, sealed on 23 August 1809, provided for an exchange of ambassadors, with the amirs promising to keep the French from entering Sind. As part of the same diplomatic initiative, Mountstuart Elphinstone of the Bombay Civil Service, whose previous political experience had included appointments as British Resident at the Maratha courts of Nagpur and Gwalior, went to Peshawar to meet Shah Shuja-ul-Mulk, king of Afghanistan since deposing his brother Mahmud Shah six years previously. Shah Shuja-ul-Mulk promised that, if the British paid him for the costs involved, he would oppose any French or Iranian army attempting to reach India through his domains. Within weeks this became a dead letter, as Mahmud Shah returned from Herat, defeated Shah Shuja-ul-Mulk and recovered the Durrani throne. Elphinstone proposed that Shah Shuja-ul-Mulk, as a British ally, should be given funds to raise fresh troops and regain power, but the British Cabinet's attention was now returning to Iran, to which two separate British missions had been dispatched.

The first of these was headed by Malcolm, who had remained in the political service and been, for a time, Wellesley's private secretary. He was now given the task of persuading Fatah Ali Shah to dismiss the French envoys at his court and, while in Iran, noting the nature and resources of the territory through which a European army might approach India. Malcolm himself, when reporting on his previous mission, had pointed to the difficulty of convincing Iranian ministers that the East India Company was not a mere trading concern and that the Governor-General of Bengal had the authority to negotiate on equal terms with the Shah of Iran. Malcolm was only allowed to deal with the Governor of Fars, south-eastern Iran, partly because the French ambassador, General Gardane, told Fatah Ali Shah that he would leave if the British were received at Tehran and partly because of this question of diplomatic status. To the very end of British rule in India, despite the common border, Iranians always resented any attempt by the British to deal with them through the Government of India, rather than through the Foreign Office.

While Malcolm returned to India, an emissary from London, Sir Harford Jones, the former British Resident at Baghdad, arrived after going first to St Petersburg with a view to mediating between Iran and Russia over the disputed Georgian territories. Despite being authorized to arrange a treaty with the Shah of Iran in the name of the King of England, his instructions came from the Board of Control, not the Foreign Office, and he was told that any aid offered to Iran was to be restricted to the local resources of the East India Company. Jones arrived at Tehran in February 1809 and within a month, after Gardane had withdrawn in protest, had negotiated a provisional treaty by which the British promised mediation, troops and money if Iran were attacked by any European power. In the event of war between Iran and Afghanistan, the British would remain neutral but offer mediation if both sides asked for it. East India Company officers would take the place of the French advisers training the Shah's new regular troops. On learning of these terms, Minto decided that the Government of India should be directly represented in discussions about their implementation and sent Malcolm back to Iran.[3]

The first British officers in Balochistan

After arriving at Bombay late in 1809, Malcolm was approached by two young officers who had served in Hankey Smith's recent mission to Sind and who now sought to join his own to Iran. The two, Lieutenant Charles Christie and Ensign Henry Pottinger, both fluent Persian-speakers, were appointed to his staff with instructions to explore the country between India and Iran while the main mission went by sea. It was decided that they should travel in the guise of horse-dealers employed by a wealthy Hindu merchant, Sundarji Sivaji, a supplier of cavalry horses to the Bombay and Madras Armies, with an extensive network of contacts along the routes to Central Asia from where these animals came.[4]

Wearing local costume (which had the added benefit of concealing money-belts full of gold coins), furnished with letters from Sundarji Sivaji and accompanied by one of his agents and two reliable Indian servants, they sailed from Bombay in a small boat after dark on 2 January 1810. The other passengers included several Afghan horse-dealers, who immediately detected them as Europeans, but were prepared to talk and gave them useful advice on the best routes to take. Two weeks later they disembarked on the coast of Balochistan at Sonmiani, where they made contact with Sundarji Sivaji's network before moving inland to the seat of the Jam of Las Bela, Mir Khan I, a tributary of Nasir Khan of Kalat. Their cover was immediately blown when a man who had been a water-carrier in Hankey Smith's mission to Sind recognized them, but they restored it by claiming they had left the Company's service and now worked for Sundarji Sivaji. One of the Jam's officials read them a letter from a Hindu merchant of Karachi, forecasting their arrival and denouncing them as spies (which, indeed, they were) but they answered that this was merely because of Sindi fears that the British might seek to develop Sonmiani as a port to rival Karachi.

The Jam summoned them to his hall of audience, where they were received with more respect than was due to mere horse-traders, and questioned them in the presence of about 150 of his subjects. Mainly he asked about the customs and religions of the English and how these compared with the French, saying that he had heard from his subjects who had travelled to India that these two peoples were constantly at war. In particular, he wanted to know about the nature of the British government, the name of their king, the organization of his armies and fleets, and the distance from London to Constantinople. An experienced ruler, who had governed his small state for over thirty years, he nevertheless expressed astonishment when they told him of British battleships that carried a hundred guns and a thousand men. Two such crews, he said, could overrun his entire country. Surely no ship could carry enough food and water for so many men, and there were scarcely so many cannon in the Khan's citadel at Kalat. After being told about the battle of Trafalgar (fought four years previously), he accepted their story, but added that had these marvels been foretold by the Holy Prophet Himself, the people of Bela would still have demanded proof. Learning of their intention to push on to Kalat, he gave orders for them to be supplied with guides and letters of transit, though urging them to stay with him for another six weeks, as the cold in the mountains was likely to kill them all. When they said that their own native land was extremely cold, he told them they should have some consideration for those travelling with them. It was clear, however, that Jam Mir Ali knew that they were no more horse-dealers than he was and, though unable to find out their real intentions, he secretly asked them to send him two wall guns from Bombay.

The party reached Kalat on 9 February 1810 and found that Sundarji Sivaji's local agent had taken a house for them on the outskirts of the city, with paddocks for the horses they were supposed to be buying. Once again, letters from Karachi had forestalled them and a Pashtun trader declared he had seen both of them in Sind the previous year. They denied this, but at first people thought this was because, as former British officers, they did not wish to admit they had come down in the world by being forced to take service under a Hindu businessman. Later their cover story was accepted and their pale complexions were accepted as those of Uzbeks from Central Asia. They found that Nasir Khan I of Kalat had gone to Kachhi to avoid the cold weather, leaving one of his sons, the capable and courageous Mir Mustafa Khan, as governor in his absence. After being questioned, on Mustafa Khan's orders, by the Daroga of Kalat they were allowed to remain but, after a month (during which they made a careful survey of the defences of Kalat fort and Christie gained a reputation as a medical practitioner) they feared they might once again come under suspicion. They left Kalat and resumed their journey by moving through the mountain passes to Nushki, fifty miles north-west of the capital.[5]

There, on 19 March 1810, Christie decided to divide the expedition and go northwards himself, through Sistan, while Pottinger took a more southerly route with the aim of rejoining him at Kirman, in eastern Iran. Christie travelled though the deserts of Helmand to Herat, where Mahmud Shah's brother, Hajji Firoz al-Din Khan, had been left as governor while Mahmud ruled at Kabul. Christie kept up his disguise as a Muslim horse-coper but after a month decided to leave, avoiding suspicion by saying he was making a pilgrimage to the holy city of Mashhad in north-east Iran. He then crossed into Iranian territory and was relieved to find that travellers enjoyed far more security than any he had experienced since leaving India.

Pottinger's route lay through the wilds of Kharan and Makran, where he had to buy the protection of a series of tribal sardars before entering Iranian-ruled Sistan and meeting Christie at Isfahan on 30 June 1810, a month after they had planned. They then made contact with Malcolm near Tabriz in north-western Iran, seven months after leaving Bombay, during which time Christie had travelled 2,250 miles and Pottinger 2,412 and both had compiled a mass of valuable military and political information. Christie was appointed one of the new British military advisers to the Iranian Army and Pottinger accompanied Malcolm back to Bombay, from where he would later be appointed British Resident in Sind.

Fatah Ali Shah of Iran

British diplomacy at Tehran had been greatly hindered by constant disputes between Jones and Malcolm and at one point there had been a real risk of a duel between the two envoys. The problem was settled by the appointment of Sir Gore Ouseley as British ambassador, answerable directly to the Foreign Office. Ouseley had previously been in the East India Company's political service and British Resident at the court of the King of Awadh. A keen orientalist, his diplomatic skills made him a good choice for this new post and in 1812 Jones's preliminary treaty was ratified as the Treaty of Tehran, an agreement that governed Anglo-Iranian relations for the next forty-two years. In return for a subsidy, Fatah Ali Shah agreed to oppose the entry into his dominions of any European power hostile to the British and to use his influence with the independent khanates of Central Asia to prevent a European army invading India through their territories.

The British also promised military aid to Fatah Ali Shah against any European power invading his dominions but this proved of no value when Shah, under nationalist and religious pressure, resumed hostilities against the Russians. Although the British advisers fought alongside their Iranian soldiers (Christie himself was killed in action on 31 October 1812), the Russians had once again become an important British ally against the French. British interests required the preservation of the Russian alliance and British aid was denied on the grounds that Fatah Ali Shah had been the aggressor. The best that Ouseley could do was to achieve some amelioration of the harsh terms imposed by the Russians at the peace treaty of Gulistan (24 October 1813). Iran was forced to abandon its claims over Georgia and neighbouring areas of the Caucasus and to concede that Russia alone could keep war-vessels in the Caspian Sea. The only sop to Fatah Ali Shah was that his younger son, Abbas Mirza, a modernizing statesman and capable general, was recognized as his rightful heir.

A new war between Russia and Iran began in 1826, with Abbas Mirza leading a campaign to recover the lost provinces. Despite their numerical advantage and their British advisers, his troops were still mostly composed of contingents raised on the traditional system of military tenure, who stood little chance against a regular army that twelve years earlier had defeated the greatest captain of the age and reached the suburbs of Paris. A series of Iranian defeats brought the Russians within five days march of Tehran itself. Fatah Ali Shah was forced to accept the humiliating peace treaty of Turkmenchai (21 February 1828), confirming all the gains made by Russia in the treaty of Gulistan.[6]

Recognizing that another war with Russia would be unwinnable, Fatah Ali Shah revived the Iranian claim on Herat, from where Kamran Shah (who had succeeded his father Mahmud Shah in 1829) continued to launch slave-raids into Iranian territory. In 1833 Abbas Mirza's son, Muhammad Mirza, led an army to Herat and laid siege to the city. Iranian dreams of emulating the conquests of Nadir Shah were shattered when Abbas Mirza died at Mashhad on

25 October 1833. Muhammad Mirza made a truce with Kamran Shah, who was left in possession of Herat in return for promising to end his raids into Iranian territory, and went back to Tehran. There, he was declared by Fatah Ali Shah to be his heir and, as Muhammad Shah, succeeded him in 1835. He continued his grandfather's policy of accepting a rapport with Russia while advancing to the east and on 22 November 1837 once more sat down before Herat.

The harsh terms of the treaty of Turkmenchai had forced British statesmen to face the prospect of Iran, willingly or otherwise, becoming a satellite of the Russian Empire. So far from welcoming the advance of Russia as an extension of European Christian civilization, British politicians saw in it only a threat to their own empire in India, where there were still a number of independent country powers to dispute the East India Company's hegemony. Foremost among these was the kingdom of Lahore, which Maharaja Ranjit Singh had built up from being a viceroyalty under the Durranis into a Sikh-dominated state comprising most of the Punjab, Kashmir and Peshawar.

Ranjit Singh's rule did not extend over all Sikhs nor over all the Punjab. Many of his subjects were Muslims and much of his territory lay outside the Punjab, the 'Five-Rivers Land'. Nevertheless, his kingdom of Lahore was, for convenience, commonly referred to as either 'the Punjab' or 'the Sikhs'. By 1830 it was, after the East India Company, the most powerful state in the sub-continent, with a professional Western-style army trained by Napoleonic veterans and regarded by itself, and by many British officers too, as a match for the Company's own sepoys. It became an important feature of British policy to be on friendly terms with Ranjit Singh, whose kingdom was seen as a valuable buffer state against any invasion of India from the direction of Afghanistan.

The British game-plan for Afghanistan

Beyond Ranjit Singh's territories lay those of Dost Muhammad Barakzai, who had ruled in Kabul since 1826, and beyond those again lay the Khanates of Bokhara and Khiva (the modern republic of Uzbekistan). Many British statesmen, seemingly quite unaware that the local rulers regarded all "Feringhi" (from *Farang*, or Frank, meaning Westerners of any kind) with equal suspicion, believed that there was a market waiting to be developed. If British piece goods could reach the area, it was thought, the economic advantages brought by the Industrial Revolution would enable them to outsell their Russian competitors. Lord Ellenborough (since September 1828, President of the Board of Control in Wellington's Cabinet) wondered what exactly the Central Asian khans had to offer in exchange for these goods but accepted that a profitable trade would encourage them to maintain friendly relations with the British and so keep Russian influence away from India.

To reach the markets of Central Asia, the British needed to open a route that would shorten the long overland journey into Afghanistan through northern India and the Punjab from their seaport at Calcutta. The answer seemed to lie along the lower Indus, so that goods could be landed at Karachi and then taken in steamboats (a relatively recent invention) up the river to Sukkur. There they would be transferred to the kafilas that would take them through Balochistan, up the Bolan to Kandahar and thence to western Central Asia. An alternative would be for the boats to continue into the Punjab, where their cargoes would be loaded onto kafilas heading through Peshawar and the Khyber Pass to Kabul and from there to the River Oxus (Amu Darya).

Access to the lower Indus required the consent of the amirs of Sind. Access to its higher reaches required the consent of Ranjit Singh. In January 1830, as a way of broaching the subject with both powers in a single move, Sir John Malcolm (by this time, governor of Bombay) was informed that the British Government was sending a team of six dapple-grey English dray-horses, as a diplomatic gift to Ranjit Singh, who was known to delight in good horses acquired in this way. The animals were to be landed at Bombay and then taken to Karachi and up the Indus to Lahore by boat, accompanied by an officer who would prepare the way for British commercial development in Central Asia and simultaneously gather intelligence about the country through which he passed. Malcolm selected Alexander Burnes, assistant political officer to Henry Pottinger, the former traveller through Balochistan and Iran, who at this time was the Resident in Cutch, the British-protected state adjoining south-west Sind.

The amirs of Sind, well aware of the true purpose behind the voyage, delayed giving permission for its passage as long as they could but eventually gave way. The horses were duly delivered to Ranjit Singh as a gift, ostensibly celebrating the accession of William IV as King of England in June 1830. Burnes reported that the river was a practicable trade route and in 1832 Pottinger concluded a new treaty with the amirs. Merchants from any part of India were allowed to enter Sind and the Indus was opened to free navigation by British subjects, with the proviso that no military stores were to be carried and that neither party would look with the eye of covetousness upon the territories of the other.[7]

Meanwhile, Burnes, after reporting to Bentinck his delivery of the horses, was selected to head another journey of exploration, this time in disguise, from the Punjab to Kabul (where he visited the Barakzai ruler, Amir Dost Muhammad), Bokhara, Mashhad, Tehran and finally back by sea to Bombay. He started in January 1832 and finished in February 1833, after which he published his account of the journey, returned to England, where he become a social lion, and then resumed his post in Cutch in 1835. From there, Lord Auckland, who succeeded Lord William Bentinck as Governor-General in March 1836, sent him on a mission to Dost Muhammad under the cover of concluding a commercial treaty. Burnes reached Kabul in September 1837 but despite prolonged negotiations no agreement was achieved.

The Iranian expeditions against Herat, 1837–38

At Herat, Kamran Shah had resumed his slave raids into Balochistan and Sistan. The British ambassador to Iran, Hugh Ellis, tried to persuade Muhammad Shah that, although a renewed campaign against Herat might well be justified by Kamran's conduct, it would only weaken his army and treasury and leave him less able to resist Russian pressure. Lord Palmerston, Foreign Secretary in Melbourne's second Cabinet, complained to his opposite number in St Petersburg, Count Karl Nesselrode, that Count Simonich, the Anglophobe Russian minister at Tehran, was encouraging Muhammad Shah to march on Herat. As, said Palmerston, this would obviously be contrary to Muhammad Shah's best interests and at variance with declared Russian policy, such action could only be detrimental to the friendly relations existing between the two Great Powers. Using standard diplomatic terminology, he expressed the belief that Count Simonich must surely be exceeding his instructions. Nesselrode replied that Simonich had no orders to encourage Muhammad Shah in his warlike course and had, indeed, officially advised him against it. The British envoy at Tehran, he thought, must have been misinformed. As evidence of Russia's good intentions, he (somewhat disingenuously) invited the British Ambassador at St Petersburg to visit the Russian Foreign Office and read the letter books of the Asiatic Department for himself.

A new British Ambassador at Tehran, John McNeill, like Ellis before him, thought that Muhammad Shah had every right and, indeed, a duty to his own subjects, to put an end to Kamran's raids but, in the Great Game, the aces of Europe counted higher than the kings of Western Asia. In consequence, when Muhammad Shah marched against Herat in July 1837, the British and Russian ministers both remained behind at Tehran to mark the disapproval of their respective governments. McNeill advised Palmerston to consider a seaborne landing on the Iranian coast of the Persian Gulf, to make it clear to Muhammad Shah that the British really meant what they said about protecting Kamran Shah.

After an exhausting march, Muhammad Shah's ill-found troops reached Herat in December 1837. Kamran Shah, inside his walls, defied him. As the siege dragged on, McNeill joined the Iranian camp in March 1838. He persuaded Muhammad Shah to call off a planned assault and personally entered Herat where he negotiated an agreement with Kamran's able though unscrupulous wazir, Yar Muhammad. On returning to the camp, he discovered that Simonich had followed him from Tehran and, during his own absence inside the besieged city, had persuaded Muhammad Shah to continue hostilities. At the beginning of June 1838, McNeill broke off diplomatic relations with Muhammad Shah and asked for his passports. On 25 June an attempt to storm the walls of Herat, led by a battalion of Russian mercenaries under a Polish-born adventurer, General Berovski, was thrown back and Berovski himself was killed.

Six days before this fight, troops of the East India Company's Bombay Army, dispatched on orders from London, had taken the Iranian island of Kharak, off the vital port of Bushir (Abu Shahr) in the Persian Gulf. McNeill turned back to Herat to deliver an ultimatum from Palmerston to Muhammad Shah that the Iranians must withdraw from Herat or face a British declaration of war. In the interests of Anglo-Russian relations, Nesselrode had already recalled Simonich on the grounds that, this time, he really had exceeded his instructions, though the slow pace of communications meant that no-one at Herat yet knew that this message was on its way.

A British political officer travelling in an unofficial capacity, Lieutenant Edred Pottinger of the Bombay Artillery (a nephew of Henry Pottinger) had been inside the city when the siege started. Aware that British policy was to support Kamran Shah against Iran, he had revealed his identity and military specialization (all artillerymen at this period were trained in siege-craft) and offered his services accordingly. Like Hector in Homer's *Iliad*, he became the inspirational leader of the defence and, as the prestige of Muhammad Shah's Russian mercenaries declined, so that of the British rose. With his Gulf coastline at the mercy of British sea-power, Muhammad Shah raised the siege on 9 September 1838 and fell back towards his capital, claiming to have asserted Iranian authority over Kabul and Kandahar (which was true only in that the Barakzais had indeed offered to help him against Kamran Shah if he would help them against Ranjit Singh) and reduced Herat to a hollow shell (which was not true at all). He denounced the perfidious British for violating their three previous treaties with his country and declared that his withdrawal was caused only by the approach of winter and a desire to protect his subjects in other provinces.

Dost Muhammad had been quite willing to encourage the extension of British trade into Central Asia and to promise he would oppose Iranian advances. The problem was that his price, British support for the recovery of Peshawar (taken by Ranjit Singh three years previously) was too high for the British to pay. They would not even give him arms against Iran, for fear that he would turn them on his Barakzai brothers in Kandahar, or, even worse from the British point of view, on Ranjit Singh. Auckland, faced on his other borders with the possibility of one war against Burma and another against Nepal and with rumours of unrest inside British India, decided that Ranjit Singh's friendship was more valuable than that of Dost Muhammad.

The Tripartite Alliance, 1838. Auckland, Ranjit Singh and Shah Shuja-ul-Mulk

Nevertheless, a friendly administration in Afghanistan was considered essential to forestall the growth of Russian influence in Central Asia. The simple solution was regime change. Shah Shuja-ul-Mulk, kept as a British pensioner against just such a need, could be brought forward as the legitimate ruler and restored to his throne with the support of Ranjit Singh, to whom he had ceded Peshawar in return for promises of aid for this very purpose. This solution had the added advantage of conciliating Ranjit Singh by British recognition of his claim to Peshawar in compensation for preventing his seizure of Shikarpur in Upper Sind. Ranjit's claim to Shikarpur was based on its notional cession to him by Shah Shuja-ul-Mulk at the same time and for the same reason as that of Peshawar. The fact that Shikarpur, like Peshawar, was not in Shah Shuja-ul-Mulk's possession (for all that he claimed to be the legitimate ruler of both on the grounds that they had been part of the Durrani empire), embarrassed neither party.

The British, however, wished to keep Ranjit Singh away from their intended trade-route to Central Asia via Balochistan and the Bolan Pass. The alternative route, via the Khyber Pass, was already under Ranjit's control, so that allowing him to take Shikarpur, on the Indus, would have given him a stranglehold over their entire scheme. In 1838, in accordance with instructions from Auckland, Henry Pottinger negotiated another treaty with the amirs of Sind. After a year's protracted negotiation, they accepted a British Resident at Hyderabad and agreed to British arbitration in any future dispute with Ranjit Singh. In effect, the British gained control over the amirs' foreign policy in return for protecting them against Ranjit Singh.

At Kabul, negotiations broke down when the British refused to give Dost Muhammad the same kind of guarantee against Muhammad Shah of Iran that they had given to Kamran Shah. On 21 April 1839 Dost Muhammad received at his court a Russian officer, Lieutenant Jan Vitkeivich, who had reached Kabul four months earlier, bearing a letter in which the Tsar of Russia expressed his goodwill towards the Amir of Kabul and his happiness at the prospect of encouraging trade between their respective subjects. Palmerston had already asked Nesselrode for some explanation of Vitkeivich's arrival, hinting broadly that the United Kingdom was perfectly able to defend its interests in the region. He was told that the letter was merely a diplomatic response to one that Dost Muhammad had sent to the Tsar and that Vitkeivich's journey was solely one of exploration, into countries so remote from Russia that further knowledge of them was necessary to prevent any ruinously costly commercial undertaking. As for any Russian threat against India, such as Palmerston's note seemed to suggest was a possibility, Nesselrode told the Russian Ambassador in London to ask the British Cabinet to look at a map of Central Asia and consider the vast distances shown between Russian and British territory. At Kabul, Burnes left the city a few days after Dost Muhammad received Vitkeivich. A decision by Auckland to restore Shah Shuja-ul-Mulk to his throne followed within a month.

Vitkeivich journeyed back to St Petersburg, hoping for some recognition of his activities. Like Simonich at Herat, he found that his government was disinclined to sacrifice friendly relations with the British for the sake of a quarrel in a faraway country of which it knew nothing. Nesselrode refused to receive him and he was found dead in his hotel room, reportedly shot with his own pistol. The general view was that, in an excess of disappointment and Slav melancholia, he had taken his own life, though conspiracy theorists suspected that he was murdered by Russian government agents to prevent him revealing the real reason for his mission to Kabul.

In 1837, when passing through Kachhi on his way to open British relations with Dost Muhammad, Burnes had exchanged letters of courtesy with the young Mir Muhammad Hasan, son and heir of Mahrab Khan II of Kalat. On returning to India after the failure of his mission, he ordered his assistant, Lieutenant Robert Leech of the Bombay Engineers, whom he had detached to Kandahar, to return to Sind. After reaching Quetta, Leech was invited to

Kalat by Mahrab Khan II, who hoped for British protection both against the Barakzai rulers of Kandahar and the Talpur amirs of Sind and also for British support against his own Brahui sardars. At first the visit went well enough but Mahrab Khan II was alienated by Leech's tactlessness and Leech, disenchanted with the Khan, rejoined Burnes at Shikarpur.

On 23 June 1838 at Simla (Shimla), the summer capital of British India, Auckland proclaimed that, by an agreement between Ranjit Singh, Shah Shuja-ul-Mulk and the Government of India, the friends and enemies of any one of the three contracting parties would henceforth be the friends and enemies of all. In consequence of what was described as Muhammad Shah's unjustified attack on Herat (something that the British diplomats in Iran did not believe), and Dost Muhammad's readiness to welcome him (something that the British politicals in India did not believe), the latter would be deposed and replaced by Shah Shuja-ul-Mulk, whose return was eagerly desired by his legitimate subjects (something that nobody anywhere believed).

In return for British support, Shah Shuja-ul-Mulk agreed to accept British control of his foreign policy and leave his nephew Kamran Shah in possession of Herat. He also gave up his claim to Sind in return for the amirs paying him the thirty years-worth of tribute that he claimed, amounting to 15 lakhs of rupees. Most of this was to be passed on to Ranjit Singh as compensation for giving up his claim to Shikarpur. Ranjit Singh agreed to station 5,000 regular troops at Peshawar under a Muslim general to provide Shah Shuja-ul-Mulk with any assistance required, funded by an annual subsidy of 2 lakhs of rupees, paid to him by the British in Shah Shuja-ul-Mulk's name.

Preparations for the invasion of Afghanistan, 1838–39

It was originally envisaged that, while Shah Shuja-ul-Mulk and the main invasion force marched into Afghanistan through the Bolan, the troops from Peshawar, accompanied by Lieutenant Colonel Claude Wade, the British Resident at Lahore, would march up the Khyber with 4,000 of Shah Shuja's own mercenaries under his eldest son, Timur Mirza. The main invasion force would be a large British formation, the Army of the Indus, led by Sir John Keane, Commander-in-Chief, Bombay. One division was provided by the Bengal Army, together with Shah Shuja's Contingent. This formation was a brigade of sepoys and British officers virtually indistinguishable from the Bengal Army (from which most of its personnel came) but paid for out of the British subsidy to Shah Shuja-ul-Mulk. It was assumed that when Shah Shuja-ul-Mulk had regained his throne, the British troops would return to India and the Contingent would remain as the regular nucleus of the army he would raise from his own revenues. That neither the men nor their officers were his own subjects was immaterial, as most of the sepoys in the Bengal Army itself came not from the East India Company's territory but from that of its subsidiary ally, the King of Awadh, traditionally the home of India's best mercenary soldiers. The position of the British officers was no different from that of many others attached from their regular regiments to the armies of Indian princes under British protection.

By the end of November the force had assembled at Ferozpur, in Ranjit Singh's territory, and the Maharaja himself came 30 miles south from Lahore to meet Auckland there. The arrival of Edred Pottinger with the news that Muhammad Shah had retreated from Herat made little difference to the invasion plans. Auckland declared that the need for a friendly (i.e. compliant) government in Afghanistan remained the same, though in view of the Iranian withdrawal, the size of the force to be employed was reduced. On Keane's insistence, the battering train was retained, just in case the Iranians returned to Herat and the British needed to retake it. Siege guns were notoriously heavy and difficult to move and would take weeks to drag even to the top of the Bolan.

The Bengal troops then marched down the Indus to Bahawalpur, where in 1835 Nawab Muhammad Bahawal Khan III had handed over control of his foreign affairs in return for British protection against Ranjit Singh. Reminded of his treaty obligations, he struggled to find fodder from his desert kingdom for the 30,000 baggage camels carrying the stores and supplies required by some 10,000 soldiers and 38,000 civilian followers who provided their logistic support. They pressed on into Sind, where Sir Henry Pottinger and his assistant Alexander Burnes negotiated their passage with the amirs. In vain did these princes protest that they had already paid their arrears of tribute to Shah Shuja-ul-Mulk in return for his recognition of their independence. In vain did they produce the Holy Korans in which this agreement had been recorded. In vain did they point to the treaties by which the British agreed not to move military stores through their country nor to station troops on either bank of the Indus. They were told that if Shah Shuja-ul-Mulk still claimed the tribute, it could only be because they had not actually paid it and that, in any case, all existing treaties had to be set aside in order to deal with the common danger from Afghanistan. The objection to troops being stationed on the Indus was met by the British forming their supply base at Bukkur, an island in the Indus, and therefore, as the treaty stipulated, not on either bank.

The main element of the Bombay division moved by sea to the mouth of the Indus, landed at Vikkur in December 1838, and began to move upstream. When the *killadar* (commandant) of the fortress of Manora delayed handing over his keys, it was bombarded by British warships on 3 February 1839 and the Bombay troops added Karachi to the list of garrisons already occupied without British loss. Two days earlier, despite warlike demonstrations from their Baloch retainers, the amirs yielded to *force majeure*, signed a new treaty and handed over 10 lakhs of rupees. Their eyes had been opened, they said, to the strength and good faith of the British.

Henry Pottinger, who had no taste for the policy he was required to implement, requested Auckland to make allowances for their previous delays, caused by the need to overcome the fears of their tribesmen 'who had always been led to think that our only object was to extend our dominion'.[8] His reluctance to impose even harsher terms only incurred Auckland's disapproval. At the end of February 1839, the leading regiments of the Bengal Division of the Army of the Indus marched out of Shikarpur, en route to restore Shah Shuja-ul-Mulk to the throne of his ancestors. With them, as evidence of the political importance of the expedition, went William MacNaghten, previously Secretary to the Government of India in the Foreign Department, and now British Envoy and Minister at the court of Shah Shuja-ul-Mulk, the revival of whose Durrani Empire he had actively advocated.

Thus a British force set out to build a strong and friendly state in Afghanistan, restore its legitimate government, bring stability and prosperity to its people, and promote the security of British interests throughout the region. It remained to be seen whether the *Iqbal* (Luck) of the East India Company, a minor local deity that had for the past eighty years brought success to the British in India, would retain its potency on the edge of Central Asia.

3

THE BRITISH ARMY IN KALAT, 1839

Courage, boys, tis one to ten
But we return all gentlemen,
All gentlemen as well as they,
Over the Hills and far away.
Over the Hills and over the Main,
To Flanders, Portugal and Spain,
The Queen commands and we obey,
Over the Hills and far away.

George Farquar, *The Recruiting Officer*

The Army of the Indus, as it passed through Balochistan, depended mostly on pack transport, predominantly camels each occupying 15 feet of road and travelling at 2 miles in the hour. The numbers required by this force swamped the capacity of the local carriers who moved the ordinary peace-time traffic of the country. Under pressure from their princes and attracted by the favorable hiring rates offered by the British, transport contractors collected every animal they could find, including those that were not baggage camels at all, but part of the local domestic or breeding herds, quite unsuited to the rigours of a campaign or any kind of long-haul work. Many died even before reaching Shikarpur and many more did so within days of leaving it. With limited supplies of fodder, beasts that were kept together went hungry. Those turned out to graze for themselves were liable to be carried off by Baloch robbers, who could scarcely believe their good fortune at the arrival of such easy prey. Others disappeared with their loads and drivers when the latter, fearing for their lives as much as their livelihoods, began to desert.

To spread the burden on local resources, the Bengal Division marched a week ahead of Shah Shuja's Contingent. The Bombay Division, bringing up the rear, found the country swept bare of supplies, and the road lined with the decomposing bodies of dead animals. On 10 March 1839, ten days and 146 miles after leaving Shikarpur, the first troops reached Dadhar, at the foot of the Bolan Pass. After halting for ten days, with no sign of the local supplies on which they had counted, they pushed on through the Bolan and ten days later arrived at Quetta, in the Afghan-ruled plain of Shal. Water was to be had, but little food, and within two days of their arrival the soldiers were on half-rations. The Bombay Division, still 10 miles short of Quetta, reported on 4 April 1839 that all were down to quarter-rations, with nothing to be obtained by local purchase. All the while, camels died and their loads were abandoned, while ever-watchful Baloch plunderers raided the supply kafilas with long-practiced ease.[1]

Negotiations with Mahrab Khan II

Despite his irritation with Lieutenant Leech, Mahrab Khan II had ordered his officials in Kachhi to co-operate with the British forces passing through his country and issued a proclamation that any disputes should be referred to the British generals for settlement. Nevertheless, there were tales that, to prevent their sale to the British, Mahrab Khan II's Hindu financier, Diwan Bacha, had confiscated the stores of grain collected by Leech at Kalat and that the Khan's brother, Muhammad Azim Khan, had seized the grain held by local Hindu dealers in Kachhi, where he had been sent to arrange the safe passage of the troops. In fact both of these occurrences derived from the internal administration of Kalat, quite unconnected with the British, but Mahrab Khan II was sent a severe letter by Burnes, who had been appointed Political Agent for Balochistan. An even less welcome letter came from Shah Shuja-ul-Mulk, re-asserting Durrani claims over Kalat, and pointedly mentioning that Shah Nawaz Khan, the Muhabatzai pretender defeated by Mahrab Khan in 1832, was present in his camp.[2]

In response, Mahrab Khan II sent two of his ministers to treat with the British. One was Wazir Mulla Hasan, whose father had been dismissed from the wazirship by Mahrab Khan II in favour of Daud Muhammad, and the other was Sayyad Muhammad Sharif, a Naib in Kachhi with grudges of his own against the Khan. Both saw in the coming of the British a chance to bring him down. Wazir Mulla Hasan, in arranging the murder of Daud Muhammad, had made it appear that he was acting under Mahrab Khan's orders. Daud

Muhammad's two brothers, Ghulam Khan and Khan Muhammad, had marriage ties with Brahui sardars whose territory lay near the Bolan. Taking the chance to be avenged on Mahrab Khan II, they secretly joined forces with Wazir Mulla Hasan and encouraged their Brahui relations to harass the British supply columns. At the same time, they assured the British political officers of their own friendship towards the British and produced letters to which Mulla Hasan had fixed Mahrab Khan II's seal (held by him as wazir), encouraging the Bolan tribes to raid British convoys.

Wazir Mulla Hasan's promises that he would persuade Mahrab Khan II to adopt a more friendly policy brought him generous financial awards from the gullible British. He then returned to Kalat, where he denounced them for attempting to bribe him and reported that there was little to be feared from their forces. Mahrab Khan II nevertheless seemed genuinely happy to meet Burnes who, with Sayyad Muhammad Sharif in his train, followed the wazir to Kalat. 'Had he had wings, he would have flown to the meeting', one of his courtiers later told Charles Masson, the British antiquary and intelligence-gatherer, who travelled extensively in Balochistan and neighbouring countries at this period. Mahrab Khan II's only stipulation was that the British mission should not include Leech, whom he considered *persona non grata*.[3]

Burnes's treaty with Kalat, 28 March 1839

At Kalat, Mahrab Khan protested to Burnes at the way he was being treated, especially by Shah Shuja-ul-Mulk, to whom he had given shelter in the days of the latter's adversity, but who now, contrary to the custom of the country, refused to return this generosity. As for the privations suffered by the Army of the Indus when passing through Kachhi and the Bolan, the Khan complained that the troops had damaged property and destroyed crops that were scanty enough even in a good year and had taken water needed for irrigation, especially so in that year of drought. Despite this, he said, he had helped the British as best he could, only to find that, when he might have allied himself with his neighbour, the Shah of Iran, or even the Russians, he was asked to accept subordination to Shah Shuja-ul-Mulk. He warned the British of their folly in choosing to support the worst possible characters, first the faithless Kamran Shah of Herat and now his worthless uncle, Shah Shuja ul-Mulk, who relied on an army of foreigners and unbelievers instead of his own people. He forecast that it would be easy enough for the British to install Shah Shuja-ul-Mulk at Kabul, but without the continued presence of their troops he would soon be driven out again.

Mahrab Khan began negotiations by asking for British help recovering Karachi from the Talpurs, but this seems to have been merely an opening gambit. Burnes reported that what little grain there was had indeed been made available to the British, and that Mahrab Khan had sent them 13,000 sheep, the staple product of the country. At the end of March 1839 the Khan accepted a treaty that had been drafted by MacNaghten and sent to Kalat with Burnes. He acknowledged that he was subject to Shah Shuja-ul-Mulk in the same way that Nasir Khan the Great had been subject to Ahmad Shah Durrani, and promised to do his best to obtain supplies, carriage and escorts for British kafilas passing between Shikarpur and Quetta. In return, the British undertook to refund the costs involved without hesitation, and to give him an annual subsidy of a lakh and a half of rupees, payable by half-yearly instalments, commencing from the date of the treaty and continuing as long as British troops were in his country. The treaty also confirmed Mahrab Khan's possession of the territories held by his ancestors since the time of Ahmad Shah Durrani, listed as Kalat, Kachhi, Kohistan (the Hill country), Makran, Kech, Bela and the port of Sonmiani. The British promised never to interfere between him and his subjects, and in particular to lend no assistance to Shah Nawaz Khan or any other descendant of Muhabat Khan.[4] With the treaty signed and sealed on 28 March 1839, Burnes started back for Quetta, leaving his Hindu *munshi* (secretary) Mohan Lal, to follow him one march ahead of Mahrab Khan.

Wazir Mulla Hasan saw that British friendship, and especially the ready money represented by their subsidy, would strengthen Mahrab Khan's position. He therefore told the Khan that if the latter went to Shah Shuja ul-Mulk's camp at Quetta to pay his respects in person, as he had agreed to do, the British would arrest him and set up Shah Nawaz Khan to rule as their puppet. As evidence, he pointed out that when Mahrab Khan had first agreed to go to Quetta with a retinue of 500 troopers, Burnes had said that twenty would be enough. This number, argued the wazir, was too small to ensure the Khan's liberty or maintain his prestige. Such a limitation, together with the idea of travelling behind an idolatrous Hindu, fell far short of what Mahrab Khan considered due to him as a ruling prince and he postponed his departure from Kalat accordingly.[5]

The theft of the treaty

Two marches short of Quetta, Burnes's kafila halted for the night and camped as usual. The camp was then raided by robbers, who killed two or three men before making off with several baggage camels. In the morning, it became clear that the missing animals included one carrying a treasure chest with 2,000 rupees (intended for travelling expenses) and the British copy of the treaty sealed a few days earlier. It was generally agreed that, because they had taken this particular camel and left most of the remainder, the robbers had possessed some inside knowledge of the loads.

When the attack was reported to Mahrab Khan, he ordered his lieutenant governor at Quetta, Naib Rahim Dad, to investigate. The Naib discovered that the camel in question was one in the personal train of Sayyad Muhammad Sharif, the Khan's minister who was travelling with the kafila and to whom Burnes had given the treaty and money for sake-keeping. He also reported that the person responsible for the robbery was Sayyad Muhammad Sharif himself, who had paid a relative 1,400 rupees to lead the raid. Mahrab Khan took no further action, but Burnes, unaware of Naib Rahim Dad's findings, was persuaded by Sayyad Muhammad Sharif that the Khan had changed his mind about the treaty and had arranged the attack in order to steal the British copy. To the British, this tale, coming after the discovery of the documents inciting attacks on their convoys in the Bolan, was enough to prove Mahrab Khan's hostility. 'The Khan of Khelat is our implacable enemy' wrote Mac-Naghten, 'and Sir John Keane is burning with revenge. There never was such treatment inflicted on human beings as we have been subjected to on our progress through the Khan's country'.[6] For the time being, the advance into Afghanistan took priority, but Kalat's turn would come.

The Restoration of the Durrani Empire

After a halt of eleven days at Quetta, the Army of the Indus marched for Kandahar. The Khojak Pass, judged to be as difficult as the Bolan itself if held by determined defenders, was "opened with a golden key", as the local expression had it, and the local sardar rode in to pay his respects to Shah Shuja-ul-Mulk and receive his pre-negotiated award of 10,000 rupees. The Barakzai princes of Kandahar, supposing that other chiefs had been promised equally generous treatment if they changed sides, fled north-westwards and took refuge in Iran. On 23 April 1839 Shah Shuja-ul-Mulk entered the city to the cheers of as many of his subjects as British funds could muster.

On 27 June, the same day that Maharaja Ranjit Singh died, leaving his kingdom of Lahore to an unsettled future, the army moved on. The four heavy guns of the battering train, dragged up the passes with such labour, were left behind. Herat was still a possible destination, but the remaining fortresses on the road to Kabul were thought likely to be as easily gained as Kandahar. Indeed, Dost Muhammad expected the British to head for Herat while Ranjit Singh's promised troops marched via the Khyber to Jalalabad, where he accordingly stationed his best troops. Ghazni, the only place to offer serious resistance, was taken by a *coup de main* on 23 July, after its gates had been blown down by gunpowder, a regular tactic in Indian sieges, where gateways were by European standards generally ill-fortified. The Army of the Indus continued its advance and Shah Shuja-ul-Mulk re-entered Kabul, which he had last seen thirty years previously, on 7 August 1839. Shortly afterwards his son, Timur Mirza, arrived from Jalalabad with the late Ranjit Singh's contingent. This was followed by six weeks of reviews, celebrations, and awards marking the restoration of the Durrani Empire and the Army of the Indus's accomplishment of its mission.[7]

But for subsequent events, this campaign would have been remembered as one of the most brilliant in British military history. The Army of the Indus had marched 1,200 miles in ten months, crossed deserts and mountains, reached the heart of a wild and warlike country, won every engagement with only minimal casualties, and effected a desired regime change. Not for the last time in the history of war, however, it was found that a mission accomplished did not mean an immediate withdrawal of the victorious troops. Thus, while part of the Bengal Division began a return to India through the Khyber Pass, a greater part remained behind. This was only partly to prop up Shah Shuja-ul-Mulk, support for whom was displayed only by his personal entourage and the British Envoy at his court. An equally important factor was the situation at Herat, where despite all the efforts of Edred Pottinger (appointed Political Agent there as a reward for his services during the recent siege), the old custom of slave-raiding had been resumed, with the consequential likelihood of provoking another Iranian invasion. In such a case, British troops might be needed to protect Herat, something that could be more easily done if they were still in Afghanistan. Apart from this, the country seemed secure enough and the perennially cash-strapped Government of India sought to achieve a peace dividend by recalling the Bombay Division as soon as Shah Shuja-ul-Mulk was enthroned at Kabul.

The British invasion of Kalat

Balochistan remained as unfinished business. When Shah Shuja-ul-Mulk and the British Envoy moved on from Kandahar, relations with Kalat had been placed in the hands of the British political agent at Quetta, Captain John Dickson Bean, 23rd Bengal Native Infantry, late commandant of the 1st Infantry in Shah Shuja's Contingent. Believing that Mahrab Khan was behind the theft of the treaty and the continuing raids on British convoys, he at first refused to receive any communications from him, but then agreed to meet Wazir Mulla Hasan. The wazir had been sent by Mahrab Khan with presents and congratulations to Shah Shuja-ul-Mulk on his occupation of Kandahar but never went beyond Quetta, from where he sent back messages to Kalat saying that the British would soon be defeated.

When Shah Shuja-ul-Mulk reached Kabul, Mahrab Khan ordered Naib Rahim Dad, his lieutenant governor at Quetta, to go there with further gifts and congratulations. Despite his earlier zeal in investigating the theft of the treaty, Rahim Dad pleaded that he was unable to make the journey and it later emerged that he was pre-occupied with rustling baggage camels from the British and sending them for sale in Sistan. Wazir Mulla Hasan assured Bean that, despite his own best efforts, Mahrab Khan was irredeemably hostile. At the same time, he continued to warn the Khan that, if he went to Quetta, the British would send him to Calcutta as a state prisoner. Bean's immediate superior, the newly-installed political agent for Baluchistan and Upper Sind, was Andrew Ross Bell, a Bengal Civil Servant, whose last appointment had been as Collector and magistrate in the British-administered districts surrounding Delhi. With no previous experience of his new area of responsibility, he shared Bean's opinion that Mahrab Khan was to blame for the raids on British kafilas.

At Kabul, the British Envoy decided that Mahrab Khan should be punished both for the theft of the treaty acknowledging his subordination to Shah Shuja-ul-Mulk (a challenge to the revival of the Durrani Empire, the whole foundation of British policy in the region) and also for encouraging (or at least failing to stop) the raids on British communications between their bases in Sind and their ally in Afghanistan. The Bombay Division, under Major General Thomas Willshire, then at Quetta on its way home, was diverted to Kalat with orders to enforce Shah Shuja ul-Mulk's authority. The presence in Willshire's train of Shah Nawaz Khan, the Muhabatzai pretender to the throne of Kalat, made the intentions of Shah Shuja ul-Mulk and his British advisers only too clear.

Willshire's staff included the thirty-seven-year-old Captain James Outram, destined to play an important part in the history not only of Balochistan and Sind, but of British rule in India as a whole. When a subaltern in the Bombay Native Infantry, he had served creditably in counter-insurgency operations in

Khandesh during 1825, where he became a political officer and during the next ten years established British authority over the forest-dwelling Bhil people. He then moved to north-western Gujerat, where he was based when his regiment was mobilized as part of the Army of the Indus. He applied to return to regimental duty, but was instead appointed an extra aide-de-camp on the staff of the army commander, Sir John Keane, though still retaining his allowances for political employment. He landed in Sind with the army and, as a political officer, negotiated with local rulers for the boats, baggage animals, food and forage needed by the advancing troops. Colonel Henry Pottinger, by this time the senior British political in Sind, despatched him to Hyderabad to negotiate with the amirs. From there, Outram followed Keane into Balochistan, through the Bolan and on to Kandahar, where he took part in the capture of Ghazni. In October 1840, after the restoration of Shah Shuja-ul-Mulk, he joined Willshire's Bombay Division on its return to India.[8]

Mahrab Khan only learnt of British intentions when Willshire marched out of Quetta on 4 November 1839, heading not down the Bolan but directly for Kalat. Determined to resist, he called on his sardars to bring their contingents to his aid. Not all did so, as there were several with unresolved blood feuds against him from the domestic conflicts earlier in his reign. Of those disposed to support him, those in eastern Balochistan were already harassing the British, and those in the west were too far away to reach him in time, as by 11 November Willshire was only two days' march away from Kalat. Mahrab Khan then sent his son and heir, the young Mir Muhammad Hasan, to safety at Nushki, some 50 miles north-east of Kalat, in the care of Daroga Ghul Muhammad. Akhund Muhammad Sadiq was sent to the British with a message calling on them to halt the invasion pending the outcome of negotiations and offering to meet Willshire in a personal parley, with each side accompanied by only a small escort; otherwise, if the British continued their advance, he would shut his gates and they would find him at the entrance to his citadel with a drawn sword. Well aware that only eight years earlier Akhund Muhammad Sadiq had attempted to seize the throne of Kalat for himself, Mahrab Khan gloomily observed that he expected to be betrayed by him once more.[9] Nevertheless, the Akhund duly delivered his message and rumours spread in the British camp that the Khan had declared he would see the sepoys damned and deal only with the English soldiers.

According to Masson, the Akhund had taken bribes from the Hindu merchants of Kalat, who stood to lose much if the British took the city by storm, to persuade the Khan to flee. Despite this, several members of the Hindu community waited on Mahrab Khan offering to fight in defence of their homes. When he sent them away, saying that the Holy Law allowed only Muslims to bear arms, some converted to Islam and later, after falling in battle with unbelievers, earned the appellation of martyrs. Akhund Muhammad Sadiq certainly sought to delay the British advance and thereby give Mahrab Khan a chance to escape. Willshire, fearing that the young Mir Muhammad Hasan and the Daroga were on their way back from Nushki with reinforcements, refused to halt and sought a battle in the open, where British drill and discipline would give him the advantage.

The attack on Kalat city, 13 November 1839

Mahrab Khan's field force amounted to some 2,000 men and five guns, with a few hundred more men gathered from nearby villages to hold the walls of Kalat. Willshire, on faulty intelligence that the road from Quetta to Kalat lacked forage and water, had sent most of his cavalry and artillery down the Bolan, together with all the infantrymen judged unfit for combat. This left him with just under 2,000 officers and men, including two British Army units, the 2nd (The Queen's) and 17th Regiments of Foot, and the 31st Bengal Native Infantry, each about 300 strong. The artillery consisted of two 9-inch howitzers and two 6-pdr light field guns from Shah Shuja's Contingent and another two from the 3rd Troop, Bombay Horse Artillery. His cavalry was provided by two squadrons from Shah Shuja's Contingent, who performed so badly in skirmishes on 11 November that they were thereafter assigned to guarding the baggage train.[10]

When the advance resumed on 13 November, the Khan's troopers realized the British had no cavalry in the field. They then adopted a conventional harassment tactic of the country whereby each man galloped up to a marching column and fired several matchlocks in succession before riding off to reload. The 17th Foot suffered several casualties but the British pressed on until they crested a ridge and saw Kalat about a mile away. They promptly came under fire from Mahrab Khan's artillery, posted with the bulk of his troops behind breastworks and redoubts on a row of three hills north of the city. Outram described the scene as 'truly an imposing sight. Some small hills in front were crowned with masses of soldiers, and the towering citadel which frowned above them in their rear was completely clustered over with human beings, chiefly ladies of the harem who had assembled to witness the discomfiture of the Feringee and the prowess of their lords, all of whom, with the Khan at

49

their head, had previously marched out to the heights, where they awaited us in battle array.'[11]

Willshire decided to assault the three hills simultaneously. Each of his three battalions was allotted a separate hill and ordered to attack with four companies. Two elite companies (the grenadiers of the Queen's and the light infantry of the 17th) led by Major John Pennycuick, occupied a series of market gardens outside the north-east corner of the city. The remaining ten companies formed a reserve under Willshire's immediate command. The British artillery moved forward and opened an effective fire on the Khan's lines, while the infantry pressed on despite the shooting of his guns and matchlocks. The Khan's troops, demoralized by both the artillery bombardment and the sight of seemingly unstoppable redcoats advancing against them, began to fall back towards the city's north (Kandahar) gate, trying to take with them as many of their guns as had not been dismounted by counter-battery fire. Willshire then sent Outram with orders to the Queen's Regiment (forming the column nearest this gate) to abandon their attack on the hill and head directly for the city. This was standard procedure in all armies when defenders retreated into a fortress, with the attackers attempting to pursue so closely that they could rush the gates before these could be closed and the retreating troops regroup.

According to Lieutenant Thomas Holdworth of the Queen's, 'We rushed down the hill after the flying enemy more like hounds with the chase in view than disciplined soldiers. The consequence was we were exposed to a most galling fire from the ramparts... the fugitives were too quick for us and suddenly the cry was raised by our leading men "the gate is shut". All was now the greatest confusion, and shelter was sought wherever it could be found. Unluckily a dash was made by the greatest part of the Regiment to an old shell of a house, which could scarcely afford cover to 20 men, much less the numbers who thronged into it and were so closely jammed that they could not move... the outside portion were exposed to the fire from the left bastion of the town, which completely outflanked them, and from which the matchlockmen kept pouring in a cool and most destructive fire... while a wide broken-down doorway to their front exposed them to fire from another bastion to their front.'[12]

Unable to return fire, the Queen's lost Lieutenant Thomas Gravatt, along with eight soldiers killed and several more badly wounded. Holdworth and others found cover behind some low walls nearby, but were pinned down by intense fire from the bastions. Pennycuik's two companies ran forward across 300 yards of open ground to reach a wall about 30 yards from the gate, losing three soldiers and a bhisti (water-carrier) to the matchlocks as they did so.

When the assault stalled, Captain Alexander Peat of the Bombay Engineers prepared powder bags with which to rush the gate and blow it down.

The storming of Kalat

From the heights abandoned by the Khan's force, two British guns opened fire on the bastions protecting the Kandahar gate and had some effect in suppressing the matchlockmen. Two other guns fired on the gate itself, in Holdworth's words, '[making] some very clever shots... but still the old gate would not fall'.[13] Lieutenant Henry Creed of the Bombay Horse Artillery, in another standard tactic of Indian siege warfare, galloped to within 150 yards of the gate with the remaining two guns, came into action and demolished it with their second salvo. Willshire arrived with the reserve companies of the 17th Foot and the Bengal Native Infantry and deployed them on the right of the British line. When the gate fell, his aide-de-camp, Outram, galloped down with orders for the Queen's to advance, followed by Willshire himself, waving his hat and shouting "Forward, Queen's, or the 17th will be in before you". The whole force, led by Pennycuick's men, surged through the ruined gateway, suffering a few more casualties as the matchlockmen fired a final volley before retreating.

When the British approached Kalat, Mahrab Khan told his brother, Mir Azim Khan, to escape and secure his own safety. At the same time he sent the ladies of the harem outside the city to keep them away from the fighting, though in such haste that some were left without transport or baggage. He also sent a messenger to his son at Nushki, with a musket bearing the names of twenty-three of his ancestors, inlaid in gold, with which the prince could prove his identity if the need arose. The young prince was commanded not to surrender too quickly to the Franks, nor to put his faith in the treacherous Brahui sardars but, above all, to avoid tobacco, as it would lead to wine-bibbing, a sin that had rendered his uncle Mir Azim Khan useless for public office. If the prince disobeyed this last injunction, Mahrab Khan said, he would rise from the grave to reproach him.

Once inside the gate, the troops found themselves in a maze of narrow streets and alleys. Holdworth recalled that his column soon became broken up into small parties, not least because men disappeared in search of loot. After groping his way through a labyrinth of passages, expecting at any moment to be rushed by enemy swordsmen, he found himself back at the gate through which they had entered. There, a man of his regiment's light company reported that he had found a route to the citadel and asked Holdworth to lead a nearby group of soldiers along it. They set off and reached a stable-yard full of horses and men just below the citadel wall. The defenders offered to surrender, with cries of *Aman* ("protection" or "mercy") but during the storming of Ghazni the Queen's had been attacked by Afghan fanatics to whom they had given quarter, and the men were disposed to shoot them out of hand. 'Not liking to see this done', wrote Holdworth, 'I stopped their fire and endeavored to make the Baluchis' (more probably, Brahuis) 'come out of their holes and give themselves up'.[14] While making this attempt, he was knocked unconscious by a shot from the citadel's walls. At first left for dead, he recovered sufficiently to hobble after the soldiers, fearing that at any moment the very men whose lives he had been trying to save would come out and kill him. Eventually his own men found him and put him in a doolie (ambulance litter) and he lived to write his memoirs.

The main body of the 17th reached the citadel by following the main street and met little resistance, apart from one group of swordsmen who launched a charge against the leading files. Several swordsmen were killed in the melee and the rest taken prisoner. After surrendering his sword to Major William Croker, one of the prisoners waited for him to turn away and then wrestled him to the ground. Croker, a veteran of several campaigns, broke free and his opponent was bayoneted by Croker's men. Hand-to-hand fighting continued in other parts of the city, sword and shield against bayonet and butt. At close quarters the English soldiers, mostly taller and heavier than their opponents, had the advantage, but matchlockmen firing from houses and roof-tops caused many casualties.

When the British entered the city, Mahrab Khan attempted to leave by its southern gate. At the same time, Willshire sent one company of the 17th and one of the 31st along the western side of the city wall, and two companies of the 17th with Creed's two guns along the eastern side. They arrived almost together to find the gate open so as to allow refugees through and forced their way in before it could be shut. Mahrab Khan, finding the gate in British hands, went back to the citadel to make his stand there. On the northern side Pennycuick's men were the first to reach the citadel gate, where they shot away the lock by placing the muzzles of a dozen muskets against it and firing them all simultaneously.

Mahrab Khan's last stand

They then had to go through an unlit tunnel before emerging at the far end to face a rush by the defending swordsmen. This was thrown back and Pennycuick regrouped his troops to continue the advance. This took them into a forecourt outside the *zanana* or harem area, held by Mahrab Khan in person. Some of his companions offered to surrender, but the Khan drew his sword and entered the fight, as he had told Willshire he would. He was wounded several times and hit by a dozen bullets before at last falling to a musket-shot claimed by Private Maxwell of the Queen's. Seven or eight sardars and many of their men died with him, as a separate group of British infantry found a different route into the palace and cut off all retreat. His body was taken to a nearby *masjid* (mosque) where it lay unattended and exposed until buried later the same day, as Muslim custom required.

The floor above the scene of Mahrab Khan's last stand was held by a group variously estimated to have been between thirty and eighty strong, led by Wazir Mulla Hasan, Akhund Muhammad Sadiq and Rahim Dad, the Naib of Quetta. The only approach was along a narrow passage and staircase, both covered by numerous matchlocks, and several British lives were lost in unsuccessful attempts to storm through. Lieutenants St George Stock and Thomas Addison, carrying the colours of the Queen's Regiment, determined to plant them on the citadel's ramparts and passed the body of Mahrab Khan on their way up. With the aid of some pioneers, who cut a hole through a wall for them, they reached the flagstaff platform, but came under such heavy fire from a lower level that they had to retreat with the loss of two men killed. An attempt to find another way up proved equally fatal and they were again forced back. The distinction of placing their colours on the citadel fell to their rivals of the 17th, who entered through a breach on the southern side created by Creed's guns. After holding out for several hours, and seeing the British preparing for another assault, Wazir Mulla Hasan realized that with Mahrab Khan's death further resistance was futile and surrendered on a promise of quarter.

Outram later wrote of the storming of Kalat, 'The soldiers displayed much greater forbearance than they normally do on such occasions. Quarter was never refused by them when craved by cries of "*Aman*", "*Aman*" and before nightfall nearly two thousand prisoners had been removed from the fort unharmed'. Another 400 defenders were thought to have been killed, either in the storm of the city or in the fighting on the heights. The local levies dropped over the lower walls and made for their homes. British casualties amounted to one officer (Gravatt of the Queen's) and thirty-two men killed, with eight officers and 107 men wounded. The Queen's suffered most heavily, with sixty-nine casualties or 23 per cent of their total engaged. The 17th incurred thirty-three (six killed), the Bengal sepoys twenty-two, the gunners three and the

Engineers and cavalry one each. It had been a harder-fought action than the more famous storming of Ghazni earlier in the year. In the subsequent distribution of honours, the entire force was voted the thanks of Parliament, Willshire was made a baronet and various field officers were decorated with the Order of the Bath or of the Durrani Empire (recently instituted by Shah Shuja-ul-Mulk) or given brevet promotion. The regiments were granted the battle honour 'Khelat' to carry on their Colours.

At Kalat, the contents of the captured palace were collected for subsequent auction by the prize agents (officers representing each unit present in the engagement), according to the laws of war then in force. Lieutenant J. T. Mauleverer of the 17th noted in his diary that the booty included 'immense quantities of flour, grain, provisions of all sorts, bales of Indian silks, Cashmir shawls, Persian carpets, English guns and pistols, Dollond's telescopes, china... the fruits of spoil and toil, levied on kafilas going through the Bolan Pass were stored here, but very little money was found, although there is supposed to be some'.[15] A reward was offered for the discovery of the Khan's jewels and a few days later an informer revealed that many had been taken to the house of Wazir Mulla Hasan, where they were discovered packed ready for transport. They were eventually auctioned in Bombay but though large and (in the Eastern fashion) uncut, many were flawed and only 60,000 rupees were realized for the prize fund.

The search of the wazir's house also produced a pile of blank sheets, bearing the Khan's seal, ready to be filled in with any message that Wazir Mulla Hasan wished to send. This was taken as evidence of his disloyalty to Mahrab Khan, though they might merely have been kept as a convenience by a busy minister. More damning was the discovery, in Mahrab Khan's personal chambers, of letters to him from the wazir advocating an anti-British policy. Realising that the wazir had duped them as much as he had betrayed Mahrab Khan, the British political officers sent him and Naib Rahim Dad under arrest to Bukkur, the British stronghold on the Indus.

Outram's ride to the sea

After the storming of Kalat, Outram thought himself lucky to have survived the battle unscathed and was convinced that, as one of the few mounted officers in the field and marked out by the dark green of his Bhil Rifle Corps uniform, he had drawn more than his fair share of fire. Willshire sent him back to Bombay with a duplicate of his despatches, the conventional way of rewarding an officer for bravery in combat and of ensuring that at least one copy would escape enemy patrols. The custom also encouraged speedy delivery, as the first officer to arrive at headquarters could expect some other award. Outram was ordered to go via Sonmiani, on the coast 360 miles to the south, and in the process to spy out the land to see if there was a practicable route for an army. Disguised as an Afghan *pir* (holy man), and accompanied by two *sayyads* (pious descendants of the Prophet) from Quetta who were also making for Sonmiani, he left Kalat at midnight on 15 November 1839, two days after the fall of the city.

In the morning, his party overtook refugees from Kalat, including the families of Wazir Mulla Hasan and Mir Azim Khan (the allegedly intemperate brother of the late Mahrab Khan). Some of the ladies recognized the sayyads as old acquaintances, and told the holy men of their misfortunes. Outram, as a supposed *pir*, was expected to sympathise with their loss. 'This I did by assuming an air of deep gravity and attention, though in reality I did not understand a single word that was uttered'.[16] Outram, despite his successful diplomatic career, never mastered Persian, the language of all Central and South Asian courts, still less the Brahui tongue in which the ladies may have been speaking. He was thankful that his disguise, taken from Mahrab Khan's looted palace, consisted of simple, unrecognisable garments. At the next camping place, the party was surrounded by villagers asking for news of what had happened at Kalat. Outram pretended to sleep while the sayyads answered questions long into the night.

Two days later, near the village of Nal, he found himself left in hiding while his companions went in search of grain for their horses. One of the sayyads eventually found him again, and the small party pushed on from village to village asking about the first sayyad, thinking he had overtaken them in the dark. They found him in a small fort, where he was leading prayers of mourning for its dead chief, news of whose fall at Kalat had arrived earlier that day. Unaware that this search had blown their cover and that a party of vengeful Brahuis was on his trail, Outram hurried on simply in order to be the first to deliver the despatches. Barely hours ahead of his pursuers, he reached Sonmiani in the morning of 23 November 1839. A friendly Hindu merchant provided him with a boat to Karachi where he reported to the astonished British authorities the first news of the fall of Kalat and the death of Mahrab Khan.

4

THE THREAT FROM THE BALOCH HILLS, 1839–40

Prince Ghul: *Look into my maps, old Mulla, and tell me what you see.*

Mulla: *I see blotches and lines.*

Prince Ghul; *And I see a wave, a wave of men; lean, hard, hungry, free men from the hills, swooping down on the fat soft comfortable slaves of the plains, their white throats ripe for the knife, a story as old as time...*

'The Drum', Alexander Korda, London Films, 1938

The Dombkis and Jakhranis

Many of the raids on British supply kafilas heading for the Bolan Pass were carried out by members of the Baloch Dombki tribe, whose territory, with their chief town at Lahri, lay in the north-eastern corner of the Kachhi plain. Their recognized sardar was Baloch Khan, a peaceful man who preferred living quietly on his jagir lands to riding out to take prey. The bolder spirits among his tribe supported his kinsman, Bijar Khan, who held jagirs around Phulji, a small town 15 miles south-east of Lahri. A man of charismatic leadership and impressive physique (the British general Sir Charles Napier, who later met him and his fellow chiefs, said he had never seen such tall men), he imposed firm discipline over his warriors, dispensed justice fairly, treated his cultivators generously and protected the merchants with whom he traded. In the late 1830s he rejected the authority of Sardar Baloch Khan and, in alliance with Darya Khan, sardar of the neighbouring Jakhrani Baloch, began a reign of terror all along the border. The Talpur amirs of Upper Sind, from where the kafilas started their northward journeys towards the Bolan, tried to buy him off with robes of honour and jagirs in southern Kachhi, but to no avail.[1]

The plains-dwelling Dombkis and Jakhranis were among the few Baloch tribes who regularly fought on horseback rather than on foot. Preferring mares to stallions, on the grounds that the latter were liable to give away an ambush by neighing, they thought little of riding 60 miles in a night, resting their horses and then emerging from cover at dawn to rob and slay in a surprise attack. With their wiry mounts well-accustomed to desert conditions, they would then ride off through the heat of the day, easily out-distancing the big, grain-fed horses of the regular cavalry sent in pursuit. With no-one able to stop them, these raiders, a few dozen bands totalling no more than a thousand men in all, brought the vital caravan traffic through the Bolan almost to a standstill. At this point, the arrival of the Army of the Indus and its weakly-guarded supply convoys offered them a series of attractive alternative targets.

During April 1839 a British kafila of 2,600 camels was continually harassed as it crossed Kachhi. Its cavalry escort tried to come to grips with the elusive raiders, but failed after losing fifty horses to thirst and exhaustion. On a report that some of the loot had been taken to Khangarh, the frontier village where the kafila route between Sind and Kandahar crossed into Kalat territory, a British detachment attacked the fort there and mistakenly killed or wounded about a hundred cultivators belonging to the friendly Khosa Baloch. Ross Bell, the British Political Agent for Balochistan, decided to send a punitive expedition against Bijar Khan's base at Phulji. On 3 June 1839 a force of about fifty European soldiers under Lieutenants John Jacob of the Bombay Artillery and S. R. Corry of the 17th Foot, set out from Sukkur on the Indus, in the appalling summer heat. Three marches later, the survivors staggered into Shikarpur, having lost Corry and fifteen men to a mixture of heat stroke and exhaustion. At the same time, the escort of a kafila of 4,500 camels taking supplies from Shikarpur to the starving troops at Quetta lost six out of its fourteen Europeans, 120 sepoys and 300 followers to heat, thirst and disease. This escort, 400 cavalry and 600 infantry, was meant to have co-operated with the European troops from Sukkur, but neither group was able to march further and the move against Phulji was called off.[2]

While the regular troops were confined to their camps by the heat, Bell formed the Baluch Levy, a para-military force of horsemen made up of local Pashtuns and Khyheri Baloch, the latter hoping that the British would help them regain territory they had lost to their Dombki and Jakhrani neighbours some years previously. The Levy, commanded by Lieutenant Philip Amiel of the Bombay Grenadiers, succeeded in arresting several desperadoes belonging to the Burdi tribe, the inhabitants of Burdeka, a border district north-east of Shikarpur belonging to the Talpur Amir Ali Murad of Khairpur. The assistant political officers riding with his patrols became familiar with the local country and its inhabitants and one of them, Lieutenant Thomas Postans, 15ᵗʰ Bombay Native Infantry, was instructed to offer Bijar Khan a free pardon and a subsidy of 3,000 rupees every month if he would 'protect' (ie, refrain from attacking) the kafilas. The offer was received with derision and the raids continued as before.

The Marris and Bugtis

The mountains between eastern Kachhi and the Indus Valley were the home of the two most feared and warlike of all the Baloch tribes, the Marris in the north and the Bugtis in the south. Secure in their mountain strongholds, they had defeated every expedition sent against them by the khans of Kalat, whose notional subjects they were, or the amirs of Sind, whose territory they bordered. Like other Baloch, they kept large flocks of sheep and goats and traded their wool with merchants from northern India in exchange for grains and piece goods. Their main income, however, came from raiding kafilas and settlements, plus a rake-off from plunder carried through their country to be sold elsewhere by the merchants with whom they traded. The Bugti chief, Babarak Khan, though disapproving of Bijar Khan Dombki's defiance of Sardar Baluch Khan, generally gave refuge to Dombki and Jakhrani bands when the need arose. In September 1839, however, after some of Bijar Khan's men had joined first the Khan of Kalat and then the Amir of Khairpur in attempted punitive expeditions against the Bugtis, he closed his borders against both tribes.

The campaign against the Dombkis and Jakhranis, October 1839

Ross Bell was at this time preparing another and larger expedition.[3] This was commanded by Major T.R.Billamore, 1ˢᵗ Bombay Grenadiers, and consisted of a wing (half-battalion) of his own regiment, amounting to 450 sepoys under Captain Charles Baillie Raitt; the light company of the 5ᵗʰ Bombay Native Infantry, some eighty strong, under Captain Lewis Brown; a bullock-drawn battery of two 24-pdrs and one 6-pdr under Lieutenant John Jacob, and an impromptu military labour company consisting of one sapper, three pioneers and about fifty lascars normally employed in pitching tents and handling stores. Their immediate military mission was to punish the raiders, kill or capture Bijar Khan and the other robber chiefs, and recover what they had stolen. Beyond this, they were to enforce British demands that Babarak Khan Bugti, and Duda Khan, the Marri chief, should wait upon Bell in person, restore the stolen property in their possession, give hostages for future good behaviour and acknowledge the authority of the newly-restored Shah Shuja-ul-Mulk by paying him one-third of their land revenue (stated to be the ruler's 'usual share', though neither the Khans of Kalat or anyone else had ever been able to collect it).

During October 1839 Billamore's troops crossed the desert from Sukkur and reached Phulji, only to find that Bijar Khan had burnt the town and taken refuge in the hills 5 miles away. Amiel announced the restoration to the Khyheris of lands taken from them by the Jakhranis and Bijar Khan's Dombkis. Sardar Baluch Khan, as chief of the main body of Dombkis, then agreed to accept a British subsidy in return for preventing further raids. Bijar Khan denounced him as a coward and remained at large. Denied entry into Bugti territory, he re-entered Kachhi with a raiding party of about 500 men. Billamore marched out from Phulji to intercept him. Amiel, with the Baluch Levy, overtook the slow-moving infantry and, on encountering the raiders, made a headlong charge only to be routed with the loss of twenty-five men, so that Billamore arrived to see the robbers disappearing over the horizon.[4]

Bijar Khan continued to plague Kachhi, but met with a check when a new cavalry regiment, the Scinde Irregular Horse (SIH), was posted to the area. 'Irregular', in the Indian Army, was at this period a technical term, meaning not partisans or para-militaries, but sepoy regiments in which, unlike the case in 'regular' regiments, the sub-units were commanded by Indian officers. The few British officers who formed the regimental headquarters were all carried on the establishment of exising regular regiments, to which they could be returned without the need for expensive redundancy payments if their irregular corps were disbanded. A major advantage of irregular service for the British officers was a higher level of appointment (and corresponding pay) than they held in their regular regiments. In outward appearance, irregular regiments differed from their regular counterparts by being dressed in uniforms of Indian rather than European style.

The first detachment of Scinde Irregular Horse, two troops under Lieutenant Walpole Hamilton Clarke of the 2nd Bombay Grenadiers, arrived at Chhatr (Chattar), 15 miles south of Phulji, to learn that a large Jakhrani raiding party was nearby. Clarke was said to be the strongest man in the Bombay

Army, 6 feet in height, a Hercules in appearance and a Centaur on horseback, handsome, witty and generous, admired by friend and foe alike.[5] He set out at midnight with ninety troopers and, before dawn, had been guided to a cornfield where 300 of the Jakhranis were dividing their spoils. The raiders scrambled into their saddles and fled, but the cavalrymen followed, killing fifty and capturing eleven without loss to themselves, and recovering most of the plunder.

Bijar Khan Dombki then moved his operations 20 miles south, to Shahpur, where one of his most notorious lieutenants, Jani, inflicted several casualties on the Baloch Levy. Billamore responded by leading a force of thirty infantry and sixty cavalry into the hills south of the Bugti country, where he surprised Jani's camp. About a hundred of the Dombkis escaped on their fleet-footed mares while those left behind placed their women and children in nearby caves and made a stand at the top of a hill. They opened fire with their matchlocks and only surrendered after Billamore, attacking on foot, had killed about twenty of them and captured their families. The next day the infantry were sent back to Shahpur with the prisoners and their livestock, while the cavalry went in pursuit of Jani and his men. The British found them waiting in a line, as if to offer fight, and charged forward only to ride into a hidden quicksand. Jacob, Billamore's well-mounted artillery commander, struggled through to the far side to find himself alone and at Jani's mercy. The chief gave a derisive shout and rode away, leaving him unharmed. While the Dombki riders disappeared into the hills, Billamore's troopers and their exhausted horses followed the infantry back to Shahpur.[6]

The campaign against the Bugtis and Marris, December 1839–March 1840

Ross Bell then decided to move against the Bugtis and Marris. Following the capture of Kalat and the death of Mahrab Khan in November 1839, their chiefs were more willing to deal with the British and on 19 Dec 1839 Babarak Khan Bugti rode into Postans's camp at Chhatr. Agreeing to allow British troops into his main town, Dera Bugti, he promised to pay tribute to Shah Shuja-ul-Mulk and agreed to aid the hunt for Bijar Khan. Babarak Khan Bugti refused to go further into Kachhi to meet Bell and returned to Dera Bugti, but left one of his entourage, Mir Hasan Nothani, as a hostage and guide for the troops to follow him. The Marri chief, Duda Khan, excused himself from making the journey to Bell on the grounds of age and infirmity, but promised his entire acceptance of whatever the British demanded and sent them a guide to his chief town, Kahan. Accordingly, on 22 December 1839, two British columns began their march into the Baloch hills. One, led by Billamore and comprising two companies of infantry, a 24-pdr howitzer under Jacob and 120 Scinde Irregular Horse under Walpole Clarke, headed for Dera Bugti. The other, led by Raitt with the rest of the Bombay Grenadiers and eighty troopers of the SIH, marched on Kahan. As they did so, a group of the most wanted Jakhranis surrendered unconditionally to Postans and were followed a few days later by Bijar Khan Dombki himself on an undertaking that his life would be spared.[7]

Signal smokes against the mountain skies warned the Baloch of Billamore's approach, but he reached Dera Bugti without opposition and was conducted into the fort by Islam Khan, Babarak Khan's eldest son. Babarak greeted Billamore cordially, but remarked on the small size of the force, saying that though he himself was too old for war, he had twice as many men inside his fort and 2,000 more in the neighbouring hills. Ill-feeling soon developed between the troops and the local people, with Baloch braves openly displaying contempt for the sepoys and traders in the bazar complaining that the soldiers were causing disturbances. Supplies were withheld or offered only at high prices. The British believed there were ample stocks in the neighbourhood, but failed to allow for the inflation and shortages that inevitably follow the sudden arrival of several hundred men in excess of the normal population of a poor area.

Islam Khan, after profuse assurances of friendship, mysteriously disappeared along with many of his men. On 3 January 1840, Billamore received information that Babarak Khan (who had moved outside the fort) was about to follow his son and that the whole fighting strength of his tribe was massing to attack. On the same day Raitt and most of his command arrived at Dera Bugti. This force had reached Kahan as planned but, unable to obtain supplies from the Marris, had been forced to march away again, leaving only one company of the 1st Bombay Grenadiers inside the fort, under Lieutenant Elliot Peacocke. Glad of these reinforcements, Billamore moved his camp close up to Dera Bugti's strong mud walls and placed a guard over Babarak Khan.

The British stood to arms all night without being attacked, but at dawn Clarke's scouts galloped in to report that about 1,200 Baloch were approaching, 'strong, fierce-looking men... with loud shouts, much flourishing of swords and firing of matchlocks'.[8] A party of horsemen attempted to rescue Babarak Khan, who was too old and frail to ride far, but his sepoy guards stood firm. Clarke rode to the scene, unhorsed one of the Bugtis, seized another by the throat, and then brought him and Babarak Khan back as prisoners. The main body of Baloch halted out of British musketry range and were eventually dispersed by shells from Jacob's howitzer, losing thirty-three men and a few horses in the process. Billamore then declared Dera Bugti a hostile town and confiscated all the grain and foodstuffs as lawful prize, while his troops took whatever private property they could find. The Baloch blocked the stream on which the fort depended for water, but after a skirmish Brown broke the dam and diverted the stream long enough fill a large reservoir beside the fort's walls.

Every camel the British could find, escorted by Raitt with 150 infantry and Clarke with 100 cavalry was then sent to Traki, about 7 miles away, the nearest source of firewood and forage. While the camels were being loaded there, the Baloch gathered in the nearby hills and launched an attack when the convoy began its return journey. They outnumbered the escort by about five to one and came on, unchecked by Raitt's volleys, to within 10 yards of his bayonets before a charge by Clarke's horsemen caught them in the flank and rode them down. British casualties amounted to three infantry and one trooper killed, with several wounded, mostly among the cavalry, including Clarke himself. The British counted seventy-nine Baloch dead, three of them chiefs, and believed that there were many wounded among those who retreated to the hills. The Baloch had hoped that the attack on this convoy would force Billamore to strengthen the escort of the next by sending his howitzer with it, in the absence of which they could make another attack on Dera Bugti itself. In fact, the convoy brought in enough stores to last for as long as the British remained there, while their heavy losses deterred the Bugtis from again challenging the British in the open. Babarak Khan, on Ross Bell's orders, was taken under a strong cavalry escort to join the Jakhrani chiefs in detention at Bukkur, with his tribesmen being told that if they tried to rescue him he would be shot.

With the Bugtis defeated in the field, their sardar in custody and their main town occupied, Billamore decided to re-establish a British presence at Marri Kahan, 25 miles away through the mountains to the north-west. Peacocke had sent word that the Marris, with all their flocks and herds, had disappeared from the surrounding area. This he regarded as a sinister development, though it might simply have been a move to fresh pastures as normally practiced by semi-nomadic pastoralists. As his own supplies were about to run out, he left Kahan and marched to join Billamore at Dera Bugti. Billamore sent Jacob with the pioneers, escorted by a company of infantry and a troop of the SIH under Clarke, to find a trail to Kahan passable by artillery. En route, they experienced some long-range matchlock fire from the hill-tops, but killed one of the Baloch snipers and found the Marris' herds, estimated at 1,000 head of cattle and 3,000 sheep. These they sent back to Dera Bugti, in the care of Peacocke whom they met on his way from Kahan. After three days Jacob returned to report that the pioneers had cleared a road and that he could reach Kahan with his howitzer and its limbers in two marches.

Billamore then left Raitt at Dera Bugti with the greater part of his command and moved on Kahan with a troop of cavalry, the artillery, the light company of the 5th Bombay Native Infantry, one company of the Grenadiers and the pioneer company. The winter had now set in and, after one march, freezing rain made the track impassable for camels. During the next two days, while the party waited for a thaw, spies reported that a large Marri war party had gathered near the only watering-place on the route to Kahan, intending to attack the British when they halted there. Billamore then advanced to Kahan without stopping and, watched all the way by the Marris, arrived to find the place deserted. Duda Khan Marri, having seen the fate of Babarak Khan, had ignored British overtures and vanished into his mountains.

Unable to locate him, Billamore's only option was to take the quickest route back to Kachhi. A Bugti shepherd who knew the area showed Jacob (who, as an artilleryman, was a trained survey officer) a trail to the pass of Nafusk, a high saddle about 4 miles south-west of Kahan. The path then descended steeply and rose again to cross another ridge at the Sartuf Pass, from where there was an easy route back to Phulji in the plains. As the way down from Nafusk to Sartuf was too steep for wheeled vehicles, Jacob used his pioneers and civil labour to cut zig-zag traverses through the rocky hill-side.

After four days' work, undertaken despite Marri sniping, the howitzer and its limbers were dragged over the pass where previously there had been little more than a sheep-walk and even infantry had had to go in single file. The way was clear for gun-bullocks, troop-horses and baggage camels along with all the rest of the column, though the gradient and length of the slopes still placed great demands on men and animals alike. After crossing the Sartuf Pass they finally returned to Phulji, where Raitt and the troops from Dera Bugti joined them a few days later.

These operations, involving 700 sepoys under eight British officers, had lasted some three months in all. The British had shown that they could defeat the tribes in open combat, enter their mountains and occupy their forts. The robber chiefs had been arrested or forced into hiding, with their captured followers sentenced to labour on the roads around Sukkur. Bombay sepoys had proved themselves quite capable of operating in cold weather and without European troops. At the strategic level, regions previously unknown to Europeans had been entered and mapped; the authority of Shah Shuja-ul-Mulk had been asserted over some of his most intransigent subjects; and most important of all, the safety of the Bolan road had been secured. Following the earlier success in Afghanistan and the taking of Kalat, it seemed that the British had won yet another hand in the Great Game.

Despite this, hopes that this expedition had achieved its purpose were soon dashed. Not all the robber chiefs were in British custody and new leaders soon emerged to take the places of those who were. Political control was retained by Bell, despite his having gone for medical reasons to Simla, 600 miles away, where it took ten days for him to be reached by express post-riders. Day-to-day political business was left to his senior assistant, Postans, who was told in any sudden crisis to consult James Outram, by this time appointed Political Agent in Lower Sind. A resumption of the previous policy of relying on local levies, deployed in small numbers and isolated posts, allowed renewed raids on weakly-guarded convoys and undefended settlements. The frontier of Upper Sind held a brigade of three regular Bombay infantry regiments and 500 irregular cavalry, based at Sukkur, but the cavalry were too few and the infantry too slow, so that the raiders attacked at will and escaped unpunished, growing bolder with each success.

The Defence of Marri Kahan

Before his departure, Bell had decided to leave an infantry detachment at Kahan, but Billamore had returned to the plains before his orders arrived. It was not until April 1840 that a force was assembled at Phulji, under Captain Lewis Brown of the 5th Bombay Native Infantry, with orders to return to Kahan. Brown's column consisted of 300 sepoys from his own regiment, under Ensign William Taylor, two 12-pdr howitzers of the 3rd Bombay Golandaz (Indian gunners) Company, under 2nd Lieutenant David Erskine of the Bombay Artillery, and fifty Scinde Irregular Horse and fifty Pashtun troopers. The cavalry was led by Walpole Clarke, who was second-in-command of Brown's entire force with Assistant Surgeon Glass, Bombay Medical Service, joining them later. To counter the Marri tactic of simply starving out an occupying force, the column was accompanied by some 600 fully-loaded camels, carrying supplies for four months. After the force reached Kahan, the camel train was to return to Phulji and bring back supplies for another four months.[9]

Before starting for Kahan, Brown was told to send back the artillery, as Erskine had become medically unfit but, after receiving intelligence that the Marris were gathering to oppose him at the Nafusk Pass, he insisted on retaining one of the guns. Erskine returned to duty, but Dr Glass ordered Ensign Taylor back and Brown was left as the only British infantry officer for the three companies of sepoys. Leaving behind the Pashtuns, whom Brown regarded as untrustworthy, they began their march on 2 May, at the hottest time of the year. Delayed by their gun, which had to be man-hauled with drag-ropes when the gradient proved too steep for its bullock-team, and by the heat, which at times reached 116° F, they made slow progress. With no water at the top of the Nafusk Pass, men and animals had to be sent back down to drink in relays. Many of the heavily-laden camels, with only one driver to every six or seven beasts, proved unable to cope with the gradient, and while Marri matchlockmen kept up a harassing fire from the surrounding hill-tops, other tribesmen rushed down to snatch the packs from beasts that had foundered. Despite this ominous shortage of water, the column reached Kahan on 11 May 1840 where, as Brown later reported, 'It was a delightful sight to see the camels and bullocks rushing to the river. I thought they would never stop drinking'.[10] The town and fort, however, had been burnt and abandoned. A sepoy straggling some 500 yards from the walls was cut down by a party of Marri horsemen, who escaped despite a long chase by Clarke and twenty troopers. There were still crops of grain standing in the nearby fields and over fifty camel-loads were harvested and brought in before Marri infiltrators set fire to the rest two days later.

On 16 May, Clarke started back for Phulji with 700 unladen camels (including a hundred found in Marri grazing grounds), escorted by his fifty SIH troopers and two infantry companies, each of ninety sepoys. The original plan had been for the escort to include only one company, but Brown had decided to strengthen it with a second one in view of the hostile attitude of the Marris. Having reached the top of the Nafusk Pass without seeing any sign of an enemy, Clarke ordered Subedar (Indian company commander) Bagu Jadeo back to Kahan with his company while the convoy continued on its way with the rest of the escort. The subedar saw the last of the camels over the pass and then headed back towards Kahan. Half-way back to Kahan, the troops (the elite light company of the 5th Bombay Native Infantry) were ambushed by an estimated 2,000 Marris. The light infantrymen doubled to the nearest high ground and formed a square, but were only able to fire two or three volleys before being overwhelmed. Subedar Bagu Jadeo, an Indian Leonidas, fell fighting to the last, his men around him like the Spartans at Thermopylae, with only a doolie-wala (ambulance-litter bearer) surviving to tell the tale.

Unaware of this, Clarke pressed on to the next pass, the Sartuf, 13 miles away from Kahan, where he found the crest held by another large force of Marris. Leaving half his infantry to guard the convoy, he advanced with the remainder to clear the way. With the advantage of ground and numbers, the Marris held him off for about two hours, after which he sent a bugler back to the convoy. Correctly deducing from this, and the slackening rate of fire, that the sepoys were running low on ammunition, the Marris launched a charge against the handful of redcoats. Clarke, the beau sabreur, himself killed two men with his sword and was wounded struggling with another before he went down. As a tribute to his valour, the Marris later buried him where he fell (the only man on the British side to be given proper burial) and the Baloch tribal bards long sang of him as a great paladin and worthy opponent. The Marri charge swept on to the camel train, their main target, and only the cavalry and a few infantrymen escaped to eventually reach Phulji.[11]

Thus in a single day, the 5th Bombay Native Infantry lost two Indian officers, five havildars (Indian sergeants) and 139 rank and file, a total of 146 out of the 180 men engaged. Clarke, perhaps influenced by his previous victories, had fatally under-estimated his Baloch opponents. To divide a force while the enemy is unlocated is always a military error. For Clarke to have done so in the presence of so wily and experienced an opponent as Duda Khan Marri (who was clearly not as weakened by age and infirmity as he had led the British to believe) was a blunder. This, compounded by his over-confident decision to attack with inadequate strength, not only cost himself and his men their lives, but also destroyed the myth of British invincibility. The Marris, who lost about twenty-five men, gained not only an immense boost to morale and prestige, but also 700 valuable camels and 150 modern muskets as the spoils of victory.

At Kahan, Brown had already begun work on strengthening the defences. The existing wall, about 25 feet high, but thin in several places, had six sides, protected by a ditch, six bastions and a fortified gateway. The gates had been removed by the Marris, but were found in a field about two miles away and, as he noted with some understatement 'afterwards proved invaluable to us'. His single piece of artillery was hauled up to one of the bastions covering the re-installed gates, but there were only 140 infantrymen to hold the remaining 900 yards of wall.

On 18 May a party of about sixty Marris rode round the walls, shouting abuse and brandishing weapons, though remaining out of range, and it was not until 21 May that Brown heard from local herdsmen of Clarke's defeat and death. He at once put his men on half-rations and sent a rider to Sukkur, reporting the disaster and stating that he would continue to hold until relieved. On 27 May a rider came in from Lieutenant Loch of the Poona Horse to say that he was coming to the rescue with 200 troopers, but Brown replied urging him not to make the attempt, as cavalry would never get through the Nafusk Pass. Another rider arrived on 4 June, informing Brown that no regular troops were available as reinforcements but that Bean, the Political Agent at Quetta, had been asked to send a contingent of Kakar Pashtuns in his pay. In the event, these never materialized, as the Kakars turned hostile and on 23 June 1840 Quetta itself had to fight off 800 Panizai Pashtuns. Soon afterwards, it was attacked by Brahuis fighting for Nasir Khan II, the title taken by the young son of the late Mahrab Khan of Kalat.

Brown continued to work on his fortifications, digging trenches and planting stakes as obstacles, pulling down houses to clear fields of fire, digging wells to ensure a water-supply (the little river on which the town depended lay outside the walls), filling empty grain bags with sand, and strengthening his manpower by arming the non-combatant camp-followers with clubs and training them as sentries. 'All working at the defences most cheerfully' he noted in his journal, 'and every man seeming to think that the safety of the whole depends on his individual bravery. Treat sepoys kindly and I do not think they will ever fail at the push'.[12] Sniping from the surrounding areas continued daily. Twenty bullock-drivers who had gone out to forage by the river came under attack and forty sepoys, under covering fire from Erskine's gun, went to their rescue, but ten of the drivers were cut down by Marri swordsmen.

On 3 July, Sher Beg Bugti, a trader to whom Brown had done a kindness earlier in the Afghan War, brought in a flock of forty-five sheep and goats for sale. The Marris, he said, were planning to attack Kahan on the night of 6 July, as a holy man had declared that British lead bullets were useless, and had demonstrated this by firing 300 rounds from the pouches of Clarke's dead sepoys at a bullock tethered a hundred yards away, without causing it any harm. The night of the forecast attack passed without incident, but Sher Beg returned unabashed with a load of sugar and chillies, charging steep prices and, in Brown's opinion, spying out the defences, but nevertheless being welcomed by the whole garrison as a friendly face. Post riders came and went, keeping up communications between Kahan and the British headquarters at Sukkur, though Brown was sure that Duda Khan Marri only allowed them to pass because he read the messages they carried.

On 14 July, Brown recorded that, because of 'ulcers' (possibly a skin condition symptomatic of incipient scurvy), 90 of his 140 sepoys could not wear their belts, though all continued to man their posts. To replace them, he armed and drilled doolie-wallas, camel-men and bullock-drivers, all from ethnic groups considered by Indian military authorities as belonging to 'non-martial' classes, though given the chance such men repeatedly proved themselves just as good soldiers as anyone else. A period of heavy rain flooded the trenches and brought an outbreak of fever that affected the three British officers and many of the men. Baloch marksmen, with their long jezails seeming to outrange the British muskets, crept closer by the day. On 7 August an attempt to rush the gates was only halted by fire from Erskine's gun.

During these weeks, the Marris pastured flocks of sheep near the walls. Although this was their normal grazing ground, Brown suspected that they did so to tempt the garrison into making a sortie out of range of its artillery. He resisted the temptation, but offered to buy the flocks from their owner, Haybat Khan, a local Marri chief. When Haybat Khan refused to sell, Brown waited for the flocks to stray within range and on 10 August captured two large flocks, amounting to 300 sheep and fifty-seven goats, most of the latter in milk. After bringing them inside the fort, he sold them to his men at four annas each and put the proceeds aside for the widows of those who had fallen on 16 May. Haybat Khan rode up to the gate to claim their return, saying that they were his personal property and that, as a poor man, he could not afford the loss. Brown was unsympathetic, as Hybat Khan had refused to sell them when offered a fair price, and told him that most had already been eaten. Enraged, the chief shouted back that Nasir Khan II, the rightful ruler of Kalat, had driven the British into Sukkur, and that he himself would take Kahan, at which Brown told a sentry to take a shot at him 'when he quickly departed'. A week later, news came that a British force had indeed left Sukkur, not in retreat but to relieve besieged Kahan.

The Battle of the Nafusk Pass, 31 August 1840

The relieving column was a strong force of all arms, including 750 sepoys of the 1st and 2nd Bombay Grenadiers, the two most senior and prestigious native infantry regiments of the Bombay Army, and three horse-drawn 12-pdr howitzers with thirty-four gunners and twenty pioneers under Captain Henry Stamford of the Bombay Artillery. With them went a long train of 12,000 camels and 600 bullocks carrying camp stores and combat supplies, including water and food for men and animals, and provisions for the re-supply of Kahan. A detachment of the 40th Foot, originally intended to form part of the force, was left behind at Sukkur, probably because European troops were judged unsuitable for operations in the intense heat of what was by this time late summer. The Bombay Grenadiers, under Captain Charles Baillie Raitt, had served in Billamore's hill campaign of the previous year, but Billimore himself had died of fever at Karachi in April 1840 and command of the column was given to Major Thomas Clibborn of the Grenadiers. Joined by 200 cavalrymen of the Poona Horse and SIH, they crossed the desert to Phulji without incident, entered the hills on 24 August and arrived at the Sartuf Pass five days later. As Brown had found earlier in the year, the steep gradient delayed the progress of the guns and the baggage animals, and it was fourteen hours before all reached the summit. No water was found there, and pack animals had to be sent back down the pass to replenish the water containers. The column made camp amid the scattered bones and clothes of Clarke's command, where the gallant Clarke's own grave was identified by his tartan trousers found lying above it.

Clibborn's march had been watched by Duda Khan's spies from the time it had left Sukkur, and the delay at the Sartuf Pass merely gave that chief more time to gather his forces. During the night of 30 August 1840, Marri braves made repeated raids on the British baggage lines, giving the exhausted soldiers little chance of rest as firing broke out all round the camp perimeter. Clibborn ordered the advance to be resumed while it was still dark, hoping to reach the Nafusk Pass before the full heat of the day. Night marches are notorious for delays and confusion, especially when there is no proper road. One of the guns, with its limber, fell into a ravine. With the dawn, the troops began to come under fire from Marri matchlockmen on the surrounding hills, but the column pressed on through increasing heat. It reached the foot of the pass only to find the way ahead blocked by trenches and stone breastworks held by large numbers of hostiles. Brown had sent word from Kahan that the rains that had caused him such problems would also have fallen at Nafusk, only 6 miles away, and that there should be water at the camping ground below the pass. In the event, none was found, and all the water carried from Sartuf had been exhausted by the time Clibborn's rearguard joined him. Unable to remain where his men and animals would die of thirst, Clibborn appreciated that the only courses open to him were to retreat to Sartuf or to advance to the top of the Nafusk, where his Baloch guides assured him that there was water. Failing that, Kahan and its little river were only a few miles farther on.

Rather than retreat, Clibborn sent his infantry forward to clear the path to the summit. Led by Captain Raitt of the Grenadiers and supported by air-burst shrapnel from the howitzers, they passed the barricades but then came under heavy fire from matchlockmen beyond them. Shouting their war cries, hundreds of Marris then emerged from the nearby ravines and poured down to the attack. The outnumbered infantry were forced to retreat and form a rallying square around the guns and regimental colours. The Marri charge almost reached the muzzles of the guns, but was stopped by volleys of musketry while the gunners switched from shrapnel to case-shot (the lethal last resort of artillerymen fighting at close range). The Marris then fell back, though they had inflicted severe losses. Raitt lay dead, along with three other British officers, two Indian officers and 179 grenadiers, with another ninety-two men wounded. Most of the transport animals and their loads had been lost and the pass remained in Marri hands.

In the British lines, the heat of the day, the exertions of an approach march lasting over eight hours, the stress of combat, and chemicals in the black powder of their cartridges combined to give everyone an intense thirst. Water had run out even before the battle started, but someone remembered that the officers' stores included some bottles of beer. This was sent across to ease the suffering of the wounded, whose thirst was made all the greater by loss of blood. On its way, it was fought over by desperate men of all castes. Search parties were sent out to look for the water that Brown had expected to be there. A Baluch guide, Sardar Mir Hasan Nothani, said that he knew where some could be found. All the water containers were loaded onto pack animals and, under cavalry escort, sent to collect it. With them went the horses of the gun teams, too exhausted for any other use. During the evening Clibborn collected his wounded and regrouped his remaining forces. Then came the report that the guide had deliberately led the water convoy into a dry ravine where the Marris were waiting. The non-combatant drivers had suffered heavy casualties and many of their animals had been lost, despite the cavalry's efforts.

Clibborn now had no option but retreat. Most of his camels had either been captured by the Marris or gone missing with their drivers, who had deserted and taken their beasts with them. Many other camp followers, including the doolie-walas (the field ambulance litter-bearers), had also deserted. When the few remaining camels had been allotted to the seriously wounded, there was no means of moving anything else. The guns, their teams now in Marri hands, were spiked and abandoned. Tents, stores, food and fodder had to be left behind, along with all official papers and 22,000 rupees from the paymaster's chest. Marching through the night, the column reached the Sartuf Pass, where discipline collapsed as men and animals rushed for the water holes. Marri pursuers then caught up with the rearguard and slaughtered the unarmed followers. With difficulty, the troops were got out of the water and formed into a defensive position, but by dawn the Marris had vanished to divide their spoils.

Remaining at Sartuf was impossible, as all provisions, for lack of transport, had been abandoned at Nafusk. The only alternative to starvation was to leave the sick and wounded to their fate while the rest set out for Phulji, 50 miles away, hoping to reach it before their remaining food and water ran out. After marching continuously through the desert for two days and two nights, and suffering further casualties from heat and exhaustion along the way, the survivors reached safety. Six out of the thirteen British officers had been killed in action, along with 190 sepoys and 200 followers. Three guns, all the baggage and most of the transport animals were taken by the exultant Marris.

Meanwhile, at Kahan, Hybat Khan had returned to parley with Brown and on 28 August told him that although the British might have entered the Marri country, 3,000 warriors had gathered to fight for their homeland. They would meet the British at Nafusk, he said and, if defeated, then at Kahan, and finally retreat into the far hills to continue the fight there. On 31 August, expecting to be relieved at any moment, Brown saw large numbers of Baloch hurrying towards Nafusk and noted their smoke signals on the tops of nearby hills. He then heard the sound of musketry and gunfire and observed shrapnel bursts in the air above the summit of the pass. Subsequently the noise of battle stopped, leading him to suppose that, as he could see no sign of British troops, there had been heavy losses.

On 3 September 1840, baffled by the non-appearance of the relief force, watchers on the walls of Kahan observed long strings of baggage camels going to and from the nearby hills. Brown tried to persuade his men that they were horses, but the sepoys did not need his telescope to tell the difference, and one old soldier said he had never seen horses moving so steadily. The next day some Marris rode up and shouted that they had cut up the convoy and captured its guns. Brown refused to believe this but on the following day, when another individual gave him the same news (and was shot at for his pains), wrote in his journal 'sadly perplexed to know what to think of affairs'. He was also concerned that inside the walls there was no grass left for his camels and bullocks.

The Retreat from Kahan

At dawn on 7 September any doubts Brown had about the fate of the relief column were ended when he looked out and saw three howitzers with their muzzles pointing towards his walls. Two days later their teams of heavy horses, complete with harness and blinkers, were galloped up and down for an hour in full view of the garrison. Finally, on 17 September 1840, a message from the brigade major at Sukkur informed Brown that the relieving force had been repulsed and that, as there were no troops, followers, transport or supplies available for another attempt, his post had become untenable. He was therefore authorized to act according to his best judgement and either attempt to break out by a rapid night march, or accept such terms as he could make with the enemy.

Brown decided that, with so many men sick and the rest weakened by hunger, a break-out would be beyond his means. Instead, he calculated that by reducing their grain rations to one quarter of the normal and eating the gun-bullocks, he could hold out until 15 October while he waited for developments. Duda Khan Marri, who quite probably knew the contents of the despatch from Sukkur, sent Brown a message of his own on 22 September 1840, offering to discuss terms. An experienced general, he had fought two victorious actions in four months against the previously undefeated British. He had enhanced his reputation as a skilled commander and his men had captured thousands of valuable pack animals and their loads. The cost in lives, nevertheless, had been heavy, with many of his boldest fighters among the fallen. Further losses would weaken his numbers in any possible future actions against the British or, equally importantly, his own Baloch neighbours. The spiked guns taken from Clibborn, though prestigious as trophies, were useless as weapons, while the single British gun inside Kahan had repeatedly proved capable of preventing any attempt to carry the walls by storm. Although the sepoys were weakened, they could still man their defences. He knew too that Brown had armed his camp followers who, though not trained to fight in the open, had effectively doubled the British strength. He had more to gain by offering terms than by risking the loss of men and his personal prestige in a costly assault.

Brown's reply, sent the next day, was 'Doda Murree, I'll give you back your fort on conditions, viz. that you give me personal security for my safe arrival in the plains. If not, I will remain here for two months longer, having provisions for that time.' Doda Khan responded on 24 September, swearing by the Holy Koran that if the British left the fort in three days' time, he would protect them down to the plains. At first, each side suspected the other of treachery, but at a wary meeting to discuss the details of the capitulation, warmer relations were established. The Marris said that they had only been fighting for their country, they had never killed any of the British except in fair fight and all those taken prisoner had been clothed and set free. On the British side, as Brown recorded, 'We found these Beloochees the most civil and polite of men… No doubt their joy was just as great in getting rid of us as ours was in obtaining our freedom.'

Preparations for the evacuation began at once. Only ten government camels were left, all 'as thin as rats', and officers and sepoys alike gave up their own private animals for the move. All personal kits, half the remaining ammunition and half the tents were left behind and the artillery wagon and forge-cart were burnt. The thirty strongest bullocks were formed into a team to pull the gun, Brown having decided to take it with him in case of an attack during the 40 miles' journey to the plain. His sepoys, to whom the gun had become a symbol of honour, also begged him to keep it, saying they would defend it and haul it on drag-ropes themselves if need be. The garrison marched out on 28 September 1840 and camped the next day among the unburied British dead at the Nafusk Pass (Brown later arranged for their proper interment). The axle-tree of the gun carriage split, but Erskine repaired it and they moved on, reaching water on 30 September. Despite this, the starving bullocks began to founder and the gun ammunition was off-loaded, with only a few rounds of case-shot retained for emergency use.

By this time half the men were unable to march and had to be carried on camels. The Marri escort, so far from showing the treachery that Brown had feared, kept Doda Khan's word and actually went beyond it by giving help to the struggling troops. On 1 October spare bullocks and camels, despatched in response to Brown's appeals, arrived and the garrison of Kahan marched into Phulji later the same day, 'emaciated, ragged, hungry, and destitute, yet bringing with them their gun and their honour'.[13] Brown's achievement in standing a siege of five months did much to restore British morale after their earlier defeats, and the 5th Bombay Native Infantry was granted the battle honour "Kahun" to carry on its colours. Nothing, however, could disguise the fact that, of its three companies that had marched to Kahan, only one returned, nor that an expedition larger than any force previously sent by the British into the Baloch hills had ended in failure. It became the Marris' boast that, of all the tribes who fought the British in the Afghan War, they alone were never defeated.

5

INSURGENCY IN KALAT, 1840–41

If then we shall shake off our slavish yoke,
Imp out our drooping country's broken wing,
Redeem from broking pawn the blemished crown,
Wipe off the dust that hides our sceptre's gilt,
Away with me in post to Ravenspurgh.

Northumberland, Richard II, *Act II, scene i.*

At Kalat, despite discovering that Mahrab Khan's alleged enmity had been engineered by his treacherous wazir, the British neither rehabilitated the late khan nor acknowledged the succession rights of the son he had sent to safety. Instead, contrary to their treaty undertaking never to support the pretensions of the Muhabatzais, they handed the throne of Kalat to Shah Nawaz Khan, in whose eyes Nasir Khan the Great and his line had been usurpers. In a new treaty, Shah Nawaz Khan recognized the supremacy of Shah Shuja-Mulk (whose own throne rested on similar legitimist claims) and ceded to him the districts of Shal and Mastung, thus securing British control of the Bolan. These areas, the wealthiest parts of a poor country, enhanced the revenue desperately needed by Shah Shuja-ul-Mulk's government but correspondingly reduced that of Kalat. Under the treaty, a British political officer, Lieutenant William Loveday, 37th Bengal Native Infantry, was installed at Kalat to give Shah Nawaz Khan moral and financial support and ensure that he governed according to British advice. At the same time, Harrand was formally ceded to the kingdom of Lahore. In fact, this move merely recognized what had long been the case and demonstrated that, although Maharaja Ranjit Singh had died on the day that the Army of the Indus moved forward from Kandahar, the Tripartite Alliance between Lahore, the British and Shah Shuja-ul-Mulk remained. To the Brahui sardars, all these moves demonstrated that Shah Nawaz Khan was a mere puppet, ready to give away their country in return for British support.

Balochistan under Shah Nawaz Khan of Kalat

Shah Nawaz Khan began his reign by rewarding the sardars of Jhalawan, who had refused to fight for Mahrab Khan. Accompanied by Loveday and his escort of sixty sepoys from Shah Shuja's Contingent, he then set out for Panjgur, in the wilds of northern Makran, to hunt for Mahrab Khan's young son, Mir Muhammad Hasan. That prince, warned by one of the leading Jhala-wan sardars, Kamal Khan of Baghwan, had escaped to Nushki, some 50 miles south-east of Quetta. Shah Nawaz Khan imposed heavy fines on those who had sheltered him and then returned with the proceeds to Kalat where he strengthened his ties with the Jhalawans by marrying a sister of Sardar Kamal Khan. During the wedding celebrations, Loveday rejoined Shah Nawaz Khan with the unwelcome news that the British government, anxious to reduce its expenditure in Shah Shuja-ul-Mulk's domains, would no longer involve itself in the internal affairs of Kalat.

Nevertheless, Loveday accompanied Shah Nawaz Khan's brother, Mir Fatah Khan, in another search for the young prince Mir Muhammad Hasan, who fled to Sardar Azad Khan Nausherwani of Kharan, the desert region beyond Makran. A charismatic figure then aged about forty, Azad Khan Nausherwani had been called on by Mahrab Khan II to send a contingent to help him against the British invasion in return for the grant of a jagir in Pan-jgur. He had accepted the jagir without sending the contingent, but now gave shelter to Mahrab Khan's son. With Mir Muhammad Hasan beyond reach, the expedition marched into the country of the Mingals, who had given him hospitality while he was at Nushki. The chiefs were fined and their Sardar, Fazil Khan, was ordered to make his submission in person at Kalat. Loveday was then told by Bean, his superior officer at Quetta, that he had exceeded his duty and he was no longer to employ his sepoys in looking for Mir Muham-mad Hasan. Without Loveday's regular troops, Shah Nawaz Khan did not feel strong enough to march into the remote sands of Kharan, but he warned Loveday that by failing to deal with Mir Muhammad Hasan while they had the chance, the British were only storing up trouble for the future (as soon proved to be the case).[1]

In the districts that had been transferred from Kalat to Shah Shuja-ul-Mulk's administration, his tax officials investigated the land revenue and found, after the rapacious nature of their kind, that there had been considerable underpayment. At the same time, it was decided that an immediate income would be generated by privatising the revenue-collection. This system of tax-farming, whereby wealthy individuals paid the state what was due and then collected it themselves, keeping a proportion to cover their costs and provide a profit, was a common practice in many other periods and places (the 'publicans' of the Roman Empire being the most notorious). Like all such privatisations, it was always open to corruption and strongly resented by those who had to bear the additional costs involved, especially when, as in this case, the rate of assessment was raised at the same time.

The Outbreak of the Brahui Revolt

In Mastung, a Sarawan Sardar, Muhammad Khan Shawani, refused to pay the new rates. Early in June 1840 Loveday sent his munshi with an escort of twenty-five sepoys to collect what was due to the aggrieved tax farmer. Sardar Muhammad Khan, not a man inclined to half-measures, responded by calling out his men and killing the munshi along with the escort. This incident, coming only a few weeks after news of Clarke's defeat by the Marris, was enough to trigger a wider revolt by the discontented Brahuis. Sardar Muhammad Khan appealed to his fellow-chiefs of Sarawan to join him in arms and called on Mir Muhammad Hasan to return from Kharan and place himself at the head of his people. Accompanied by Sardar Azad Khan Nausherwani and the ever-faithful Daroga Ghul Muhammad, the young prince marched to Mastung, where they were joined by Mahrab Khan's widow, the Bibi Ganjan, and her retainers. They all then turned against Quetta, from which most of the garrison had been sent on to Kandahar.

Their initial plan was to attack in co-operation with the same Pashtuns whom Bean had hoped to employ for the relief of Brown at Kahan. As Quetta was believed to contain a large amount of government treasure, the Pashtuns decided to take it themselves without waiting for the Brahuis. The Pashtun attack, on 23 June 1840, was driven off and the Brahuis arrived to find that the British political officers had hired some local contingents and the troops sent to Kandahar were being recalled. The Brahuis prepared an escalade, but dissensions over which tribe should lead the assault led to mutual accusations of treachery and they returned to Mastung.

A few weeks previously, the traveller Charles Masson had returned to Kalat after various journeys in Iran and Afghanistan. An outspoken opponent of British policy in Afghanistan, he had formed a general dislike of the political officers who carried it out and now found several of his old acquaintances in reduced circumstances from the sack of Kalat by Willshire's army. His prejudices were confirmed by his first meeting with Loveday ("Labadar Sahib" as he was known to the Brahuis), who had become very unpopular through setting his bulldogs on a builder with whom he was in dispute, resulting in the man dying of his injuries. Loveday, who had received a warning from Outram, the Political Agent in Lower Sind, that a Russian agent had been reported travelling in Balochistan, thought that this might refer to Masson, and accordingly treated him with suspicion.

Shah Nawaz Khan had responded to the news of the Sarawan rising by sending Mir Fatah Khan to the Jhalawans, summoning them to assemble at Kalat. There, the first alarm subsided with the arrival of the Jhalawan levies and news of the insurgents' discomfiture at Quetta. Various measures were taken to strengthen the city walls and gates, though the usual procedure of bricking up the gates was not followed. Likewise, garden walls and a mosque outside the city were left intact, as Shah Nawaz Khan refused to damage either an orchard planted by his father or a religious building, even though these offered cover for an attack. Following rumours in the bazaar that the Sarawans were marching on Kalat, Shah Nawaz Khan instituted a routine of night patrols and placed his brother Mir Fatah Khan in charge of the citadel. Loveday made his peace with Masson, who was invited by Shah Nawaz Khan to join them in preparing for a siege.

Shah Nawaz Khan at bay

Masson, who had served in the ranks of the Bengal Artillery, began by looking at the guns, most of which were unserviceable. One, indeed, had been cast in Modena, Italy, over 300 years earlier, leading Masson, the antiquarian, to wonder about how it had reached Kalat. Loveday, constrained by orders not to interfere in the domestic affairs of Kalat, played little part in the preparations, apart from fortifying his Residency, and handing over his grain stores for general use. Stocks of food were low, but there was ample lead for ammunition. The Jhalawans and Shah Nawaz's household troops were each allotted their own sectors of the walls, and the leading sardars were presented with *khilats* (robes of honour) and gifts of money. Loveday's remaining sepoys were kept as a mobile reserve. Early in July 1840, Mir Muhammad Hasan, having taken the title Nasir Khan II, appeared before Kalat with Daroga Ghul Muhammad and the other loyal supporters who had stayed with him during the long months of exile. With them were between one and two thousand Sarawan tribesmen, ready to fight for their rightful prince and lower taxes.

As they approached, they came under fire from the guns in the citadel. Dismounting from their horses and camels, they attempted to rush the gates, possibly expecting that these would be opened by sympathizers within. They were beaten off, with a few men killed or wounded on either side. Loveday and Masson toured the walls and congratulated the defenders. The men led by Sardar Kamal Khan (Shah Nawaz Khan's new brother-in-law), who had born the brunt of the engagement, greeted them enthusiastically and declared that they were fighting for the *Sarkar Kampani* (the East India Company's government) more than for Shah Nawaz Khan. Kamal Khan himself, face blackened with smoke and powder, asked for more gunpowder and food for his men, who had been fighting all day on just a little parched grain. Loveday sent a few dates, but Shah Nawaz Khan, whom Masson asked to send some sheep, refused, an imprudent measure that weakened the Jhalawans' loyalty to his cause.

The second day of the siege was taken up by sniping from each side. Masson found that the gunners in the citadel, all formerly in Mahrab Khan's service, had abandoned their posts under Sarawan fire. Shaming them back to the embrasures, he took over as a gun-layer, first on the ancient Italian cannon, and then on the other pieces, but found their shooting so inaccurate that he feared to hit the defenders on the lower walls. One lucky shot passed close to Nasir Khan II's tent and killed Sardar Azad Khan Nausherwani's charger, picketed nearby.

At nightfall, the Sarawans attacked with scaling ladders, covered by heavy matchlock fire. At one point, about fifty of the stormers got over the wall with the aid of Jhalawans who were meant to be defending it. A handful of sepoys shot down about fifteen of them, along with the treacherous Jhalawans, but the remainder concealed themselves inside the city. They emerged to encounter Shah Nawaz Khan himself, on his way with a few men to the scene of the fighting. In the melee, the Khan personally cut down one of the Sarawans, but two or three of his own men were killed and he was forced to retreat. The stormers, finding themselves cut off, surrendered to Sardar Kamal Khan and were disarmed.

The third day began well for the defenders. An attack on Kamal Khan's sector, made in the mistaken belief that the captured stormers were still at large there, was driven off after two hours of hard fighting. Shah Nawaz Khan sent sweetmeats to the defenders and his military band played to celebrate their success. Kamal Khan, however, had formed the view that the city was indefensible and spent most of the day persuading Shah Nawaz Khan that such was the case. His own resolution was weakened by reports that the Sarawans had sent men to Baghwan to destroy his home and capture his wives and children for use as human shields in the next attack. Throughout the city, men lost heart and work on the defences was abandoned. At sunset, a *vakil* (accredited representative) arrived from the rebels and, in return, an *elchi* (ambassador) from Shah Nawaz Khan was sent to their camp.

The next day, Kamal Khan produced a copy of an agreement between the sardars of Sarawan and Jhalawan, acknowledging Nasir Khan II as ruler of Kalat but leaving Baghwan and central Jhalawan to Shah Nawaz Khan if he abdicated and left Kalat city within three days. Loveday was promised safe conduct to Quetta with his sepoys and property. In the course of further negotiations, Atta Muhammad Khan, a brother of the Akhund Muhammad Sadiq, assured Loveday that Nasir Khan II, the Daroga and the Queen Mother, Bibi Ganjan, all had nothing but goodwill for him, and that the Bibi had adopted him as a son. When Masson, suspicious of these assurances, pointed out that a letter said to be from the lady did not bear her seal, he was told that she had given this to Postans (acting as senior political officer in Balochistan in the absence of Bell at Simla), who was undertaking some business on her behalf. Shah Nawaz Khan, encouraged by Masson, was disposed to continue resistance, but Loveday, influenced by Sardar Kamal Khan, advocated accepting the terms.

Despatches arrived from Quetta and Shikarpur to warn that no troops could be spared for Kalat from either garrison. Loveday then decided to abandon Shah Nawaz Khan, who accordingly left Kalat on the third day of negotiations. The deposed khan, knowing how unpopular Loveday had become, begged him to leave at the same time. When Loveday chose to stay, Shah Nawaz told the sardars that it was the British Government, not Loveday the individual, who had placed him on the throne of Kalat, and that Loveday was as dear to him as his beard. Nasir Khan II replied that Loveday, by remaining, had also become as dear to him as his own beard, and would be treated as a brother (scarcely a reassuring remark given the incidence of fratricide among Brahui princes).[2]

Loveday and Masson at the court of Nasir Khan II

As Shah Nawaz rode out, the new Khan rode in, to the cheers of his subjects. The chief offices of state were resumed by those survivors who had held them under Mahrab Khan. These included Akhund Muhammad Sadiq, who still held his late master's seal, and began by ordering the closure of the Bolan Pass to British kafilas. After receiving Loveday's reports, Bean informed the Brahui sardars that, subject to their acknowledging the supremacy of Shah Shuja-ul-Mulk, he would recommend the recognition of Nasir Khan II as khan of Kalat. They refused, saying that Shah Shuja-ul-Mulk had wronged Mahrab Khan and was a shah in name only, though they were willing to submit to MacNaghten, the British Envoy, whom all knew to be the real ruler of the country.

Masson, somewhat quixotically, had decided to remain with Loveday, but their position became more perilous by the day. Their houses were ransacked and their possessions stolen (Masson losing the notes and records of his fifteen years of exploration). Loveday's hated bulldogs were killed and as many of his sepoy escort who had not deserted were disarmed and imprisoned. Masson and Loveday were then arrested and taken through a hostile crowd, being spat on by women and pelted with stones, to the Khan's palace. Daroga Ghul Muhammmad assured them they were then protected by the laws of hospitality, but lodged them under guard in the ominously-named Chamber of Blood, a room whose most recent occupant had been Mahrab Khan's murdered wazir, Daud Muhammad. There they were visited by the Shahgasi Wali Muhammad, who mentioned that his brother, Shahgasi Nur Muhammad, had fallen beside Mahrab Khan in the storming of Kalat, after killing his own wives and female dependents to preserve their honour. He nevertheless promised that Loveday and Masson would be treated generously and sent in various items of furniture and provisions taken from their houses.

Some days later, Masson was summoned before the Daroga, whom he described as a 'tall, spare, aged and harsh-featured man, blind of one eye and his head affected with palsey'.[3] The conversation began unpromisingly, with the Daroga saying that he never saw a *farangi*, or even thought of one, without blood being ready to gush from his eyes by reason of the wrongs and injuries he had suffered at their hands. He spoke of Sikandar (Sir Alexander Burnes) who in that very room had sworn by Hazrat Isa (Holy Jesus) that the British had no designs on his country; of the aid that Mahrab Khan, in accordance with his treaty, had given the Army of the Indus; of the way this had been rewarded and the way that his late master's body had been left unhonoured and uncovered. He also drew Masson's attention to a hole in the room's wall, made by a British cannon-ball during the storming of the city. Particular complaints against Loveday were his attempts to capture the young Nasir Khan II, and his having put a price on the head of the Daroga himself. It then emerged that one of Loveday's most trusted clerks was actually an agent of the Daroga, who thus had been kept informed of all British intentions.

Daroga Ghul Muhammad then said that he was willing to forget the past and desired only to make peace with the British. To that end, Loveday would be taken to Mastung to meet Bean there, but the British should remember that, if a peace settlement was not achieved, their communications with Afghanistan could be cut by the Brahuis. Negotiations continued for several more days before Loveday and Nasir Khan II, followed by the Daroga and the Brahui sardars, set out for Mastung. Kalat was left under the new khan's uncle, Mir Azim Khan, who had returned from Las Bela complaining of the poor hospitality he had been given by the Jam. Unable, for lack of funds, to indulge in the wine-bibbing that, in his late brother's view, made him unfit for office, he seemed to have abstained while in exile but, once back at Kalat, resumed his old habit.

Bean, meanwhile, had sent his assistant, Lieutenant William Frederick Hammersley of the 41st Bengal Native Infantry, with a strong force of local levies and horse artillery, towards Kalat. They surprised and routed a group of Brahuis near Mastung but Bean then decided that the likely opposition was too strong and recalled them to Quetta. Loveday promised one of the daroga's servants 2,000 rupees in return for horses with which to escape, but this was discovered and thereafter Loveday was chained to a tent-pole whenever the party camped for the night.

After reaching Mastung, the prisoners were treated increasingly harshly. News came of Clibborn's defeat in the attempt to relieve Kahan, but as Doda Khan, the Marri Sardar, declined join Nasir Khan II in arms, the daroga declared that once peace was made with the English he would deal with the Marris himself. Loveday once more promised the Brahuis that he would write to Bean urging British acknowledgement of Nasir Khan II. Bean's reply, that the young khan must first surrender Kalat, go to Kandahar, and thereafter comply with whatever was asked of him, was received with outrage. Eventually, after Loveday's repeated requests, the daroga allowed Masson to leave for Quetta to explain to Bean how dangerous the situation at Mastung had become. Many Brahuis believed that Masson would not return, but he gave his word to them, and to Loveday, that he would do so. Escorted by a few horsemen, he was led out of Mastung by a back way, to avoid any hostile demonstrations, and reached Quetta after dark the same evening.

The next day Bean listened to Masson's story, but declined to act on it. Loveday, he said, was safe enough, as it was well known that Brahuis never killed their prisoners. Masson's suggestion of offering to exchange him for Rahim Dad, formerly Mahrab Khan's naib of Quetta, was dismissed, on the grounds that Nasir Khan II's advisers would not value the release of one who had betrayed his father. Masson himself had no documents from the daroga to prove the authenticity of his claims, nor anything authorizing him to travel in Shah Shuja-ul-Mulk's dominions. To disguise his position as a deserter from the Bengal Army, he had at times pretended to be an American citizen, and Bean wrongly suspected he was the Russian agent of whom Outram had sent word. He was therefore not allowed to return to Mastung, despite having given his word. Instead, he was placed under arrest while further enquiries were made. By his own account, he was given only the most disgusting food until one of his guards carried it to Lieutenant Colonel Robert Stacy of the 43rd Bengal Native Infantry, an officer in the force recently sent back from Kandahar, who intervened to improve his conditions. Masson then demanded to know why he, a British subject, had been deprived of his liberty by British political officers.

This began a correspondence lasting over four months, involving Mac-Naghten at Kabul and John Colvin, his successor as secretary to the Government of India in the Foreign Department. Masson was eventually released on 9 January 1841 on the orders of the ailing Ross Bell, who had returned from Simla and learned from the Brahui sardars that Masson's story was the truth. Masson later returned to London, where he carried his grievances to the East India Company's Court of Directors. He received some compensation, but little sympathy, as the Directors felt that by choosing to travel in a war zone he had brought some of his misfortunes on himself. He played no further part in the affairs of Afghanistan or Balochistan, but achieved lasting fame for his exploration of their previously little-studied antiquities.

The British return to Kalat, November 1840

Meanwhile, the British prepared to re-assert control over Kalat. Major General William Nott, an experienced officer of the Bengal Army then commanding at Kandahar, was on 3 September 1840 ordered to offer Nasir Khan II recognition as chief of Kalat in return for his submission to Shah Shuja-ul-Mulk (the terms previously offered by Bean). Nott, writing to his daughters, said that he was disgusted by the proposal. Mahrab Khan, he said, had been most unjustly dethroned and replaced by a tool of Shah Shuja-ul-Mulk. 'Had they taken this boy by the hand when he was a wanderer in the land of his ancestors, there would have been a generous and honourable feeling; but to bend the knee to him and his bloody chiefs now is disgraceful.'[4] Nott was already on bad terms with the political officers, having been censured after MacNaghten complained of his punishing corrupt officials of Timur Mirza, Shah Shuja's son and heir, who had been appointed governor of Kandahar. When Bean had specified the reinforcements he wanted after Hammersley's failed attempt to relieve Loveday in Kalat, Nott himself had complained to Sir Willoughby Cotton (Keane's successor as Commander in Chief in Afghanistan) that to send them in the numbers demanded would risk the entire position in southern Afghanistan. 'Captain Bean confines his ideas to that miserable dog-hole Quettah and *dictates* the troops to be sent to that place from Candahar without noting the object in view... no officer of common understanding would pay the least attention to such a call.'[5]

Nott marched to Mastung with 300 men, reaching it on 25 October, while the insurgents avoided an encounter by moving into northern Kachhi. There, they attacked Dadhar on 30 and 31 October, but the post commandant, Captain John Watkins, 23rd Bombay Light Infantry, held them off. A small force, hastily assembled from nearby lines of communications troops by Captain Hugh Boscawen, 54th Bengal Native Infantry, routed the Brahuis in an action outside the town on 2 November. When the British entered the abandoned Brahui camp, they found in one of the tents the body of Loveday, dressed only in the cotton *pajamas* worn by Muslims, still chained at the ankles. A weeping Hindustani attendant told them that, contrary to the wishes of the Khan, Daroga Ghul Muhammad had ordered that the last man to leave the camp should cut Loveday's throat. It later emerged that Loveday tried to save his life by telling his guard that Nasir Khan would be angry if a British officer was killed except on the Khan's direct orders. The guard was later tried for murder by a British court at Quetta, where he said that he went to search for the Khan but, unable to find him in the confusion, returned and killed Loveday on his own initiative. This brought him to the gallows, but at least exonerated Nasir Khan II.[6]

Nott occupied Kalat unopposed on 3 November. As the British approached the city, the governor (the alleged wine-bibber Mir Azim Khan) fled, taking with him the survivors of Loveday's sepoy escort. These, with the exception of their elderly subadar who disappeared as the party traversed a mountain track, were subsequently liberated by Hammersley. Nott returned to Kandahar, leaving a garrison at Kalat, where Lieutenant Colonel Stacy was appointed political agent in Loveday's place. Bell, as a goodwill gesture, released the political prisoners held at Bukkur and agreed to open negotiations with the insurgents who, after their defeat at Dadhar, had fled south and re-assembled at Kotra, in western Kachhi. Major General George Brooks of the Bombay Army, commanding the troops in Upper Sind, sent a force of 900 sepoys, drawn from the 2nd Bombay Grenadiers and the 21st and 25th Bombay Native Infantry, with two guns and eighty Scinde Irregular Horse, to disperse them. The troops reached Kotra on 1 December 1841 and made an immediate attack, taking the Brahuis by surprise. Nasir Khan II escaped on foot with two attendants, but four sardars and about 500 men were killed in the fighting, and another eight chiefs and 132 men were captured. The remainder, estimated to number about 3,000, escaped into the nearby hills. The sepoys plundered the Brahui camp and their officers were congratulated on a brilliant success.

The Brahuis later claimed that the reason why they were taken by surprise was that they had been in daily negotiations with the British political officers as the Bombay troops approached and that, at the time of the attack, the Khan's emissaries were actually in the British camp. As Daroga Gul Muhammad (who scarcely needed a further cause for his anti-British views) told Stacey, 'It is not the custom to send proposals of peace and friendship in the evening, and in the morning make an attack. Who shall say how many men were killed wounded or taken; how much property was seized; what was the extent of our misfortunes?'.[7] The episode brought the British a reputation for treachery that was repeatedly referred to both by Brahui and Baloch spokesmen in later diplomatic exchanges. Its origins clearly lay in a failure of communication between the military officers, looking to enhance their careers by a quick victory over hostiles who had already attacked British posts, and the diplomats, who were trying to negotiate a peaceful settlement.

Outram's Treaty with Kalat, 6 October 1841

A month after the Kotra incident, Bell decided to make a fresh start by sending an officer from the British force at Kalat to re-open negotiations with Nasir Khan II in Kachhi. Stacy volunteered for the mission and, disregarding the fate of his predecessor, rode unescorted into the Brahui camp on a promise of safe conduct. Adopting a conciliatory attitude quite different from that of the discredited Bean, he spent the first months of 1841 negotiating with the Brahuis, so successfully that in July 1841 Nasir Khan II re-entered Kalat city, with the British garrison paraded in his honour. The ailing Bell never lived to see the fruits of his new policy, as he died at Quetta on 31 July 1841, when Nasir Khan II was actually on the way to meet him.[8] The proposed talks were then delayed pending the arrival of Bell's successor, Major James Outram, the same officer who less than two years earlier had carried the dispatches reporting the British storming of Kalat.

Outram's services had brought him to the attention of the Governor-General, Lord Auckland, who appointed him Political Agent in Lower Sind (Hyderabad) in January 1840, when Henry Pottinger, increasingly out of sympathy with Auckland's policy towards Sind, returned to England. Outram gained the personal friendship of the Hyderabad amirs and did much to improve relations between them and the British who had occupied their country in the name of Shah Shuja-ul-Mulk. His success was recognized in August 1841 when, following Bell's death, his area of political responsibility was extended over Upper Sind (Khairpur) and Balochistan. Aware that Stacy had recently succeeded in persuading Nasir Khan II to agree to a conference, he immediately hurried up the Indus by steamer to Sukkur and passed through Kachhi at the hottest time of the year to reach Quetta on 2 September 1841.[9]

Two days later, Nasir Khan II and his entourage also arrived at Quetta, to be received by Stacy with a guard of honour. The following morning, at a formal darbar, Outram greeted the young Khan with all the courtesy due to a reigning prince. In Stacy's words, 'The youth was rather embarrassed at first, but on Major Outram's assuring him of the kindly feelings of the Government towards him, he expressed his desire to become an ally of the Company... to enroll himself amongst the number of their servants, to live under the shade of their flag... and to agree to whatever terms the Company might prescribe.'[10] It seems that Outram, who both in Sind and later in Awadh, felt much sympathy for wronged Indian princes, was able to convince the Khan and his ministers of British good faith and, after further negotiations, both parties set out for Kalat with a ceremonial escort of British troops.

A new treaty, signed at Kalat on 6 October 1841, began, as had that agreed between Mahrab Khan and Alexander Burnes, by confirming that the Khan of Kalat, his heirs and successors, were vassals of Shah Shuja-ul-Mulk, King of Kabul, in the same (unspecified) way that his ancestors had been vassals of Shah Shuja-ul-Mulk's ancestors. Of the districts resumed on the death of Mahrab Khan (cause diplomatically left unstated), Kachhi and Mastung would be restored to Nasir Khan II 'through the kindness of His Majesty Shah Shuja-ool-Moolk'. Shal, containing the strategically vital town of Quetta, remained under Shah Shuja-ul-Mulk. Troops of either the British government or Shah

Shuja-ul-Mulk were allowed to be stationed anywhere in the dominions of the Khan of Kalat, who bound himself always to be guided by the advice of the British officer resident at his court. Merchants and others travelling from the Indus or from the seaport of Sonmiani were to be protected, 'as far as possible', from any aggression or undue exaction, and only those transit dues agreed between the Khan and the British government were to be imposed. No political contact with foreign powers was to be undertaken without British or Shah Shuja-ul-Mulk's consent, though 'the usual amicable correspondence with neighbours' was to continue as before. In return, the British guaranteed to aid Nasir Khan II against any open enemy and, should he be in dispute with any foreign power, to use their good offices for the maintenance of his rights. Finally, Nasir Khan II agreed to provide for Shah Nawaz Khan, either by funding a pension, payable through the British as long as that prince resided in British India, or by granting him estates inside Kalat territory.[11]

In the presence of the leading Brahui sardars, Outram then conducted Nasir Khan II to the throne of his ancestors, a public recognition (though no apology was issued) of the wrong done by the British to Mahrab Khan two years earlier. A royal salute was fired by the Khan's gunners, while the Khan himself shook hands with all the British officers in attendance, including Major General Richard England (a British Army officer who had succeeded to the command of the troops in Upper Sind), Captain Bean (from Quetta) and Captain Lewis Brown (the defender of Marri Kahan). Outram wrote to John Colvin that 'The young chief was visibly affected—almost to tears—by the good feeling displayed towards him by the English gentlemen'.[12] The Brahui sardars made a special point of expressing their appreciation of Stacy's part in achieving the settlement, sentiments that, while those conventionally exchanged on such occasions, might well be taken at face value. The day ended with displays of Brahui horsemanship and traditional dances, in which, as Outram reported, 'all ranks and classes heartily joined'.

The assignment of John Jacob to the Upper Sind Frontier

After the conclusion of the 1840 hill campaign, Billamore's artillery commander, Captain John Jacob, took the widely-held view that there was little chance of further active service on the Sind frontier and returned to his previous post in civil employment with the Survey Department in Gujerat. On his way down the Indus, he visited Outram, whom he had long admired for his work in western India and who at this time was still the British Political Agent in Lower Sind. Jacob readily accepted Outram's request to survey a route by which troops returning from Afghanistan to Bombay overland could avoid the worst of the deserts between southern Sind and Gujerat and the two officers began a long-lasting friendship. After Clibborn's defeat by the Marris, Outram wrote to Jacob urging him to return to regimental duty, in the anticipation of a new campaign and during October 1840 Jacob led a party of reinforcements through the desert to Sukkur, where he joined the 4th Troop of Bombay Horse Artillery en route to Quetta.[13]

When this unit was ordered back to India following the conclusion of the peace treaty with Nasir Khan II, Outram obtained Jacob's services to survey the water sources along the kafila route between Shikarpur and Dadhar, granting him an extra allowance to compensate for the loss of income from his civil post in Gujerat. Within three weeks Jacob produced a plan for the excavation of large tanks or reservoirs at all the main halting points. These would be filled during the annual flooding of the normally dry Nari river, which follows a hundred-mile course through Kachhi, and thus collect in a few hours enough water to last the rest of the year. Outram gave his support to the idea and proposed that the cost of labour and materials should be shared equally between the British and the Khan of Kalat, whose subjects would be the immediate beneficiaries.

Although the scheme was eventually abandoned, Outram continued to rate Jacob extremely highly. In November 1841, he endorsed Jacob's application for the vacant command of the Scinde Irregular Horse, an appointment within the patronage of the political rather than the military authorities. Jacob, he said, had proved himself an able and zealous officer, whose survey work would be assisted by the command of a regiment whose posts all lay in Kachhi or along the frontier of Upper Sind. As an artilleryman, he would be able to command a mountain train in the Baloch hills, the terrain of which he knew better than anyone. Outram also arranged Jacob's appointment as a 3rd Class Political Assistant for Kachhi (authorized in January 1842), thereby combining the local military and diplomatic powers in a single individual.[14] Jacob, a good rider and a formidable swordsman, arrived on the frontier of Upper Sind at a time when the local Baloch tribes, subjects of the Khan of Kalat on one side and the amirs of Sind on the other, were growing restive. He was destined to play a decisive role in the pacification of the Balochistan border and the extension of British control beyond it.

6

THE FIRST NORTH-WEST FRONTIER, 1842–46

... stories of border warfare...of ambush, firing on the rear-guard, heat that split the skull better than any tomahawk, cold that wrinkled the very liver, night-stampedes of baggage-mules, raiding of cattle, and hopeless chases into inhospitable hills, when the cavalry knew they were not only being outpaced but outspied.

[conversations with US Cavalry officers, Yellowstone, July 1889]

From Sea to Sea, Rudyard Kipling.

Outram's agreement with Nasir Khan II (most of which could have been achieved two years earlier without the subsequent costs in blood and treasure) came just in time. During the summer of 1841, a British general election brought a new ministry to power in London. Auckland resigned as governor-general and Lord Ellenborough, a former President of the Board of Control, was appointed to succeed him, with orders to reduce the immense costs of the Afghan adventure. Before he even reached India, the plan of reconstructing the Durrani Empire as a friendly and powerful British ally had collapsed. During November 1841 first Burnes and then MacNaghten had been murdered at Kabul. This marked the beginning of a major insurgency against Shah Shuja-ul-Mulk and his British paymasters and in January 1842 the British garrison of Kabul, 4,500 soldiers and 11,000 followers, had perished (mostly from exposure) attempting a winter retreat to Jalalabad. The politicals (of whom Edred Pottinger was the senior survivor), the married officers and their families were surrendered as hostages to the insurgency's leader, Sardar Muhammad Akbar Khan, son of the exiled Amir Dost Muhammad, who protected them under the laws of hospitality.[1]

The British withdrawal from Afghanistan, 1842

With the British political service in Afghanistan left leaderless. Auckland, in the dying days of his administration, decided that political control should be exercised through the local military commanders, Major Generals George Pollock at Peshawar and William Nott at Kandahar. In Balochistan and Sind, Outram thus found himself under the orders of Nott, who had previously been subordinate to him in political matters. Nott, however, made it clear that he did not wish every question to be referred to him and, in response to a query from Hammersley at Quetta, replied 'When the Government gave me political authority, it could only have been intended [as] the power of putting my veto on what I may deem injurious. It could not have been meant that I should interfere with details. The charge of an army of 25,000 men is quite enough'.[2]

Ellenborough reached Calcutta on 28 February 1842. Two weeks later he ruled that, as Shah Shuja-ul-Mulk had repudiated his British allies, their treaty with him was ended and the troops in Afghanistan were to be withdrawn to India as soon as British military prestige had been restored. A fortnight later, however, learning that Ghazni had been lost and that Major General England had been defeated at Haikalzai, he ordered Pollock to return at the earliest practicable date after relieving Jalalabad. Nott was told to pull back from Kalat-i-Ghilzai and Kandahar to Quetta, and from there to Sukkur as soon as the season allowed.

England had been ordered forward to resupply and reinforce Kandahar. After reaching Quetta, he left most of his brigade still moving up through the Bolan and pushed on with four companies of the 41st Foot, six of Bombay Native Infantry, four horse artillery guns and two troops of cavalry. On 28 March, at Haikalzai, just below the Khojak Pass, the last major defile on the route to Kandahar, he found the road barricaded and held by local tribesmen. After suffering casualties, he decided that the position was too strong to force and retreated to Quetta. He subsequently blamed this defeat on Hammersley, the political officer, for failing to provide him with intelligence of the likely opposition. Ellenborough accepted this, and ruled that Hammersley should be returned to regimental duty, thus forfeiting the extra pay that went with political appointments. Outram's opinion was that England was to blame, first for advancing without his full force (contrary to Outram's advice and Nott's orders) and secondly for not pressing home the attack on the barricade. Furious at an injustice to a valued subordinate, he disregarded the orders to remove Hammersley, arguing that at such a critical time local experience was indispensable.[3]

Outram's view was that the British could hold Balochistan. There was, he reported, no fellow-feeling between Baloch and Afghan; Quetta was impregnable; British troops were invincible in the open plains; the reinforcements pouring into Sind would discourage any ideas that the amirs might have of rising against the British; and the lines of communication through Kachhi were secure. There, in November 1841, the Jakhrani chief, Turk Ali, after two years service in the para-military Baluch Levy, deserted with the intention of joining a Bugti raid, but was pursued and arrested by Baluch Khan, the Dombki sardar. In February 1842, learning of the British disasters in Afghanistan, Turk Ali (whom Outram, with characteristic chivalry, had pardoned) again deserted, this time with all his men. He joined forces with a band of Bugtis and made off with 200 camels laden with grain intended for the troops above the Bolan.

One consequence of the cession of Kachhi to Shah Shuja-ul-Mulk in 1839 had been a closer inspection of its revenues. As a result, the former Naib in Kachhi, Sayyad Muhammad Sharif, was convicted of fraud and imprisoned at Sukkur. Early in 1842 he escaped with the aid of Fatah Muhammad Ghori, chief minister of Mir Rustum Khan, the senior amir of Upper Sind. Outram suspected a conspiracy to weaken British control in Sind by raising a new rebellion in Balochistan. Muhammad Sharif reached Sardars Babarak Bugti and Bijar Khan Dombki, both of whom had been released by the British in return for undertaking to keep the peace, but neither saw any benefit in breaking their recent agreements. He then tried to raise the Brahuis but, with Kachhi now back in their hands, none were anxious to lose the benefits of the recent treaty. Nasir Khan II kept his promises and met Outram's request for transport under the terms of the treaty by supplying several thousand of the camels needed by Nott for any move from Kandahar.

Pollock, with his men reinforced and their morale restored, advanced from Peshawar at the end of March. On 16 April 1842 he reached Jalalabad, where the garrison, on a false report that he had been defeated in the Khyber, had already sallied out and dispersed its Afghan besiegers. At the other end of the country, responding to explicit orders from Nott, England advanced from Quetta on 26 April 1842, traversed the Haikalzai defile and Khojak Pass without difficulty and reached Kandahar on 10 May. Ellenborough then expected Nott and Pollock to comply with his former orders to withdraw as soon as practicable, especially as Shah Shuja-ul-Mulk had been assassinated at Kabul on 5 April. Neither general was in a hurry to leave Afghanistan with the hostages unrecovered and the Kabul garrison unavenged and so they prevaricated, reporting that they were short of transport and that the season was against them.

Finally, with the costs to Indian revenues becoming heavier by the day, Ellenborough found a face-saving solution. At the end of July 1842 he told Nott that he could return to India via Kabul, and Pollock that he could advance to co-operate with him. Then, after demonstrating British power and inflicting suitable retribution, they were to leave the country without further delay. On 10 August, after the arrival of several thousand camels collected by Outram from Kalat and elsewhere, Nott marched with the greater part of his troops for Kabul. The remainder were placed under England's command and ordered back to Sind via the Bolan. Nott and Pollock fought their separate ways to Kabul and on 16 September hoisted the British flag there. Then, having gained their victories and rescued the hostages, they marched out on 12 October 1842 and returned to India via the Khyber.

The handover of Quetta, 1842

Meanwhile, Ellenborough had discovered that there were more political officers beyond the northern frontier of British India than there were British diplomats in the whole of Europe. On 22 May 1842 he officially informed Outram that, following the withdrawal from Afghanistan, large reductions would be made. Outram's achievement in producing the camels for Kandahar had been favourably noticed and Ellenborough promised that he would be appointed Envoy to the amirs of Sind. Outram remained responsible for the conduct of British relations with Kalat, from where Stacy had joined England's march to Kandahar and served at the two engagements at Haikalzai. Auckland, shortly before leaving office, had expressed vague support for a proposal by Outram that Shal (Quetta) and Sibi (a neighbouring district, some 4,000 square miles in extent, lying to the east of the Bolan) should be handed over to Nasir Khan II as a reward for having fulfilled his treaty obligations. Outram renewed the proposal after Ellenborough's arrival. It would be better, he said, for these two districts to be granted to Kalat while they were still occupied by British troops, rather than left to whatever government came to power in Afghanistan, especially as the British were treaty-bound to defend Kalat against invasion. He was told that political responsibility for Kandahar and Balochistan had been handed to Nott as the commanding general and therefore all proposals should be submitted through him. On 28 June 1842, Nott sent a brief acknowledgement but, occupied by military affairs, made no other comment.[4]

Anxious to smooth the way for the planned return of the Kandahar garrison, Outram told Nasir Khan II that he had been authorized to return Shal to Kalat. Nott, in charge of local political affairs, responded to this decision by telling Outram 'I daresay the Government will approve of your proceedings regarding Shal, but it was my wish to retain Quetta until my army encamped there; this would have been convenient. I regret you did not wait for my orders'. Ellenborough objected even more strongly 'to resort to fiction in communications to a native chief, without the shadow of justifying necessity, if any such there can be, is conduct inconsistent with the character which... [the Governor-General] desires the diplomacy of India to maintain. The Governor-General trusts that he shall never again have occasion to remark upon similar conduct, which he has witnessed with the greater regret on the part of an officer so able and so zealous in the performance of public duty as you have heretofore shown yourself to be'.[5]

Outram did his best to answer what was in effect an accusation of lying. There had been no reply, he said, to his urgent proposals on a question that had to be settled as part of the British decision to withdraw from Balochistan. The timely cession of Shal had been well received by the Khan and the Brahui sardars, and within hours of its announcement, Hammersley had been able to arrest Muhammad Sharif, the troublesome ex-Naib in Kachhi. Had the Brahuis not been conciliated in this way, said Outram, Muhammad Sharif's intrigues might well have united them with the dissident Afghan sardars around Kandahar and started a new war in Balochistan. He had no orders or precedents to guide him about the disposal of Quetta, he had not been told the intentions of the authorities at Kandahar, despite being expected to implement them, and was working with 'a fanatical and treacherous people... naturally opposed to us by religion, and by awe of our enemies their neighbours—besides being goaded by recent recollections of the many hardships they have suffered at our hands, such as spoliation of their territory, sacking of their capital, and slaughter of their Khan and principal chiefs'.[6]

Ellenborough was unmoved, and no more was said about Outram's appointment as Envoy. The governor-general had already been irritated by Outram's defence of Hammersley, who died at Quetta on 9 August 1842, officially of fever. Outram himself was stricken with 'brain fever' (possibly viral encephalitis) after several nights spent at the dying man's bedside. He noted that the medical officers thought Hammersley's condition was worsened by his being scape-goated to save General England's face. Quetta remained in British hands until England's columns passed through on the way home from Kandahar, and the whole province of Shal, with the co-operation of the Khan's officers, provided supplies. Sibi, however, continued to belong to Kandahar as it had in the days of Ahmad Shah Durrani, though now separated from it by the Khan's possession of Shal.

'The Bayard of India'

Outram rode with the troops as they withdrew from Quetta, through Kachhi, to Sukkur. There on 12 October 1842 he met the 60-year-old Major General Sir Charles Napier, a Peninsular veteran recently appointed commander of the British forces in Sind and Balochistan with full political authority from the sea to the Afghan border. Expecting to serve under Napier as Envoy to the amirs of Sind, Outram was instead, on 26 October, informed that his department was to be broken up and that he and all his officers would return to regimental duty. Disheartened, he decided to take the furlough that he had long earned and was granted permission to go to Bombay and sail for England. Many officers sympathized with him and, before he left Karachi, he was dined out by over 200 officers. Napier proposed a toast to him as "The Bayard of India, sans peur and sans reproche".

Although Ellenborough had been anxious to withdraw from Afghanistan at the earliest opportunity, he was equally determined to maintain the British hold over Sind. Napier was instructed to negotiate a new treaty with the amirs, obliging them to cede in perpetuity the port of Karachi and all the other places of importance occupied by British troops in support of Shah Shuja-ul-Mulk. In Hyderabad (Lower Sind), Mir Sobdar Khan was to be recognized as Rais or senior chief. In Khairpur (Upper Sind), Mir Ali Murad was to be made Rais in the place of his elder brother, the aged Mir Rustum. This would give the British only two princes to deal with, both of whom had proved co-operative during the Afghan war and could be expected to accept the new terms. It soon became clear, however, that neither were ready to do so.[7]

To deal with the growing diplomatic crisis, Napier recalled Outram before he could sail and appointed him commissioner in Sind. In the course of January and early February 1843, the amirs reluctantly submitted to all the British demands except for the supersession of Mir Rustum by Mir Ali Murad, whom most of his peers thought of as a traitor. If the British could set up one amir over another, they said, then the position of all would be in danger, and even if they themselves assented to it, their Baloch retainers would see their jagirs at risk and take up arms of their own accord. Napier believed that the amirs were prolonging their discussions with Outram simply to gain time while they gathered their forces. He continued to move his own army towards Hyderabad, where Outram, personally sympathetic to the amirs, but bound by Napier's instructions, did all he could to achieve a peaceful settlement. On 12 February all those present agreed to put their seals on the new treaty, though Mir Rustum's position was not mentioned.[8]

Napier's Conquest of Sind, 1843

Nevertheless, each side saw the other as intending to provoke hostilities. News that a group of Marri chiefs settled in Sind had been arrested en route to Hyderabad was taken as evidence that the British were determined on war. Baloch jagirdars and their men had been streaming into Hyderabad during the preceding weeks, ready to fight for their land and their freedom. Now, ignoring the orders of their amirs, they attacked the British Residency in Hyderabad. Outram and his small escort made a spirited defence but eventually retreated to their river-steamer and escaped down the Indus. Mir Nasir Khan, a leading advocate for peace, was presented by his Baloch sardars with a woman's dress. Rather than be deemed a coward, he rode out with them, living up to his earlier declaration "We gained this country by the sword and if it is to pass from us it shall not do so without the sword".

In two closely-contested battles (Miani, 17 February 1843 and Hyderabad, 24 February 1843) Napier's army, though greatly outnumbered, routed its brave but poorly-led Baloch opponents.[9] Most of the amirs surrendered and were made prisoners of state. Ellenborough declared the annexation of Sind to British India and appointed Napier its governor. Only Mir Ali Murad of Khairpur was left as a ruling prince, and even he was forced to accept British control over his foreign policy. By the middle of June 1843, the last resistance was ended. The heavy casualties suffered in the two pitched battles had convinced the Baloch that they could not defeat the British and they became reconciled to the new Raj when Napier confirmed them in their existing jagirs. Unemployment among their former soldiers was eased when Napier formed a 'Baluch Battalion', armed and uniformed in the local fashion, under a few British officers as their regimental staff, and stationed in Sind to support the new authorities. Sind was divided into three Collectorates, two in lower Sind (one on either side of the Indus, governed from Karachi and Hyderabad respectively), and the third, Upper Sind, governed from Sukkur. The capital of the new British province of Sind was established at Karachi.

The Upper Sind Frontier, 1843

The North-West Frontier of Sind thus became that of British India. Along its lower stretches the inhabitants were mostly peaceful shepherds or farmers. The un-demarcated frontier of Upper Sind, on the other hand, long disputed between the amirs of Sind and the khans of Kalat but rarely protected by either, was a scene of constant cross-border raiding. The Scinde Irregular Horse, previously deployed to this area, had been withdrawn during the Sind war to make up for Napier's deficiency in cavalry, leaving the countryside defenceless. During May 1843, within weeks of having become British territory, the districts north-east of Shikarpur were laid waste by Baloch robbers. With nothing to stop them but four troops of the 3rd Bengal Irregular Cavalry, hastily sent to the area under Captain Thomas Tait of the 2nd Bombay Europeans, raiders descended at will on the settlements between Shikarpur and Larkana. At the end of 1843, a band of 300 Dombkis and Jakhranis sacked several villages and drove stolen cattle back to their own territory, 80 miles way to the north-east, easily evading the troops sent in pursuit. On 25 March 1844 another large war-party rounded up 1,500 animals from Larkana district, the sixth major raid in as many months. At much the same time, the Kalpars, a major clan of the Bugtis, came down from their hills on the south-eastern side of Kachhi and attacked a village north of Shikarpur. On 1 April 1844 a thousand Dombkis, Jakhranis and Kalpars, led (regardless of his previous peace agreement) by the notorious Sardar Bijar Khan Dombki, descended on a prosperous village only 17 miles north of Shikarpur, killing forty people, burning the houses and committing various atrocities, including cutting off children's hands to take their bangles.

Napier reported this outrage to Ellenborough and asked for permission to take severe reprisals as the only way of protecting those who had become British subjects. On 8 May 1844, Ellenborough replied that reprisals did not accord with British principles of civilization and humanity, and would in any case only provoke blood feuds. It would, he said, be better to rely on defensive measures, such as filling in the desert wells (except those on the route to the Bolan) and fortifying the frontier villages, but the decision would have to be made on the advice of those who knew the country. Bijar Khan, if taken, could be hanged, but only after a public trial.[10]

Ellenborough, however, was about to leave office. His annexation of Sind had been unpopular with the Court of Directors who saw it as an expensive mistake. Outram had returned to London, where his account of Ellenborough's treatment of the amirs raised a public outcry. The Cabinet was embarrassed and the Directors, who had several other grudges against Ellenborough, invoked their never previously exercised right of recall. Against that, any hopes that the amirs had of retrieving their lost independence faded when, in May 1844, his successor was named as Lieutenant General Sir Henry Hardinge, a veteran of the Napoleonic Wars, a member of the existing Cabinet and Ellenborough's own brother-in-law.

Frontier Operations, 1844

In Sind, Napier decided that action had to be taken against the robbers. He gave conditional approval for a proposal by Lieutenant Robert Fitzgerald of the 12th Bombay Native Infantry, commandant of a recently-formed camel corps, to make a dawn attack on Bijar Khan's base at Phulji and capture the chief as he slept. Despite being ordered to wait until artillery and reinforcements reached him at Shikarpur, Fitzgerald decided that any delay would lose the element of surprise and, accompanied by Tait and his four troops of cavalry, ordered a rapid march across the desert. As commonly happens in such missions, the column made slower progress than planned. Stragglers had to be left behind at Chhatr, a village 10 miles south of their destination, and the main force, arriving at Phulji in broad daylight, found itself long expected and the town's crumbling walls lined with Dombki matchlockmen. Lacking artillery or scaling ladders, Fitzgerald advanced with a forlorn hope under covering fire from the camel corps, intending to blow in the gate with a powder bag, just as the British had done when taking Ghazni five years previously. The attempt failed with the loss of eleven men killed, one of them a British sergeant who had carried the powder bag at Ghazni. Running short of water (the wells were inside the town), Tait abandoned the mission, retrieved his stragglers and retreated to his base at Khangarh. A subsequent Court of Enquiry into this debacle found that the decision to retreat was correct in the circumstances, but that the circumstances should never have been allowed to arise in the first place.

On 16 June 1844, the 6th Bengal Irregular Cavalry, newly-arrived at Khangarh, sent out its grass-cutters (non-combatants skilled at gathering fodder from even the most unpromising country) some 11 miles into the desert, with an escort of 150 troopers under an Indian officer. There, with the escort relaxing in the heat of the day, they were surprised by a band of Jakhranis and Dombkis. In the panic, the cavalrymen abandoned their grass-cutters and fled, many being cut down without resistance when the Baluch riders caught up with them. Almost 200 men, including the grass-cutters, were killed and fifty more were wounded. When the regimental commandant, Captain James Mackenzie of the 8ᵗʰ Bengal Light Cavalry, eventually reported this disaster, a furious Napier published a general order on 22 June 1844 censuring him for his men's indiscipline and cowardice, the one being, he said, a consequence of the other, and for not having commanded the detachment in person. 'The Major-General desires that the European Officers of the 6ᵗʰ Irregular Cavalry shall never quit their saddles, night or day, when a detachment is out of their cantonment. The European Officer who commands at an outpost must be eternally on his horse, with his sword in his hand; he should eat drink and sleep in his saddle'.

During July and August 1844 Baloch raiders plundered a total of five settlements near Larkana, where Fitzgerald's Camel Corps was stationed. The township of Kambar, a mere 14 miles east of Larkana Fort, was torched in broad daylight. Troops sent to the rescue found their way blocked by flooded irrigation canals and did not arrive until long after the raiders had ridden off. At the end of August, Mackenzie received a report that raiders were again crossing the desert, heading for the country north of Shikarpur. He rode east from Khangarh to intercept them and, on the border of Burdeka, a district still ruled by Mir Ali Murad Talpur, encountered a large body of Khosas and Burdis, subjects of the British and Ali Murad respectively. These Baloch tribesmen had gathered to protect their own homes, but Mackenzie mistook them for the raiders. Determined to retrieve his regiment's reputation after Napier's earlier criticism, he at once charged into them and when they cried out that they were on the side of the government, ordered them to throw down their weapons. He then rode off in fruitless pursuit of the raiders, while his rearguard, arriving under an Indian officer, compounded the original error by cutting down over a hundred unarmed men and maiming as many more.

Troops humiliated by previous defeats in unconventional warfare are especially prone to such 'blue on blue' mistakes when they believe that they have at last cornered their opponents. Mackenzie reported a body count of 200 hostiles and basked in Napier's approval until stories of what had actually occurred reached the general's ears. A court of enquiry established the facts and four years later the villagers received generous compensation. At the time, Mir Ali Murad told Napier that Baloch of any kind were all robbers and the troops' mistake was quite understandable, but this demonstration of British military incompetence merely encouraged Bijar Khan to continue his depredations. In September 1844, two other Baloch tribes, the Chandios and the Magsis, both of whom had suffered from Dombki raids, joined forces and attacked Phulji, only to be defeated just as Fitzgerald and Tait had been. Dombki and Jakhrani marauders prowled around Khangarh itself and in early October 1844 a war party 150 strong was at large inside British territory, robbing, burning and killing. All along the frontier, farmers abandoned their fields and sought safety under the walls of government forts. In the Baloch hills, old feuds forgotten, old quarrels set aside, thousands of the finest light horsemen in the world prepared to ride together against the scattered British garrisons.

Napier's Hill Campaign, January–March 1845

Napier decided that it was time to take the field in person. Believing that all the hill tribes together, Baloch, Brahui and Pashtun, could muster 18,000 men if they united against him, especially if he suffered any kind of a reverse, he assembled a force strong enough to meet any challenge. The mounted troops consisted of the 6th Bengal Irregular Cavalry from Khangarh, the Scinde Irregular Horse (recalled to the frontier from Hyderabad) and the Camel Corps from Larkana, anxious to make up for its failure to save Kambar. The conventional infantry comprised the 2nd Bengal Europeans and three battalions of sepoys while the Bundelkhand Legion, a 1,700-strong Irregular contingent of the Bengal Army, provided more cavalry and infantry. The field artillery, mostly from the Bengal Army, amounted to four 9-pdr guns, nine howitzers and three mortars, and was accompanied by a battering train of twenty-one pieces. Sardar Wali Muhammad Chandio brought 500 clansmen, and Mir Ali Murad promised 2,500 of his Baloch retainers, with ten guns.

A further contingent came from the 13th Foot, veterans of the Afghan war who were due to return to the United Kingdom. It was the normal practice, when a British regiment left India, for men to be invited to volunteer for transfer to other regiments remaining in the country. This suited both the Army, as these latter units were thus brought up to strength by seasoned reinforcements, and the soldiers themselves, because a bounty was paid to those who transferred from one corps to another. Those without close families at home often preferred life in India, where the drudgery of military life was mostly undertaken by camp followers, to the hardships of a barrack room in the United Kingdom. In October 1844, at Karachi, 446 of the 13th's rank and file volunteered to remain in India. Of these, 192 were assigned to the 39th Foot in Bengal. Napier decided that, before they departed to join their new regiment, he could use them in his coming campaign and formed them into a separate unit, mounted on camels.[11]

Aware that he would be crossing the border to wage war against nominal subjects of the Khan of Kalat, Napier sent a vakil to Nasir Khan II, at that time in Kachhi, to seek a conference. Nasir Khan, possibly on the advice of Daroga Ghul Muhammad, who always remained suspicious of British intentions, declined the invitation and the vakil returned to Sind empty-handed. Lieutenant E. J. Brown of the Bengal Engineers, on Napier's civil staff as Secretary to the Government of Sind, had previously met Nasir Khan II and was now sent to his camp at Bagh to obtain agreement to the coming campaign. Brown discovered that the Khan's unenthusiastic response to Napier's proposal for joint operations was because he needed all his troops to establish his authority in Shal. After admitting that the border tribes were beyond his control, Nasir Khan II agreed to the British entering his country to punish them for crimes committed on either side of the border. As Brown carried the agreement back to Napier, he narrowly escaped a large band of Bugtis who, possibly tipped off by anti-British elements at Nasir Khan's court, had ridden out to intercept him.

By January 1845 all was ready. As disinformation, Napier sent a message to Kalat saying that sickness among his troops would prevent any immediate move. This was allowed to fall into the hands of Bijar Khan, who relaxed his guard while Napier began the campaign. On the left (western) flank, the Chandios were sent to make another attempt on Bijar Khan's stronghold at Phulji. John Jacob, with the Scinde Irregular Horse and the camel troops, was ordered to move from the frontier post of Rojhan, 15 miles west of Khangarh, timing his march to reach Phulji twelve hours after the Chandios. In the centre, Napier himself would advance with his main force north-eastwards from Khangarh, twelve hours after Jacob's departure from Rojhan, while the 69th Bengal Native Infantry, on Napier's extreme eastern flank, moved forward to keep contact with Mir Ali Murad's contingent. The cavalry would then secure the routes down from the hills while the main force, preceded by its Chandio allies, marched into the heart of Bugti territory.

On 13 January 1845 Napier issued a manifesto, explaining that he was entering the territory of the Khan of Kalat, a friend of the British, to punish his subjects who had robbed and murdered in Sind. He declared that he was doing so with the Khan's permission, but that even without it he would still have invaded, as it was his duty to protect British territory and British subjects from those whom the Khan, when called upon, had proved unable to control. Even without this manifesto, the movement of 8,000 troops, with all their followers and baggage animals, could not be concealed. Bijar Khan realized that even his much-feared warriors could not hope to defeat twice their number of regular soldiers, and the presence of a battering train showed that Napier intended to attack his towns, whose mud walls could withstand muskets and matchlocks, but not siege guns.

Consequently, when the Chandios reached Phulji, they found the town burnt and abandoned. Napier then ordered Jacob, who was at this time 10 miles east of him, to divert to Shahpur, where Bijar Khan's son, Wazir Khan, was reported to be at the head of a large Dombki war-band. Jacob left the slow-moving camel corps behind and, starting at noon on 15 January 1844, made a dash for Shahpur. At the same time, the 6th Bengal Irregular Cavalry, now under Captain George Salter of the 4th Bengal Native Infantry, moving from Khangarh ahead of Napier, encountered Sardar Darya Khan Jakhrani at Uch, 10 miles south-east of Shahpur. The cavalrymen, at last finding a legitimate enemy, succeeded in inflicting heavy casualties and the Jakhranis dispersed, leaving behind a herd of 3,000 cattle.

Meanwhile Jacob, after a forced march of 37 miles, reached Shahpur just before midnight and surrounded the town before the alarm was given. Knowing the place well, he rode into an area normally occupied by the Jakhrani horsemen to find it almost deserted. The Jakhranis then opened fire with their matchlocks from the town's rooftops, killing three men and wounding two. When Jacob dismounted a troop and attacked on foot, the Jakhranis ceased resistance, but sixty-two of them, found with matchlocks that had recently been fired, were made prisoner. Wazir Khan, alerted by the sound of firing from Uch, had departed some hours before Jacob's arrival.

Napier was then delayed by the discovery that neither the military nor civil departments had sufficient funds for the local purchase of supplies or to pay transport contractors. His infantry were still trudging through the desert and Mir Ali Murad had yet to appear in the field. Making a virtue of necessity, he allowed Bijar Khan to retreat unmolested, believing that, if cornered, the Baloch would kill their women and children to preserve their honour. After a week at Uch, Napier moved on to Shahpur, where he concentrated his forces and collected a fortnight's supply of food and forage. The Bundelkhand Legion was sent forward from Shahpur to Phulji and thence through the passes to Dera Bugti, which it entered unopposed on 30 January 1845. At the same time, Napier marched eastwards across Mir Ali Murad's front and entered the Bugti hills from the south.

Nevertheless, it was clear that raiders were still active. Patrols saw signs of them along the lines of communication and found the bodies of murdered camp-followers. Post riders were intercepted, one of them carrying the proofs of *The Conquest of Sind*, written by Sir Charles Napier's brother, William, the historian of the Peninsular War. At the end of January 1845, 500 camel-drivers, who had already refused to go beyond Shahpur, deserted after receiving neither pay nor protection. Napier assigned half of the Camel Corps's mounts to the commissariat, reduced the number of baggage camels allotted to his headquarters staff, called on all officers to hand over as many private camels as they could spare and asked Nasir Khan II to provide more camels from Kachhi. Foraging parties were sent out to look for local food supplies, but a poor country that scarcely produced enough for its ordinary inhabitants could not sustain an army of several thousand. The troops went hungry until the camel train, after covering 50 miles in two days and three nights, re-appeared on 8 February 1845 with 2,000 pounds of flour from Shahpur.

On 22 January 1845 Jacob had been authorized to negotiate in Napier's name with the Khan of Kalat, the Chandios, and the Marris. 'Fancy my making a Political!' the general (whose dislike of such officers was well known) had written to him, '—yet such I am going to make of you'. Napier's policy was to resettle the Dombkis and Jakhranis inside the borders of Upper Sind, and hand over their lands in eastern Kachhi to the Chandios. Jacob found the Chandios unwilling to accept these lands without promises of British protection, but Nasir Khan II sent word that the Marris would be prepared to do so. The Marris, warned by their old rivals, the Bugtis, that the British would seek to destroy them in their turn, initially resisted Jacob's overtures. Eventually, on 12 February 1845, he persuaded them to send Napier forty guides and a vakil. They still declined the offer of lands around Phulji and Chhatr, upon which Jacob recommended that these be returned to the Khyheris.

Napier's Advance to Traki, 'The Robbers' Cave'

While Napier waited for supplies, Mir Ali Murad reported that Bijar Khan had offered to negotiate. Napier replied that his terms were that the Dombkis should all be re-settled inside Sind. Not waiting for an answer, he resumed his march eastward but then, on Ali Murad's advice, agreed to halt until 14 February. He then swung his main force north, into the Bugti heartland. Raiders remained active and on 20 February made off with 150 laden camels from near his camp, but he pressed on and four days later reached Dera Bugti. As Napier prepared to march further, news came that an attack was in progress on a convoy 3 miles from his camp. He put himself at the head of his escort, and rode towards the scene of the action, ordering the 6th Bengal Irregular

Cavalry to follow. The attackers proved to be about fifty mounted Baloch, at whom the young officers on his staff charged 'like schoolboys on holiday' as their irritated general complained. The raiders made off and disappeared down a narrow defile.

This proved to be the entrance to Traki, a natural stronghold long used as a bandits' lair, where Napier had hoped they would stand at bay. He posted cavalry to prevent their escape and returned to camp, where he learned that Bijar Khan had entered Traki from the north side. A company of infantry was sent to help guard the southern portal, while the Bundelkhand Legion and the men of the 13th Foot, supported by Mir Ali Murad's contingent, moved round to Traki's northern side. Traki proved to be a rocky basin covering about 10 square miles. All the approaches were through cliffs and precipices, some rising up to a thousand feet above their surroundings. Inside, there was ample water, but food for neither men nor animals. The British siege train could not create a breach in solid mountains nor could the howitzers, even at maximum elevation, shoot over them, but Bijar Khan could not escape unless the climate or lack of supplies forced Napier back to the plains.

Napier was not prepared to wait. While his artillery created a diversion by bombarding one side of the southern entrance, the infantry approached the other under cover of night, with the sound of their movement drowned by the guns. The troops were ordered not to form a storming column, but rather to advance in open order until their natural fighting spirit carried them on to their objective. Napier, a veteran of Wellington's sieges, knew how men, once committed to a storm, would press on almost regardless of casualties, which in this case he expected to be high. He also knew how British soldiers behaved once they were inside a captured town and hoped that the Baloch did not have their families with them.

On 8 March 1845, the volunteers from the 13th Foot spearheaded an attack on the northern entrance to Traki. As they advanced into the defile, Sergeant John Power and the sixteen men of his section took one side of a fissure and became separated from the rest of their company. The fissure suddenly became a deep chasm and their officer signalled them to fall back. Power mistook the waving arm as a signal to advance and led his men up the mountainside in full view of the enemy. All the soldiers were veterans of the Afghan campaign and had at least one campaign medal to their credit. Eleven of them reached the top, where they met some seventy hostiles waiting for them behind a breastwork. In a hand-to-hand struggle, six soldiers were killed and the remaining five, all wounded, were driven back down the slope. On the Baloch side, seventeen men died, including their chief, bayoneted by Private Samuel Lowrie before he himself fell.

All the survivors received commendations and Wellington, as Commander in Chief of the British Army, ordered that Sergeant Palmer should be considered for a commission. When the bodies of the slain were later recovered, they were found stripped but, instead of being mutilated in the usual way, left with a red thread tied around each wrist. Napier was told that among the Baloch it was the custom for the courage of heroes killed in battle to be recognized with a red or green thread on the right or left wrist respectively, the red being the greater honour. The episode was held to reflect much credit on the fighting men of both sides and became the subject of a popular poem by Sir Francis Doyle, *The Red Thread of Honour*.

For all their bravery, the deaths of these men served no useful purpose. None of the troops on the north side of Traki then knew that four days earlier, Sardars Bijar Khan Dombki, Islam Khan Bugti and Darya Khan Jakhrani had waited on Napier, dressed in black and with Korans on their head (corresponding to a white flag in European warfare) to ask for an armistice. Napier offered the same terms as before. If they wished for peace, they must lay down their arms and settle with their followers wherever in Sind he ordered. The next day, 5 March 1845, the Jakhrani chiefs Darya Khan and Turk Ali, accompaied by several minor chiefs, came out and surrendered. Napier's infantry passed the southern defiles unopposed. The families of the Dombki chiefs were captured and Bijar Khan himself was taken on 9 March. Islam Khan Bugti and his family escaped through an unguarded northern pass and found asylum with his brother-in-law, Haji Khan, sardar of the Khatrans, whose extensive country lay between the Marris, Harrand (in the Punjab), and Pishin (bordering southern Waziristan). Most of the other Bugti leaders also escaped, and the only one of note to fall into British hands was Mir Hasan Nothani, the guide who had led Clibborn's water-party into the trap at Nafusk.

The Results of the Hill Campaign

Nevertheless, enough had been achieved to allow Napier to return in triumph with his prisoners. Bijar Khan and his immediate followers were handed over to Mir Ali Murad, who granted him a jagir in Burdeka but kept him under close supervision. The Jakhranis and the rest of the Dombkis were granted jagirs under the supervision of a British district officer at Janidero, a few miles south of Khangarh, where they were encouraged to build houses and take up agriculture. Napier met Nasir Khan II at Shahpur and obtained agreement for restoring Chhatr and Phulji to the Khyheris and establishing a British outpost at Shahpur to deter the Marris. The colours of the 64th Bengal Native Infantry, taken away from them by Napier after their earlier refusal to march into Sind without the allowances they expected, were restored.

The relocation of the Dombkis and Jakhranis was at first welcomed by those on whom they had preyed for generations. It soon became clear, however, that the vacuum left by the removal of these tribes had been filled by the even more fearsome Bugtis and Marris. The Bugtis, re-assembling from their various refuges, needed to replace the grain and livestock they had lost during Napier's invasion. Led by the Kalpars, in September 1845 they descended on the new Jakhrani settlement at Janidero and carried off seventy head of cattle. Napier allowed the Jakhranis to mount a counter-raid, supported by some cavalry and police, but they were unable to come up with the robbers. When the Marris sent to ask Napier if the Bugtis were under his protection, he replied that the more Bugtis they killed, the more honour they would gain and sent them powder for their matchlocks. On 8 January 1846 he ordered that any Bugtis approaching the frontier were to be treated as outlaws and taken or destroyed on sight.

The First Sikh War, 1845–46

In December 1845, the government of Lahore launched an invasion of British India.

Hardinge had long anticipated this and had exchanged views with Napier on how the army in Sind might be used. By 8 February 1846 Napier had installed a deputy as governor of Sind and concentrated a field force 6,000 strong at Rohri. He planned to lead this into the Punjab and capture Multan, but was ordered to join Sir Hugh Gough, Commander in Chief, India, and Hardinge while his troops marched into Bahawalpur without him. Neither Napier nor his men met the enemy before the British victory at Sobraon (10 February 1846) ended the fighting. A peace treaty at Lahore (9 March 1846) imposed punitive terms, including extensive territorial losses and large reductions in the Sikh Army.

The expansion of British rule into the Punjab placed extra demands on the Bengal Army. Hardinge therefore decided that Sind should be garrisoned solely by the Bombay Army and agreed an increase in its establishment accordingly, including a second regiment of Scinde Iregular Horse and a second

Baluch Battalion. In August 1846, the Bundelkhand Legion, as a Bengal Army formation, handed over the frontier of Upper Sind to the 3rd Bombay Light Cavalry and the 4th Bombay Rifles. Napier repeated his orders that no troops should cross the border without his authority and placed Lieutenant Ross Moore of the newly-arrived Light Cavalry under arrest, for sending troops to aid the Khyheris at Phulji.

Operations on the Upper Sind Frontier, 1846–47

Napier had believed that his Hill Campaign had left the Bugtis too weak to pose a serious threat to Upper Sind. Nevertheless, in July 1846 he received reports that Sardar Islam Khan Bugti was gathering men for a raid and ordered the officers commanding outposts to be on the alert. He offered a reward of 10 rupees a head for any Bugtis brought in as prisoners, thereby encouraging the Dombkis and Jakhranis he had resettled inside British territory to assist in their own defence. At the same time, he suspected that these tribes were likely to resume their old ways by complaining that they were the victims of raids and then robbing kafilas for which the Bugtis would be blamed.

When allegations were made that the resettled tribes were indeed raiding Kachhi from inside British territory, Lieutenant J. Hamilton, the district magistrate at Janidero, said this was impossible, because their mares had been auctioned off by Napier's orders.

The Deputy Collector of Shikarpur, Major Goldney, 4th Bengal Native Infantry, and his lieutenant of police, Captain J.W.Younghusband, 8th Bombay Native Infantry, agreed and accordingly Major General George Hunter, commanding at Sukkur, allowed them to keep their arms for self-defence. In October 1846 Hamilton had to admit that Balochis from his district had raided Bugti territory and Hunter then warned that, if there was any repetition, the offenders would be imprisoned and their communities disarmed.

The Great Bugti Raid of December 1846

Napier's orders confining patrols to British territory had the effect of blinding him to movements beyond them. Islam Khan Bugti was thus able to complete his preparations undisturbed and on 10 December 1846 entered the unsuspecting borderland with a thousand fighting men and 500 lightly-armed followers. Ranging more than 50 miles from their own country, they penetrated to within 15 miles of Shikarpur itself. Moore, by this time out of arrest, met them as they approached but, with only twenty-five troopers, decided he could do nothing to stop them, though one of his Jakhrani guides fired a matchlock at a venture and killed a Bugti chief. Another small patrol of the 3rd Light Cavalry also encountered the approaching raid, but retreated to join the main body of the regiment at Mirpur. Their commanding officer, Lieutenant Colonel Maurice Stack, recently promoted after seven years as superintendant of the Bombay Stud Department, sent an urgent message to Shikarpur, 20 miles away to the south-east, asking for reinforcements. He was sent the rest of his regiment, supported by 200 infantry of the 4th Bombay Rifles, but it took a day for them to reach him, during which time the Bugtis plundered the countryside unopposed and started for home. The garrison at Shahpur (one troop of light cavalry, two companies of infantry and a field gun), made no move to intervene, and its commandant later excused his inaction by claiming that he received no reports of the raid being in progress.

Stack set out in pursuit but the infantry slowed him down, he left them behind and went on with his 250 troopers. At dawn the next day he sighted the Bugtis in the desert immediately ahead of him. Beyond them were great clouds of dust as their followers drove a herd of 15,000 stolen animals towards the hills. Clashing their shields, the Bugtis formed up and offered fight. Stack, outnumbered four to one, turned back to Shikarpur. Napier doubted Stack's claims about exhaustion of his men and horses, or the existence of a hill on which Stack reported that the Bugtis had taken up their position. In any case, he considered that Stack should have used his carbines to engage the Bugti line while a mounted detachment rode round to recover the stolen herd. As it was, the Bugtis returned home with all their plunder, having lost only one man.

The Return of John Jacob

Napier then took a decision that would usher in a new era on the frontier. Jacob and the 1st Scinde Irregular Horse were ordered to return from Hyderabad, where they had been stationed since the end of the Sind War, and take over the defence of the Upper Sind Frontier. Napier had noticed Jacob favorably during the conquest of Sind, calling him 'the Seydlitz of the Indian Army'. Personal relations between the two officers, originally cordial, had cooled when Jacob took Outram's side in the latter's dispute with Napier over the conduct of the Sind campaign. Outram and Napier accused each other of falsehood and letters to the Bombay newspapers by their respective supporters only intensified the quarrel. Napier suspected Jacob of feeding information to Outram and thought him a disloyal ingrate. Jacob felt that Napier had failed to acknowledge the value of the Hill campaign and of the maps he had made during Billamore's earlier operations. Billamore had died at Karachi on 27 April 1840 and Jacob (writing as 'One of his Subalterns') now published his own narrative, making it clear that in his view the history of Napier's Hill Campaign, recently written by William Napier, was full of exaggerations and inaccuracies.

Nevertheless, Napier held Jacob in high esteem as a cavalry commander and posted him to the desolate frontier of Upper Sind, not as a banishment, which most officers considered it to be, but because of his previous success there. He gave Jacob full discretion to place his troops wherever he wished, as long as this did not involve expenditure on new accommodation, and placed the Khyheri guides under his authority. The brigade commander at Shikarpur gave him similar discretion, though forbidding him from entering the dominions of either the Khan of Kalat or Mir Ali Murad of Khairpur except in close pursuit. This was in accordance with Napier's close-border policy, except that everyone knew that Shahpur lay 20 miles inside Kalat territory and that Khangarh was still claimed by Mir Ali Murad. 'On 20ᵗʰ Decmember [1846] Jacob's trumpets sounded the advance, and the 1ˢᵗ regiment of Scinde Irregular Horse, with its commander at its head... marched out on service. But this time they would return no more to Hyderabad'.[12]

7

THE PALADINS OF THE UPPER SIND BORDER, 1847–54

Tell the Constable,
We are but warriors for the working day;
Our gayness and our gilt are all besmirch'd
With rainy marching in the painful field;
There's not a scrap of feather in our host,-
Good argument, I hope, we will not fly,-
And time hath worn us into slovenry:
But, by the Mass, our hearts are in the trim;

King Henry, Henry V, *Act V, scene iii*

According to his own account, Jacob arrived at Khangarh to find its light cavalry garrison (which seemingly failed to notice his approach) inside the fort, in the middle of the morning, with the gates closed for fear of marauders. Its commandant, when handing over, warned that there was only enough water and forage obtainable locally for a single squadron, and that supply convoys required strong escorts if they were to get through at all. Jacob, from his local experience and own temperament, disregarded most of this, knowing that regular troops hated serving on this desolate frontier and could not wait to be posted elsewhere, but discovered that all the frontier posts were provisioned by the commissariat department at Shikarpur, 'as if on shipboard', to the extent that the rations included a daily issue of lime-juice to compensate for lack of fresh fruit or vegetables.[1]

Meanwhile, Napier had ordered an inquiry into the recent Bugti raid. Jacob, sent to examine the area, found only a slight rise in the ground where Stack (possibly deceived by the mirage) had seen a hill. Jacob's second-in-command, Lieutenant William Lockyer Merewether, sent with one troop to take over at Shahpur, went through the records and found that the raid actually had been reported while it was in progress. Stack himself deposed that it was on the advice of his officers that he had decided not to attack. Napier, writing to Major General George Hunter, the brigade commander at Shikarpur, commented 'The story of his officers riding up to him beats all I have heard yet. However, Jacob will settle the matter; his officers won't ride up to him to run away, and if they did the only turn he would make would be upon them, or I am much mistaken!' Napier finally decided against issuing one of his General Orders with the inquiry's findings. The affair was, he told Jacob, too disgraceful to be made public.[2]

Jacob's border protection measures.

It soon became clear that Jacob's arrival meant more than the French-grey hussar jackets of the Light Cavalry being replaced by the olive-green long kurtas of the Scinde Irregular Horse. Taking the view that a regiment of cavalry should be its own defence, he ordered his forts' gates to be burnt and their walls abandoned. The various outposts became open cantonments, as in any ordinary station. The miserable shacks clustered outside the forts were replaced by houses and shops from which tradesmen provided services for the troops and the passing kafilas. Khangarh, where Jacob established not only his headquarters but his home, laboratory and gardens, became a thriving, tree-lined settlement to which the locals soon gave a new name, Jacobabad (Jacob's Town).

On reaching the frontier, Jacob found that there was no system of patrols linking the eleven existing posts, whose garrisons seemed to him to spend most of their time waiting to be attacked. To improve communications, he built roads and bridges linking his headquarters at Khangarh to the outposts, whose commandants had previously each reported separately back to Shikarpur. The troops were kept constantly ready for field service and no wheeled transport was allowed. Rather than standing on the defensive, as had previously been the case, the troops were now deployed entirely with a view to taking the offensive. Under the new arrangements, standing patrols from each outpost met each other at regular intervals and exchanged information. Local Baloch guides collected intelligence of movements beyond the border, and noted any tracks crossing into or out of British territory. Later, this system was enhanced by a ploughed strip along the frontier line, allowing all such movements to be instantly detected.

To broaden experience of the country and the people, at the beginning of each month the garrisons at each end of the line were relieved by troops from regimental headquarters and each then moved along to its neighbouring post. The last two garrisons then returned to base at Jacobabad, thus ensuring that a strong reserve was always available. A hearts and minds campaign persuaded the local inhabitants to regard the cavalrymen as their protectors and they began not only to produce food and forage for sale (thus ending the reliance on expensive supply columns from Shikarpur) but also to provide information about the robbers. Writing in August 1854, Jacob claimed 'Every man of the Sind Irregular Horse is looked on and treated as a friend by the country-folk.'[3]

While Jacob and his men began their new routine, the new-caught Dombkis and Jakhranis at Janidero continued to raid Kachhi despite their apparent lack of mounts. It was then discovered that the auctions to dispose of their mares had been rigged, as genuine dealers were kept away by Baloch threats. When the animals were knocked down for a song, the unwitting British authorities paid their owners the difference between the auction price and the estimated normal market value. These mares were actually so valuable that they were usually owned not by individuals but by syndicates, whose members shared the cost of their upkeep and the plunder taken in raids in which they were used. After these auctions, the mares had been boarded out with their new owners, who were mostly local landholders secretly in league with the syndicates. When a raid was planned, the original owners quietly collected their mares and gathered in out-of-the-way places before riding off to kill and rob. Afterwards, they returned them in the same way, with each landholder receiving his share of the loot.[4]

On 20 January 1847 a band of 200 Jakhranis was reported to have left with the intention of raiding into Mir Ali Murad's domains. Towards evening, a patrol of eighteen Scinde Irregular Horse troopers under a dafadar (Indian cavalry sergeant) intercepted them near the outpost of Garhi Hasan, 20 miles east of Jacobabad. The dafadar, in accordance with standing orders, at once reported a contact and then advanced towards the Jakhranis, who split up into three groups and rode away at full speed. The patrol caught up with one party and sabred several of the robbers, though all then escaped into the night. When the dafadar's report arrived, Jacob immediately rode to join him but, despite covering 80 miles in twenty-four hours, failed to find the raiders. At the scene of the engagement, grain in discarded saddle bags was identified as typical of that found in Sind, as was the pattern of horse-shoes in the prints left by the raiders' mounts. All the tracks led out of British territory. None came in from the direction of the Bugti hills.

Once more, Napier was infuriated. This time, the subjects of his ire were Forbes, Younghusband and Hamilton, as it was on their recommendation that the Jakhranis had been allowed to keep and bear arms. All that was needed to deal with raids, he said, was activity and reflection, and 'neither seem to have been employed till Captain Jacob arrived'. Jacob was therefore appointed magistrate over Janidero, and the re-settled Baloch were forbidden to leave the district without permission. They were likewise forbidden from carrying unlicensed weapons or owning horses and were told that anyone caught plundering would be hanged. The new policy was put to the test within days. On 28 January 1847 a cavalry patrol found fifteen mounted Balochis making their way back to Janidero with a herd of stolen cattle. Their swords had fresh blood on them, and they openly boasted of raiding into the Bugti hills and killing six of the stockmen. They were sent for trial in Shikarpur and their mares confiscated, while Hamilton was ordered to locate and sieze the animals boarded out with landholders.

To provide an outlet for the bolder spirits, and to boost the authority of their chiefs, Napier agreed to Jacob enlisting a force of Baloch guides. Initially this amounted to a mere fifteen Jakhranis, chosen by their reformed sardar, Darya Khan, but this number was later increased and extended to include other Baloch tribes. The riders were recruited and paid by their chiefs, using British funds. If any man turned criminal, the whole contingent would be discharged and the chiefs' allowances discontinued. This scheme, which resembled the long-established arrangements for the protection of kafilas, was readily accepted. With the guides being the only men allowed to carry arms, and would-be raiders finally deprived of their mares, raids out of British territory gradually died away.

Raids into British territory were countered by constant patrols. In February 1847 a large band of Bugtis was routed by Younghusband's mounted police, operating out of the outpost nearest to the junction of Burdika, Bahawalpur and the Punjab. In April, Merewether, with Scinde Irregular Horse patrols from Shahpur, twice intercepted small raiding parties, whose members refused to accept quarter and perished to a man. Two further parties were wiped out in June and July. When Bugtis attacked Phulji, Sardar Abdulla Khan Khyheri, encouraged by Merewether's presence at Shahpur, drove them off and led the

British-paid guides in pursuit, killing four and recovering the little plunder that they had taken.

At the same time, the long-established dealings between the Bugti sardars and Hindu merchants in Upper Sind were stopped. The merchants had for years sold grain and arms to the Bugtis and acted as receivers of their stolen property, as well as giving them useful information about the troops and police. Trade between British subjects and the Bugtis had been forbidden ever since Napier declared the whole tribe outlaws, but no-one on the British side had been able to prevent it, or even, until Jacob's patrols began to intercept their kafilas, been much aware of it. These measures led to much hardship among ordinary Bugtis and in September a large group of starving individuals came into Jacobabad to beg for food. Jacob fed them and asked Napier how to proceed, recommending that sanctions should only be against the chiefs, not the common people. Napier ordered that the women and children should be kindly treated and that any men who surrended peaceably should be pardoned.

The fight at Zamani River

In the Bugti hills, Sardar Islam Khan decided it was time to repeat his great raid of the previous December. Late in September 1847 reports reached Jacob that Bugtis were gathering in strength with the intention of attacking Chhatr. In response Jacob sent one of his officers, Lieutenant Henry Green, to reinforce Merewether at Shahpur, but remained himself at Jacobabad with 250 men, in case the Bugtis entered British territory. Some Kalpar Bugtis under Sardar Alim Khan crossed the frontier at the end of the month but Jacob decided this was a diversion and left them for his outposts to deal with. At 1.30 in the morning of 1 October 1847, on receiving firm intelligence that the Bugtis were heading for Chhatr, Merewether left Green to guard Shahpur and rode out with 133 horsemen. Despite their numbers, amounting to 700 men on foot and twenty-five on horseback, the Bugtis achieved little. At one village, the Khyheris under their local headman Din Muhammad withstood three determined attacks in which the raiders lost several men killed and one captured.

At first light on 1 October, crossing the little Zamani river east of Chhatr, Merewether found the tracks of a large raiding party. His chief Khyheri guide, Jan Muhammad, then reported sounds from a short distance ahead. Merewether changed his formation from a column of troops into a line and galloped forward. He then saw the raiders occupying an area of brush-covered broken ground. As they seemed to be heading for a patch of jungle, he rode rapidly across their front to prevent them escaping. The Bugtis, perhaps remembering their success against the 3rd Bombay Light Cavalry, rushed forward to meet him, with 'much firing, loud shouts, and howls'.[5]

Merewether changed direction to the left, a manoeuvre that, as he later reported, his men executed as steadily as if on parade, and charged. The Bugtis formed a solid mass to receive the cavalry, whom they outnumbered five to one, but many were ridden down. The remainder rallied, standing shoulder to shoulder, and headed for some hills about 3 miles away. As well as their swords, the troopers carried short-barrelled carbines of a pattern specially made to Jacob's own design. Small enough to be fired like a pistol, these weapons had a devastating effect at close range. The Bugti matchlocks, long emptied, could not easily be reloaded on the move and a swordsman on the ground stood little chance against one in the saddle. Even so, the Bugtis fought on, crouching behind rocks and bushes, using their thick hide shields to turn the cavalrymen's sabres and cutting up at their bridle-reins to make the horses unmanageable. Driven down to the open plain by repeated charges, they still tried for the distant hills but one of Merewether's Indian officers, Risaldar Shaikh Ali, acting on his own initiative, led his troop to cut them off. They then turned back the way they had come and continued fighting, despite repeated offers of quarter, until even the bravest saw that further resistance was futile and threw down their arms.

The fighting had been unusually fierce. Merewether mentioned the names of four troopers, each of whom he saw kill several opponents 'in fair stand-up fight, hand to hand' and thought that the rest of his men must have done as much.[6] The five Khyheri guides fought equally valiantly and their chief, Jan Muhammad, killed several opponents before breaking his sword over the head of the last. Only two riders escaped to carry the news back to Islam Khan and the hungry families in the Baloch hills.

Bugti losses amounted to 560 dead, nine chiefs among them, and 120 captured. All the prisoners able to march were led off to Chhatr. The wounded were treated by the British medical officer, Assistant Surgeon J.Pirie, and left under guard at the nearest village, to await collection. The British lost one man killed and eleven wounded, of whom one later died of wounds. Nine horses were killed and another ten wounded, seven of whom later had to be destroyed. Jacob's own charger, which Merewether had taken on leaving Jacobabad, suffered two severe sword cuts. The Bugti prisoners were sentenced to hard labour on the frontier roads, but were later freed to return to their hills and some were taken into British service as guides.

The fight at Zamani entered Bugti folk-lore, with names of Jacob and Merewether featuring prominently in their bards' songs. It broke the power of the Bugtis for a generation for, as Jacob pointed out in respect of frontier warfare generally, demography was always on the government's side. If a soldier was killed, there were many potential recruits available to take his place the next day. If a tribesman was killed, it took a generation to replace him, during which time his tribe was weakened not only against the government, but against its rivals. The impact of Zamani on Bugti society was as powerful as would be that of Gettysburg on the Southern Confederacy, or the Somme on the home towns of Kitchener's Pals' battalions.

Many who had joined in expectation of profitable raids now left Islam Khan's camp. Together with Sardar Alim Khan Kalpar, he decided to make peace. Warned by Darya Khan, the reformed Jakhrani sardar, that if they surrendered to Jacob he would put them in prison, they gave themselves up to the Indian officer of police at the extreme eastern end of the frontier. They were sent to the Collector of Shikarpur, who ordered them to Mahmuddero, near Larkana, where Bugtis who had submitted previously were settled. It was hoped that, like the Dombkis and Jakhranis at Janidero, the captured Bugtis would abandon their predatory ways and become husbandmen. For a time, the two sardars feigned to accept this. They were then allowed to go to buy plough oxen at Shikarpur where, in a carefully planned move, they evaded their escorts and joined Islam Khan's son, Ghulam Murtaza, waiting for them outside the town. All three then rode at high speed to the Bugti hills, where Ghulam Murtaza had rallied their remaining men.

On 1 October 1847 Sir Charles Napier sailed for home from Karachi. The post of Governor of Sind, directly under the Government of India, was abolished and replaced by that of Commissioner in Sind, under the Government of Bombay. The new Commissioner, R.K.Pringle, was a member of the Covenanted or first division of the Bombay Civil Service, the only such official of this level in the whole of Sind, which Napier had staffed with either military or non-covenanted nominees. Described by one of his successors as 'a barn-door fowl in an eagle's nest',[7] he was appalled to find that few records had been kept, and baffled to find that Jacob, commandant of two regiments (in itself an anomaly), was performing political duties normally undertaken by the nearest civil authority, in this case Major Goldney, the Collector of Shikarpur. He accordingly placed Goldney in charge of relations with the trans-frontier tribes and instructed Jacob (under command of the GOC [General Officer Commanding], Sind Division) to co-operate with him in military matters.

115

Jacob lobbied vigorously against these instructions, insisting that the strong measures by which he had brought peace to a troubled frontier could only be implemented if all local military, political and civil authority remained in the hands of a single individual. His protests were supported by his old patron Outram (at this time British Resident at Satara, one of the Indian princely states controlled by Bombay) and Captain P.T.French, political agent in Sibi when Jacob served in Kachhi during 1842 and now private secretary to George Clerk, the newly-appointed Governor of Bombay. Colonel the Honourable Henry Dundas, brigade commander at Shikarpur, wrote to the Commander in Chief, Bombay, supporting Jacob's cause. Clerk, who was already familiar with Jacob's political record, over-ruled Pringle and early in 1848 appointed Jacob to the dual post of Political Superindendant and Commandant, Upper Sind Frontier.

Jacob was thus able to negotiate directly with the vakils of Nasir Khan II of Kalat and Mir Ali Murad of Khairpur respectively, and with the sardars of Baloch tribes outside as well as inside British territory. His troops were authorised to cross the border in close pursuit of raiders. Any taken were sent to Jacobabad, where Jacob and his officers acted as local magistrates. Those accused of crimes beyond their powers of punishment were sent for trial in Shikarpur. Subjects of Nasir Khan II or Mir Ali Murad accused of offences outside British territory were handed over to the officers of these princes for disposal. Known malefactors who fled to them for asylum were extradited through the agency of the respective vakils. Member of tribes such as the Marris and Bugtis, who denied the jurisdiction of the Khan of Kalat, were punished by British courts if captured raiding near British territory.

The British annexation of the Punjab and operations on the Upper Sind border

More far-reaching developments began at the end of April 1848, with the outbreak at Multan of a revolt against British control over the government of Lahore. The insurrection turned into a major war, with much hard fighting before the British were finally successful in March 1849. Lord Dalhousie, who had succeeded Hardinge as governor-general in January 1848, announced the annexation of the former kingdom of Lahore to British India as the province of the Punjab. Its south-western frontier region, Harrand, once a dependency of Kalat, but most recently of Multan, became the administrative division of Derajat, consisting of two districts, Dera Ghazi Khan in the south and Dera Ismail

Khan in the north (colloquially known to the British as Dreary Ghastly and Dreary Dismal Khan respectively), each under a Deputy Commissioner. The western border of Dera Ghazi Khan ran alongside the hills inhabited by Baloch subjects of the Khan of Kalat, the Khatrans and the Kalpar Bugtis in particular, and its own population included the Mazaris and other Baloch tribes who lived on both sides of the frontier line. Its southern boundary, some 15 miles of desert, adjoined the Frontier District of Upper Sind. In principle, this regime change should have made peace-keeping easier, as the entire border was now under British rule. In practice, turf wars between the frontier officers of these neighbouring British provinces would escalate until eventually the governance not only of the border, but of Balochistan as a whole, became a major issue.

The insurgency in the Punjab inevitably affected Upper Sind and the neighbouring parts of Kalat. Before his defeat, Diwan Mulraj of Multan paid the Marris to distract the British from their operations against him by raiding into Upper Sind, where the frontier force was weakened by the departure of one regiment of Scinde Irregular Horse to take part in the campaign. True to form, they raided easier targets in Kachhi. Kalat officials reported that an Afghan army was on its way down the Bolan to assist Mulraj, but it transpired that the force was merely that normally sent to collect the revenue due from the Afghan enclave of Sibi. Nasir Khan II's Brahui contingents had refused to enter the Marri hills and his officials had hoped that any British troops sent to counter the imaginary Afghan threats would help them deal with the Marris.

In April 1849, knowing that the Scinde Irregular Horse post at Shahpur was due for its monthly relief, Sardar Alim Khan Kalpar, with Sardar Mir Haji Khatran (the brother-in-law of Sardar Islam Khan Bugti), and Gul Gawar, a cousin of the sardar of the Marris, assembled a raiding party about 600 strong. Under cover of night, they rode 40 miles across the desert and then, taking advantage of the bustle of the handover, entered the camp as if friends and cut down most of the guard before the alarm was raised. About fifty then dismounted and, holding their mares on long ropes, made for the Indian officers' quarters, only to find them empty. The few troopers left inside Shahpur rallied and the forty men of the new garrison who had not yet come in prepared to meet a second rush. Having distracted the troops by this attack, the raiders made off with a thousand camels, the real object of their raid.

About 4 miles away, the commander of the departing garrison heard the firing on his way to the next post, Kumri. Leaving eight men to guard the baggage and carry the word to Kumri, he rode back through the night with his remaining thirty-two sabres. At dawn, en route to Shahpur, they encountered 300 raiders with the stolen camels, who dispersed as soon as the cavalry attacked. The Indian officers commanding at Kumri and its next post, Kandhkot, who had ridden out with their men as soon as the alarm was given, intercepted the Baloch as they headed for their hills, killing a number of riders and capturing their mares, one of which was recognizd as having carried Sardar Alim Khan Kalpar on many previous raids. In the entire episode, the British lost four cavalrymen killed and four badly wounded, with two Baloch guides, two cultivators and nine horses also killed. The raiders' losses were estimated at forty killed and eighty wounded, with all the stolen camels being recovered. Army headquarters in Bombay demanded to know how so large a body of hostiles could have approached Shahpur undetected, but Jacob pleaded that they had only done so under cover of the disruption caused by the relief and this proved to be the last major attack on one of his outposts.

Raiders continued to enter Kachhi, though with diminishing returns. In September 1849 Sardar Alim Khan Kalpar, having found a new mount, made two descents into the plain. Each time he narrowly avoided meeting British patrols and was chased back to his hills with the loss of the camels he had stolen. Nevertheless, the tribes were still dangerous. In 1850 Jamadar (deputy troop commander) Durga Singh of the Scinde Irregular Horse received word that some camels had been carried off from his nearby post. Starting with twenty men, he found the robbers' tracks and followed them for 30 miles, losing seven of his horses to exhaustion along the way. He then caught up with the raiders, who abandoned the camels and fled. Durga Singh pursued, with more of his horses (two of them under Durga Singh himself) dropping dead in the chase until he had only two cavalrymen and a guide with him. They then encountered a party of about fifty Baloch. The guide urged discretion, but Durga Singh replied he would be ashamed to report to Jacob that he had turned his back on robbers. The little party then charged against their enemies, in a desperate encounter in which three cavalrymen were literally cut to pieces, with only the guide surviving, badly wounded, to tell the tale. The jamadar's courage was greatly admired by the Baloch, who tied the red thread of courage around his wrist, and a century later the place was still pointed out as Durga Kushta, or Durga's slaughter-place. Jacob commended his bravery but, in his utilitarian way, noted that he would have achieved more by conserving his mounts, and pointed to the more effective conduct of Risaldar Hyder Khan, commanding the next post. This officer saddled up and moved out with his troop as soon as the alarm was sounded but, by careful horse-management, kept it fully operational. He reached the scene of action soon after Durga Singh's death, recovered the stolen camels, picked up the stragglers and returned to base without losing a horse or man.[8]

In March 1851, following the death at Khairpur of the old robber chief, Bijar Khan Dombki, his son Wazir Khan sought permission to lead his people back to their ancestral home in Kachhi. The petition was supported by Nasir Khan II of Kalat (whose subjects they had notionally remained), Sardar Baloch Khan Dombki and Sardar Islam Khan Bugti, who asked that his family and the others held at Mahmuddero should be allowed to return to their hills. All were released on promises to keep the peace, with Sardar Baloch Khan, who was glad to have them as reinforcements against Marri incursions, guaranteeing their future good conduct. Sardar Alim Khan Kalpar decided to co-operate, and in February 1852 was wounded while arresting men wanted by the British. A few months afterwards, Jacob added thirty Bugtis to his Baloch guides, with Sardar Alim Khan as their commander, an arrangement advantageous to all sides.

Five years of constant vigilance and rapid reaction by the Scinde Irregular Horse, the Ironsides of India, had persuaded potential raiders that plundering British-protected territory was not only unprofitable but unlucky. Jacob had described his first year on the border as 'one of enormous bodily labour; we had, literally, to lie down with our boots and swords on, for many months together'.[9] By 1851 he was writing to his brother in England that he almost wished for a return of one of the old raids, for the sake of excitement. The Dombkis and Jakranis, once the terror of the borderside, had become peaceful husbandmen and vied with each other in digging irrigation canals to improve their land-holdings.

On the Punjab border, raids and counter-raids continued regardless of the advent of British rule. In 1852 a party of Mazaris from Dera Ghazi Khan attacked the Bugtis, who had recently made peace with the Khan of Kalat and the British. Captain William Merewether, as assistant political superintendant, Upper Sind Frontier, contacted his opposite number in the Punjab, the deputy commissioner of Dera Ghazi Khan, asking him to punish the raiders. At a higher level, Henry Bartle Frere, a thirty-five-year old Bombay civil servant who had succeeded Pringle as Commissioner in Sind in January 1851, wrote to his own opposite number, John Lawrence, the forty-two-year-old Bengal civil servant who in early 1853 had become the first Chief Commissioner of the Punjab. Frere supported Merewether's request for action against the Mazaris and suggested that patrols from the Sind and Punjab frontier forces should meet and operate together.

Differences between the frontier policies of Sind and the Punjab

Lawrence's response was unenthusiastic. The Mazari raid, he said, was a reprisal for one made on them by the Bugtis the previous December. The Scinde Irregular Horse troopers were paid half as much again as those of the Punjab Frontier Force, which would make it difficult for them to serve together. He did not say why this would be so, but may have feared that his men would agitate for the same pay. As a cheaper solution, he would raise a body of local tribesmen under their own chiefs to fill the unpatrolled gap between the Sind and Punjab outposts. Jacob told Frere that it seemed as if the Punjab government was justifying the practice of individuals making war on their neighbours, and thereby adopting the views of the Baloch themselves, which were quite unworthy of British officers. He was in agreement with Lawrence's objection to the two frontier forces serving together, though in his case it was because he saw no point in patrolling a border where, he complained, every man was allowed to bear arms and wage private war on the slightest pretext.

The question of private arms was a major point of disagreement between the Punjab and Sind authorities. Jacob had forbidden anyone not in the service of the government to bear arms on the public highway, though men were allowed to keep them at home for defence against raiders. Previously everyone had gone about armed, so that it was impossible to tell the intentions of any approaching party and the bearing of weapons could not be taken as evidence of criminal intent. Lawrence agreed to Frere's request that his tribal levies on the border with Upper Sind should carry certificates signed by a district magistrate, as was the practice on the Sind side, to show to any Scinde Irregular Horse patrols they encountered. Jacob then asked that no-one in the parts of the Punjab adjoining Upper Sind should be allowed to bear arms without a similar license. Lawrence delayed a response while he considered the whole subject of disarmament. After touring Derajat in the cold weather of 1853–54, he declared that so far from disarming the frontier inhabitants, he would incite and encourage them to go well armed against the hillmen. Nevertheless, to meet the wishes of Frere and Jacob, he ordered that any Punjabi found to have entered Sind carrying arms would be dealt with by the Punjab authorities in the same way as if he had been arrested by those of Sind.[10]

Frere and Jacob nevertheless continued with their criticisms. On the Punjab side, they said, the close border policy meant that the British had no contact with the Amir of Kabul or neighbouring tribes. As a result they made little effort to recognise his authority over the tribes. When provoked into launching punitive expeditions, they imposed collective punishment on innocent and guilty alike and then withdrew (a policy later summarised as 'butcher and bolt'). By contrast, they claimed, on the Sind side, the British authorities acknowledged the Khan of Kalat as sovereign over the tribes in his country, officers freely crossed the border to establish friendly relations with his subjects, and local law and order was enforced by troops remaining in the areas affected.

Jacob's impressive qualities of leadership and innovation were inhibited by a stutter that always impeded him in verbal discussions. In writing, however, he found the facility to free himself from this constraint, and to express himself forcibly and fluently. His official correspondence on the differences he saw between the frontier policies of Sind and the Punjab was couched in the strongest terms, vehemently resented by those who found themselves the target of his criticism. In February 1854 he reported to Frere an outbreak of raids and counter-raids between Bugtis and Mazaris and complained that, whereas such retaliation was forbidden by the Sind officers, it was permitted, even encouraged, by their opposite numbers in the neighbouring districts of the Punjab. 'So little are the principles on which we have since 1847 acted on the Sinde Frontier understood by our neighbours that not long ago, on the occurrence of one of these lawless attacks by the hillmen against their neighbours, the officer commanding at Asni wrote to congratulate me on the success of *my* Boogtees, I having informed the Boogtees when they wrote me boasting of what they had done... that, had they been British subjects or living in British territory, I would have had them all hanged for their robbery and murders.' As the same tribes and families lived in adjacent districts of Sind and the Punjab, proceedings on one side inevitably affected those on the other. British policy, he said, should be the same on both sides and the Punjab officers should adopt his policy of stopping inter-tribal warfare.[11]

This opinion, when it eventually reached the Government of India, brought down on Jacob's head the wrath of Lord Dalhousie, the Governor-General. Dalhousie saw the recently annexed Punjab as the model province of British India, whose officers, unrestrained by the legal codes of the older 'Regulation' provinces, were regarded as the elite of the British Raj. This reputation for excellence grew out of a variety of factors, including in the first instance the patronage of Dalhousie as their founding father. His response to Jacob's complaints against his prestige project was to minute that grave accusations had been made against the Government of India or its officers in the Punjab or both. 'Blame must be somewhere', he told the Secret Committee in London, 'Wherever it may be proved to be, there the consequences shall fall.' At the same time, he also minuted that Jacob had recently been censured by the Court of Directors for publishing his views on the Indian military system (comparing the caste-ridden Bengal Army unfavourably with that of Bombay) and had now 'thought proper to denounce to his superior officer on official record the policy he asserts is pursued by the Supreme Government of India on the frontier districts of the Punjab'. Jacob was ordered to produce evidence of his claim that retaliation was encouraged.[12]

Lieutenant H. Bruce, the officer commanding at Asni, whose congratulatory letter had provoked Jacob's outburst, was equally indignant. He agreed that encouraging private retaliation would lead to constant petty warfare but pointed to the peace and order existing all along the Punjab frontier as evidence that such a policy was not, in fact, being followed. '... nothing from me to Major Jacob can be construed into my approval or abetment of retaliating raids by border tribes, as will be seen should Major Jacob be required to produce the correspondence he has improperly and without scruple abused'.[13] He was supported by the Punjab government, which observed that it was not improper for an officer to have expressed satisfaction at the discomfiture of a predatory tribe without approving, still less encouraging, the act that caused it.

The Punjab government answered Dalhousie's enquiry by admitting that there were some differences between its own frontier security arrangemnents and those of Sind, but maintained that it had to deal with a different, and more difficult, problem. In Upper Sind, it said, the entire frontier force of 1,400 sabres was available for the defence of a border 70 miles long, with 30 miles of level desert between the settlements and the hills. Jacob could therefore use his cavalry to prevent raids without assistance from the local population, whom he accordingly had been able to disarm. In Derajat, on the other hand, there were only 800 cavalry (with again the point being made that Jacob's troopers were paid half as much again) and 400 infantry to guard a line 300 miles long and, on average, only 6 miles away from the hills. The frontier terrain was unsuitable for cavalry and therefore all the outposts, widely separated and held only by small garrisons, were located well back from it. Many areas had no troops at all. Settlements were close to the hills, and flocks grazed right up to the mouths of the passes. The same families lived on both sides of the British border. 'We could not, even if we wished, disarm these people, and it would be still more difficult to protect those we did disarm. If we took away the weapons of the people who adjoin these tribes in the plains, we deliver them up virtually to be a prey to their ancient plunderers.' Nevertheless, the Punjab government insisted, retaliatory raids, far from being encouraged, had been prohibited time after time, even if this resulted in robbers going unpunished.[14]

Jacob still denied the validity of the Punjab arguments. His actual frontier was 185 miles long, he told Frere, and was held with less than two men per mile, compared with four per mile in the Punjab. During his first year he had held the line with only one regiment, 800 sabres; he had found it an advantage to have posts near the hills; so far from the Derajat frontier being prey to hordes of robbers, the threat from the cross-border tribes amounted to no more than 300 men. He then appealed to Frere for support against arguments 'founded on imperfect information, incorrect as to fact and unjust as to conclusion'. Unable to produce evidence in support of his allegations that the Punjab frontier officers encouraged retaliation, he was nevertheless obliged to say that he had not meant to criticise the policies of the Goverment of India. This did not prevent him incurring the displeasure of that government, and he was told that to aid in the defence of one's own property, and to bear arms for that purpose, did not amount to retaliation or waging private war.[15]

Jacob's philosophy of border control

At Frere's request, Jacob drew up a memorandum of his proceedings and policies on the Upper Sind Frontier. In this, he tried to show that the reasons for his success were moral rather than physical. 'The highest moral ground always being taken with the predatory tribes, treating them always as of an inferior nature as long as they persist in their misdeeds: as mere vulgar criminal and disreputable persons with whom it is a disgrace for any respectable persons to have any dealings.' Every soldier was taught that he was the good man against the bad, and that the raiders were not warriors but wrong-doers. Robbery and murder were treated as equally criminal, whether the victims were British subjects or not. Blood feuds and retaliation were regarded not as justification for such actions, but rather as evidence of malice aforethought. No private person was allowed to bear or possess arms without a licence. Summing up, he expressed his policy as follows 'At first, put down violence with the strong hand; then, your force being known, felt and respected, endeavour to excite men's better natures, till all men, seeing that your object is good and of the greatest general benefit to the community, join heart and hand in putting down violence'.[16]

Arguments over the differences between the Punjab and Sind frontier policies, or indeed, over whether there was in fact much difference between them at all, affected British relations with Balochistan for at least the next twenty years. At this time, however, developments in the Great Game required Dalhousie to use Jacob as a piece in moves beyond the Upper Sind Frontier. The struggle on the ground was left to itself while the British opened a new diplomatic initiative with Kalat.

8

THE GREAT GAME RENEWED

INDIA, IRAN AND BALOCHISTAN, 1854–58

Vouchsafe to those that have not read this story,
That I may prompt them: and of such as have,
I humbly pray them to admit the excuse
Of time, of numbers, and due course of things,
Which cannot in their huge and proper life
Be here presented.

Henry V, Act V, Prologue.

In March 1851 Nasir Khan II sent his wazir to Jacobabad to discuss various local matters with the British officers there. This wazir was Mulla Muhammad Hasan, who twelve years earlier had held the same office under Mahrab Khan II. Imprisoned by the British after the capture of Kalat, he had been freed during their subsequent negotiations with Nasir Khan II, who re-appointed him wazir despite British allegations about his treachery towards Mahrab Khan II. Nasir Khan II's ministers, rebuilding their country after a period of occupation and civil war, may well have welcomed him and the others released from British captivity as valuable and experienced former colleagues. Reports from the British (whom few in Kalat had any reason to believe) that Mulla Muhammad Hasan was a traitor could have seemed disinformation, shifting the blame for Mahrab Khan II's death from themselves onto his chief minister.

These allegations seem not to have been known to Jacob, who on meeting Wazir Mulla Muhammad Hasan thought him a loyal and efficient servant of

125

the young Khan, with many suggestions for the better government of Kalat.[1] At a second meeting, held the following year, believing that the British saw him as the man to bring order to a turbulent country, the wazir proposed that they should set him up as khan in Nasir Khan II's place. Jacob ordered him to leave British territory at once and denounced him to Nasir Khan II, who nevertheless kept him in office. Following this, the extradition from Kalat of a group of Baloch wanted for murder in Upper Sind was refused. Marri hostages were allowed to leave Kalat and the Marris resumed their raids against the Khyheri villages in Kachhi. Jacob reported that the wazir was in league with the Marris and, with Frere's support, urged that British troops should be ·sent to protect the Khyheris. The Government of Bombay decided that the Khyheris were subjects of the Khan of Kalat, not of the East India Company, and the Sind officers were told to confine themselves to the defence of their own frontier. The Khan was to be encouraged to protect his own people and warned that he would be held responsible for any attacks by his subjects on British territory. Responding to British pressure, Nasir Khan II's ministers complied with the extradition demands but the Marris continued their raids, unsettling the Baloch tribes inside Upper Sind and menacing the kafila route to the Bolan.

Jacob once more sought permission to ride against the Marris, promising that with only a few troops he could easily bring a permanent end to their raids. Writing to Barrow Ellis, Assistant Commissioner in Sind (Frere was at this time absent on furlough) Jacob commented that 'It would be unreasonable to call on the Khan of Khelat to assert his influence in controlling the people who owe him only a nominal or doubtful allegiance, while he himself is continually and hitherto in vain begging the British Government to afford him aid in reducing his subjects close at hand to obedience'.[2] Alternatively, Jacob suggested giving the Khan financial aid to enable him to send his own troops against the Marris. Frere, on his return, backed this scheme and in November 1853 the Government of Bombay put forward a plan to subsidise Nasir Khan II with 50,000 rupees (£5,000 at the then rate of exchange) for this purpose.[3]

Outram and a new treaty

Outram himself had remained in the Bombay Political Service and in 1847 been appointed British Resident at the court of the Gaekwar of Baroda. There he found a long-established system involving corruption at all levels of government. In tackling this he made himself unpopular both with the Gaekwar, whose servants tried to poison him, and with the Government of Bombay, whose senior officials he suspected of complicity in the abuses. When his report was submitted to the Court of Directors in 1851, the Government of Bombay condemned it as disrespectful and ordered him to leave Baroda within the month. He returned to London, where the Directors were torn between approving what he had done and censuring his manner of doing it. They decided to place the Baroda Residency under Dalhousie and told him to employ Outram in an appointment 'where his talents and experience may prove useful to the public service'.[4]

Outram reached Calcutta in September 1853, where Dalhousie informed him 'I have officially told the Court that if I am to take charge of Baroda, as they desire, I must appoint my own agent; and that my first act would be to replace you in that Residency'.[5] He was still in Calcutta when the Bombay proposal to aid Nasir Khan II arrived and on 7 December 1853 Dalhousie wrote to him, as an acknowledged expert on Balochistan, for advice about recent reports of Iranian advances into Makran and the proposals for a Kalat subsidy. Dalhousie was doubtful about the latter. 'Give him Rs.50,000 tomorrow, it is to my mind very uncertain that he would prevent transit dues (or, in plain Scotch, black-mail) being collected even if he wished, while it is quite certain that if it is not taken there it will be taken somewhere else. If he can't sustain his own power then our Rs.50,000 won't do it. If we are to support him by force of arms, I conceive we shall engage ourselves in obligations without end and in a policy without bottom'.[6]

Outram waited upon him the next day with a detailed memorandum on both these questions. Makran he dismissed, as the country was too poor to support an organized invasion force and, if the Iranians tried to supply it by sea, one or two steam frigates of the Indian Navy could easily blockade it. In any case, he thought that it would be no bad thing if the Iranians did occupy Makran, as their possessions in the Persian Gulf were always vulnerable to British sea-power, whereas there was no way of imposing sanctions on 'the wretched Mekranees'. Regarding Kalat, he referred to a suggestion he had made when the British withdrew from Afghanistan in 1842. This had been to replace the British guarantee against foreign enemies with a subsidy to the Khan of 50,000 rupees annually, in return for safeguarding the kafila route to Kandahar. In fact, he said, he had not expected the Khan to be able to do this, but the British would have been rid of an inconvenient obligation and would not have had to pay the subsidy if the kafilas were not protected.

Technically, as Outram pointed out, the existing treaty did not bind the British to help the Khan against the Marris, who were not foreign invaders but domestic subjects. Even so, he supported the plan of giving Nasir Khan II a chance of showing what he could do with 50,000 rupees. It was too late in that year's campaigning season for a British expedition but if one was later judged necessary, it should be controlled by Jacob. 'That officer's prudence and fore-sight is as remarkable as his gallantry and enterprise. And so thoroughly impressed am I with the superior qualifications of Major Jacob for such an undertaking that I would confidently leave him to conduct it when and how he thought fit.'[7] On 19 Jan 1854 Dalhousie forwarded the subsidy proposal to the Court of Directors' Political Committee in London, saying that he doubted whether the Khan, if given the money, would really use it to stop the Marris or any other tribes from levying tolls on the kafilas, or give up his own undoubted right to do so.[8] The Committee told the Board of Control that it shared his reservations, on the grounds that Nasir Khan II was a weak ruler but that, if he did use the subsidy to extend his authority (something that the Committee said it thought unlikely, if Wazir Mulla Muhammad Hasan was as great a villain as reported), he might not use his new-found power to British liking.[9]

The approach of war with Russia, 1854

While this discussion continued, moves in the Great Game between European powers once more affected Balochistan. France after the Napoleonic Wars, like Germany after the Second World War, had changed from being an old enemy of the British into a new friend against the Slavic hordes and their tyrannical rulers. In 1852, for domestic political reasons, the future Emperor Napoleon III asserted long-neglected French rights to the guardianship of the Holy Places in Jerusalem, part of the Turkish Ottoman Empire. In June 1853 the Russian Emperor, Nicholas I, asserted his own rights as protector of all Orthodox Christians under Ottoman rule by occupying the Ottoman Dan-ube provinces of Wallachia and Moldovia. The Ottomans, counting on Anglo-French support, declared war on Russia on 5 October 1853.

The President of the Board of Control for India at this time was Sir Charles Wood (later 1st Viscount Halifax), in the Whig Cabinet formed under the Earl of Aberdeen in December 1852. On 24 November 1853 he wrote to Dalhousie that the United Kingdom might become involved in a war with Russia over the Turkish question. He did not fear the Russians would invade India but thought they might try to stir up trouble on the North-West Frontier. Dalhousie should therefore anticipate the Russians by establishing trade links with countries east of the Caspian. Echoing Outram, he thought that even if Iran established control over Makran, the British would be better-off dealing with a civilised government than with a lawless collection of tribes that lacked central leadership. Nevertheless, Dalhousie was to gather a force at Bombay ready for service in the Persian Gulf if Russia encouraged the revival of Iranian claims to Herat and Sistan. This force was also intended to deter the young Nasir-al-Din Shah of Iran (who had succeeded his father, Muhammad Shah, in 1848) from attacking his Ottoman rivals while they were distracted by war with Russia.[10]

The Great Game beyond the Frontiers

On 4 January 1854, as the Near Eastern crisis deepened, Wood instructed Dalhousie to strengthen British influence in Afghanistan and Balochistan. The Khan of Kalat could be given the aid recommended by Bombay the previous November but at that time disallowed. If he could be helped to establish an orderly government, he would probably become a firm ally reliant on British protection. 'A barrier against Persia and the Candahar Afghans, able to control the Murrees and other plunderers among his subjects, the protector of Kafilas from Kurachee to the upper country, he would be precisely the sort of person we require on that portion of our western frontier'. Dalhousie was accordingly authorised to send the Khan 50,000 rupees for a campaign against Marris, taking the final decision on his own judgement after consulting experts on Kalat, specifically Jacob and Outram. Official confirmation from the Secret Committee followed nine days later.[11]

Outram, still in Calcutta waiting for a new appointment, told Dalhousie there was no need for the British to enter Afghanistan. An enemy coming down the Khyber Pass should be met on British ground as he debouched at Jamrud. Likewise, invaders coming through Balochistan should be met below the Bolan, with their supply lines at the mercy of the robber tribes (something Outram himself had experienced during the Afghan War). He forwarded his memorandum of 1842 in which he had suggested giving an annual subsidy to the Khan of Kalat while avoiding any impression that this had been forced on the British.[12] That consideration, he stressed, had become even more important since the British had ignored the Khan's request for aid under the existing treaty. Any new agreement should be presented as stemming from that request, with the delay attributed to the time it took to consult the authorities in England.

At this period, it took about six weeks for letters to pass from London to Calcutta. Wood's letter of 24 November 1853 therefore passed one to him reporting that, at the end of November, Jacob's patrols had intercepted letters between Wazir Mulla Muhammad Hasan and the Marris showing that the wazir encouraged their raids. Jacob forwarded the letters to Nasir Khan II and soon afterwards heard from the Khan's vakil at Jacobabad, Mulla Ahmad, that the wazir had been dismissed.[13] Jacob then persuaded Nasir Khan II to visit Jacobabad in February 1854 to meet Bartle Frere, the Commissioner in Sind. At this conference, Nasir Khan II told Frere that, though his advisers had told him not to trust the English nor to enter their territory, he had disregarded this and come on his own judgement. He said that he had discovered that Wazir Mulla Muhammad Hasan, for his own ends, had misrepresented the previous interviews with Jacob, but his main reason for coming to Jacobabad was to seek British friendship against the Barakzai rulers of Kandahar.[14] Dalhousie was able to tell Wood on 18 March that, although there was some doubt about Amir Dost Muhammad's likely reaction to British overtures, there was none at all about that of Nasir Khan II.

By the next monthly mail, on 18 April 1854 Dalhousie reported that Jacob had been directed to negotiate the replacement of the existing treaty of 1841 with a new one that 'would bind the Khan to us wholly and exclusively'. The British, while retaining the right to station troops in Kalat at need, would incur no obligation 'except the annual stipend of £5,000 which you have already sanctioned', to be paid only if the caravans had been protected during the preceding year and tolls kept to a standard rate set out in the treaty. A few days earlier he had written privately to Jacob saying that he had previously been opposed to a subsidy, but had been convinced by Outram of its merits and of the advantages of a new treaty. The immediate need stemmed directly from 'the unlooked-for change which has passed over the affairs of Europe during the last few months, and which it is very generally believed in England may materially affect us in India'. A public statement by the Khan that he was a friend of the British and enemy of anyone passing through his country to attack India would be regarded everywhere as a great diplomatic success. Dalhousie told Jacob that although he did not expect to see Russian troops at Kalat, Russian agents might try bribing the Khan to cause trouble. It would nevertheless 'take a good many paper roubles and paper promises to outweigh with the Khan and his people the 50,000 solid Company's rupees which I propose should be annually paid to him and which would be spent among his followers and chiefs'.[15]

Jacob's Treaty with Kalat, 1854

Wood received this news in early June 1854. He at once wrote to Lord Elphinstone, the Governor of Bombay (where the mails from London arrived a week earlier than at Calcutta) telling him to stop Jacob, if there was still time, before he made any treaty on these terms. 'Dalhousie has construed my sanctioning a donation of Rs.50,000 in order to enable the Khan of Khelat to put down the Murrees into an annual subsidy in order to enable him to keep them down. We never intended this, and I shall tell him so by the next mail'.[16] The same day he wrote to Dalhousie 'You have gone beyond my letters and our sanction in proposing an annual stipend'. Everyone in London, he said, had understood that, if the Khan were given a single payment to put down rebellion, that would be enough. 'I see no reason for paying him annually to do what it is so clearly for his own interest to do for himself'.[17]

Three weeks before these letters were even dispatched, and barely a month after receiving the instructions sent him by Dalhousie on 11 April, Jacob reported from Mastung that the treaty had been concluded, though he had met far more difficulty in obtaining agreement than he had anticipated. To the Khan, he had written:

> The matter stands as if a man, being sick and weakly, were assaulted by an enemy, and a friend at hand strike that enemy down; in this case one enemy may be overthrown, but the weak man is no stronger than before, nor in any way permanently benefited. But if, instead of acting thus, the friend, when the other is threatened, administers food, medicines, etc., and thus causes the weak man to become healthy and vigorous, and able to support himself by his own strength, the assistance thus afforded is far more important than the other, and the benefit is infinitely greater.

He urged the Khan to go beyond his treaty obligations and secure life and property throughout his country. Oppression and violence should be stopped, justice administered impartially to all men, cultivators and traders encouraged, roads made safe, and no private tolls or similar exactions allowed. 'The pecuniary aid now to be afforded to your Highness will, with proper arrangement, materially assist your Highness in establishing a strong government, in improving your own resources in various ways, and in making such arrangements as will cause your country to become rich, flourishing, and powerful, as it is the wish of the British Government that it should be.'[18]

Though the British Government, in the person of Sir Charles Wood, indeed wished Kalat to be all these things, it was unenthusiastic at the prospect of paying an annual subsidy to achieve them. Dalhousie wrote to Wood on 30 May 1854 (a week before Wood even knew that Jacob was on his way to Mastung) reporting that the new treaty had been signed and recommending it as advantageous to both parties.[19] Wood had to put the best face on things that he could. 'You have done your work so rapidly with Kelat that there is no more to be said. It is a good thing to be relieved from the old treaty, which was a very bad one, and I hope that the mercantile advantages will make good the £5,000 per annum... but it is odd enough that the misapprehension occurred, for neither the Chairman, Deputy [of the Court of Directors] or myself, had the slightest idea of an annual stipend'.[20]

'Even the Kelat treaty did not please Sir C.Wood', Dalhousie complained to a friend, 'As if a chief would... make himself the enemy of our enemies, agree to give us military possession of his country when we demanded it... and large commercial advantages, all for one trumpery £5,000. I certainly believed Sir C.Wood had sanctioned the grant of £5,000 a-year. At any rate, he may be thankful for what has been achieved for him at that price'[21] Nevertheless, Wood was quite justified in complaining that London had never been consulted about the subsidy being permanent, rather than one-off. The idea can only have come from Outram, who had first proposed it twelve years earlier and whom Wood himself had recommended to Dalhousie as an expert on Kalat affairs.

The Consequences of the 1854 Treaty

There can be no doubt that only an annual subsidy would have achieved the new treaty. It was certainly in the Khan's interest to suppress the Marris, but every report from the frontier made it clear he was unable to do so without British help. He lost more from the treaty's permanent reduction in his transit fees than he gained from even the annual subsidy, still less than from a single grant. The real benefit to the Khan was that he now had a steady cash income in place of the unreliable customs tolls. His reluctance to accept restrictions on his freedom to raise these rates whenever he needed additional income may account for Jacob's initial difficulty in securing the treaty. By sacrificing this freedom, the Khan obtained a regular income that gave him the means to fund a regular army. This force was never large enough for him to do without the contingents produced by the sardars nor, by itself, to defeat them, but it was a factor that altered the balance in the Khan's favour. If the contingents were no longer his only troops, he could reduce, or resume, the jagirs granted for their upkeep. A standing army, however small, threatened the personal wealth of the tribal sardars just as it did their monopoly of military power.

The treaty introducing the new annual subsidy that was to have so profound, though unintended, consequences for Kalat ultimately sprang not from that backwater at all, but from the swirling eddies of the distant Great Game. Devised as a precautionary measure in a time of increasing international tension, it was signed some six weeks after the United Kingdom and France had declared war against Russia on 27 March 1854. During the following months, British troops were sent to the Near East. The Duke of Newcastle, Secretary of State for War, asked if Indian cavalry from the Sind or Punjab frontier forces could join them. Dalhousie, who had already protested in vain against the withdrawal of two British infantry battalions for the coming campaign, replied that the cavalry was needed on the frontier. On 13 September 1854, he minuted 'We are perfectly secure so long as we are strong and are believed to be so' but such a belief would be weakened if the British appeared unable to meet the Russians without troops from India, where the existing garrison was never stronger than it needed to be. The next day, Allied troops landed in the Crimea. No Indian troops were despatched to this theatre, though several of the East India Company's officers served with Turkish irregular units. Two officers of the Scinde Irregular Horse, the brothers Henry and Malcolm Green, joined the siege of Sevastopol as volunteers, armed with a rifle designed by Jacob and capable of firing explosive bullets effective at ranges of over a mile.

In approving the new treaty, the Directors told the Government of India not to exercise any more interference in the Khan's affairs than its objects required.[22] Jacob nevertheless secured the appointment as wazir of Mulla Ahmad, formerly the vakil at Jacobabad, who seemed more amenable to British influence than the discredited Mulla Muhammad Hasan. Dalhousie's original intention had been to pay the first grant of 50,000 rupees when the treaty was signed, with only the subsequent grants paid in arrears, conditional upon the Khan fulfilling his obligations. After the hostile reception that the annual subsidy received in London, he had changed his mind, with the result that Nasir Khan II still had no funds with which to raise troops against the Marris and would therefore be unable to comply with his new treaty obligations. Frere, when Jacob pointed out the problem, authorised immediate payment on the grounds that even a short delay would make it impossible for the Khan to take the field before the 1855–56 campaigning season.[23]

Dalhousie agreed not to reverse Frere's decision, but warned him that he must not again depart from the principle of payment in arrears. 'This change would sap the foundations of the main argument by which I have justified the conclusion of the Treaty in the eyes of the Court [of Directors], who were by no means prepared to agree to the annual payment'. If the first payment had already been made, then the next could not be paid until April 1856.[24] In February 1855 Nasir Khan II, having received his subsidy, was persuaded by Jacob to spend it on preparing a campaign against the Marris. To pre-empt this, the Marri chiefs attended the Khan's camp and promised their future good conduct.

Far away from the Baloch hills, the Great Game continued. In February 1855 Palmerston succeeded Aberdeen as prime minister and the war against Russia was pushed on with vigour. Wood remained President of the Board of Control and in March 1855 Dalhousie concluded a treaty of mutual friendship with Amir Dost Muhammad. In the same month the Russian Emperor Nicholas I died of pneumonia and was succeeded by his son, Alexander II. The Russians abandoned most of Sebastopol on 9 September 1855 but captured the Ottoman fortress of Kars in Armenia on 26 November 1855 and encouraged Nasir al-Din Shah to distract the British by renewing Iranian claims to Herat.

Herat, 1842–56

In Herat, the Sadozai ruler Kamran Shah was murdered in 1842 by his wazir, Yar Muhammad, who ruled until his own death ten years later. Yar Muhammad's son and successor, Sayyad Muhammad Khan, sought help from Nasir al-Din Shah against the Barakzai brothers Dost Muhammad of Kabul and Kohan Dil Khan of Kandahar, each of whom had their own claims on Herat. Despite warnings from the British minister in Tehran, Nasir al-Din sent troops against Herat early in 1852 but was forced to recall them by British moves in the Persian Gulf. On 25 January 1853 he formally declared he would not interfere in the affairs of Herat unless it was threatened from the east.

Sayyad Muhammad Khan was murdered in September 1855 and his place at Herat was taken by Muhammad Yusuf Khan, a nephew of the late Kamran Shah, thus restoring the legitimate Sadozai line. In the previous month Amir Dost Muhammad had taken advantage of his brother Kohan Dil Khan's death to seize Kandahar. Muhammad Yusuf Khan, fearing that the Amir's next move would be against Herat, turned for help to Nasir al-Din Shah of Iran who sent troops to re-assert his own claims there. Now threatened from both sides, Muhammad Yusuf Khan hoisted British colours over his citadel and appealed to the nearest senior British officer, the Commissioner in Sind. As he did so, the Crimean War was ended by the Treaty of Paris (30 March 1856), an agreement that left Russia weakened in Europe, but unhampered in Iran and Central Asia.

Three months earlier, John Jacob, newly promoted to lieutenant colonel, had been appointed acting Commissioner in Sind while Frere took medical leave in England. It was therefore Jacob who, in May 1856, received the message from Muhammad Yusuf saying that Herat had been invaded by an Iranian army and asking for a British response. Jacob, unaware that Dalhousie's successor, Lord Canning, had just received instructions from London that if Iran threatened Herat, the British response would be decided at Cabinet level, replied that the British had no intention of intervening. This response therefore brought him a personal rebuke from the new governor-general, though after further correspondence Canning accepted that Jacob could not be blamed for failing to conform to government policy if he had not known what it was. He explained that there were disputes with Iran on other issues (including strained personal relations between the British Ambassador, Sir Charles Murray, and the Iranian chief minister) so that the Herat question could not be settled in India.

With this crisis in mind, Canning invited Jacob to express an opinion on the various routes through which a British force might advance into Iran, should hostilities occur, saying 'The more I examine it, the more I am brought to the conclusion that there never was a country, an attack on which would entail so much risk and cost with so little certainty of an impression'. Jacob replied on 30 June with an outline plan of campaign based on Bushir but at the same time urged a policy that would, he said, achieve the security of the Indian frontier in a far easier and more certain way. This was the establishment of a British position at Quetta. The Khan and his people, Jacob declared, would welcome a British presence, the road through the Bolan could be improved and a railway could be laid from Upper Sind to the foot of the Pass. Quetta had a climate suitable for European troops and the cost of the garrison there could be funded by disbanding that of Sind. The whole should be an enlarged version of his own frontier force, with an increase in the powers, pay and prestige of its commander. From Quetta, the British could reach Herat before an invading army could reach Kabul, and could operate on the rear and flanks of any enemy force heading for the Khyber. 'Such a position would be the bastion of the front attacked and nothing could, with hope of success, be attempted against us until this salient were disposed of', he later wrote, forecasting that the establishment of a division-sized force at Quetta would result there, as it had at Jacobabad, in the growth of a large commercial town, able to supply an army from its own resources. Fifty years later Quetta would be as he prophesied, but at the time Canning thought the scheme would only hasten Russian expansion.[25]

At Herat, Muhammad Yusuf was arrested by his wazir, Isa Khan, and sent to the Iranian camp. The Iranian commander, Murad Mirza, installed Isa Khan as governor. When Murad moved on, the Heratis rose up and massacred the garrison he had left behind. Isa Khan put himself at the head of his fellow-citizens, claimed British protection and offered to hold Herat for Dost Muhammad. Murad Mirza returned and laid siege to the city, but Dost Muhammad, with two of his Barakzai nephews in the Iranian camp claiming he had usurped their claims to Kandahar, decided not to intervene.

The Iranian invasion of Balochistan

In June 1856 Nasir Khan II told his wazir to inform the British that an Iranian force had entered Makran and to remind them that, at the time of a previous incursion (in 1853), they had assured him that the Iranians would never raise their hand against his country.[26] Canning decided that although the British were no longer obliged to defend the Khan against an invasion, it would be prudent to encourage him. Any question of alienating Nasir al-Din Shah could be disregarded, because his troops were known to be in front of Herat, if not already in possession of it and 'the occupation of that city by a Persian force will be followed by instructions from England to proceed to hostilities'.[27] At the end of July 1856 Jacob was told to assure the Khan that in the event of an unprovoked invasion from Iran, money and arms were available for his assistance, though not to promise troops.[28]

Before Jacob could take action, news came that 3,000 raiders had crossed from Sistan and descended on the Sarawan border town of Nushki, 50 miles north-east of Kalat city. They had stolen large numbers of camels, sheep and goats and returned to Iranian territory with their loot. The local naib levied a force to go in pursuit but was stopped by the Khan, who feared that the Iranians had instigated the incident to provoke such retaliation, and decided to take no action until British intentions were clear. Further south, one of the Khan's officers in Makran, Babar Shah Khan, reported on the Iranian moves there. He thought it possible they were intended against the Sultan of Muscat (who held Gwadar on the Makran coast and was in dispute with Iran elsewhere) but that their more likely target was the Khan's territory. If so, he could not stop them. 'The forts in this country are merely earthworks...The state of the army is known to you. They have no pay. Your name is great. In your forts however there are no stores'. He himself had not been paid for three months.[29]

Canning authorised the immediate commencement of aid to Kalat. Jacob's proposals for sending a lakh of rupees in cash, four 3-pdr mountain guns, each with 200 rounds, and 2,000 muskets, complete with percussion caps, bayonets and 200 rounds of ammunition, were accepted. At the end of August 1856 the Bombay government was ordered, by the newly constructed electric telegraph, to implement them at once.[30] In Kalat, Nasir Khan II answered a message from the Iranian governor of Bampur by saying that he was a British ally and had no reason to correspond with officers of the Shah of Iran. The Iranians then approached Sardar Azad Khan Nausherwani and offered him the fort and revenues of Jalk, in Sistan (150 miles west of his base at Kharan). Sardar Azad Khan Nausherwani had played an important part in Nasir Khan II's struggle for the throne of Kalat and had given the young Khan his favourite daughter, Bibi Mahnaz, in marriage. Putting aside these ties, he joined the Iranians with few men but much money, offering to pay whatever was wanted for the rest of Makran. 'The Persians', wrote Babar Shah Khan, 'have thus spread a net, namely Jalk, to keep Azad Khan. His province of Kharan being dry and very unproductive, he would thus fall into the snare.'[31]

Nasir Khan II responded by repairing his forts and paying his officers. He told the British that, though he was grateful for the promised aid, nothing would deter an Iranian invasion so much as the presence of British troops, however few, alongside his own. Failing that, he begged the British to exercise their treaty rights to station troops in his country, saying that a British post at Quetta, or anywhere in Kalat, would deter an invasion by the Iranians or anyone else. Although troops were not sent, British arms and money were, and in early September 1856 the muskets, guns and ammunition came up the Indus from the arsenal at Hyderabad to the Begari canal. This watercourse, intended primarily for the irrigation of the Upper Sind frontier, had been extended under Jacob's direction and by this time was supporting fine crops where formerly, for fear of marauders, not even goats could be grazed. Now it was used as a navigation to bring the munitions and rupees to within 50 miles of Gandava. Merewether reported 'the astonishment of the people of the country was very great, and they flocked from all directions to see the fleet of sixteen boats in the heart of the Desert, where boats had never been before'.[32]

As Outram had forecast, the Iranian force in Makran found it impossible to maintain itself. It replaced a few local chiefs with collaborators willing to accept

Iranian authority and then moved north to join Murad Mirza outside Herat. Canning decided to send arms and money to strengthen Amir Dost Muhammad and in October 1856, with the local temperature several degrees below freezing, a strongly-escorted kafila of 550 camels went up the Bolan and delivered them to the amir's representatives at Quetta. They were not in time to save Herat, where Isa Khan, despairing of aid from either Dost Muhammad or the British, surrendered to Murad Mirza. In accordance with his existing instructions, Canning responded by declaring war on Iran on 1 November 1856.

War with Iran, 1856–57

Jacob had previously obtained Canning's agreement to the creation of a new post, Assistant Political Agent at Kalat, to be held by Major Henry Green, whose presence at such a critical time, Jacob declared, would be worth 10,000 soldiers. The establishment of a Kalat Agency was not mentioned in the 1854 treaty, but Nasir Khan II (who had not actually been consulted) accepted it as the British support that he sought. Jacob wrote to him on 28 October 1856 informing him of the imminent arrival of Green, 'whose words and advice I request that you will consider as coming from myself'.[33] Green's first task was to urge Nasir Khan II to take action against the Marris who, despite their promises, had raided Kachhi while the Khan's troops were concentrated on his western borders. Little was achieved before the British too were distracted by Iranian hostilities.

During 1854 Major General James Outram had briefly returned to Baroda before being appointed Political Agent at Aden. In December, he became the British Resident in Oudh (Awadh), where he implemented Dalhousie's decision to depose the king, Wajid Ali Shah, for misrule. Oudh was annexed as a province of British India on 7 February 1856, with Outram becoming its first Chief Commissioner. Two months later, Sir James Outram, as he had become, was ordered to England on medical leave. On 13 November he was called urgently to the Board of Control and told that the Cabinet had selected him to command the British expedition against Iran, with full diplomatic powers and promotion to lieutenant general. His command was to consist of two divisions from the Bombay Army, of which one was already embarked for the Persian Gulf.[34]

In his first official letter as a GOC, written five days after appointment, Outram asked for a large cavalry contingent composed of British dragoons and Scinde Irregular Horse, the whole to be commanded by his old friend Jacob.

Jacob protested at weakening the Upper Sind frontier while the Marris remained unsettled, but was over-ruled and made a brigadier general, commanding Outram's cavalry on 13 January 1857. The 1st Scinde Irregular Horse was ordered to the Persian Gulf under Major Henry Green. Malcolm Green, previously on leave in England, accompanied Outram as his military secretary. Lieutenant Lewis Pelly, in civil employ as assistant to the Commissioner in Sind and highly-regarded by both Frere and Jacob, became Jacob's aide-de-camp. Merewether was left as officiating political superintendent, Upper Sind Frontier, and ordered to raise a third regiment of Scinde Irregular Horse. Jacob's place in Sind was taken on 12 February 1857 by Barrow Ellis of the Bombay Civil Service, pending the return of Bartle Frere from leave three months later.

The campaign in the Gulf proved a success for British arms, but Palmerston, with a divided Cabinet and hostile Parliament, became as anxious for a speedy settlement as was Nasir al-Din Shah. By a peace treaty concluded at Paris on 4 March 1857 the Iranians agreed to withdraw from Herat and respect its future independence. Three months were allowed for ratification, during which Outram was forbidden from taking any action that might weaken Nasir al-Din Shah. Any question of remaining on Iranian soil longer than necessary was pre-empted by the outbreak of the Indian Revolt at Meerut and Delhi on 10 and 11 May 1857. Havelock's division was already en route back to India, where every British soldier was needed. Outram hurried back to Calcutta, leaving Jacob to hold Bushir until the Iranians evacuated Herat.[35] Murray, on returning to the Tehran legation in July 1857, was greeted with every sign of friendship, including an offer of military aid to help the British restore order in India.

The constitutional changes following the Revolt of 1857 resulted in the abolition of the East India Company and the transfer of all its engagements and servants to the Crown in India. The Board of Control and the Court of Directors were merged into a new India Office, under a Secretary of State advised by a Council whose members were appointed for their Indian experience and whose approval was required for any significant expenditure. Army officers would be re-organized into staff corps, bringing automatic promotion by length of time served. The Governor-General of India was given the additional title of Viceroy, and his Council later adopted a portfolio system, with each Member taking charge of a separate department under its own permanent secretary. The Political Department was reserved for the Viceroy, who thus became his own Foreign Minister. British relations with Iran passed from the Foreign Office to the India Office, so that, at Tehran, Murray was replaced by Henry Rawlinson of the Indian Political Service.

Muhammad Yusuf, the last Sadozai ruler of Herat, was murdered by a Tehran mob protesting at the peace terms. His successor, Sultan Ahmad Khan, a Barakzai prince who had been driven into exile by his uncle Amir Dost Muhammad, was accepted by the British and Iranian governments as a suitably independant candidate. Alienated by Murray's subsequent clumsy attempts to unseat him, he agreed to accept a Russian agent. Rawlinson persuaded Nasir al-Din Shah to refuse consent, after which Sultan Ahmad Khan offered to accept a British agent. Lewis Pelly spent some weeks there in 1860 while returning to India from the British mission in Tehran (which at much the same time was transferred back to the Foreign Office, in response to Iranian sensibilities and the Goverment of India's reluctance to pay for it).[36] Sultan Ahmad Khan ruled at Herat until his death in 1863, after which the province, with British encouragement, was annexed by Amir Dost Muhammad.

The death of Nasir Khan II

On 2 June 1857 Nasir Khan II of Kalat died suddenly, in the seventeenth year of his reign. He was still in his early thirties, so most people thought that he had been poisoned. Over a century later, the last Khan of Kalat, Mir Ahmad Yar Khan, wrote that the British had killed him because he had begun to assert his independence, but there is little to support this view. At the time of the 1854 treaty, Jacob had commented that the Khan had no son and feared that this would cause problems if he were to die young. Moreover, of all the times when the British would seek to destabilise a neighbouring state, June 1857, with mutiny and insurgency spreading rapidly throughout northern India, was not one.

At Kalat, it was rumoured in the bazar that the Daroga Ghul Muhammad had conspired with Bibi Kujis, a widow of Mahrab Khan II (said by her enemies to be of low birth and infamous character), to replace Nasir Khan with his half-brother, her son Mir Khudadad Khan, born posthumously to Mahrab Khan II in 1840. The Daroga was violently anti-British, as he himself had told Charles Masson, so that Nasir Khan II is more likely to have been poisoned for being too friendly towards the British rather than the reverse. It cannot be denied that Daroga Ghul Muhammad had served both Nasir Khan II and Mahrab Khan II faithfully for many years, but the sudden death of the pro-British Wazir Mulla Ahmad in the following August strengthened the conspiracy theory. It is more probable that Nasir Khan II's death had nothing to do with the British at all and some said that it was caused by a secret but long-standing illness.

Khudadad Khan had been brought up in the seclusion of the harem and until his accession his very existence was little known. His name, which can be translated as 'the gift of God' (cf the Greek 'Theodore') may have been bestowed with reference to his posthumous birth. He was then sixteen years old and said to be weak-minded, a condition that may have led the great Brahui sardars to accept him as a ruler whom they could control. Merewether, still officiating as Political Superintendant, Upper Sind Frontier while Jacob was at Bushir, reported that the new khan was using the subsidy to protect the kafilas in accordance with the treaty and had proclaimed he would maintain Nasir Khan II's policy of friendship with the British. Frere, by this time back in post as Commissioner in Sind, told Merewether to express British regrets at Nasir Khan II's death and send Captain G.W.Macauley of the Scinde Irregular Horse to fill Henry Green's vacant post at Kalat.[37]

In September 1857 the sardars of Kalat assembled to pay their respects to their new ruler. Those who might have thought to dominate him found that he already had his own advisers. The leading figures were Daroga Ghul Muhammad and his son Atta Muhammad; Shahgasi Wali Muhammad (who had befriended Masson during his captivity at Kalat in 1840) and his two sons Taj Muhammad and Ghulam Jan; Naib Abdul Aziz of Mastung; Sher Khan, the commandant of Nasir Khan II's new regular troops; and Ganga Ram, a Hindu *bania* (businessman), who had been given the office, though not the title, of wazir in succession to the late Mulla Ahmad. Ganga Ram was very wealthy and had connections with the chief trading houses of Central Asia and northern India. His family was influential in Sind, where many of his relations were government servants. Jacob suspected him of being in Iranian pay and believed that he had assisted Khudadad Khan's accession in return for the office of wazir. Frere later told Elphinstone 'A Jewish Prime Minister could scarcely have been more obnoxious to the Barons of Robert the Bruce than was the Hindu Wuzeer to the haughty, ignorant, and bigoted chiefs of Beloochistan.'[38]

The sardars' spokesman was Mir Khan II, since 1830 Jam of Las Bela, who had treated Nasir Khan II with little respect and ignored his summons to take the field against the recent Iranian incursions. On behalf of his fellow nobles, he claimed the awards normally distributed on the accession of a new ruler, and sought the release from arrest of Muhammad Amin, brother of the discredited ex-wazir Mulla Muhammad Hasan. The ex-wazir was married to a sister of Mulla Muhammad Raisani, the chief sardar of Sarawan, through whom he continued to influence Kalat politics. Ganga Ram, Khudadad

Khan's new chief minister, rejected all these petitions and the sardars withdrew to their camp in a garden below the city. On 10 September 1857 Sher Khan's gunners opened fire on them from the citadel. Taken by surprise, the sardars fled, with the Jam heading southwards for Las Bela and the rest, including Mulla Muhammad Raisani and Taj Muhammad Zahri, the chief sardar of Jhalawan, into the hills east of Kalat.

Merewether believed that the dissidents were a minority, and that most sardars supported the Khan. Nevertheless, he wrote to Frere on 18 September 1857 'it is certain that if he [Khudadad Khan] does not exert himself and administer severe punishment speedily on these rebels, his power will rapidly diminish and the discontent spread widely. I have written to His Highness to this effect, and pointed out that proper energy displayed by him now will establish his power for ever.' At the same time, to strengthen the Khan's position and keep the disorders away from Sind, he ordered Macauley to patrol the foot of the Baloch hills and personally encourage the sardars to remain loyal.

The Upper Sind Frontier and the Indian Revolt of 1857

When the 1st Scinde Irregular Horse was ordered to the Persian Gulf, Jacob protested that this would leave the Bolan unguarded against a possible descent by the Iranian forces in Sistan, or by their ally, Azad Khan Nausherwani of Kharan. The Government of Bombay asked for a regiment of cavalry to be sent from the Punjab to take its place, but it was not until March 1857 that the 6th Bengal Irregular Cavalry reached Jacobabad from Multan. As mutiny spread throughout the Bengal Army during May and June 1857, this regiment became disaffected. Jacob and his officers had long despised the Bengal Army for its lack of discipline and this view, held widely throughout the Bombay Army, was shared by their troopers. When the Bengal cavalrymen taunted their comrades of the 2nd Scinde Irregular Horse as Christians and cowards for refusing to join them in revolt, the latter merely reported the plan to their British officers. A plan by Sardar Darya Khan of the resettled Jakhrinis to return to the old days by concerting a surprise attack on Jacobabad with a mutiny by the Bengal cavalry and the garrison of Shikarpur came to nothing. The plot was discovered by British agents, the sardar was quietly arrested by the police when he entered the cantonments, and the troops remained quiet.

Outram, after reaching Calcutta, had urged Jacob's appointment to command the Central India Field Force then being formed at Bombay, but Iranian delay in evacuating Herat kept him at Bushir. The command went to Sir Hugh

Rose, while Outram himself joined Havelock in the advance to relieve Lucknow, where together they would achieve lasting fame. Jacob returned to the frontier in November 1857 to find that of the three regiments of Scinde Irregular Horse, the First had gone straight from Iran to the campaign in Central India, the Second had to watch the unreliable Bengal Cavalry, and the Third existed only as a few recruits. He had been authorised to raise two infantry regiments and arm them with his own double-barrelled rifles, but these units too were not yet formed. When he and Frere protested at the continued absence of the First Scinde Irregular Horse, they were told that their frontier was quiet and they could use the horses and equipment of the Bengal cavalry for the new Third regiment. Jacob responded that a regiment was not a mere collection of men and horses such as could be raised in a day. He was promised the return of his First Regiment as soon as the emergency allowed and in December 1857 the Bengal cavalry was moved to a less critical station.[39]

British intervention in Kalat

After escaping from Kalat, the Brahui sardars prepared to settle their differences with Khudadad Khan by force. The granaries in Kachhi were plundered and contributions levied from merchants and shop-keepers. Azad Khan Nausherwani wrote from Kharan offering to act as an honest broker and urging all parties to unite against the British. Merewether, to whom Khudadad Khan copied this letter, considered that the sardar was only trying to get his favourite daughter, Bibi Mahnaz, a widow of Nasir Khan II, away from Kalat and was, moreover, in league with Jam Mir Khan II of Las Bela. Macauley, en route to Kalat, was met by a petition from some of the Brahui sardars. He replied that he would have no dealings with men in arms against their king, but would hear their case if it were put to him via the Khan. The sardars, believing that Macauley would give them a fair hearing, dispersed and when Green returned to Kalat in November 1857, Macauley told him that the sardars had been most respectful and had no alternative to acting as they did. Their lives, he said, would never be safe and the country never pacified as long as the Khan had such advisers as Ganga Ram and Daroga Gul Muhammad. In January 1856 Frere, Jacob and Green met the Khan and the Brahuis at Jacobabad. The sardars were told that they should set aside their grievances and work for the good of the country. Khudadad Khan reluctantly agreed to dismiss Ganga Ram and Daroga Gul Muhammad. Shahgasi Wali Muhammad, with British approval, was appointed wazir.

Despite this, when Green rejoined the Khan's court at Bagh a month later, he found Ganga Ram and the Daroga still there, daily forecasting the end of British rule in India and openly expressing surprise that, with their own dominions in turmoil, the British offered advice to others on how to govern. Green discovered that Ganga Ram was kept informed of confidential British correspondence by one relation who was a munshi in Jacob's office at Jacobabad and another in Green's office in Kalat. He also found that Ganga Ram had several sardars in his pay and had promised that if they petitioned the British for his restoration, he would free Sardar Mulla Muhammad Raisani's brother-in-law, Muhammad Amin. Green suspected that Azad Khan Nausherwani of Kharan had been behind the previous disturbances, with the aim of gaining the throne for himself. 'It will be a bad day for the British Government that sees Azad Khan established as Khan of Kelat', he wrote to Jacob, 'He is our bitter enemy, hates us with all his heart and soul and is most ready and willing to join any party against us'. Frere, reading these reports, feared that Sardar Azad Khan Nausherwani would make all Balochistan an Iranian province.

In February 1858 Sardar Azad Khan Nausherwani sent a force south to take Makran. Khudadad Khan was unable to drive it out without the sardars' contingents, which they refused to send until Muhammad Amin was released. Green's own safety seemed at risk at this time. A dish of apricots sent to him by Daroga Gul Muhammad was suspected to be poisoned and Commandant Sher Khan vainly tried to suborn Green's escort. The escort feared for Green's life and on one occasion, when he was absent in the Khan's palace for longer than expected, fell in ready to go to his rescue. The Khan told Green that he cared nothing for his throne if he could not keep Ganga Ram. Suddenly, he had a change of mind and at the end of February 1858 ordered Ganga Ram out of Kalat. Green thought this was in consequence of the return to Jacobabad of the First Scinde Irregular Horse, thus discrediting those who had claimed British power in India was at an end. Though he had no legal power to do so, he followed up this advantage by refusing permission for Ganga Ram to reside anywhere in the Khan's dominions, on the grounds that it would become a centre for intrigue.

Green then arranged a betrothal between Khudadad Khan and a daughter of Sardar Taj Muhammad Zahri and summoned all sardars to attend this ceremony and acknowledge the Khan's sovereignty. They came reluctantly and, after a harangue by Green, promised their future loyalty. The release of Muhammad Amin was announced, after which Green made another speech, rose and gave his hand to the Khan. The sardars flocked round and kissed the young Khan's feet. 'This was quite a spontaneous gesture and certainly expressed real feeling', Green wrote to Jacob on 4 March 1858, 'I assure you the scene was most affecting... His Highness has only now to act with justice, manliness and truth—he will then have everything in his hands'.

Jacob was less optimistic and told Frere that there was no great hope of Khudadad Khan behaving in this desirable way 'The youth is, I fear, naturally low-minded and nothing really noble, generous or manly has yet appeared in him...There is no doubt that the Khan does not treat his Chieftains properly. He continually tells Major Green, in private, that they are all scoundrels (loochas), but scoundrels or not, His Highness cannot, as Major Green explains, rule without them. The truth is that these men are a rough bold manly race, whom a man can govern readily, but not a feeble false or cunning boy. When Major Green takes them to task for disobedience, they...know well what must really be passing in the mind of the English gentleman with regard to their Khan as he sits silent and sullen in his chair'.[40]

At the end of March 1856 Green persuaded the great sardars Mulla Muhammad Raisani, Taj Muhammad Zahri and Jahangis Khan Lahri to lead their contingents against Azad Khan Nausherwani. Before leaving Kalat, they told Green that if Azad Khan promised obedience, they would be reluctant to see him punished. Green saw the difficulty of relying on men who only recently had been fighting against the Khan, but thought the situation in Makran was very serious and told Khudadad Khan to regard Azad Khan as an enemy of the British as well as Kalat. Azad Khan had recently entertained a rival claimant to Khudadad Khan's throne, Fatah Khan Muhabatzai, a brother of the deposed Shah Nawaz Khan. Fatah Khan found little other support and subsequently crossed into Iran but, while travelling from Karachi to Kharan, he had been aided by Jam Mir Khan II of Las Bela. In response to a protest from Frere, the Jam insisted that he was loyal to Khudadad Khan. 'Ever since you directed me to remain in my own place, I have looked upon that order as graven on stone and remained quiet... How can any person say that I have kept company with the seditious?'.[41]

Vakils sent to Frere by the Jam blamed Ganga Ram and Daroga Gul Muhammad for bombarding the sardars who had come to acknowledge Khudadad Khan's accession. In the recent gathering of chiefs, they said, Major Green had gone to much trouble in inviting the Brahuis but the Jam had been ignored. It was customary for the Jams of Las Bela to be summoned by a prominent chief or official, but this courtesy had been disregarded and their master could not attend without loss to his honour. He had not been given the assurances of personal safety offered to the others and 'if the Sahib were personally acquainted with the Khan's advisers, he would be satisfied that the precaution was necessary'. The Jam, they said, had obeyed Nasir Khan II's call for troops as far as his means allowed and had sent 500 men in the direction required. The Iranian border was far away, 'but he did all he was directed to do and would, if able, have done more'.[42]

At Kalat, Henry Green still believed the Jam and Azad Khan Nausherwani to be in league with Daroga Gul Muhammad. Jacob, fearing for Green's life, ordered him to terminate his mission, but Green remained in Kalat, arguing that, by his influence, he prevented it from falling to Kandahar. On 8 September 1858 he was able to report that the Khan's authority had been re-established in Makran, revenue unpaid for the previous two years had been collected and Sardar Azad Khan Nausherwani forced to withdraw to Kharan. The Kalat troops were thus freed to act against the Marris, the original purpose for which the British subsidy had been granted. A force was mustered at Kalat consisting of 8,000 men from the sardars' contingents (eventually including that of the Jam of Las Bela), and 400 sepoys from Khudadad Khan's regulars. Green was not impressed by the latter, describing them as 'scoundrels of sorts, deserters from our Belooch regiments, Pathans and Afghans, with men from all parts of Central Asia...a scourge to the country...commanded by a knave formerly in the Bengal Army and ready for any villainy'.

The death of Jacob

Jacob had long advocated a campaign against the Marris, but was not destined to see them crushed, as he became seriously ill at the end of November 1858 and died at Jacobabad, aged forty-five, on 5 December. His influence on the history of Upper Sind and Baluchistan can scarcely be underestimated. After his death he became an object of veneration, literally so to the ordinary country folk whom he had protected and virtually so to the officers who had served under him. Henry Green, who had reached Jacobabad just before his old chief's death, hastened back to the Khan's army, fearing that so large a body of armed men assembled near the British frontier would be unsettled by the news. Jam Mir Khan II had already proposed that, with the great General Jacob dead, the whole force should turn against Jacobabad, as offering better prospects of plunder than the barren Marri hills.

9

CIVIL WARS, 1858–1872

... the nimble gunner
With linstock now the devilish cannon touches
And down goes all before them. Still be kind
And eke out our performance with your mind.

Henry V, Act III, Chorus

The Khan of Kalat's long-planned punitive expedition into the Marri country was accompanied by Henry Green, the Poltical Agent at Kalat, and a squadron of Scinde Irregular Horse under his brother Malcolm. During December 1858 Marri villages were burned, harvests destroyed and cattle confiscated, though Jacob and Frere had always insisted on individual rather than collective punishment and condemned the latter when practised by the Punjab government. The Marris, accustomed to boasting that in the Afghan War they alone had never been defeated by the British, were obliged to yield to the despised Brahuis and give hostages for future good behaviour. The myth of the impregnability of the Marri hills was destroyed and three of the guns lost by Clibborn were taken back in triumph to Jacobabad. The fourth would remain in Marri hands until 1918, when it was handed back at the conclusion of a serious rising that was suppressed only by a large-scale British punitive expedition including the use of aircraft.

Encouraged by this success, Henry Green urged Khudadad Khan to lead a force into Makran to see as much of his dominions as possible and mix with his chiefs and people while still at an impressionable age. This, he thought, would

147

help unite the tribes of Balochistan under a single responsible ruler and keep any potential invader away from the route between Kandahar and Sind. The Khan promised to prepare another expedition but in October 1859 told Green that not one of his sardars had produced their contingents when summoned. The following year Green persuaded the Brahuis to assemble their men and, early in 1860, a successful campaign in Panjgur and Kech ended with the local chiefs acknowledging the Khan's authority. In April 1860 Green wrote to Merewether (Jacob's successor as Political Superintendant, Upper Sind Fontier) that, despite all advice, the Khan obstinately refused to recognise the rights of the sardars, though 'the constitution of this country is such that the Khan is only able to collect a force by keeping on good terms with his Chiefs.' He complained that Khudadad Khan lacked the force of character to dominate the independently-minded sardars, leaving Green himself obliged on the one hand to show the outward respect due to the Khan's position but, on the other, to deal directly with the sardars in order to keep the country quiet.

Citing Sir Thomas Munro, a former governor of Madras, Green pointed out the danger that British support could keep bad rulers in power, because they were protected from the two traditional sanctions against misgovernment, a domestic rebellion or a foreign invasion. In April 1860 he formally warned Khudadad Khan to change his ways, telling him 'there is neither faith, confidence nor justice in the land, the roads are as unsafe for traffic as for life, and if the country is not in actual rebellion it is merely through fear of the displeasure of the British Government'. He urged the Khan to draw up agreed lists of what was due to each sardar, reduce the regular army to a bodyguard of 400 men, and confirm Shahgasi Wali Muhammad as wazir, with responsibility for collecting the revenue and enforcing order.

The Coup d'Etat

Khudadad Khan paid little heed to these strictures. To make things worse, in 1861 he formed a violent passion for Bibi Mahnaz, the widow of his late half-brother, Nasir Khan II, and the favourite daughter of Azad Khan Nausherwani of Kharan. Ignoring her express wishes to the contrary and repeated declarations that she would rather die, Khudadad Khan got possession of the lady's person and forced her to marry him. She later regained the protection of her father who, by one account, sent a large body of horsemen to rescue her and, by another, kept her safe when, after being allowed to visit him, she refused to return to Kalat. At the time, it was generally agreed that the Khan's actions caused great and justifiable offence to Sardar Taj Muhammad Zahri, whose daughter's betrothal to Khudadad Khan had been arranged by Green as part of the 1858 accord. Taj Muhammad responded to this insult by plundering some of the Khan's granaries in Kachhi.

In March 1863 Khudadad Khan was attacked and wounded by his cousin, Sher Dil Khan, who then took the throne with Taj Muhammad Zahri's support. Commandant Sher Khan and many of his sepoys went over to Sher Dil Khan, while Khudadad Khan fled westwards with those who remained loyal and found asylum with the Naib of Kech, Sardar Fakir Muhammad Bazanjau. After a month, with his wound healed, he attempted to retake Kalat but his army melted away and he was given refuge by Sardar Mulla Muhammad Raisani. Henry Green then asked him to disband his remaining followers, on the grounds that keeping up a hopeless cause was liable to create disturbances on the British frontier. At higher levels on the British side, Frere, appointed Governor of Bombay in April 1863, Lord Elgin, Canning's successor as Governor-General, and Wood, at the India Office, all approved Green's decisions and Sher Dil Khan was recognized as the *de facto* ruling Khan of Kalat.

Sher Dil Khan's reign lasted little over a year. Lavish grants of jagirs and money to the Brahui sardars merely depleted his resources and left him more at their mercy. Emissaries from Kandahar, offering him aid in return for the cession of Quetta, Dadhar and Mastung, were turned back by the Brahuis. In May 1864, at a review of his regular troops, Sher Dil Khan was shot and killed by one of the sepoys after a violent argument with Commandant Sher Khan about their pay. Kudadad Khan then recovered his throne with the aid of Sardar Mulla Muhammad Raisani but found there was no money left in the Treasury and most of the revenue had been alienated. As a gesture of conciliation he married the daughter of Sardar Taj Muhammad Zahri as had been arranged previously. Despite these disturbances, kafilas continued to pass in safety and in November 1864 the British paid Khudadad Khan the annual subsidy of 50,000 rupees in accordance with their treaty.

The Khan spent most of this on rebuilding the regular army so as to make himself less dependant on the sardars. To overcome the ill-feeling between the sepoys who had followed him into exile and those who had remained under Sher Dil Khan, he used the former as the nucleus of his Foot Guards and the latter as that of a regiment of infantry of the line. Their establishment was brought up to strength with men at that time being discharged from the Indian Army in the Government of India's perennial search for financial savings. Within a few years the Western-style regular army amounted to 200 cavalry, 400 foot guards and 800 infantry of the line, supported by 75 artillerymen stationed at various garrisons and the arsenal at Kalat. In addition, Khudadad Khan recruited 400 Pashtun horsemen, dressed and equipped in the local manner, as his personal bodyguard.

The value of these troops soon became evident. In March 1865 Sardars Mulla Muhammad Raisani and Taj Muhammad Zahri, leading the Sarawans and Jhalawans repectively, rose against the Khan with the aim of replacing him with his infant son. They plundered Kachhi but their tribesmen were then defeated by the Khan's regulars. Mulla Muhammad Raisani fled to Kandahar while Taj Muhammad Zahri was brought back to Kalat as a state prisoner. In July, the Jam of Las Bela, joined by his Jhalawan brother-in-law, Sardar Nur al-Din Mingal, also rose in rebellion, only to be defeated and taken to Kalat, where they spent some time under arrest before being pardoned and released. Sardar Taj Muhammad Zahri remained in custody at Kalat, where he died two years later. There were the usual conspiracy theories that he had been poisoned (in this case by his son-in-law, the Khan) but Henry Green reported that such stories usually arose in Balochistan when any great man died. He could find no evidence to support them and thought that, as Khudadad Khan had not previously put any sardar to death, it was most probable that Taj Muhammad died of natural causes.

Sardar Mulla Muhammad Raisani returned from Kandahar in October 1867 to avenge Taj Muhammad's death and reclaim his own rights. He was easily defeated by the Khan's troops and took refuge with the Marris, from where he appealed to Green to intercede for him and other dissidents. Green agreed to do so only if the Khan invited him and if all parties promised to accept his judgement. With Khudadad Khan's consent, Green then convened a meeting at Jacobabad between Sardar Mulla Muhammad Raisani and the wazir, Shahgasi Wali Muhammad. He achieved a provisional agreement and prepared a permanent settlement for confirmation during the coming cold weather, when the Khan planned to tour Kachhi for the first time since his restoration.

British Ministers and Indian Frontier Policy

On the British border, the differences between Sind and the Punjab continued unresolved. The Punjab system of encouraging British subjects to keep arms for protection against the hillmen also allowed them to raid or counter-raid their neighbours at will. Sir Bartle Frere, knighted in April 1859 and promoted from Sind to the Governor-General's Council at the end of the same year, had vainly continued his criticism of this policy. The Punjab school was at the peak of its prestige as rulers of the province that had saved India during the Revolt of 1857 and neither Canning nor Elgin was persuaded of the need for changes. Frere returned to Bombay as Governor in April 1862. Elgin died of a sudden illness in November 1863. His successor, Sir John Lawrence, whose Punjab frontier policy Jacob and Frere had so often criticised, was strongly opposed to any involvement by the Government of India in affairs beyond its frontiers. Scarred by the experience of the Afghan War and the events of 1857, he took the view that all the Government's resources should be concentrated on improvements within India and keeping down taxation, so that the population would see benefits from British rule.

Amir Dost Muhamad had died in June 1863, after a reign of thirty-seven years, broken only by the period in which he was driven from his throne by the British. Not a prince to bear a grudge, he became reconciled to his powerful neighbours and took no part against them in the Indian Revolt of 1857, when their own position seemed for a time in the balance. In return, they had given him arms and money to take Herat in May 1863. This was a time when, once again, British statesmen feared that Russian expansion across the steppes of Central Asia was bringing the Tsar's troops ever nearer to Afghanistan. Some Russian statesmen, however, believed that Russia, the great land power, and Britain, the great sea power, if working in co-operation together rather than rivalry, could achieve much for the peace of the world and especially the advance of Christian civilisation in Asia. Among these were Prince Alexander Gorchakov, the Russian Foreign Minister, who in September 1864 responded to British complaints in a memorandum justifying this expansion. The Russians in Central Asia, he said, were faced with the same problems as the Americans in their Western plains, the French in Algeria, the Dutch in the East Indies and the British on their Indian North-West Frontier. In each case, the government had to defend its subjects against savage tribal raiders from beyond their borders. If the government's soldiers withdrew after an expedition, the tribes saw it as a victory for the forces of barbarism and repeated their raids. The only way was to defeat and disarm them, but this then left them open to attack from other wild tribes. The civilised government therefore had a moral duty to protect the newly-tamed tribes and were thus almost inevitably drawn forward to fill a power vacuum.

Despite this, said Gorchakov, the Tsar wished only to prove to the khanates of Central Asia that, though aggression would be punished, their independence would be respected, and that peaceful trade was more profitable than raiding caravans and pillaging settlements. Nevertheless, as elsewhere, the braves of Central Asia continued their traditional practices of robbing and killing, leading to the Russian annexation of Tashkent in 1865, Samarkhand in 1868 and Bokhara in 1869. The suspicious British saw not a proffered hand of Russian friendship, but Russian gunboats on the Upper Oxus, within easy reach of the Afghan border.

In June 1866 the Conservatives returned to power under the Earl of Derby. The Secretary of State for India in the new Cabinet was Viscount Cranborne, who two years later would succeed to the peerage as the third Marquess of Salisbury. During August 1866, Henry Green, then in London, presented him with a confidential memorandum headed 'Suggestions for the protection of the North-West Frontier of India with reference to the Advance of the Russians in Central Asia', advocating the eventual British occupation of Quetta and the immediate despatch of a mission, headed by himself, to Russian Central Asia. British interests lay solely in protecting the kafila traffic, he said, and there was no need to intervene in Kalat. To secure the Bolan, the Marris and other tribes should be taken into British pay as local police. The Sind frontier political officers should visit Kachhi and camp regularly at Quetta with their escorts. After a time, a British presence there would be accepted as normal, and the occupation effected without disturbing public opinion in the United Kingdom.

Cranborne passed this on to Lawrence, who replied privately on 4 October 1866, 'I don't know Sir Henry Green but from what I have heard of him I suppose him to be a brave and hardy soldier, but with no great ability'. He agreed with Cranborne's view that there would be nothing gained by the proposed mission as the Russians would only allow Green to see what they wanted him to see. As for the occupation of Quetta, 'it is the old scheme of General John Jacob rechauffé by a very inferior soldier'. Jacob, he said, was such an able officer that few plans, 'however wild', would altogether fail in his hands, but he himself had opposed it when Jacob first raised the idea. The Khan's government was almost nominal and he merely presided over a confederation of feuding chiefs. If invasion threated, he might be helped, but until then his country should be left alone. Lawrence then went on to denounce schemes concocted by officers with time on their hands, trying to justify their own existence and hoping to gain distinction for themselves by achieving some change in policy. Such schemes, he said, were often difficult to refute but would lead to disaster just as Burnes's ambition had led to the Afghan War.

Cranborne accepted this with regard to Quetta, saying 'I would as soon sit down upon a beehive', but asked for the official views of the Governor-General in Council for future reference. Bartle Frere, by this time Governor of Bombay, wrote that he had always considered the opinions of Jacob and Green on this subject to be fundamentally sound. A British presence in Kalat would ensure the protection of trade and cultivation. Quetta should be a British outpost, as every day that passed increased the risk of some less friendly power than the Khan of Kalat establishing itself there. Against this, the Commander in Chief, India, Sir William Mansfield, condemned the plan as one that would place an isolated force more than twenty days away from its nearest support on the wrong side of a difficult country, and thought that Green's idea of 'creeping over the country like a mist, unobserved by the public or those affected' was not an honourable way of implementing policy. On 23 February 1867, Lawrence and his Council formally rejected the plan. By the time their letter reached London, Cranborne had resigned from the Cabinet over the question of Parliamentary Reform. His successor, Sir Stafford Northcote, indicated general support for the Laurentian view.[1]

The arrival of Robert Sandeman

Early in 1866 a new Deputy Commissioner had been appointed to Dera Ghazi Khan, the southernmost district of the Punjab frontier. This was an ambitious thirty-one-year-old Scotsman, Lieutenant Robert Groves Sandeman, who had fought in the Revolt of 1857 before transferring to civil employment in May 1859. In his new district he established friendly relations with the sardars of the Baloch tribes living inside British territory, much as Jacob had done in Sind, by finding government employment for tribesmen they selected, an arrangement that strengthened their authority. In these negotiations he employed a chief of the local Mazaris, Imam Baksh Khan, with whom he became increasingly close.

Sandeman's hagiographer, T.H.Thornton, who at the relevant period was Secretary to the Punjab Government, later wrote '... with his usual keen insight into character [Sandeman] at once recognised the merits and ability of Imam Baksh Khan, acting *tomandar* or chief of the Mazari tribe—now Nawab Sir Imam Baksh Khan, K.C.I.E., whom he constituted his chief native henchman. This remarkable man had formerly served as a native commissioned officer in the 3rd Punjab Cavalry, and during the great Mutiny commanded the levies which had been raised to protect the district in the absence of the regular troops. His loyalty to the British Government was undoubted and his character singularly upright. At the same time he was a Baluch to the backbone. He was thus an excellent intermediary between the British Government, or its representatives, and the Baluch tribes beyond the border'.[2]

A far less favourable view was expressed in 1875 by Sir Henry Green when developments in the Great Game were giving officials at the India Office a new interest in Balochistan. 'The real actor on the Punjab Frontier between Sind and Mithancote, in connexion with the Murres and Boogtees, is one Imaum Bux, Muzzaree... a very clever Asiatic [who] has obtained a great reputation amonst the Punjab officials and is also a magistrate. He knows, and also thoroughly understands, the jealousy and rivalry which has so long existed between the Sind and Punjab officials, and has done his best to turn it to his advantage. Sandeman is totally under his thumb; Imaum Bux is the agent employed on all occasions between Sandeman and the mountain tribes, and he, of course, makes out the advantages to be derived from his friendship and the power he possesses for good or ill. It is he who advises these Chiefs to be insolent to the Sind authorities—it is he who encourages them to plunder in the Khan's territory and the Bolan, with a view to bring discredit on the Sind system, and to raise that of the Punjab—it is he who purchases the cattle stolen from the Khan's territory and resells it in that of Bawalpoor just across the river—it is his object to prevent the Murrees getting thrashed and brought into subjection, as by doing so he would be the loser—it is he who makes up pretended tribal feuds, and allows of Sandeman making rose water reports to the Punjab Government and pointing out how superior the Punjab system is to that of Sind, and which the former are only too glad to spout about in all directions. Jacob tried, Merewether tried, and I tried to bring this man's conduct to light, but it was useless; the Punjab, with Lord Lawrence as Lieutenant-Governor, and then Viceroy of India, was too much for us'.[3]

In January 1867 a 1,500-strong party of Marris, Bugtis and Khatrans, led by a notorious Bugti chief, Ghulam Hussein, crossed the border into Dera Ghazi Khan. There they attacked Harrand fort, burned villages, killed British subjects and stole several hundred head of cattle belonging to the local Gurchani tribe. Sandeman put himself at the head of the Gurchanis and, joined by thirty troopers from the Punjab Frontier Force, caught up with the robbers as they re-entered their hills. In the ensuing fight Ghulam Hussein Bugti and 120 of his men were killed and 200 captured, against losses on the government side of seven dead and 60 wounded.

Basking in the congratulations of the Punjab Government, Sandeman then wrote to Sir Henry Green (knighted following his appointment in 1861 to succeed Merewether as Political Superintendant, Upper Sind Frontier) to seek compensation from the Khan of Kalat for the damage caused by his subjects. Green replied that the Khan had no more power over the Bugtis than Amir Dost Muhammad had over the Afridi Pashtuns of the Khyber 'and any complaint of their conduct to the Khan would be of about as much use as the Commissioner of Peshawur bringing to the notice of the Ameer of Cabul the conduct of the said Afreedees'. He told Sandeman that the Marris occasionally tried to raid Upper Sind, but the risk was reduced by a prohibition on cattle being grazed beyond his outpost line. If any were stolen, he held his own Indian officers to blame. It would be unfair to ask the Khan to pay for losses caused by a lack of vigilance on the British side, especially as he suffered more from Marri depredations than anyone. Green repeated the criticisms of Punjab policy that Frere and Jacob had made a decade earlier. 'By the employment of border militia you have established a very neat little blood feud between Murrees, Boogtis and Khatrans on the one side and the Gurchanis on the other'. Using such forces only kept alive the old plundering spirit and re-opened old feuds between hill and plain. 'We ought to be able to depend on our own strength without the assistance of these people...I hope I have not spoken too plainly: if so you must excuse me, but long experience has proved to me what I say is correct'.

Sandeman was quite prepared to accept this and asked Green if he could consult him again, especially about what to do with the prisoners taken after Ghulam Hussein's raid. Green answered 'Write whenever you like and as much as you like' but added, echoing the old Sind reservations about Punjab policy, 'Our arrangements and yours are so different that it is difficult for me to advise what to do'. He repeated that disarming the tribes living inside Upper Sind had made them peaceful and prosperous. 'You ask me if I am not in favour of a conciliating policy. My whole conduct on this frontier has shown that I am so; but unless very careful, semi-barbarians...mistake our kindness for weakness. No! I do not think your policy soft...your foundations are sound, and as you gain experience and grey hairs, will stand.' He advised that the Baloch prisoners be dealt with as in the Upper Sind frontier, either by being handed over to the Khan's officers or, as he recommended in this case, tried summarily by the local British magistrates.[4]

Instead, Sandeman decided to use them as hostages to bring Sardar Ghazan Khan Marri to a meeting in the border town of Rajanpur. There, the Marri, Bugti and Khatran chiefs agreed to refrain from raiding Dera Ghazi Khan in return for Sandeman's employing a number of their men as post-riders, much as he had already done with the tribes living inside British territory. Green endorsed this arrangement and supported Sandeman's idea of establishing a military outpost on the edge of the Marri country. As for relations between these tribes and their nominal overlord, in which Sandeman had begun to express an interest quite outside his proper area of responsibility, Green told him 'Never mind the Khan of Khalat's affairs, I will work them for you.'

During the cold weather of 1867–68 the Commander in Chief, Bombay, Sir Robert Napier, toured the edge of Bugti territory with a strong brigade from the Sind Frontier Force. Green, as its commandant, accompanied him. Neither the Khan nor the Bugtis raised any objection and Sandeman, accompanied by his assistant commissioner, R.I. Bruce, joined them with an escort of para-military tribal levies from Dera Ghazi Khan under their own sardars. It seemed that the long feud between Sind and the Punjab was over, the Baloch hill tribes had been pacified and British mediation was about to reconcile the Khan of Kalat with his sardars.

The arrival of Phayre and the return of Merewether

The subsequent departure of Henry Green, permanently, and Robert Sandeman, temporarily, delayed these outcomes for another ten years. In 1868 a diphtheria epidemic in Dera Ghazi Khan killed Sandeman's young wife and two of their small children. The following winter he returned briefly to England with his surviving child. Henry Green too returned to England on medical grounds and shortly afterwards, having become a major general in the Bombay Staff Corps, retired altogether. Green's old comrade Merewether served as Military Secretary, Bombay, until 1865, when he became Political Resident and commandant in Aden, dealing with the Arab Fadheli tribe of the interior much as he had dealt with the Baloch of the Upper Sind Frontier. His political responsibilities included British relations with Ethiopia and he played an influential part in the decision, taken in 1867, to send an expedition to free Europeans held hostage by the Emperor Tewdros (Theodore).

The expedition was mounted by the Bombay Army, led by its Commander in Chief, Sir Robert Napier, with the forty-seven-year-old Colonel Robert Phayre as his Quartermaster-General (QMG). A Bombay Army officer, Phayre had been briefly a political assistant in Balochistan during the Afghan War and later fondly recalled his meetings with Brahuis sardars and sharing the pleasure they took in their greyhounds. He served in the Sind War, where he was wounded at Miani, and subsequently in Napier's Hill campaign. He made his career as a staff officer in the Quartermaster-General's branch, dealing with operations and intelligence as well as logistics, there being no General Staff in the British service at this period. In 1857 he was appointed Quarter-master-General of the Bombay Army.

Always noted for his physical energy, during the Ethiopian campaign Phayre made a habit of conducting reconnaissance in person and climbed hills at a speed outpacing officers half his age. In the final battle outside Theodore's capital at Magdala (April 1868), he was blamed for allowing the supply train to move ahead of the main army and thereby almost causing a British disaster, but nevertheless was decorated with the usual awards given to a principal staff officer in a successful campaign, becoming a CB and aide-de-camp to the Queen. After eleven years as QMG, Bombay, it was time for him to be re-assigned and, with Jacob's school of frontier officers dispersed or unavailable, was appointed as Henry Green's successor in the prestigious and well-paid post of Political Superintendant and Commandant, Upper Sind Frontier.

Phayre took up his new command a few weeks before the arrival of the new Commissioner in Sind, Colonel Sir William Merewether, created a Knight Commander of the Order of the Star of India (KCSI) in recognition of his previous services, including the Ethiopian expedition, which he had accompanied as the senior political officer. The two men, in charge respectively of civil and military intelligence in that campaign, would certainly have known each other, but whatever their previous relations, they soon disagreed so strongly over Kalat policy that Sandeman was able to benefit from their differences.

Rebellions against the Khan, 1868–9

At the end of 1868 fresh disturbances broke out in Kalat. Sardar Mulla Muhammad Raisani, at that time a refugee in Sibi, informed Phayre that the Jam of Las Bela and his brother-in-law, Nur al-Din Mingal, had again risen against the Khan and had invited him to join them. At Phayre's request, he sent Ala al-Din Kurd and other Sarawan sardars to the Jam urging him to keep the peace. Despite this, the Jam wrote to Sardar Fakir Muhammad Bazanjau, Naib of Kech, calling on him to join the rising and avenge the murder of Sardar Taj Muhammad. The Naib, a faithful servant of the Khan, to whom he had given refuge when Sher Dil Khan seized the throne, answered 'Who are you that I should blacken my face with rebellion... you people will soon reap the reward of your evil counsel'. Sardar Nur al-Din Mingal wrote to Shahgasi Wali Muhammad that the insurgents were not supporting any other Ahmadzai against the Khan and only wanted the restoration of their ancestral holdings. 'It does not become the Khan to destroy the whole country for the sake of a little land'. The wazir replied 'in the last rebellion the Khan listened to my petition for you and pardoned you... He is still your Ruler... come and pay your respects to him at once.'[5]

The insurgents now included the Jam of Las Bela (who brought two field guns served by artillerymen formerly in the Bombay Army), Nur al-Din Mingal and a nephew of Azad Khan Nausherwani of Kharan, Baloch Khan Nausherwani, who arrived with 500 horsemen and a thousand foot. Khudadad Khan left Kalat at the head of his regular troops on 11 December 1868. When he reached the rebels, they sent a message to Bibi Ganjan (Khudadad Khan's stepmother, still as active in politics as she had been when helping her son Nasir Khan II gain the throne nearly thirty years earlier) asking her to arrange a parley. The Khan saw this merely as a delaying tactic and bombarded their position until his ammunition ran out, but then judged he was not strong enough to attack. Bibi Ganjan, aided by Mir Kayra Bazanjau, the son of Naib Fakir Muhammad, then brokered a settlement and the rebels dispersed. Both sides claimed victory, the Khan declaring that he had pardoned the rebels in return for their promises of future obedience, and the rebels that he had granted all their demands.

Phayre believed that the sardars would be satisfied with a small part of their claims, if only the Khan would be amenable to reason and listen to British advice. Merewether commented that if the Khan did not live up to the agreement, a fresh outbreak was certain and he would again be deposed. The post of Political Agent at Kalat, held by Malcolm Green between May 1862 and February 1867, but vacant since his retirement on medical grounds, was then filled by the appointment of Captain C.H.Harrison, one of Jacob's last subalterns in the Scinde Irregular Horse. Phayre proposed that Sardar Mulla Muhammad Raisani should accompany Harrison to Kalat, but both Merewether and Harrison thought this would make the sardar appear a British protégé. Instead, after a visit to Jacobabad, Sardar Mulla Muhammad went to Las Bela, accompanied by Sardar Ala al-Din Kurd and others, including one Mairab Jamali, who had asked to travel with them carrying a petition to the Khan. From Las Bela they set out for Kalat. When they camped for the night, Mairab Jamali took a sword and went to the tent of Mulla Muhammad Raisani, where he found a sentry posted. He then went to the tent of Sardar Ala al-Din Kurd, whom he attacked and wounded along with two of his sons, and killed the sardar's second son, Jani Khan. He was arrested and, before himself dying of wounds received in the struggle, declared (or was said to have declared) that he had been acting under orders from the Khan.

Early in 1869, Sandeman had returned from England with ambitions to expand his involvement in Balochistan. Since the days of Lawrence, the Punjab government had forbidden its officials to enter tribal territory, partly as an element of its close-border policy and partly for fear that they would be murdered by religious extremists and have to be avenged by expensive punitive expeditions. Sandeman, on good terms with the Baloch sardars whom he paid not to raid his district, decided to disregard this rule. Acccompanied by several chiefs already in British pay, he crossed the border to meet those who hoped to benefit similarly. When they agreed to accept British funds for employing their tribesmen as post-riders, he was able to report that he had secured the peace of his frontier by establishing his influence over them. The gamble paid off and the unauthorised mission was approved by Sir Donald McLeod, Lieutenant-Governor of the Punjab.

Finding that Sir Henry Green, to whose long experience of Kalat affairs he had been obliged to defer, had been replaced by a Political Superintendant unfamiliar with the frontier, Sandeman hastened to Jacobababad to meet his new neighbour. The two established an instant rapport, and Phayre soon began to question the policy of supporting the Khan against the sardars. On 23 March 1869, following the attempted murder of Ala al-Din Kurd, he sent Merewether a long memorandum saying he had 'recently' (presumably from Sandeman) gained a great deal of information showing that all the troubles of the previous four years resulted from the Khan's violation of the constitutional rights of his sardars. The Khan, he said, was merely the first among equals in a Brahui confederacy, but had assumed despotic powers, appointed his household slaves (khanazads) as ministers and surrounded himself with over 2,000 mercenaries 'of the lowest description'. Remonstrance had gone unheard, armed resistance had been condemned and the attack on Ala al-Din Kurd had undoubtedly been instigated by the Khan. According to Phayre, the sardars claimed that the Khan should rule with their advice and consent as in the time of Nasir Khan the Great. In particular, they sought the disbandment of the mercenaries, who were maintained from revenues previously allotted to themselves; compensation for the blood of Taj Muhammad and others; a revocation of the appointment of the Khan's infant son as sardar of the Jhalawans in Taj Muhammad's place; the dismissal of the wazir and the right to nominate his successor according to ancient custom.

Pringle, Frere and their two successors as Commissioner in Sind, all Civil Servants, had been happy to accept the views of their political officers on the

Upper Sind frontier in dealings with Balochistan. Phayre, by contrast, was under a Commissioner in Sind who had made his name in the fight at Zamani River and been not merely Jacob's successor in office but his adopted son. Merewether knew the country at first hand and had little time for the opinions of a newcomer barely six months on the frontier, especially when these conflicted with his own and were derived from an opportunistic junior official of a rival province. He therefore instructed Phayre to follow a policy 'of friendly counsel to his Highness the Khan as the sole person in Beloochistan with whom we have any right or reason to communicate... we are in no way entitled to interfere directly between himself and his nobles and subjects.' The British should not be seen to identify with those opposed to him, and Phayre should give no countenance to allegations that he was responsible for the attack on Ala al-Din Kurd.[6]

Harrison, on his way to present his credentials to the Khan, was met on 11 May 1869 by Sardars Mulla Muhammad Raisani, Ala al-Din Kurd and others, at the head of 3,000 armed men, demanding the dismissal of the wazir, the disbandment of the regular troops, and the restoration of all land and water grants resumed by Khudadad Khan. He told them that the British government did not believe the Khan was behind the attempt on Ala al-din Kurd's life, and thought highly of the wazir but, if they approached the Khan respectfully, he, Harrison, would use his influence to restore their ancestral holdings, with which they should be content.

The Khan, on Harrison's advice, offered the sardars these terms. They then withdrew their demands regarding the wazir and the regular army, but the Khan still refused to pay blood money for Taj Muhammad and other chiefs, saying that two had died from natural causes while in detention and the rest been killed fairly in battle when fighting against him. He promised to return ancestral holdings, but any grants made by himself he declared forfeit for rebellion. The sardars discussed the offer at another meeting with Harrison and, finding it too expensive to keep their men under arms, eventually dispersed.

The Jam remained unreconciled and seized the grain-revenue of Kamal Khan, a village that he claimed in Jhalawan, despite Harrison's decision to settle the dispute in the Khan's favour. The Khan offered to overlook the matter if the grain was handed back, but the Jam refused and called on the Jhalawan sardars to join him in arms. In October 1869 Wazir Shahgasi Wali Muhammad led the Khan's regular troops against Sardar Nur al-din Mingal and occupied his principal town at Wad. The Jam advanced to support the Mingals with his own regulars, tribal levies and seven guns. When the wazir attacked their position on 15 November, the Jam and Nur al-Din fled back towards Las Bela, followed by the Jam's mercenaries, whose last advice from their employer was reported as being to plunder the town before the wazir arrived. The wazir occupied Las Bela early in December 1869, while the Jam, Nur al-Din and their families took refuge across the British border in Karachi.

The beginning of the Merewether-Phayre controversy

Phayre continued to press for a change of policy. In December 1869 he presented Merewether with a narrative of events in Kalat since 1854, quoting criticisms of Khudadad Khan and his ministers made by Frere, Jacob and the Greens and comparing these with their more favourable mentions of the sardars. Given the strategic importance of Baluchistan, he argued, the British should in their own interests cease supporting an unpopular ruler and instead seek the goodwill of the sardars, describing them as the true strength of the country who would be valuable allies in case of war in Central Asia. Less than tactfully, he drew attention to the way that Sandeman was allowed by the Punjab authorities to deal directly with Baloch sardars in the Khan's dominions bordering Dera Ghazi Khan.

Sandeman was convinced of the importance of supporting the sardars. Indeed, the whole policy by which he was rapidly making his reputation depended on it. The Rajanpur agreement had bound the Marris and others not to raid into the Punjab, but said nothing about Kachhi, where outrages continued. These, the Baloch sardars claimed, were justified by the tyrannous rule of the Khan, with whom they considered themselves at war. Sandeman took these complaints at face value, just as did Phayre those of the Brahuis. That the two were working together became apparent when Sandeman wrote to his own superior officer, Lieutenant Colonel S.F.Graham, the Commissioner of Derajat, at the very same time that Phayre sent his memorandum on Kalat affairs to Merewether, with much the same arguments and vocabulary appearing in both documents (including the reference to a Brahui 'confederacy', a term previously unknown in this context, though widely familiar from the recent American Civil War). Sandeman claimed that by treating solely with the Khan, as if he was 'a despot' rather that the head of a confederacy, the Sind officers were acting contrary to the constitution of Kalat and weakening the Punjab officers' influence over the Marris (with whom Sardar Mulla Muhammad Raisani was at this time hiding out). 'It is surely time to interfere when we find that the Khan's… mismanagement has led to the peace and administration of that part of the Punjab border being placed in such jeopardy'.[7]

Nevertheless, if Sandeman's influence over the Baloch tribes was as great as he claimed, conflicts inside Kalat would have posed no risk to his own district. These conflicts had, in fact, subsided, with the Jam, Nur al-Din Mingal and Mulla Muhammad Raisani all defeated and in exile. Upper Sind had been quiet for years, due to the vigilance of the Sind Frontier Force and the disarmament of its population. The Punjab government, however, after years of having the shortcomings of its frontier policy pointed out by Sind officers, was readier to return the compliment than to change the policy and Sandeman's paper was forwarded from Lahore to the Government of India.[8]

Merewether made detailed comments on almost every paragraph of Phayre's narrative, dismissing the quoted criticisms of the Khan's government as out of date, pointing out khanazads had been employed as ministers by previous khans, defending Shahgasi Wali Muhammad as 'the best and most true man in Beloochistan' and justifying the regular army as a necessary counterweight to the demands of the sardars. It was better, he said for the British to support a strong central government rather than to leave a strategically vital region in the hands of factious contending chiefs. Sandeman had no dealings with the government of Kalat and Phayre had been ordered not to deal with the rebel sardars solely because of his open sympathy with them.[9]

Harrison defended the Khan's sepoys, pointing out that, by this time, the cavalry of the line were mostly former troopers of the Scinde Irregular Horse, and the foot guards included many men with certificates of honourable discharge from the Bombay Army's Baloch regiments, all generally well-behaved and much respected. He also produced a list of sardars showing fifty-one friendly to the Khan and only twelve sympathetic to the Jam or Sardar Mulla Muhammad Raisani. Phayre, thus contradicted by his own assistant, against whom he subsequently bore a grudge, was reduced to claiming that no-one could really say who the sardars supported, and that the claims against the regular troops related to those deployed outside the capital, beyond Harrison's knowledge. For good measure, he passed on reports from Sandeman blaming the Khan's misgovernment for recent outrages by the Marris and Bugtis. Merewether advised him not to accept Sandeman's views and later told him 'I feel that you have been unfortunate in not taking advantage of the assistance of those near and under you. You unluckily leaned on Sandeman instead'.[10]

In January 1869 Lawrence had been succeeded as Governor-General by the 6th Earl of Mayo. A Conservative politician who sat in the Derby-Disraeli Cabinets as Chief Secretary for Ireland, he had not even reached India before the administration that appointed him was turned out of office to be replaced by a Liberal one under Gladstone. Mayo assured the new Secretary of State for India, the 8th Duke of Argyll, that he was even more strongly opposed to the Government of India becoming involved in affairs beyond its frontiers than Lawrence had been. The emergence of this new controversy was therefore especially unwelcome to him. 'It appears that those who call themselves the Punjab and Sinde authorities differ materially, not only as to the policy to be pursued, but as to the constitution of the Khelat State...' he told Argyll in March 1870. 'To my mind this state of affairs is fraught with danger, and I have no hesitation in saying that the sooner these gentlemen are taught that they are not Punjab or Sinde officials, but are officers of the Queen serving under the Government of India the better... both appear to be in favour of extension of the frontier—though they don't admit it'. He thought the arrangement by which not all frontier affairs were directly under the Government of India was 'most unsatisfactory' but ordered that Merewether's policy, having previously been approved, should be maintained.[11]

The Mithankot Agreement, February 1871

On the frontier, relations between Phayre and his colleagues grew worse. In July 1870 he accused Harrison of trying to hinder Sandeman by telling the Khan, who had asked what Sandeman was doing in Marri Kahan (in fact he was en route to visit Phayre) that he did not know, 'thereby raising a question as to the very propriety of Captain Sandeman's conduct on that occasion—conduct which you very well know had my approval'.[12] Harrison appealed to Merewether, claiming that the implication that he had acted to discredit Sandeman was an attack on his public character and personal integrity. Merewether supported Harrison and complained that Phayre persisted in following his own policies towards Kalat, despite being repeatedly told they were wrong, while Sandeman, without Phayre's permission but apparently believing it would be given (a successful gamble similar to his first crossing of the border), had met the rebel sardars at Kahan and promised redress of their grievances. 'He has therefore not merely meddled and shown therein great discourtesy to His Highness the Khan but he has exhibited marked disrespect to me in acting contrary to the instructions I had issued to the Officer in charge of the Sindh Frontier'. Merewether then proposed to Sir Seymour Fitzgerald, who had succeeded Frere as Governor of Bombay in 1867, that relations with Kalat be conducted directly by himself as Commissioner in Sind, thus restricting Phayre to his military duties as commandant of the Sind Frontier Force.[13]

Once again the question came before Mayo, this time with a ninety-two-page history of Kalat, plus appendices, compiled in the Government of India's Foreign Department. This concluded that Merewether was correct in regarding the Khan as a sovereign; the idea of a 'Brahui confederacy' was a novel and unjustified one; the Jam and the other exiles had been justly punished; and the less the British had to do with either party the better.[14] Nevertheless, Mayo decided that in view of the strong differences of opinion between the Sind and Punjab officers, there should be a conference between Merewether and Sir Henry Durand, the recently appointed lieutenant-governor of the Punjab. Phayre and Sandeman were to be in attendance to provide local knowledge. This loaded the dice against Merewether, since both these officials were known to oppose his views, despite Phayre being his subordinate. Durand, originally of the Bengal Engineers, had been in the powder-bag party at Ghazni, and had held a number of influential posts, including membership of the Council of India and the Governor-General's Council. Though he might have have been expected to support Sandeman, the Punjab representative, he never reached the conference. At the end of December 1870 he was fatally injured when the elephant on which he was riding during an official visit to the Nawab of Tank panicked and ran into a low archway.

On Mayo's orders the conference nevertheless went ahead at Mithankot early in February 1871. Durand's successor, Sir Henry Davies, acknowledged his own lack of knowledge about Kalat affairs and declined to express a view. He agreed with Merewether that the Commissioner of Derajat (Sandeman's direct superior) should have no dealings with the Marris and Bugtis and that, although Sandeman should continue his own contacts with them, these should be under the control of the Political Superintendant, Upper Sind Frontier. This was approved by Mayo's government, and extra funds were made available to be paid to the Marri and Bugti sardars by Phayre, in the Khan's name, for the employment of tribesmen as guides and messengers inside Kalat (much as Sir Henry Green had recommended in his memorandum to Cranborne four years earlier).[15] Thus Merewether's policy of upholding the Khan's authority was maintained and Sandeman, in his contacts with the Marris and Bugtis, was placed under Merewether's subordinate, Phayre. Merewether's triumph, nevertheless, was short-lived, as neither of these officers was prepared to follow his orders and Sandeman, for the first time formally associated with the Upper Sind Frontier, was one step nearer achieving his ambitions.

Insurrection, 1871–72

During 1871, Khudadad Khan made his long-delayed tour of Kachhi, a province he had not visited since his restoration in 1867. His arrival was not much welcomed, partly because it involved the cost of providing for him and his retinue, but mostly because his revenue officials examined the sanads (charters) of local land-holders. It was found that some had been granted by the late Sher Dil Khan and others were completely fraudulent. Harrison and the Wazir urged a liberal approach, but the Khan could not afford to lose his revenue and ordered full payment by all whose holdings were in doubt. Among these was Sardar Jahangir Khan Lahri, a man noted for his boldness, who openly declared he would not submit. Secretly, he plotted with others aggrieved by the Khan to kill him, seize Mastang and Quetta, recall Sardars Mulla Muhamamad Raisani and Nur al-Din Mingal from exile, and join them in ruling Kalat.

The assassination plot came to nothing, either because the Khan received warning or because Harrison visited him on the planned day, but on 3 October 1871, with most of the Khan's regulars still absent in Makran and Las Bela, the conspirators seized Mastang. On hearing this, the Naib of Quetta shut the gates of his fort, thus forestalling any *coup* there. Wazir Wali Muhammad set off from Kalat for Mastang with 400 regular cavalry and infantry, two guns and the contingents of several loyal sardars. In an unusually fierce battle the rebels sought to counter his advantage in firepower by closing to fight hand–to-hand. The bold Jahangir Khan Lahri was killed along with two other leading sardars. Among the Khan's troops Commandant Sher Khan, commanding the artillery, and Risaldar Hyat Khan, the cavalry commander, both fell fighting. The rebels fled to the Bolan and the Khan's army re-occupied Mastang on 8 October. Wazir Wali Muhammad was wounded in the fight, not seriously, but he was an old man and slow to heal.

At the end of October 1871 the rebels, reinforced by Sardars Ala al-Din Kurd and Wadera Adam Khan Bangalzai, laid siege to Dadhar. The Khan ordered Nawab Muhammad Khan, his vakil at Jacobabad, who was at this time in Kalat, to take 150 troopers and ride to its relief. The vakil objected to going without infantry so his departure was postponed until the troops recently returned from Las Bela were ready to march. At Bagh, Sardar Imam Baksh Rind pleaded with the Khan's officials to relieve Dadhar. Instead, they decided to await a Brahui attack. When news came that Dadhar, after holding out for three days, had fallen and its Naib been burnt alive, they fled. Sardar Imam Baksh Rind found it impossible to defend the town without trained sepoys and later reported to the Khan 'your officials deserted us and left us to be plundered by these dogs and wolves... The Brahooees have only two hands and so have we, and had we been assisted we would have fought... During one month the Brahooees plundered... cattle, household property, money, jewellery and wearing apparel. Many people buried their treasure, but the Brahooees drew their swords and threatened to kill them if they did not show where it was hidden. Having done this they set fire to many of the villages.'[16]

Vakil Nawab Muhammad Khan neared Bagh with his troops in mid-November 1871. Deciding that the best way of preventing further losses to the people would be to achieve a peaceful settlement, he opened negotiations with the rebels, who had been joined by Sardars Mulla Muhammad Raisani, Nur al-Din Mingal and Ali Khan Jamot, son of the exiled Jam. It was then agreed that, if the Khan pardoned them and agreed to restore their confiscated grants, the rebels would drop all claims for blood-money and loss of property, play no part in future disturbances and acknowledge him as their sovereign, with the future of Las Bela left to him. The Khan promptly repudiated this agreement and wrote to Nawab Muhammad Khan that there had been no need to negotiate, since Azad Khan Nausherwani of Kharan had rejected an approach by Nur al-Din Mingal and the British had expressed disapproval of the Brahuis. Quoting a Persian poet, he wrote 'War and peace out of time and season are useless. The rose remains in its own place and the thorn in its own'. Far from benefitting the people, he said, these terms would neither encourage the return of those who had fled, nor dissuade others from following them.

Nawab Muhammad Khan re-occupied Gandava on 23 November 1871 and promised compensation to the remaining inhabitants. Contingents from the Rinds and Marris joined him, eager to raid the Brahuis, and Commandant Shakar Khan was also keen to take the field as the Khan ordered. Nawab Muhammad Khan forbade this and continued to strive for a negotiated settlement, writing to the Khan, 'By one fight the whole tribe of Brahooees cannot be exterminated, neither can the Chiefs be apprehended nor any other advantage gained... I have treated with them as the only means of restoring peace'. He went on to report that the rebels said they would not abide by the agreement unless it was made in the presence of the British and that all parties were therefore en route to Jacobabad.[17]

The Khan told Harrison that this agreement virtually acknowledged the sardars as the ruling power in the state and that as he and his late brother, Nasir Khan II, had always considered themselves dependants of the English

Government, if Kalat was of any value to the English, the time had come for them either to take possession of it themselves or give him assistance. Failing which, he would do his best but might eventually have to seek protection from either Afghanistan or Persia.[18] Phayre, reporting the Khan's opposition to the agreement, asked if he should allow Nawab Muhammad Khan and the rebel sardars to enter Jacobabad. His telegram was ostensibly to Merewether, but he copied it directly to the Government of India, which replied that they should be allowed in to lay the facts of the quarrel before the British officers there. Merewether, in the meanwhile, had ordered that only Nawab Muhammad Khan, as the Khan's vakil, should come in.

On 20 November 1871 Mayo ordered Merewether to meet Phayre and Sandeman at Jacobabad to investigate the causes of the insurrection and offer mediation. Fitzgerald, the Governor of Bombay, telegraphed to Mayo on 27 November 1871 pointing out that the rebels had already been offered pardon and the return of their ancestral holdings, so that mediation would only subvert the Khan's authority. He added that, in a minute of 10 February 1871, he had pereviously expressed his disapproval of Phayre's opinions and suggested his removal to another post, while Sandeman's district was too far from Kalat for his information to be reliable. Meanwhile, Khudadad Khan should be given a lakh of rupees as Merewether had asked. 'If Khan overthrown no one to take his place and anarchy on the frontier the result'.

Merewether had asked for the lakh of rupees to help the Khan reward the faithful, compensate the robbed, and pay his troops. The reply from Mayo's foreign department, telegraphed on 6 January 1872, was to ask if the Khan really needed the money, as the Viceroy had heard (source unspecified) he was very rich, adding 'It is hardly possible that the Chiefs and tribes in arms have not some good cause of complaint'. Merewether was told to promise them justice if they submitted. 'Viceroy looks on the state of things in Khelat as most dangerous seriously affecting British influence and likely to have an injurious effect in Persia and Afghanistan... A speedy settlement is all important'.[19] Of course he was not rich, retorted Merewether, 'How could he be? Seven years ago he was a fugitive having lost everything; since his restoration he has had great expenses'.

Merewether complained to Fitzgerald that, by calling a conference, the Government of India seemed to be showing a lack of confidence in his judgement. Fitzgerald replied 'You have my entire confidence... but as my views of the merits of the dispute and course to be adopted have not been concurred in, I am obliged to refer to the Viceroy'.[20] This brought a sharp response from the Foreign Department, to the effect that the Government of Bombay could have removed Phayre at any time without consulting the Government of India and that all its proposals regarding Kalat affairs had been accepted, apart from the extra lakh of rupees, with even that now having been authorised. In any case, it was told, there was no point in including such remarks in instructions sent to subordinate officials.[21] The grant was authorised only on condition that the Khan accepted British mediation and allowed the sardars a share in the government, so it was clear that the views of Phayre and Sandeman had indeed been preferred to those of Fitzgerald and Merewether. Mayo wrote as much to Argyll privately on 5 January 1872. 'I thought it right to approve of the Bombay policy from time to time, though I never thoroughly put full confidence in it... it has certainly failed... I doubt if Merewether is on speaking terms with Phayre'.

While this quarrel among the British continued, fresh disturbances broke out in Makran. There, in August 1871, the previously loyal Naib of Kech, Sardar Fakir Muhammad Bazanjau, resigned after being asked to keep proper revenue accounts instead of just submitting a lump sum. His place was taken by the Daroga Atta Muhammad, who introduced a more conventional system but, as Captain S. B. Miles, the Political Agent at Gwadur, reported, showed 'more zeal in collecting revenue for His Highness the Khan than the inhabitants altogether approve of'.[22] The Daroga also found that for the previous thirty years Sardar Fakir Muhammad had been misappropriating state revenues which, Merewether observed, 'was doubtless true, but he managed to keep order... which was worth quite as much as he took'. In December 1871 Daroga Atta Muhammad was besieged inside Kech by 2,000 Gichki and Zahri tribesmen, whose sardars' income had suffered under his new system. At the same time Sardar Ali Khan Jamot, supported by his uncle, Sardar Nur al-Din Mingal, advanced towards Las Bela to reclaim it for his father, the exiled Jam. At this news, the Naib, Shahgasi Ghulam Jan, abandoned the city and retreated with his troops towards Kalat.[23]

In Kachhi, disturbances were renewed when the Brahuis heard that the Khan refused to ratify their agreement with Vakil Nawab Muhammad Khan, and that the British also disapproved of it. They attempted a surprise night attack on the Khan's troops outside Bagh, but were beaten off. Commandant Shakar Khan followed up this success and drove them out of Bagh, but was halted there by the vakil's orders. He then took his troops into Sibi, claiming to search for the families of rebels who had taken refuge there, though Merewether, who had warned him not to do so, believed it was to pay off some private grudge. In his absence, the Brahuis continued to plunder Kachhi and at the beginning of March 1872 raided a kafila emerging from the Bolan. Sandeman reported this was retaliation for their defeat at Bagh. Merewether commented that this was a strange way of looking at things and described it as an outrage committed by rebels who had been led by 'some unscrupulous person' to believe that such acts would invite the attention of the British government to their grievances.[24]

The remnants of the kafila were encountered by a British survey party en route to join the Anglo-Iranian boundary commission set up to determine the Sistan border between Iran and Afghanistan. Dr Bellew, the party's medical officer, treated the wounded survivors and noted that the route through Kachhi was marked by depopulated villages, with the corn-bins emptied, cattle and crops all taken, the very doorposts of houses stolen and the people stripped even of their clothes, much as Sardar Imam Baksh Rind had reported at the beginning of the outbreak. The party avoided the raiders by going up the Mulla Pass to Kalat and were greeted along the way by the local Naibs with guards of honour from the Khan's regular troops, of whom Bellew wrote 'Where the Khan collected such a unique set of villains I cannot understand. I never saw anything to equal their barbarous attire and rascally looks anywhere'. At Kalat the party met the wazir, whom Bellew described as looking like a bundle of dirty rags, with a beard that, with a little soap and water, would have been white, but who was nevertheless (an echo of Merewether's words) the best and truest man in Balochistan. The Khan received his British visitors, who put on their best uniforms for the occasion, finding them uncomfortably thin for a poorly heated palace in the cold of a Balochistan winter. He told them that he had sought peace with his sardars, regarding them as the limbs of his state, but they had turned bad, so he had cut them off and cast them from him. Turning to Bellew, he asked, "Is this not what the English hakims do?".[25]

The rival Kalat policies, 1872

At the end of December 1871 Merewether wrote to Khudadad Khan asking him to accept British mediation and to send Wazir Wali Muhammad to a conference at Jacobabad. The Khan prevaricated, saying that the wazir had still not recovered from the wounds he had received at Bagh and there was no-one else suitable to represent him. Merewether insisted that, as the Khan seemed unable to prevent disturbances near the British frontier as he was required to by his treaty, he must accept mediation. Going beyond his orders, he issued a proclamation calling on all those in rebellion against the Khan to lay down their arms and submit to his authority, after which the British, in his name, would examine their grievances.

Mayo objected that, if the sardars remained in arms, this proclamation would give the Khan an excuse to reject British mediation. To Argyll he complained that Merewether's wish to arrange matters in the Khan's name, but without his agreement, might ultimately lead to British military intervention in Kalat. Once again, he deplored the system by which the Government of Bombay conducted diplomacy without keeping the Government of India fully (or sometimes, at all) informed of its proceedings. Supported by his Council, he formally asked for the political officers at Zanzibar, Muscat, Aden, Gwadur and the Persian Gulf states to be brought directly under the Indian Foreign Department. Kalat affairs would have to remain with Sind until such time as that province was placed under the Lieutenant-Governor of the Punjab 'as we believe it will ere long', when relations with the Khan would be conducted in the same way as with the Amir of Afghanistan.[26]

Mayo's approach to the Great Game had changed since his arrival in India in 1869. By May 1870 he was writing to Disraeli, then in Opposition, about 'the success of my departure from Masterly Inactivity' and a few weeks later he had told Durand that the idea of the British maintaining 'a Thibetan policy' in the east had been tried and failed. At the end of 1871 he formally stated his wish to establish close and friendly relations with Afghanistan, Kalat, Burma and Yarkand (at that time maintaining a short-lived independence from the Chinese Empire). These states were to be assured that the British desired only to preserve their independence and that the days of annexation were over, thus making them friendly outworks of the Indian Empire. It was, he said, to keep other European states (i.e. Russia) out of these border countries that he had pushed on with the demarcation of Iran's eastern boundaries with Afghanistan and Kalat.[27]

This policy of re-establishing British contacts without extending British territory may go some way to accounting for Mayo's stance over the Kalat question. Having been persuaded by Phayre and Sandeman that the Khan was a tyrant who had driven his sardars into rebellion, he feared that Merewether, by supporting the Khan, was involving the British in the internal affairs of a neighbouring state. He also feared that if the disorders continued, the British would find themselves drawn into occupying the country. Such proposals, he told Argyll privately on 5 January 1872, had been advocated by Jacob and rejected by every governor-general since Canning, and he felt even more strongly on the subject. 'If ever there was a time when such an advance on our part would be a blunder and a crime it would be now'. A move into Kalat would belie his assurance to other border states that there would be no more annexations and, if the British occupied Quetta, which Jacob himself had described as the key to Kandahar, Herat and Kabul, how could they complain at Russian advances in Central Asia?

Mayo's decision to disregard the advice of his own Foreign Department that there was no merit in the idea of a 'Brahui Confederacy' can only be explained by his fear that supporting the Khan would lead to British expansion, the very thing that he wished to avoid. Paradoxically, intending to strengthen British influence in states where it was weak, he weakened it in Kalat, where it had been strong. His proposals for transferring Sind to the Punjab, like those for ending Bombay's political responsibilities outside India, owed much in origin to the dispute over Kalat. In the event, before those proposals left India, he was assassinated by a Pashtun Wahabi convict while visiting a penal settlement in the Andaman Islands.

The Jacobabad Conference, February–March 1872

Mayo's death left Sandeman and Phayre unsupported at Jacobabad. Merewether considered that, whatever had been the original purpose of their attending a conference with him, later instructions required him only to listen to what they had to say and record where he differed. He therefore ordered Phayre not to allow Sandeman to play any part in the mediation betweeen the wazir (whom Khudadad Khan had eventually sent) and the sardars. Sandeman replied that he considered it his duty to offer advice. Merewether commented that he had pushed himself in 'where he was not wanted... but he had not the good taste to see or understand this'.[28] Phayre argued that he employed Sandeman just as anyone would use any means to save a house on fire, and took the chance to complain that Harrison, his official subordinate, gave him far less information than Sandeman, while at the same time keeping up a demi-official correspondence directly with Merewether. He also complained that Merewether had only just told him of the decisions of the Mithankot conference taken twelve months earlier.[29] Merewether answered that if Phayre believed correspondence was being carried on behind his back, it was 'exceedingly improper that he should have allowed such a supposition to enter his mind' and again told Phayre not to allow Sandeman to become involved in the mediation.[30]

Similar exchanges continued throughout February 1872 until Merewether plainly told Phayre that he was insubordinate in continuing to query orders. Phayre responded by writing to Merewether 'as an officer of high military rank, superior to your own' and asking for the correspondence to be referred to 'Government' (he did not specify whether of Bombay or India) for an explanation of the way he was being treated.[31] In fact, Merewether and Phayre were both colonels in the Bombay Staff Corps, promoted in 1868, and Phayre was therefore not in a superior rank, as he claimed, although he was the senior as a colonel by seven months. In any case, his relationship with Merewether at this time was entirely a civil one, where their military rank was immaterial.

Ignoring this issue, Merewether wrote to Fitzgerald on 27 February, 'Colonel Phayre is certainly the most impracticable wrong-headed man I have ever met', adding that Sandeman had become to him 'a sort of necessity, a second self'. On the same day Fitzgerald telegraphed to Aitchison, Secretary in the Indian Foreign Department, that the wazir and the sardars were about to reach Jacobabad and Sandeman had claimed he could not complete his report before taking statements from them. Sandeman's continued presence, Fitzgerald said, was a source of danger, and it was impossible for Merewether to conduct negotiations while he was there.[32] Aitchison replied that if there had been a conference as ordered, Sandeman should leave Jacobabad at once. Otherwise, it should be held without delay as the Punjab Government was anxious for Sandeman to return to his duties at Dera Ghazi Khan if he was doing no good at Jacobabad.[33]

When Merewether expressed further reservations, Aitchison ended the question of a tripartite conference between the British officials by telegraphing to Fitzgerald on 2 March 1872 that Sandeman should present his report and leave Jacobabad within three days. Phayre was to place himself 'in cordial relations of advice and co-operation' with Merewether, and Fitzgerald was to ensure that Merewether did not offer the Khan more than the Government of India's good offices. Fitzgerald considered that these instructions to Phayre to co-operate with Merewether were contrary to the previous subordination of the Political Superintendant to the Commissioner in Sind, and never sent them on.[34] Phayre almost certainly did see them, because he continually referred to instructions 'from the highest authority', leading Merewether, who had not received any such, to accuse Phayre of obtaining them through a channel other than Bombay, the sole proper one. This could only have been the Government of the Punjab, which forwarded to Sandeman its own copy of the Government of India's instructions, though Fitzgerald had decided not to send them to either Merewether or Phayre. When the wazir and sardars reached Jacobabad, Fitzgerald ordered that Sandeman was not to meet them but to submit his report to Merewether without delay. Sandeman claimed it had not yet been copied and, when he refused to present it verbally, the exasperated Merewether told him to leave Jacobabad within twenty-four hours.

During the first two weeks of March 1872 the sardars put their grievances before Merewether. The wazir answered each point in detail, generally stating that the actions of which the sardars complained were in accordance with the long-standing custom of the country and neither unlawful nor unprecedented. He told Harrison that, despite having repeatedly been shown clemency, the rebels would not change their ways. 'As a well-known poet has said, the colour of a negro cannot be changed from black to white if he is washed as many times as it is wished'.[35] On 18 March, Merewether telegraphed to Fitzgerald 'Clear the line—Colonel Phayre's conduct is ruining everything. He deliberately encourages Sirdars and they have submitted unjust and utterly unreasonable demands... if Colonel Phayre is not removed at once, I cannot answer for the consequences... I now distinctly assert, after enquiry, that Sirdars are in the wrong'.[36]

On Mayo's death, the Governor of Madras, Lord Napier of Merchistoun, the senior of the two minor Presidential governors, had automatically taken over as officiating Governor-General pending the appointment of a permanent successor. His caretaker administration now had to cope with a breakdown in relations between officers on a distant frontier, exacerbated by the determination of his colleague at Bombay to defend that Presidency against encroachments from its old rival at Calcutta. Fitzgerald forwarded Merewether's telegram on to Napier, adding that 'I have so urgently represented the danger of leaving Phayre at Jacobabad that I can add nothing to the above.' Napier replied that if Phayre had received the orders to adopt cordial relations with Merewether (implying that the Indian Foreign Department suspected that he had not, as was indeed the case) and if he had made his report in writing, he might be removed by being sent on leave, or if he refused to take leave, as Fitzgerald feared he would, by being recalled. Merewether was to ensure that the sardars were given a fair hearing and the Khan was to be told that the British would not intervene to protect him.[37] On 20 March 1872, in obedience to Fitgerald's orders, Phayre handed over to Colonel W.G. Mainwaring, who had served on the Upper Sind frontier in command of Jacob's Rifles from the time of its being raised in 1858. An able and sensible officer, he made no difficulty about following Merewether's instructions while waiting for further developments.

Phayre still had friends in high places. His elder brother, Sir Arthur 'Burmese' Phayre was Chief Commissioner of British Burma, the last province to be visited by Mayo prior to his assassination, and it is likely that the grievances of Robert Phayre, whose view of the Kalat question Mayo accepted, had been discussed then. After returning from leave in England, Robert Phayre was in March 1873 apponted Resident at Baroda, a post since Outram's time in the gift of the Government of India rather than Bombay. There, he accused the Gaekwar, Mulhar Rao, of misgovernment and in November 1874 claimed Mular Rao had tried to poison him. The Government of India had already decided to remove Phayre and on 25 November he was succeeded by Sir Lewis Pelly, who, under Frere's patronage, had been British Resident in the Persian Gulf. Nothing was proved against Mulhar Rao, despite a trial that attracted attention throughout the sub-continent (including Kalat), but in April 1875 he was deposed by the British as unfit to rule.

Sandeman's own ambitions for a greater part in the affairs of Balochistan remained unabated. In the cold weather of 1872–73 he showed visitors to his district of Dera Ghazi Khan a map of the frontier and pointed to Quetta, saying "That is where we should be and that is where I hope to be some day".[38]

Such a view was not in accord with that of the London government. There, in January 1873, Gladstone's Cabinet had secured an agreement with the Russians for a neutral zone in Central Asia, with Amir Sher Ali's dominions accepted by both sides as being outside the Russian and inside the British spheres of influence. Argyll approved building on this by sending a British mission into Aghanistan to inform him of the Anglo-Russian accord and announce the results of British arbitration between him and the Shah of Iran over the disputed Sistan border. Amir Sher Ali replied that he had no wish for a British officer in his country, especially to tell him about Sistan where the British had awarded the most fertile areas to Iran. His foreign minister, Nur Muhammad, journeyed to Simla in July 1873, and made it clear that the Amir had no faith in Russian promises nor British assurances of support. If the British had failed to help him against Iran, which was weak, how would they help him against Russia, which was strong. Rather than end the system of military conscription he had recently introduced, he would accept the unpopularity it had brought him, and build up his regular army so that he could rely on his own resources. Refugees from Khiva (recently defeated by Russia) had entered his country and might try to carry on the struggle, so provoking a Russian invasion. His nephew, Abdul Rahman, who had reigned briefly at Kabul during the wars of succession after Dost Muhammad's death, was a pensioner of the Russians in Tashkent. Who could say that they would not use him just as the British had used Shah Shuja-ul-Mulk?

Amir Sher Ali's suspicions about British intervention in his affairs were heightened when, early in 1874, Mayo's successor, Lord Northbrook took up the case of the Amir's eldest son, Yakub Khan. This prince had become estranged from his royal father when the Amir recognised his favourite son, Abdulla Jan, as heir to the throne. After a series of revolts and reconciliations, Yakub Khan was appointed governor of Herat, but at the beginning of 1874, after having gone to Kabul on a promise of safe conduct, he was arrested. Northbrook attempted to ameliorate Yakub Khan's treatment, writing, in the conventional formula, as 'a friend and well-wisher'. Amir Sher Ali replied that 'sincere and intelligent friends do not like under any circumstances to put their faithful friends to such shame, least of all by interceding on behalf of an undutiful son whose misdeeds his own father was ashamed to repeat'.

10

THE KAFILAS AND THE COLLAPSE
OF BRITISH CONTROL, 1872–76

> "In a turquoise twilight, crisp and chill,
> A kafila camped at the foot of the hill
> And the picketed ponies, shag and wild,
> Strained at their ropes as the feed was piled;
> And the bubbling camels beside the load
> Sprawled for a furlong a-down the road;
> And the Persian pussy-cats, brought for sale,
> Spat at the dogs from the camel-bale..."

> Rudyard Kipling. *The Ballad of the King's Jest.*

Jacobabad Award

At Jacobabad, freed from the counter-productive presence of Sandeman and Phayre, Merewether delivered his findings.[1] He told the sardars that they were entirely in the wrong and that their demands were such as no previous Khan had ever accepted, and utterly incompatible with proper government. In the Khan's name, he ordered them to restore everything stolen from the kafilas or the cultivators. If they accepted the Khan's authority, they would not be required to compensate him for plundered government property and would be pardoned, with the restoration of all grants made by Nasir Khan II.[2]

Merewether's generosity to the rebels owed much to his belief that they had been encouraged 'by one high in authority on this frontier' (i.e. Phayre), but was also intended to give them terms they could afford to meet. He asked again for a lakh of rupees, this time to compensate the Khan for the liberal terms granted in his name. The Kalat treasury, he explained, had been drained by the campaign in Kachhi, and there would be no land revenue there that year because the fighting had brought agriculture to a stand-still. Aitchison congratulated him on the 'exceptionally well chosen terms' of his remarks to the sardars. Nothing was said about the lakh of rupees. On the contrary, the Khan was to be told that the British would not support him if he drove his subjects into rebellion and Nur al-Din Mingal (excluded from the Jacobabad conference because he had remained in arms and plundered another kafila) was to be offered mediation if the Khan could not defeat him.

The attacks on the kafilas, April–May 1872

Early in April 1872 at Abigum, the plain between Quetta and the top of the Bolan, a 600-strong band of Samalani Mingals (Brahuis) attacked the camp of the Baloch Sardar Sher Dil Mazarani. The Mazaranis, taken by surprise, fled to the nearby hills with the loss of all their belongings. These included their sheep, for whose fleece they had already been advanced 3,000 rupees by a Pashtun merchant, Khush Muhammad (who had warned both them and the Naib of Mastang of the impending raid). Many around the Bolan believed that the Khan was behind this attack, either out of annoyance because the Mazaranis (a Marri clan) had received payments from Sandeman, or to stir trouble and to evade the terms of Merewether's award. From Quetta and Mastang the Naibs reported that, before the raid, they had ordered the Samalanis to disperse and, although their messengers had not arrived in time to prevent the raid, thousands of the Mazaranis' sheep had been recovered and were being held by the Naibs. Daroga Atta Muhammad, who had set out with troops to intercept the Samalanis, confirmed their stories.

The Samalanis at first claimed that this raid had been in retaliation for Marri depredations elsewhere but later alleged that it had been incited by the two Naibs in return for a one-fifth share of the proceeds. This figure was mentioned to Harrison by both Khush Muhammad himself and Sayyad Sher Dil, a Pashtun horse-coper and supplier of remounts to the Bombay Army (generously described in the Kalat Diary reporting this raid as 'a respectable merchant'). It may, however, represent no more than the kind of fee commonly paid in pastoral societies to those who cared for animals impounded after being found strayed or stolen. As with the 'pounders' of medieval England and the early USA, it was commonly believed that officials whose income was boosted in this way worked in league with cattle thieves.

Blaming the Kalat authorities for the loss of his sheep and the death of his son, who had been killed during the raid, Sardar Sher Dil returned to Abigum with 200 Mazaranis and on 18 April attacked a kafila coming down from Quetta. This was partly to injure the Khan, whose British subsidy depended on the safety of the caravans, and partly to allow his tribesmen to make up for what they had lost to the Samalanis. The merchants and drivers offered resistance and the Mazaranis, with several of their number killed in the fighting, succeeded in carrying off only a few camels. The Khan sent a message to Sardar Sher Dil telling him that the local naibs had been ordered to recover his sheep, by force if necessary, and that he should keep the peace. Meanwhile, the naibs were ordered to close the Bolan and divert all kafilas via Kalat and the Mulla Pass. This route, though longer in time and distance, kept the kafilas away from the Marris, with the added benefit to the Khan that all the transit tolls would go into his depleted treasury.

At Dadhar another kafila was waiting to go up the Bolan. The Naib, Abd al-Wahad, had not yet received the orders to close the pass, but scented trouble when the six Mazarani riders sent to provide the token escort in return for Sardar Sher Dil's one-third share of the transit tolls (an arrangement newly agreed with the Khan), refused to accept responsibility. The merchants, anxious to reach their markets and possibly emboldened by the escape of the last kafila, rejected the naib's advice to postpone their departure and demanded a passage. He therefore put together an escort of seventy horse and foot from local Brahui contingents, but took the precaution of securing a bond from the kafila-bashi agreeing that, if the kafila were attacked, any compensation claimed by the merchants would be set against blood money payable to the escort. He then recorded that he took 110 rupees as transit fees for a total of sixty-three camels and 205 donkeys.

On 6 May 1872, when the kafila was two days inside the pass, Sardar Sher Dil Mazarani attacked with a thousand men from various Marri clans. The escort was overwhelmed and only one man returned to Naib Abd al-Wahad. The merchants and drivers banded together to defend their property, but several were killed, many wounded, and all suffered serious financial loss by the theft of animals and loads. Sardar Ala al-Din Kurd, in the area claiming to collect stolen property as part of the Jacobabad agreement, arrived while the raid was in progress and forced the Marris to disgorge some of their loot. He ordered the wounded to be cared for and sent them on to Quetta with what he had recovered. Merewether was unimpressed by the presence of Ala al-Din Kurd, whom he described as 'a subtle character, most unscrupulous in his sayings and doings. Much of the evil that has occurred in the country during the past nine years may with justice be laid at the door of this restless schemer'. Other survivors made their way to Kalat, meeting Harrison on the road as he returned from Jacobabad.[3]

Harrison at first was inclined to believe that the raid was in retaliation for the defeat inflicted on the Mazaranis by the previous kafila but early in June 1872 heard rumours that the Khan was responsible. When he raised the matter, Khudadad Khan showed him a report from the Naib of Dadhar, who had written (with remarkable prescience, as events were later to prove) 'Your Highness, I am perfectly convinced that Captain Sandeman has caused all these disturbances in the Bolan, in hopes that he may ultimately get charge of this country'. The Khan himself blamed the dissident Sarawans who, having plundered Kachhi, now wished to discredit Sardar Sher Dil Mazarani and obtain his share of the Bolan transit tolls for themselves. As for the stolen sheep, he said his naibs had recovered 5,000 animals from the Brahui thieves and were waiting for Sardar Sher Dil Mazarani to collect them.

There had now been four kafilas attacked in six months (one by the Sarawans in January 1872, one by Nur al-Din Mingal during the Jacobabad conference, and two by Sher Dil Mazarani). Many survivors were at Kalat, starving and penniless. Others had gone to Kandahar, leading Amir Sher Ali of Afghanistan (Dost Muhammad's son and successor) to call on the Government of India to make the Bolan safe and compensate the merchants. The Amir's son, Sardar Nur Ali Khan, governor of Kandahar, wrote to Khudadad Khan asking for compensation for 6,000 rupees worth of the Amir's property lost in these raids, unless the Khan needed the money in which case, for friendship's sake, he should keep it. The Khan's reply was that the whole country had suffered from robbers, himself more than anyone, and surely the Amir knew this. He expressed surprise at being asked for compensation and said the best he could do was to attempt recovery of the stolen property or its cash equivalent from the Brahuis. He refused to be held responsible for the Marris, whom he regarded as outside his control.

The Khan's new ministers

By this time, Harrison had come to believe that Khudadad Khan was indeed out to destroy the Jacobabad settlement. It would, after all, not have been unreasonable for the Khan to resent the terms awarded by Merewether in his name. He had followed British advice about extending his authority only to find that, when this provoked a rebellion, he was denied aid and left worse off than before. He had never really expected the rebels to accept mediation, and although Merewether's terms were not very different from those he had himself previously offered, it was now more likely that, as they had British support, he would be forced to implement them. During the absence of Harrison and Wazir Wali Muhammad at Jacobabad, he turned to other councillors. Among these were Nawab Mulla Muhammad Khan, the former vakil, whom the Khan had recalled but later restored to favour, and Commandant Shakar Khan, an officer who had been dismissed for misconduct from one of the Bombay Army's Baluch battalions. He had found this no bar to promotion in the Khan's service and, having performed gallantly during the recent campaign in Kachhi, hoped to succeed the late Commandant Sher Khan as Commander in Chief of the Khan's regular troops.

The Khan also leaned towards Abdul Aziz, a Pashtun merchant, who hoped to become Wazir through the support of the Khan's influential stepmother, Bibi Ganjan, and sister, Bibi Fata Khatun, who had a son old enough to succeed to the throne. The courtiers whom Harrison regarded as having the most pernicious influence were two munshis, Gul Muhammad and Salah Muhammad. They had been secretaries under Wazir Mulla Muhammad Hasan in the time of Nasir Khan II, who had them beaten, fined and imprisoned for their involvement in the wazir's schemes to dethrone him. Released by Khudadad Khan, they were employed by his anti-British minister Ganga Ram and then, after Ganga Ram's dismissal, by Wazir Wali Muhammad. Harrison believed that, having made fortunes by corruption during the recent troubles, they feared the coming of peace, when their accounts would be examined and their wrong-doing discovered.

Harrison blamed these new counsellors for Khudadad Khan's refusal either to give relief to the starving merchants at his gate or promise them some redress. In vain did he tell the Khan that his naibs had no right to take fees for safe conduct they could not provide. In vain did he point out that the Khan was still responsible for the acts of his subjects, even of those in revolt. Relations grew worse still when on 14 June 1872 Wazir Wali Muhammad came to Harrison's tent to seek protection, claiming that the Khan was about to arrest him and have him killed for his part in the Jacobabad settlement. Harrison went to see the Khan, who swore that he never intended to harm the wazir nor was he displeased by Merewether's award. He declined to discuss the subject unless the wazir disclosed the name of his informant and proved all the allegations. He later gave the wazir a written guarantee of safety, but further messages reached Wali Muhammad advising him to put no trust in this nor on any account to leave the English camp.

Smarting under the wrongs he had endured at the hands of rebels encouraged by Phayre and Sandeman, and aware of developments in the Great Game beyond his border, Khudadad Khan believed that the British would not dare break with him for fear that he would welcome the Russians. He told Harrison that Russia was backing the Iranian claims to Sistan and that, if the Afghans resisted, there would be serious fighting, with Balochistan becoming very important to the English government. The least the British should offer him was ten lakhs of rupees annually, as they gave the Amir of Kabul twelve.

Merewether formed the view that there was more behind this change of attitude than mere caprice, to which Khudadad Khan had always been considered prone, and agreed with Harrison in attributing it to the new counsellors. He wrote to the Khan, as his 'oldest and best friend', urging him to hold back from his 'reckless and unreasonable course', investigate the charges against his naibs, honour the terms of the agreement awarded in his name, restore his confidence in the British Agent and Wazir Wali Muhammad, 'the most faithful and true servant a sovereign ever had' and turn away the evildoers who only sought his ruin. The Khan replied that his naibs were not to blame for Sher Dil's raids. 'You, my friend, know how lawless the Murrees are, and their thieving propensities'. He said that he could not afford to pay compensation on their account and he looked upon the Political Agent as his elder brother. 'I therefore do not act without his advice; consequently the hint you give about recalling him does not please me.'

As for Major Shakar Khan and the two munshis, the Khan stated that they had served him faithfully and honestly in their respective duties and had never been guilty of a single bad action. He had agreed to all the terms made in his name and accepted Merewether's forgiveness of those who had devastated his country. The wazir, accordingly, had committed no fault by his involvement in the award. 'Why therefore should I commit any injustice towards him?... As long as I live it cannot be proved against me'. He ended on a note of reproach. 'My friend, from the day I was first obedient to the English Government to the present day, I have followed the same course and entrusted my life and property to God and the English Government... I am hopeful that the more I am supported by the English Government, the greater service I and my country will be to them.'

Attempts to recover property stolen from the kafilas continued, with limited success, throughout June 1872. The merchants, as the price of wool had fallen, wanted its original cash value rather the actual fleeces. The Khan told Harrison he hated his sardars so much that if they eventually entered Paradise he would rather go to Hell. Azad Khan Nausherwani of Kharan wrote to the wazir 'I have heard that you and His Highness distrust each other. This is the way of the Ahmedzais; they would murder their most devoted servant for Rs 5... I myself served the present Khan to the best of my ability, but from first to last derived no benefit'. As tension increased, Merewether sent a company of Jacob's Rifles to reinforce Harrison's cavalry escort. Commandant Shakar Khan riposted with noisy patrols that shouted and howled around the British camp at all hours of the night and encouraged his men to talk of *jihad* (Holy War). One sepoy fired a shot into Harrison's tents, but Khudadad Khan had no intention of allowing matters to go so far and threw him into prison, where he remained for the next five years.

Faced with British threats to break off diplomatic relations, the Khan reluctantly dismissed Commandant Shakar Khan and the two munshis but still refused to pay compensation for the plundered kafilas. Only when Harrison produced a message from Merewether recalling him to Jacobabad and set about hiring camels for his journey did the Khan give way. Rather than risk losing the British subsidy, he promised to settle all outstanding claims as soon as he could. The master of the caravan plundered by Nur al-Din Mingal was advanced 5,000 rupees, to be recovered from that sardar's jagirs in Kachhi. The merchants robbed by Sardar Mulla Muhammad Raisani were given 30,000 rupees, the difference between what they had lost and what the Brahuis had returned. Shahgasi Wali Muhammad resumed his duties as wazir and Sardar Fakir Muhammad Bazanjau was re-instated as Naib of Kech, experience having proved that no-one else could control the country. Against this, the ex-vakil Nawab Mulla Muhammad remained at court and visited the Khan after dark, and the Naibs of Quetta and Mastang were retained in post.

British relations with the Khan

Mayo's successor as governor-general was Thomas Baring, 2nd Baron Northbrook, a Liberal peer who had served as Under-Secretary of State for India from 1861 to 1864 and as the junior minister for War from 1868 to 1872. Touring his new areas of responsiblity, he went up the Indus in the steamer *Outram* during November 1872 and Khudadad Khan, hoping to appeal unto Caesar, accepted an invitation to meet him at Sukkur. Little good came of this. Northbrook merely continued the line taken by his officials and told the Khan to be reconciled with the sardars and forget his evil counsellors. Khudadad Khan offered to perform any service the British wanted, but insisted he could not govern his country without sometimes taking harsh measures. He asked for permission to re-instate Commandant Shakar Khan and the two munshis, who had accompanied their master to the conference, but this was denied and the three were detained by Merewether as political prisoners. The Khan, who spoke no English, was not able to express all he wanted to say and took his leave, fearing that he too would be arrested. Back in Kalat, he was taunted by his ladies for having returned with a few presents instead of his own good servants.

Khudadad Khan sought another meeting with Merewether in the hope of securing their release, but was told that all claims from the plundered kafilas must be met first. He agreed to a scheme devised by Harrison and the wazir, whereby the merchants compensated at a rate of ten annas for every rupee claimed (sixteen annas equalling one rupee). Cash and bonds amounting to 90,000 rupees were handed over and claims against the robbers were thereby transferred from the merchants to the Khan. He wrote to Merewether that he saw no possibility of recovering the money without causing another rebellion and had paid the merchants only in order to achieve a meeting with him. This took place on 21 Frebruary 1873, and although longer than the perfunctory audience with Northbrook, was equally unsatisfactory to both sides. Merewether refused to release the three 'favourites', as he called them, because they would supplant the British-nominated Wazir Wali Muhammad. The Khan refused to discuss anything else and spoke of abdicating on the grounds that, if he could not keep even such poor creatures at his court, he obviously had no power over his country, and that everyone, even Harrison, had turned against him. The wazir also spoke of resigning, to make way for someone in whom the Khan had more confidence.

Merewether had to accept that the policy by which, for nearly twenty years, control of Kalat had been exercised through a Political Agent working with a British-approved wazir had collapsed. He made one last effort to persuade the Khan to become reconciled to his sardars, urging that if peace was established, all parties would benefit; the planned extension of irrigation works from the Indus into Kachhi would produce work and good crops for many of the Khan's subjects; the new Sind railway would attract more traffic down the Bolan; and the 1871 Mithankot arrangements, at last about to be implemented, would bring steady wages to the hill tribes, paid by the British in the Khan's name. He advised that a Naib should be sent to Las Bela, out of control since the rising led by the son of the exiled Jam in 1871. He even promised to try once more to remedy the Khan's long-standing grievance that, under the 1854 treaty, his treasury lost more through the lowering of the transit fees than it gained from the subsidy.

The Khan's answer was to forbid his subjects to have any part in the Mithankot settlement, saying that the Bolan was safe when his government was strong and would remain unsafe until his authority there was re-established. He told Merewether that Phayre and Sandeman had interfered so much with the Marris that he no longer considered them his subjects. As for Las Bela, if the wazir wanted to recapture it with Brahui contingents, as he had often claimed was possible, he might do so, but all the regular troops who could be trusted were needed as a personal bodyguard and it was useless to send those who could not be trusted. His best offer would be the appointment of Sardar Azad Khan Nausherwani of Kharan as governor of all Makran, thus making him an ally and separating him from Sardar Mulla Muhammad Raisani. Khudadad Khan then irritated Merewether further by raising a third regiment of infantry, commanded by the former Naib of Dadhar, though his existing troops had not been paid for many months.

The final decision to break off relations with Kalat arose from a query by Colonel F.A.E. Loch, who took over from Mainwaring as Political Superintendant and Commandant, Upper Sind Frontier, in February 1873. Originally an officer in the 3rd Bombay Light Cavalry, and commandant of the 3rd Scinde Horse since 1870, he soon formed the view that in view of the deteriorating situation at Kalat, Harrison's escort should be increased to two troops of cavalry and a double-company of Jacob's Rifles. Such a force would need to be accompanied by 40,000 rupees in the paymaster's treasure-chest, a sum Loch thought large enough to attract the Khan's unpaid troops into attacking the British camp (a scenario resembling events that would in fact occur at Kabul six years later). As it seemed to him increasingly likely that the Political Agent would have to be withdrawn and the Khan and sardars left to their own devices, he asked Merewether for a decision before the troops and the treasure were sent. On 5 April 1873 a formal note was delivered to the Khan at Gandava, in which Merewether stated 'All that has passed lately and is passing now goes to show that it is utterly useless attempting to aid Your Highness with advice... [it is] derogatory to the honour of my Government to allow the Political Agent to remain any longer at your court.' Four days later, despite the Khan's pleas, Harrison and Wazir Wali Muhammad, with two hundred of the wazir's friends, family and retainers, left for Jacobabad.

The extent to which British influence in Kalat had collapsed was not immediately appreciated. Northbrook accepted Harrison's recall as a logical outcome of decisions he had already approved. Merewether forecast that Khudadad Khan would realise how weak he was without British support and agree once more to British advice, or else be driven from the throne by a new rebellion. At the India Office, John Melville, assistant secretary to the Political and Secret Committee, questioned the wisdom of Merewether's actions. 'The Government of India say that not only will they withhold the subsidy, but continue to hold the Khan responsible for the acts of his nominal subjects, whom, even with its aid, he cannot control. This is a thorough case of making bricks without straw.—A more certain way of throwing the man into the hands of bad advisers, perhaps, eventually, of Russia, and of shaking his confidence in the British Government, could hardly be devised.' The Committee, however, agreed with Argyll, the Secretary of State, that it was out of the question to intervene, as Northbrook had threatened this action in his personal interview with the Khan at Sukkur.

From Gandava, the Khan returned to his citadel at Kalat, where the fruit trees that year were barren, widely held to be a consequence of the British Agent's departure. Daroga Atta Muhammad declined appointment as wazir (though later was persuaded to accept) and urged the Khan to seek the return of Shahgasi Wali Muhammad and Harrison. Nawab Muhammad Khan remained the Khan's most influential adviser. The Brahui sardars, whom Merewether had expected to dethrone Khudadad Khan, failed to unite against him, and continued to plunder Kachhi, which offered their tribesmen better prospects of loot. When kafilas between Karachi and Las Bela were attacked by a bandit chief, Nausherwan Chuta, the Khan sent Sardar Nur al-Din Mingal to arrest the thieves and murderers and recover the stolen property. The sardar reported that he had secured an offer of camels as alternatives to those stolen from the kafilas, but no-one would consider giving compensation in cash as there were rumours that Jam Mir Khan II (Nur al-Din's brother-in-law) was about to return from India and recover his country. Having recovered as much stolen property as he could, and collected the land revenue, Nur al-Din then retired with the proceeds to the Mingal stronghold at Wad. Further north, Iranian incursions into Sistan (intended to influence the decisions of the Afghan-Iranian boundary commission) were repulsed by local Rind sardars, acting on Azad Khan Nausherwani's orders.

The raid on the Lower Sind fronter

In February 1874, three families of cultivators entered Lower Sind from Jhalawan seeking refuge in British territory. They were pursued across the border by Sardar Pahar Khan with 200 armed Brahuis, claiming that the asylum-seekers were his runaway slaves and that the animals in their possession belonged to him. A constable of the Sind Police, sent by the Collector of Shikarpur to investigate, was detained by the Brahuis, and while the men fled, their families and animals were taken back across the border. The Collector asked Loch, as Political Superintendant, Upper Sind, to arrange for those responsible to be arrested and sent to Shikarpur, on the grounds that once the cultivators entered British territory, they became free. Loch replied that, if the police allowed thieves to enter British territory, it was not to be wondered at if their victims crossed the border to recover the stolen property. Nevertheless, he admitted that this did not excuse Pahar Khan's conduct, and asked Merewether (to whom, as Commissioner in Sind, both parties answered) for further orders.

The most serious aspect of the incident, in Merewether's view, was its location, the previously quiet frontier of Lower Sind, guarded only by a few policemen. On 10 March, arguing that, without an immediate response, others would copy Pahar Khan's example and the whole border line would have to be held by troops, he recommend a full-scale military expedition into Kalat. One column would march from Karachi into Las Bela and restore order there. Another would go from Jacobabad to Kalat and occupy the city until the Khan complied with his treaty obligations. The Khan should be prevented from fleeing to Sistan, but no countenance given to the dissident sardars. Shahgasi Wali Muhammad should be re-appointed wazir, and a Regency Council established under the guidance of the newly promoted Major Harrison. A proclamation should be issued saying that the British came only to enforce the treaty and re-establish good government. Asserting that the British had the moral right to intervene in a neighbouring state when their wider interests were at stake, and pointing out that the existing treaty allowed them to station troops anywhere in Kalat, he asked for approval before the onset of the hot weather made movement difficult.

In the same month as Sardar Pahar Khan was disturbing the peace of the Sind frontier, a British general election replaced Gladstone and the Liberals by Disraeli and the Conservatives and the Marquess of Salisbury (formerly Viscount Cranborne) returned to the India Office as Secretary of State. In a reversal of the way in which Mayo, appointed by the Conservatives, had become responsible to a Liberal Ministry, Northbrook, appointed by the Liberals, became responsible to a Conservative Ministry. It was therefore to Salisbury that, on 27 March 1874, Northbrook privately forwarded his own views on Merewether's proposal to invade Kalat. 'The Khan, whom I saw in the autumn of 1872 in Scinde, is a mere savage... and we had to withdraw the payment he received on condition of keeping the routes through his country open. He has quarrelled, moreover, with his Barons, and the chances are that before long he will be dethroned or otherwise disposed of. Our policy was to leave him alone but the other day Sir W Merewether sent a telegram to report there had been a raid of some sort on our people, and that we ought to advance at once into the Khan's country in force. We have asked for further information and my feeling is strong against such an expedition.'[4]

The influence of the Great Game

Salisbury had told Northbrook on 6 March 1874 that the Cabinet as a whole was against making an issue of Russian moves against the Turkmans because, as St Petersburg had given repeated assurances that none were planned, another protest could achieve no more if the Russians were sincere, or be met with another falsehood if they were not. The official reply to Merewether, sent by Aitchison on 21 April 1874, therefore said that the Russians were threatening to march into Turkman territory, between the Atrek and Khiva, which would bring them within striking distance of Herat and Afghanistan, but the British could not object if, at the same time, and for similar reasons, they were themselves marching into Kalat. Such a move, Aitchison wrote, would revive Afghan suspicions of British intentions and undo all that had been achieved there in recent years. Although the cessation of Russian advances and the goodwill of the Afghans were not to be purchased at the cost of humiliation in Kalat, wider considerations than obtaining satisfaction for a border outrage had to be taken into account. Merewether was reminded that the instructions previously given to him had distinctly envisaged the possibility of negotiating directly with the sardars if the Khan proved unable or unwilling to fulfil his treaty obligations.[5]

In May 1874 Aitchison, on furlough in London, attended the India Office for a series of discussions on Central Asia. The new Permanent Secretary, Sir Louis Mallet, (previously a member of the Council of India, to which he had been appointed for his experience at the Board of Trade) formed the view that Aitchison and other Indian Political officers wanted 'a sort of protectorate over Afghanistan or Persia', involving indefinite expenditure at a time when the demands of famine and public works placed Indian finances under strain. 'Nothing could be gloomier than Aitchison's predictions' he wrote to Northbrook on 5 June 1874. 'Settlement officers, engineers, soldiers and lawyers all conspire to spend money, and who is to pay in the end?'.[6]

After seeing Aitchison, Salisbury decided that the Indian intelligence sytem was inadequate, and that agents should be installed at Herat and Kabul. If possible, this was to be done openly, with Amir Sher Ali's consent. If not, then secretly. 'Of course, it would need a large expenditure of Secret Service money, but it would be well laid out. You may be sure the Russians are not stinting it'. Salisbury continued that, although he was against making a Russian occupation of Merv a *casus belli*, if only because it was beyond British reach, Herat was a very different matter, and he asked Northbrook to send him the Government of India's views on the feasibility of a British army marching there from the Indus.[7]

Northbrook's first response, in June 1874, was to suggest that information from Herat could be gathered by installing a consulate at Mashhad (thus transferring the cost to the Foreign Office). He opposed Salisbury's idea of setting up a separate Intelligence Department, on the grounds that it would only collect 'a mass of lies... and some truths which we are better ignorant of'. Tension with Russia seemed to be easing, with the expedition to Merv having been cancelled and the Duke of Edinburgh (Queen Victoria's sailor son) having earlier that year married a Russian princess, the Grand Duchess Maria, only daughter of Tsar Alexander II (a love-match, strongly opposed by the Queen herself). 'Is it quite impossible', Northbrook asked Mallet in June 1874 'for us to have an *entente cordial* with Russia upon Central Asia affairs?... [eventually] these semi-barbarous tribes will come more or less under Russian or English control'. He thought that although an expedition to Kalat was still possible, an advance to Herat would be just as dangerous as the policy that had led to the Afghan War.[8] Salisbury wrote to Northbrook in July 1874 that the British should be as ready for a march on Herat as the Prussians had been for a march on Paris (a reference to the recent Franco-Prussian War) and that Sir Frederick Goldsmid, due to return to India in September 1874, might be employed on surveying a route from Dadhar to Herat, under the guise of anxiety about the Bolan traffic and further arbitration of the Sistan boundary.[9]

Thus it was that on 18 August 1874 there came to Merewether not permission to invade Kalat, but a private letter from Northbrook asking for whatever information he had about the route from Jacobabad to Quetta, Kandahar and Herat. 'We are putting together all we know in the Quarter-Master-General's Department; and if you can help, I should be much obliged; only nothing must be said about it'. Merewether sent the desired information with the comment that the roads to Kalat and Quetta were well known to the local (Sind) officers, and the route to Herat was perfect for any army. He added that in Kalat things were 'as bad as can be' and everyone on the border was asking why something was not being done 'to bring the Khan to book for what he has done or allowed to be done, and to enforce good, or some, government' and that he was about to raise the subject of an expedition again, in a formal memorandum.[10]

The official reply to this memorandum was sent on 9 October 1874, rejecting Merewether's proposals out of hand. 'It cannot be too distinctly asserted that His Excellency in Council does not consider it to be the duty of the British Government by armed intervention to settle the administration of Khelat, or to adjust the quarrels between the Khan and his nobles, or to help the Khan assert a nominal suzereignty over tribes who refuse to recognise his authority'. British aims were limited to the prevention of outrages on or near the frontier and securing the safe transit of trade. As the raid of the previous February had not been repeated (this was due largely to the police reinforcements Merewether himself had sent there) there was no need for a military response. The post of Political Agent, Kalat, was abolished as there seemed no likelihood of a British presence being re-established, a decision that negated Merewether's plan of controlling an occupied Kalat through the Agent and the ex-wazir until a new khan was installed.

On the protection of caravans, the policy of treating the Marris and Bugtis as subjects of Kalat was declared to have failed 'after long and patient trial'. The blockade of their country advocated by Merewether was rejected as likely to injure British subjects on the Punjab border, alienate Baloch chiefs friendly to the British, and require extra troops. As Ghazan Khan, the Marri sardar, had recently disgorged part of what he had stolen from the kafilas and sent his nephew to pay his respects at Jacobabad (though he had declined to appear in person), the Government of India saw no need to strain this deference by forcing him to admit subjection to the Khan. A joint party of officers from the Punjab and Sind would therefore be sent into the Baloch hills to come to an agreement with Ghazan Khan Marri, explain that the British wanted only the protection of trade, try to settle inter-tribal disputes and, at last, arrange the employment of tribal levies as decided at the Mithankot conference of 1871.[11]

This marked the triumph of Sandeman and the Punjab Government. The only sop to Merewether was a private letter from Northbrook telling him that an expedition had been ruled out, and the tribes were to be dealt with directly, but inviting him, in view of the delicacy of the problem, to visit Calcutta for a personal discussion. Merewether, in a strongly-worded response, condemned the idea of negotiating with Sardar Ghazan Khan Marri. 'The Murrees have no grievances against the Khan and never had... they have persistently plundered his country and killed poor unoffending people as and when they pleased... such people as these wild mountaineers do not understand forbearance. They regard it as weakness and increase in audacity and insolence in proportion'. He went to Calcutta at the end of 1874, but Sandeman's presence there at the same time indicated that Northbrook was listening to other counsels. Merewether's forecasts that the Khan would be deposed and that raids on the Lower Sind border would continue had proved wrong and from then on his star began to wane.

On 5 January 1875 Aitchison officially notified Merewether that he was to cultivate friendly relations with the tribes for the defence of his border and the protection of trade. To secure unity of action between the Punjab and Sind authorities, Sandeman was to be the sole channel between the British and the Marris and Bugtis, but under the orders of the Commissioner in Sind, to whom he was to report through the Political Superintendant, Upper Sind Frontier, on all matters regarding these tribes, and from whom he should receive his instructions. Regarding tribes whose affairs concerned mainly Sind rather than the Punjab, he was to take no action without first referring to the Commissioner in Sind. Nevertheless, if Ghazan Khan Marri did not give up the loot he had acquired from Sher Dil Mazarani's attack on the Bolan kafila in 1872, relations with him would be broken off, 'a result which His Excellency in Council would much regret'. Sandeman was therefore to proceed into the hills at an early date, as the Punjab Government had proposed. Northbrook wrote to Salisbury privately on 8 January 1875 that Sandeman's party would include a military officer to examine the route from Dera Ghazi Khan to the Bolan, 'bearing in mind your desire for more information about Afghanistan and the neighbourhood'. On the same day he wrote privately to Sir Henry Davies, Lieutenant Governor of the Punjab, to select a young officer of the Punjab Frontier Force who would accompany Sandeman, reconnoitre the passes and report secretly anything of military value.[12]

The view from the India Office

At the India Office, these proceedings were noted without enthusiasm. In October 1874 Sir Henry Rawlinson had handed over the chair of the Political Committee to Sir Bartle Frere, formerly Commissioner in Sind and Governor of Bombay. The Committee's new permanent secretary, Major Owen Tudor

Burne, had been Mayo's private secretary in India before returning home when his wife became ill. He had been found a post as Political Aide-de-Camp to the Secretary of State for India, an appointment that now passed to Gerald Vesey Fitzgerald, son of Sir Seymour Fitzgerald, the former Governor of Bombay (succeeded in May 1872 by Sir Philip Wodehouse, late of the Colonial Service). In response to a note by Burne covering these papers, Salisbury commented 'The policy of the Government of India strikes me as rather feeble... These caravans are the only ghost of a civilising agent between the Russian outposts and our own... it is expedient just now not to give the Amir a pretext for pretending to be alarmed... but it looks like the only two evils the Calcutta F.O. cared about were blame and trouble'.[13]

Among the authorities consulted by Burne in preparing the India Office's response was Sir Henry Green, who wrote that, although he regretted opposing 'an old and valued comrade', he thought Merewether was inconsistent in advocating an expedition against Kalat while also admitting that, prior to Phayre's arrival, the Khan had been faithful to the British. Was it unreasonable of the Khan to change his policy, Green asked, when he found Phayre degrading him in the eyes of his subjects, and forwarding 'every frivolous complaint... by a set of restless, semi-barbarous, intriguing Chiefs, who when called upon over and over again to state their real grievances did not know what they were?' Green stressed that the Khan could only rule by setting chief against chief and tribe against tribe, and as this could only be done with money, depriving him of his subsidy left him powerless. 'I listened to the complaints of his Chiefs, but only through the Khan and with his permission... I never called on him to do what I knew he could not do, therefore there was no breach of the conditions of the treaty... but the moment an officer came who knew nothing of the politics or social status of the country, and who never listened to those that did, and further set himself up as a champion of the Chiefs against their ruler, then all things went to pieces'.

As for the Marris and Bugtis, he admitted that it was Jacob's insistence that they belonged to Kalat, coupled with the persistent antagonism between the Sind and Punjab frontier sytems, that had brought about the current difficulties and 'there can be no doubt that the silly cry of their being subjects of the Khan should finally be put on one side.' In the same letter, Green denounced Sardar Imam Baksh Mazari, Sandeman's go-between in dealing with the Marris and Bugtis, as a malign influence who profited personally from their raids, and claimed that Phayre's alliance with Sandeman had allowed Imam Baksh to begin intrigues with the Brahuis. A note on this letter in the India Office files, signed undecipherably except for an initial M, reads 'Sandeman in all the correspondence is a regular Bismarck'.[14]

A memorandum produced by the young Fitzgerald, echoing views previously expressed by his father when Governor of Bombay, blamed Phayre and Sandeman for the gravity of the rebellion in 1871, arguing that when Green and Merewether were in charge of the Upper Sind Frontier, no such serious disturbances occurred (failing to mention that Khudadad Khan had been deposed and his successor assassinated), although the personalities and circumstances in Kalat were the same. The Government of India's orders to Merewether to mediate officially in the quarrel (when previously such mediation by Green and Harrison had been informal and personal) had only alienated the Khan and 'the effect of that mediation is evidenced by the course advocated by Sir W Merewether. Originally strongly averse to interference, he had been led by circumstance, step by step, to interfere, until he now proposes an armed expedition, to depose the Khan and set up a new Government'.

Fitzgerald concluded that the safety of the Bolan, which depended on the hill tribes' respect for British power achieved by Napier and Jacob, had been lost by divided authority. Subsidizing the Marris directly would only encourage other tribes to plunder in the hope of being bought off similarly, while the Khan, deprived of his own subsidy, was unable to act against them. Fitzgerald's recommendation to Salisbury and the Council of India was to renew British friendship with the Khan and, in so doing, occupy Quetta. 'Thus you, without in any way committing yourself to a policy of advance, have a base above the passes, ensuring the safety of, at any rate, one trade route, the importance of which, looking to the fact of Russian advance, it is impossible to exaggerate, and which can be secured in no other way. The presence of our troops, also, would tend to pacify the country... besides the moral effect which a determined policy would have not only in Khelat, but in Central Asia generally'.[15]

Burne, his immediate superior, endorsed the view that the situation would not be helped by dealing with the tribes and ignoring the Khan. 'The Government of India appear to think that by placing Captain Sandeman under Sir William Merewether... they have the means of future bliss and comfort. They are, I fear, mistaken, and must in reality be conscious of it'. At the same time he drew attention to Mayo's idea of placing all the North-West Frontier from Peshawar to Karachi under a single Agent to the Governor-General, responsible for relations with all the frontier tribes and the border states beyond them. The frontier districts would have been exempted from the laws and regulations of the more civilised parts of India and the officers employed there would have formed an elite, trained in political duties, and paid at higher rates. 'In short, the scheme was intended to be an attempt not only to encourage activity and unity on the frontier, but to be the nucleus of a political school, the want of which is much felt in India'.[16]

Frere, as chair of the Council of India's political committee, entered the controversy by writing privately to Northbrook to support the occupation of Quetta. He also forwarded Henry Green's views about Sandeman and Imam Baksh amd added 'It will take long to undo all the evil done by the abolition of the school of frontier officers at Jacobabad, and by foolish obstinate men like Colonel Phayre, but I believe it might yet be done by Sir William Merewether, who so thoroughly knows that part of the country and its people'. Northbrook replied that he thought Green's 'bitter and unjust attack' on the Punjab frontier officers much weakened his arguments. As for Central Asian affairs in general, he told Frere, he still shared the opinions of Lawrence (Frere's old opponent, who at much the same time was writing to Northbrook in support of maintaining the close-border policy).[17]

After reading Burnes's note about frontier administration, Salisbury took up the subject in a private letter to Northbrook, saying it was not desirable for India's most exposed frontier to be under a divided rule, especially in view of the independent attitude often assumed by the Government of Bombay. He thought that the imminent completion of the Indus valley railway might help unify the North-West Frontier provinces but, if Sind was to be placed directly under the Government of India, then Bombay would have to be compensated with the Central Provinces, as it was undesirable to diminish either of the two minor presidencies. Northbrook answered that, although in 1872 he had decided against Mayo's plan to 'put Scinde under the Punjab', he now thought that, in view of the 'difficulty of working the Scinde authorities in harmony with the Punjab officers in dealing with the Murrees and Boogtis', they should be under the same local government. It is clear from this which of the two local governments enjoyed Northbrook's favour, not least because the Lieutenant-Governor of the Punjab came directly under the Government of India, whereas the Commissioner in Sind came under the Government of Bombay. Increasingly, Northbrook supported Sandeman against Merewether.[18]

The rise of Sandeman

While these exchanges between London and India were taking place, Sandeman, newly appointed as the sole channel for British relations with the Marris and Bugtis, met the Marri chiefs to negotiate the return of property stolen from the kafilas. Rather than risk losing the income received for not raiding the Punjab frontier, Sardar Ghazan Khan Marri (who had previously claimed to be so devout a personage that he could not enter lands under infidel rule) agreed to pay his respects to Loch at Jacobabad, with Sandeman remaining a hostage for his safe return. During 1875, under pressure from Sandeman, the Marris, despite having denied responsibility for any raids, handed over a large amount of property or its cash equivalent, including cattle stolen from the British border and Sibi. Sandeman, continuing his line that Marri raids in Kachhi were encouraged by the Khan or his officials as a means of acting against the dissident Brahui sardars, asked the Government of India's permission to enter Kalat territory and offer mediation to all the tribes involved. Merewether objected that it would be unwarrantable, after breaking off relations with the Khan, for the British to send an officer to deal with his chiefs. Sandeman should confine his dealings to the Marris and use the 1870 Mithankot subsidy to stop them plundering in Kachhi.

He was answered by a Resolution of the Government of India in the Foreign Department (which came directly under Northbrook as Governor-General) dated 16 October 1875, a document that would lead to far-reaching changes on both sides of the frontier. The recent agreements with the Marris, it began, were 'not only creditable to Captain Sandeman, but give reason to hope that the arrangements by which the conduct of our relations has been entrusted to that officer will in time produce more substantial results'. Policies that had secured the peace of the Punjab border were not to be discontinued because they had failed in Kachhi. Subjects of the Khan were not to be punished by either Sind or Punjab officers for crimes committed outside British territory, except that outposts of the Scinde Horse might deal with outrages within their reach if these threatened the Sind frontier. Frontier officers might use their personal influence to settle inter-tribal disputes, or disputes between the tribes and the Khan or the inhabitants of Sibi, but the Government of India would not be responsible for the peace of the country.

On the grounds that the causes of the disturbances that threatened the safety of the Bolan were imperfectly known, Sandeman was instructed to enter the hills 'at an early date' and gather what information he could about the various quarrels among the Marris, Bugtis, Brahuis and the people of Sibi. He was to settle as many of these as he could and to report, through the Commissioner in Sind, on those he could not, and also on relations between the Marris and Bugtis and the Khan. 'Sir William Merewether may, if he thinks fit, depute an officer from Sind to be associated with Captain Sandeman, but in subordination to him.' In addition, Sandeman was to examine and report on measures to protect caravans passing through the Bolan, and was given discretion 'to make any arrangements he may think advisable within the total sum sanctioned after the Mithankot conference, namely, Rs 66,960 per annum'. If these measures succeeded, and the Khan proved willing to accept them and express regret for the past, then friendly diplomatic relations, including the annual subsidy, could be restored.[19] Sandeman's victory was completed by his being authorised to investigate the re-opening of a route from the Punjab to Thal and Chotiali (districts lying north of the Marri country and roughly midway between Quetta to the west and Dera Ghazi Khan to the east), a project he had long advocated as an alternative to Kacchi and the Bolan. Salisbury's response to this Resolution was to tell Northbrook he would leave Kalat policy to be decided in India. 'If there had been no such person as the Ameer of Kabul' he wrote on 5 November 1875, 'I should have thought that the object of keeping the Bolan open was the ruling consideration, but the exact proportion of humouring and terrifying which are required for the treatment of his unstable mind cannot even be conjectured, except by the physicians who have charge of the case'.[20]

On 21 October 1875, before the Resolution reached him, Merewether had complained to Calcutta about Sandeman on several counts. One was that he apparently desired to deal with every tribe in Balochistan, 'citing the procedure of the late General Jacob years ago'. A second was that he had failed to stop the Marris from raiding kafilas in Kachhi. A third was that he had secured the installation of a new chief of the Bugtis. This was Sardar Shabaz Khan, whose father, Sardar Ghulam Murtaza, had lost control of his tribe, according to Sandeman because he was mentally ill, but according to Merewether because Sandeman withheld the funds that had supported his position. Shabaz Khan, contrary to the wishes of his father and the Commissioner in Sind, had betrothed himself to a Pashtun woman of known bad character in Jacobabad, and when the Sind authorities prevented her from leaving to join him, took revenge by plundering a kafila. He had been caught by a patrol of Scinde Horse and confined in Sukkur fort. Sandeman intervened and, going through the Punjab Government, obtained the Government of India's approval for his release. This had the effect of adding Sardar Shabaz Khan Bugti to the number of Baloch chiefs whose personal friendship and cooperation Sandeman claimed to have. At the same time, it worsened his own relations with Merewether, his official superior in dealings with the Marris, whose decision had thus, at Sandeman's instance, been over-ruled.

Sandeman's Mission to Balochistan

Having received no response to his complaints, Merewether drafted instructions to Sandeman ordering him to enter the hills and collect information as the Resolution of 16 October required, but on no account to deal with the tribes west of the Marri and Bugti countries, nor to attempt a settlement of their disputes with Brahuis without first reporting back.[21] These instructions were written at sea, while Merewether was returning from a conference at Bombay. He landed at Karachi on 20 November to find a telegram in which Sandeman reported he had gone into the Baloch hills in compliance with the Resolution (which had been sent to him direct by the Government of the Punjab, by-passing Bombay and Sind). Whether Sandeman had hurried on his 'early date' departure after learning that Merewether was about to be for several days at sea and so beyond reach of the telegraph can only be conjectured. He certainly gave Merewether no warning of his intended departure, though there was ample time to do so. He and his Punjab superiors also pre-empted the appointment of a Sind officer to accompany his mission, even in a subordinate capacity, and ensured it was exclusively a Punjab affair, with all the credit, if it proved a success, going to themselves. The only other officer was Captain Henry Wylie, 1st Punjab Cavalry, commanding the mission's escort. Although the official report makes no mention of it, it must be assumed that Wylie's real task was the secret survey of the route from Dera Ghazi Khan to the Bolan, as Northbrook had promised Salisbury and arranged with Davies, the Lieutenant Governor of the Punjab, early in 1875.

At Jacobabad, reports reached Loch that the dissident Sarawans had gathered in Sibi to confer with the exiled Sardar Mulla Muhammad Raisani. At the same time, Sardar Ali Khan Jamot, son of the exiled Jam, was reported to have joined Sardar Nur al-Din Mingal at Las Beyla, intending to march on Kalat and depose Khudadad Khan in favour of his eldest son. Many of the Khan's regular troops there, including their commandant, Fakir Muhammad, were expected to defect in return for promises of better pay. Nur al-Din Mingal wrote to the Sarawans at Sibi urging them to raid Kachhi as a distractrion from his advance. On 13 December Merewether telegraphed to Calcutta that a revolution in Kalat was clearly imminent and that he was going to the frontier to watch events. 'Sandeman in Murree hills by last accounts. Have told him of above and instructed him to be most careful to avoid any communication with Brahooee Sirdars... and on no account to go beyond Murree Hills towards Bolan, Seebee or Kutchee'. On 16 December Calcutta replied 'Policy of non-interference approved', though it soon became clear that this did not quite mean what it said.[22]

On 21 November, the day after learning that Sandeman had already left for the Baloch hills, Merewether had sent his own instructions after him, with a post-script to say that the mission should henceforth be conducted in accordance with them. By then, however, Sandeman was well on the way to achieving his own aims. He left Dera Ghazi Khan on 18 November, while Merewether was still at sea, and crossed the border at Harrand on 22 November. In addition to Wylie's troopers, he was accompanied by over a thousand riders from the Baloch tribes living inside British territory, led by their own sardars. Though in their reports both Sandeman and his Punjab superior, Colonel Munro, Commissioner of Derajat, imply that this was a spontaneous gathering of public-spirited peace-loving individuals, so large a body could scarcely have been assembled other than through the funds paid to the Baloch sardars for keeping the peace of the Punjab. As the mission proceeded on its way it was joined by the Khatran and Bugti sardars (including Sandeman's latest adherent, Shabaz Khan Bugti) with their own tribesmen. It reached Kahan on 2 December to be cordially welcomed by Sardar Ghazan Khan Marri. Writing on 10 December to his father in the United Kingdom, Sandeman recorded that he had marched in perfect security straight through the Marri hills, 'which is a political triumph in itself' and added that, though still with much to accomplish, he hoped to restore peace to a distracted country.

Sardar Ghazan Khan declared that although the Marris were willing to accept British mediation and had refused to join the imminent Brahui rising, there was no prospect of the Baloch tribes settling down while the Brahuis and the Khan of Kalat remained unreconciled and the consequent temptation to raid on behalf of one side or the other continued. If this could be achieved, he, Ghazan Khan, would personally guarantee that the hill tribes ceased plundering Kacchi. Sandeman pressed on to reach Sibi on 8 December, where he met Sardars Mulla Muhammad Raisani, Ala al-Din Kurd, and the other Sarawan dissidents. When they admitted they were about to begin hostilities, Sandeman said that if they really wished to avoid bloodshed, he would send their petition to the Khan with two of the Baloch sardars who had come with him from Dera Ghazi Khan. After discussions among themselves, the Sarawans agreed to this proposal, but insisted that they could not protect the Bolan traffic without the Khan's co-operation, nor could the Khan without theirs.

The petition, with a covering letter from Sandeman explaining his presence in the Khan's country, was therefore sent to Kalat. On 12 December the whole mission, increased to a force over 2,000 strong by the addition of the Sarawans and their retainers, set off for Dadhar pending the Khan's response. The Naib came out to meet Sandeman and assured him that the Khan would be delighted to hear of his coming, but at the same time told the Sarawans, in a triumphant manner, that Sardar Nur al-Din Mingal had accepted appointment as Naib of Las Beyla and thereby made a seperate peace with the Khan. Sandeman entered the town, where the merchants waited upon him to complain of the losses they had suffered through the continued closure of the Bolan.

Sandeman had by this time gone west of the Marri-Bugti country, entered Sibi (an Afghan enclave) to meet the Brahuis, and directly addressed the Khan, all contrary to Merewether's instructions, which he claimed did not reach him until 15 December 1875, three weeks after they had been despatched. He was thus able to say that they had been overtaken by events and sent his favourite Baloch henchman, Sardar Imam Baksh Mazari, to open negotiations at Kalat. Meanwhile he moved up the Bolan with his entourage, justifying this on the grounds that the Resolution of 16 October authorised him to investigate the protection of the caravans there. Just before reaching Quetta, he received a message from Loch at Jacobabad, sent on 13 December, a mere eight days earlier, warning him that a revolution in Kalat was imminent and repeating that he should not communicate with the Brahuis or proceed towards Sibi and the Bolan. Sandeman replied the next day, 22 December, with studied insolence. 'I left the Murree hills on the 10th instant or three days before your letter under reply was written. It will, however, doubtless afford the Commissioner in Sind pleasure and relief to know that the state of Khelat is so far tranquil that the contending parties, notwithstanding their differences, express their desire to maintain the peaceful state of the country'.[23]

The mission reached Quetta in 24 December, where the Naib received it with honours and handed over a letter in which the Khan expressed regret at the misunderstandings between himself and the British Govenment and offered to meet Sandeman at any place he cared to name. The Khan also wrote that he had made every effort to live at peace with his sardars since the Jacobabad settlement, although they had constantly attacked his subjects and plundered their crops and property, but was now willing, yet again, to suspend operations against them. Another letter, to the sardars, promised them a peaceful restoration of the rights they had enjoyed under Nasir Khan the Great if they accepted his authority.

Sandeman then made his way to Kalat. He was received on behalf of the Khan by Nawab Muhammad Khan, the former vakil at Jacobabad, who asked him if he had received any letters from the authorities in Upper Sind. 'On my replying in the affirmative, he asked in a very significant manner as to their purport', Sandeman wrote later. He evaded answering, but the vakil had a son living near Jacobabad who had sent to warn him that Sandeman lacked proper credentials. Nevertheless, the Khan granted Sandeman a series of audiences, repeating his claim that, as the current disorders resulted from the Jacobabad settlement, the terms of which neither he nor the sardars could fulfil, he was morally entitled to military and financial aid. He told Sandeman that he had an office filled with papers from the Commissioner in Sind advising him to adopt the policy he had followed and had, in consequence, 'spent many lakhs of rupees in fighting and coercing my Sirdars, whom I hate and who hate me'.

Eventually, he told Sandeman plainly 'No power has been given to you to dispose of my quarrel with Sirdar Mulla Muhammad and the other Brahooee Sirdars. Their quarrel with my Government has been settled by the Sind officers, and I cannot alter it without the authority of the British Government or I may fall between two stools. Did I listen to you and enter upon new agreements with the Murrees and Brahoees and afterwards did I find that the Sind officers had to put them into force, I would get no help from them, and my Sirdars would in consequence get their help and support to my great loss'.[24] This virtually ended the mission. A durbar was held at which, as usual, the dissident sardars promised the Khan their submission, and the Khan promised to forgive them for their past offences after he had heard from the British Government. After a further exchange of courtesies, Sandeman had to be satisfied with a letter from the Khan offering to explain himself to the Viceroy of India, either in person or through Sandeman, after which he began a chastened return towards British territory.

Shortly after leaving Kalat, Sandeman received a message from the Khan informing him that Sardar Nur al-Din Mingal, who had reached Kalat with his Jhalawan followers just before Sandeman and the Sarawans, had been killed. The sardar, invited there to be invested as Naib of Las Beyla, had been accommodated as a guest by the Wazir (former Daroga) Atta Muhammad, who pledged his safety by an oath on the Koran. Acccording to the Khan, the wazir and Nur al-Din conspired to assassinate him when he was at prayer inside the palace but their plot was discovered, leaving him no choice but to strike first to save his own life. Others said that the Khan, having lured Nur al-Din and other leading Jhalawans into Kalat, attacked them with 400 sepoys of the Foot Guard Regiment while Commandant Fakir Muhammad and his

Line regiment assaulted their main camp outside the walls. All accounts agree that Nur al-Din was killed along with about fifty of his men and that Wazir Atta Muhammad, either as an ally or mindful of his oath of the Koran and the laws of hospitality, fought alongside him. Two of the wazir's sons and his brother, Muhammad Ali, were among those killed, and the wazir himself was wounded by gunfire before fleeing with the surviving Jhalawans.

As Sandeman continued on his way, reports came of fighting in Kachhi, where on the Khan's orders a detachment of his troops had attacked a Brahui camp in retaliation for their recent raids, killing several men and seizing many sheep and goats. So far from Sandeman's mission having brought the peace and conciliation he had promised, affairs in Kalat were no better than they had been when it crossed the border. Northbrook told Salisbury on 14 January 1876, 'I shall be glad to hear that Sandeman is well out of the country. There is no doubt that the state of affairs is both intricate and critical. I hope nothing we have done has aggravated it, but it is not easy to say'.

The fall of Merewether

When Merewether learned of Sandeman's contact with the Brahuis at Sibi, he told Loch to order his immediate return to Dera Ghazi Khan. Though communications between Jacobabad and Sandeman's camp could go no faster than the express post-riders could gallop, those on the British side of the border moved with the speed of the electric telegraph. On 20 December Merewether was warned by the Calcutta Foreign Department to be careful not to interfere in the orders it had given Sandeman. He replied on 22 December that he did not understand and could not suppose that Sandeman had orders for what he was doing 'as it is directly contrary to policy laid down by Government of India and gravely insubordinate to me'. He forwarded the Kalat Diaries for 12 and 19 December, recording that Sandeman had reached Dadhar and opened peace talks just at the very time that the Sarawans had agreed with Nur al-Din Mingal and Azad Khan Nausherwani to seize Kalat and replace Khudadad Khan with his eldest son (an outcome that Merewether had long awaited). 'The Commissioner cannot express too strongly his disapproval and condemnation of the proceedings of Captain Sandeman... The Government of India desired that a policy of non-interference should be followed... yet a young officer with only a limited knowledge of what has previously passed comes in and issues orders where he has no business to appear'.[25]

Northbrook's Foreign Department made no immediate response. Possibly no-one cared to tell Merewether that 'policy of non-interference approved' did not mean what it said. Possibly it thought Sandeman was returning to India as Merewether had ordered. Possibly it was celebrating Christmas. In the event, it was Sandeman himself who forced a decision. On receiving Loch's orders (sent on 17 December) Sandeman answered that he was on special duty acting directly under the orders of the Government of India in accordance with the Resolution of 16 October. At the same time he sent another post-rider to the Punjab (but not to Jacobabad, though this was the nearest telegraph station) with a telegram direct to Calcutta, reporting that, although his mission had been welcomed enthusiastically by all parties, 'Loch directs me to return to Ghazee forthwith... My engagements with Khan and Murree Brahooe Sirdars do not admit of my attending to order. Doing so would in all likelihood involve the peace of the country. It is in my opinion opposed to the instructions contained in Government Resolution of 16th October... Please telegraph final instructions to Commissioner, Colonel Loch and myself'.[26]

Despatched on New Year's Day 1876, when Sandeman's riders reached the Punjab telegraph, this obliged Northbrook to settle the question of who was to implement British policy towards Baluchistan. Aitchison telegraphed to Merewether on 7 January that it was he, not Sandeman, who had not properly understood the Resolution of 16 October, that Sandeman seemed to have stopped the outbreak of a civil war and that his conduct did not warrant Merewether's strong expressions of blame. Accordingly, Sandeman was to be gazetted a Political Agent directly under the orders of the Government of India (a solution suggested by the Punjab Government) keeping Merewether informed of all his actions and communicating through him if possible. When Merewether objected, he was told 'Your telegram of 9th January and previous papers exhibit views and policy in regard to Khelat quite incompatible with those of the Government of India. Governor-General in Council has no other course left than to relieve you of responsibility for Khelat affairs. Colonel Munro will be ordered from Punjab to Jacobabad to take political charge. Colonel Loch will be relieved of all responsibity for affairs in Khelat except his military duties'. Merewether was ordered to take no action regarding Kalat without prior reference to Calcutta, remain at Jacobabad until Munro arrived and comply promptly with all police or military requisitions he might make along the entire Sind-Kalat frontier.[27]

This abrupt decision gave the Punjab the final victory in its thirty years' war with Sind over frontier policy. Punjab officers now exercised political authority from the border of Afghanistan to that with Iran. Sandeman, after ten years of agitation, had succeeded in extending his political remit from the few miles of his own district frontier not only to the Baloch hills and the Bolan Pass, but the entire Khanate of Kalat. As a favourite son of the Punjab Government, he had allies in Calcutta, while Merewether, identified with the Sind school and, moreover an officer of the Bombay Government, Calcutta's ancient rival, was without support. He had not been told that Sandeman's mission was cover for Wylie's secret survey of routes through the Baloch hills. Indeed, as he had previously reported that all these routes were well known to the local Sind officers, he could scarcely have supposed it existed. Northbrook, having promised just such a survey in response to Salisbury's pressure, had every reason to countermand Merewether's orders for its recall.

This sudden transfer (by telegram) of political control of the Sind frontier to the Punjab also went some way towards Northbrook's long-term aim of placing the entire province of Sind under the Punjab Government and removing it from Bombay. There is no evidence that Sandeman's instructions were deliberately drafted to engineer a constitutional crisis, but many in Bombay thought that he would not have openly defied Merewether without special instructions from someone senior.[28] Sandeman's own insistence that he was directly under the orders of the Government of India gives credence to this, unless he himself had either misunderstood the orders or was simply gambling on a ruling in his favour. Nevertheless, the Resolution of 16 October showed that Northbrook had been persuaded that, where Merewether had failed to safeguard the Bolan traffic (as Salisbury wanted), Sandeman, given the chance, might succeed.

Merewether's error was in not accepting that the decision had gone against him, the Commissioner in Sind, who had held its frontier since the heroic early days of Baloch-hunting. Seeing Sandeman once more trespassing on his turf, just at the very time when it seemed that a Brahui rising would deliver his plans for a British-controlled Regency in Kalat, drove him to exasperation. Northbrook wrote privately to him saying 'I am very much pained at having to support Captain Sandeman against you [but following] your comments upon his conduct we really had no alternative', and adding that, just as had been the case with Phayre, it was the duty of officers to implement the wishes of those they served. When Merewether protested that he would have complied with Northbrook's wishes if he had been put in possession of them, Northbrook replied that the Resolution of 16 October 'seems to me to say, in the clearest language consistent with the courtesy due to your position... that we approved of Captain Sandeman's policy with which you disagreed... and desired to give him a fair chance of trying to arrange the inter-tribal disputes and to open the Bolan Pass' and that Merewether's restrictions on Sandeman's movements would have made his mission 'simply futile'.

It was his vigorous language that really brought Merewether down. Northbrook's opinion was that Sandeman had been carrying out the Government of India's orders and was entitled to support, especially as he seemed to have prevented the outbreak of a civil war just as any British officer should have done. 'I am very sorry Merewether has got into trouble, for I like him personally very much, but I cannot approve of his conduct to Sandeman, nor the manner in which he seems to a have habitually dealt with his rough neighbours'. Salisbury replied concurring with Northbrook's decision. 'My impression is that Merewether was decidedly insubordinate and ill-tempered and you could hardly have submitted to him'. In a note appended to these papers, later papered over but still legible if held up to the light, he wrote 'My impression is that the Govt of India is riding the policy of non-intervention to death. But they had no choice as to superseding Sir Wm Merewether'.[29]

The question left unaddressed was the constitutional propriety, not of superseding Merewether in the conduct of British relations with Kalat, but of replacing him in that capacity (though in that capacity only) with an officer of a completely different local government. Relations with Kalat, like those with the Gulf States and East Africa, were (and officially still remained) matters for the Government of Bombay. Northbrook, like other governor-generals before him, regarded this as an inconvenient, even dangerous anachronism. Merewether's false moves provided him with the opportunity to transfer Kalat affairs to a Punjab officer who, though with no more knowledge of the country than he had gleaned from Sandeman's own limited experience, was answerable more directly to the Government of India. This was in accord with Northbrook's plan, following Mayo, to secure unity of the frontier by putting Sind under the Punjab. Meanwhile, however, Bombay was the channel for diplomacy with Kalat and, when Northbrook wished to supersede Merewether in that function, the constitutionally proper action would have been to replace him with another Bombay officer. Northbrook's hurried selection of Munro rather than a Bombay officer can most easily be accounted for by the observation of his successor, Lord Lytton, that, on reaching India, he found Northbrook 'completely fascinated by all that is Punjab and in a state of complete exasperation against all that is Bombay'.[30]

11

QUETTA AND THE SETTLEMENT OF KALAT, 1876–78

Now there arose up a new king over Egypt, which knew not Joseph.

Exodus, ch.I, v.8

Returning from Kalat, Sandeman reached Dadhar to learn of his victory over the Sind officers. He hastened to Jacobabad, where Munro had already arrived. Loch remained responsible for the internal administration of the Frontier District, but under orders to comply with Munro's requisitions for troops and police. Relations between the two were at first polite, but changed after the arrival of the triumphant Sandeman. They soon became impossible, with the Punjab officials accusing Loch of hindering their political work by allowing his head munshi to resign and arresting a messenger from Kalat to Sandeman. It later transpired that Munro had been notified of the munshi's intended resignation by Loch, in Merewether's presence, without raising objections, and that the messenger, who had never said he had a message for Sandeman, and was released at Sandeman's request, had been arrested by Loch in his capacity as the civil magistrate, because he was a known bad character who had been forbidden to enter Jacobabad. Nevertheless, on the orders of the Government of India, Loch's civil duties were handed over to the Deputy Collector of Shikarpur and on 1 April 1876 he was relieved of command of the Sind Frontier Force, with the Bombay Government instructed to replace him by 'an officer of good judgement with positive orders to co-operate heartily with Colonel Munro'.[1]

Feelings in Bombay and Sind ran high at Loch's dismissal and consequent loss of allowances without the chance to defend himself. On 8 April Gonne, Secretary to the Bombay Government, wrote to Thornton, who had been moved from the Punjab to become officiating Secretary to the Government of India in the Foreign Department, 'this Government does not hesitate to say that, without a very marked change in the bearing of Colonel Munro, no officer possessing proper self-respect can be expected to co-operate heartily with Colonel Munro. Colonel Loch's communications with him were perfectly courteous, while the replies were quite the reverse. And His Excellency in Council would be very sorry to be again instructed to suspend an officer for want of hearty co-operation with Colonel Munro'.[2]

Salisbury's Frontier Policy

Salisbury's main interest continued to be in extending British influence beyond the Indian frontier. In an official Despatch of January 1875, he argued that if Amir Sher Ali of Afghanistan was friendly towards the British, he could have no objection to accepting a British representative at his court. Northbrook expressed reservations but, in November 1875, Salisbury gave the Government of India direct orders to open negotiations for the establishment of a British Resident at Kabul, who would advise the Amir against oppression at home or adventures abroad. Northbrook, supported by his Council, replied that Amir Sher Ali was popular and strong enough in his own country and neither friendly to the Russians nor unfriendly towards the British; what he dreaded was foreign interference such as would be signalled by the arrival of a British Resident. 'We deprecate, as involving serious danger to the peace of Afghanistan and the interests of the British Empire in India, the execution under present circumstances of the instructions in your Lordship's Despatch'.[3]

Salisbury had corresponded privately with Northbrook throughout 1875 on the concept of uniting Sind and the Punjab to form a new frontier province and compensating Bombay with the Central Provinces. He formally proposed this in February 1876, saying that in the event of further Russian advances in Central Asia, the Kalat border would be an object of great concern. 'It would then be vitally necessary that all the officers, both civil and military, in the valley of the Indus should obey a single will and should look for their advancement to a single authority'.[4] Northbrook, by this time, had notified Salisbury of his intention to resign office on health grounds, though a more likely reason was his reluctance to implement Salisbury's forward policy. In his last official

Letter from India, sent on 7 April 1876, he and his Council expressed support for the idea of joining Sind to the Punjab, but not for transferring the Central Provinces (which would have meant the Government of India ceding control of them). In a memorandum of 22 March 1876, forwarded from the India Office to the Governor-General in Council, Frere had supported the union of Sind and the Punjab, but with a separate government for the border districts, under joint military and civil administration as, he meaningfully added, was the case in Upper Sind. Northbrook's government, who regarded Frere as a trouble-maker, rejected the idea of a separate frontier province on the grounds that it would adversely affect the experienced local (Punjab) government that had previously carried out the Government of India's frontier policy with success. The Punjab, they said, was just as well fitted to deal with Balochistan as with Afghanistan. The transfer of the Upper Sind Frontier to the Punjab was an urgent necessity and the details of the complete unification of the Punjab and Sind could be worked out later, in negotiations between the Governments of India, Bombay and the Punjab.[5]

The struggle on the ground in Upper Sind led Northbrook to secure a Resolution of the Government of India on 14 March 1876, pressing for the immediate transfer of the Upper Sind Frontier District to the Punjab.[6] Salisbury, with his own plans for a new frontier province, decided to wait until Northbrook's successor reached India. The transfer of Upper Sind, telegraphed to London on 14 March for urgent approval, was therefore rejected by the same means, ostensibly on the grounds that, by law, all such major changes required careful deliberation and agreement by the Council of India. Salisbury ordered the details of the proposal to be sent to London by normal mail (thus delaying any final decision until after Northbrook left office) though the Government of India could make provisional arrangements in the meanwhile.[7]

Northbrook protested that 'Colonel Munro, who is a very calm steady man,' (not a view shared in Bombay) had urged that the proposed transfer was essential for the management of Khelat affairs. 'I should not have telegraphed unless there had been very strong grounds; but I must do the best I can under the circumstances...We have sent Sandeman back in with a very strong escort, and I am myself pretty confident that he will settle matters; but it is very difficult to judge when such diametrically opposite opinions are held by men who ought to know what they are talking about'.[8] Northbrook made it clear which side he backed by telling Salisbury 'I am very sorry to have had to direct the Bombay Government to remove Colonel Loch, but it is but too evident that there was no hope of his acting in unison with Colonel Munro'.[9]

Wodehouse and his Council at Bombay complained that Munro's scheme had been prepared in haste and merely extended the confusion that he claimed it would correct. Munro already had political authority down to the sea but would still have no military or civil powers in Lower Sind. Despite this, he had 'already demanded of Sir William Merewether the delivery of his records respecting those Districts, in terms of which the Government of India has been obliged, at our suggestion, to point out the impropriety'. Merely to aid yet another attempt at mediation in Kalat, 'the whole administration of Sind is to be thrown into confusion, a very important district is to be severed from it, and divided and conflicting authority is to be established from end to end of its Border'. If the Government of India was not prepared to accept Bombay officers in the border administration of Sind, it should transfer the whole province to the Punjab or the Central Government and compensate Bombay with the Central Provinces.[10]

Lytton and the Forward Policy

To Northbrook's successor-designate, Lord Lytton, all these questions were merely local manifestations of 'the great Russian problem'.[11] A career diplomat, he had been chosen by Disraeli and Salisbury as an enthusiast for their policy of strengthening the British hand in the Great Game. His personal staff were selected from men with the same views. His private secretary (transferred from the political department at the India Office) was Colonel Owen Tudor Burne, who under Mayo had drawn up the plan of a united frontier province with its own elite officers. His military secretary (a new post, created so that Lytton could by-pass the Indian military establishment that, to a man, opposed adventures beyond the border) was Colonel George Pomeroy Colley, one of the 'Wolseley Ring'. A former professor at the Army's Staff College, he dismissed the opinions of the Indian veterans as obsolete, arguing that, unlike himself, they had not studied the impact on warfare of the new breech-loading rifles used in recent Continental wars. The professional opinion of Sir Frederick Haines, Commander in Chief, India, that any expedition would need the kind of proper logistic support that the limited finances of the Governemnt of India were in no shape to provide, led Lytton to describe him as one of 'the powers of military darkness'. Haines, for his part, put a wealth of meaning into his assessment of Colley as 'the finest theoretical soldier' he ever met.

Prior to leaving London in February 1876, Lytton was invited to the residence of the Russian ambassador, Count Shuvalov, who showed him a letter from General Kaufmann, Governor-General of Russian Turkestan, complaining of British hostility. Kaufmann urged that the British should join Russia in disarming the Central Asian Khanates and dividing their territories to achieve a common Anglo-Russian border. European civilisation would replace Islamic barbarism, and in the event of another Muslim-led revolt in India, a friendly Christian power would be at hand to aid its British co-religionists. To show his own goodwill, he offered to send a letter of congratulations to await Lytton's arrival at Calcutta, forwarding it via the Amir of Afghanistan. Lytton refused to consider these proposals or the idea of joining any kind of crusade, and declared that he would prefer to strengthen the border states as portals of British India. He also asked why, if Kaufmann was so well-disposed, he had mobilised a column to advance in Central Asia just when diplomatic tension between Russia and the United Kingdom was again rising; and how could he order the Amir to forward his messages to India? Shuvalov's diplomacy proved equal to the challenge. He was evasive about the Amir and said that Kaufmann, as a patriotic soldier, had only done what he thought best for his country, and had demobilised the column now that the international situation had eased. Lytton merely became the more suspicious of Russian intentions and more determined to implement a new frontier policy to counter them.[12]

Expecting resistance from the Council that he took over from Northbrook, Lytton obtained a set of Secret Instructions (drafted by himself) as evidence that his radical new foreign policy had Cabinet approval.[13] These stated that the Home Government's anxiety over the unsatisfactory state of affairs on the North-West Frontier had been increased by Russian advances in Central Asia; the Government of India had failed to secure an alliance with the Amir and sardars of Afghanistan, while watching the Russians advance to within a short distance of the Afghan border; and the weakness of British influence in Afghanistan was a prospective peril and the disruption of it in Kalat an immediate inconvenience; (Lytton's alliterative prose style, here and in his other correspondence, illustrates his *alter persona* as a man of letters).

The new Viceroy was therefore to begin the restoration of British influence by sending a Mission to the Amir of Kabul and the Khan of Kalat, ostensibly to inform them of his assumption of office, but actually as cover for the establishment of British intelligence agents in their countries. Such a mission could be used to impress them with British strength by announcing the intended assumption by Queen Victoria of the title Empress of India. It could go first to Quetta to be received by the Khan and then to Amir Sher Ali at Kabul, or directly to Kabul, depending on the Amir's attitude. If the Amir declined to receive it, the mission should be limited to Kalat and the restoration of the British position there under the treaty of 1854. Relations with the Khan should be resumed and the British hand against Amir Sher Ali strengthened by British troops gaining unrestricted access to Quetta. Of the forty paragraphs in these Instructions, thirty were concerned with Afghanistan and only three exclusively dealt with Kalat, which was clearly regarded as a fall-back option. In the event, while the Amir refused to accept a Mission, one to the Khan, led by Sandeman, was about to depart.

Sandeman's Second Mission to Balochistan

In its Resolution of 14 March pressing for the transfer of the Upper Sind Frontier to the Punjab, Northbrook's Government had also expressed itself well pleased with Sandeman's previous mission, admitting that he had failed in all its declared aims, but claiming he had proved (what was scarcely in doubt) that mediation by a British officer would be welcomed by 'the chiefs of Kalat'. It decided that because of the disorders following the death of Nur al-Din Mingal and the Khan's doubts about his accreditation (arising from Merewether's letters of recall) he had not had a fair chance of carrying out his original orders. Munro, having been given political jurisdiction along the whole length of the Kalat border, was therefore instructed to try for another meeting between the Khan and Sandeman. Until this attempt failed, 'the Government of India is not prepared to abandon the line of action taken in October last'.[14]

Northbrook accordingly informed Lytton, still en route to India, that Sandeman had been sent back to Kalat with an escort strong enough to command respect and a letter calculated to bring the Khan to obedience. This added to Lytton's exasperation for, as he told Salisbury, he put no faith in a policy of sharp letters and weak action. If Sandeman failed, the British would have to intervene in Kalat at the very time when, if the Amir of Afghanistan refused to accept the proposed British diplomatic mission, they would need the Khan's goodwill to send it to Kalat instead.[15] Northbrook's letter was answered by Lytton saying that the Kalat despatches showed that the maxim 'divide and rule' was not inapplicable to the ruling powers themselves.[16]

By the following post, he told Northbrook that he had insisted on a free hand in frontier policy as a condition of accepting office; he had the full support of the Cabinet; he had selected Pelly (Frere's protégé and a former Sind frontier officer) to be his confidential agent in frontier matters and Sandeman's employment was not in harmony with that; and that he, personally, would not have used an officer connected with 'the recent official jealousies that have caused such a difficult situation'. Sandeman should therefore be prevented from going further, at least until Lytton was told more about the contents of the letter he was carrying.[17] Northbrook replied that Sandeman's mission was the result of a Resolution of the Government of India in Council, which could not easily be undone, and said he would wait for Lytton's views about this before acting. This delay meant that once again Sandeman was well across the border before he could be stopped. Lytton's request to Northbrook was dated 10 April but this, even with a telegram despatched on the same day, was too late.

Munro's orders to Sandeman, dated 3 April, included the triumphalist assertion, 'none of the impediments which clogged your progress on the first occasion will, on this your second mission, be permitted to interfere with your freedom of action.' Sandeman was to escort through the Bolan a large collection of kafilas gathered at Jacobabad in anticipation of his return to the country; hand over a letter from the Viceroy to the Khan with a suitable display of ceremony; acquaint himself with the Jhalawans as he already had with the Sarawans; assure himself his mediation would be acceptable to all parties; and to protect the people of Kalat from exactions by his escort or its camp followers. Since the death of Sirdar Nur al-Din Mingal, the Jhalawans had taken revenge by plundering four kafilas that were using the Mulla Pass as an alternative to the direct route to the Bolan, hence the traffic jam at Jacobabad while the caravan-masters waited for the roads to become safer.

The escort was chosen from both Frontier Forces, with troops from the 4th Punjab Cavalry and 3rd Scinde Horse, companies from Jacob's Rifles (Bombay Native Infantry) and the 4th Sikhs, and two guns from the Jacobabad Mountain Train. Military command was given to Captain Frederick Humfrey of Jacob's Rifles, Munro deliberately having selected an officer junior in rank to Sandeman (since February 1876 a major in the Bengal Staff Corps) to ensure Sandeman's control of the entire expedition in case of emergency. Most of the impromptu tribal levies hurriedly assembled for the previous mission were left behind, but Sandeman's usual associates, Sardars Imam Baksh Khan Mazari and Jamal Khan Laghari were included, along with other Baloch sardars and their retainers. In a private letter to his father in the United Kingdom, Sandeman had previously quoted Imam Baksh's unctious response to the news that Munro had been given charge of Kalat affairs. 'Yes! Sahib. Honesty triumphs in the long run. We have worked for the Government and people and God has prospered us.'[18]

Munro wrote to Khudadad Khan that he had taken over from Loch and that Sandeman would be returning with the Viceroy's answer to the message sent by the Khan at the end of the previous mission. The Khan responded in suitably diplomatic terms, though with the gloss that Major Sandeman should not bother himself with the Bolan, as he was already aware of the Khan's view that all traffic should be diverted through the Mulla Pass.[19] Munro ignored this and on 4 April 1876 (just six days before Lytton telegraphed Northbrook to stop the mission), Sandeman marched out with the kafilas from Jacobabad, joined by one from Karachi and another two from Shikarpur. The whole procession amounted to some six thousand merchants, drivers and followers, with four or five thousand camels and donkeys carrying their goods and supplies, and a thousand soldiers with their followers, cavalry horses, gun mules and baggage camels. It passed through Kachhi, where the Naibs of Bagh and Quetta arrived with orders from the Khan to accompany the British mission. On 11 April 1876 it entered the Bolan, where the Naib of Mastang joined it, having similarly received the Khan's instructions to lend every assistance.

This was soon needed, as cholera, one of the few plagues the Army of the Indus had been spared on its *via dolorosa* through Balochistan thirty-seven years earlier, was by this time endemic throughout northern India. Poor hygiene and limited supplies of clean water, the result of so many thousand men and animals being gathered together, led to its outbreak first of all in the escort, which suffered 140 cases, and then among the kafilas. Some of the Baloch contingents promptly fled home. The remainder, with the troops weakened by disease (Sandeman himself was laid low by some kind of gastro-enteric affliction) were insufficient to protect a convoy worth between six and seven lakhs of rupees. In his biography of Sandeman, Thornton states that while the mission was halted by this outbreak, Sandeman came under pressure to return to India and await further instructions. Such pressure could only have come from the Sind officers in his escort, to whom Sandeman was an unwelcome interloper. He was being attacked in the Bombay newspapers for his part in the victory of the Punjab over Sind and, if the mission turned back, a new Viceroy, whose views were already being speculated about, might reverse Northbrook's decisions.

Sandeman, as aware as anyone of this danger to his ambitions, resisted the idea. He was saved by the arrival of Sardars Mulla Muhammad Raisani, Ala al-Din Kurd and other Sarawans, offering to protect the kafilas on the usual terms. The merchants, who had hoped the British escort would make this outlay unnecessary, objected on the grounds that it would take a fortnight to assess the whole convoy and that it was imperative to move out of the cholera zone as quickly as possible. Eventually they agreed to accept an estimated assessment for transit fees to the naibs and escort fees to the sardars, with any balance being paid to the Naib of Quetta when he carried out a proper inspection after they emerged from the Bolan. Escorted by Sardar Ala al-Din Kurd's son Yar Muhammad Khan, the kafilas moved on, followed by the frontier force troops who continued to lose men until they left the source of infection behind and halted at Abigum.

By this time Lytton had reached Calcutta. He was not impressed by the quality of his advisers, telling Salisbury that Sir Arthur Hobhouse, the Law Member of his Council,was 'a treacherous psalm-singing sneak' and Thornton, the officiating Foreign Secretary, 'a scrubby little Scotsman on the make'. En route to India he had met Frere, returning to the United Kingdom after accompanying the Prince of Wales's tour of India. 'Clever man', he wrote to a friend, 'much relieved to find he concurs in all my views (which strengthen daily) as to frontier policy'.[20] Frere's influence is evidenced by a whole volume of Lytton's private papers being devoted to Frere's letters about Kalat. He certainly shared Frere's criticism of the Punjab school, telling him that 'nobody connected with the Punjab attempts to think for himself on any subject. My Council, my Secretariat, and most of the officers at present in active employment are all saturated with Punjabi traditions and sympathies, and I have to fight them all round single-handed'.[21] He later apologized to Pelly for the continued delay in appointing him to the frontier because he could not recall Sandeman's mission, 'a singularly ill-advised and ill-managed business', without, as the first act of his viceroyalty, alienating the same Members of Council who had agreed to it.[22] To Salisbury he wrote that he had no confidence in Major Sandeman or his mission and that nothing but bad could result from sending an officer to negotiate between the Khan and his own subjects with no more orders than a Resolution forwarded through the Lieutenant-Governor of the Punjab. 'I really cannot understand this kind of diplomacy'.[23]

Therefore, on 20 April, with Sandeman still halted at Abigum, Thornton was obliged to send Munro a telegram reading 'Viceroy expects Major Sandeman to return to British territory at the earliest date compatible with the object of his mission after delivering Lord Northbrook's letter to the Khan'.[24] In his Kalat Diary for 26 May, Sandeman wrote 'some short time after the mission has arrived in the Bolan Pass, a report was industriously spread that His Excellency the Viceroy had ordered it back after the Kafilas reached Quetta'.[25] This unhelpful 'report', which was very close to the truth, was likely to have originated with the Sind officers, of whom Sandeman seems to have been suspicious. To deliver Northbrook's letter he selected Wylie, who had commanded his escort in the previous mission and was present with the Punjab Cavalry squadron in the new one. Surgeon Duke and the usual Baloch trusties, Sardars Imam Baksh Khan Mazari and Jamal Khan Laghari, all of whom had been with the previous mission, went with him. Northbrook's letter stated that the suspension of diplomatic relations, which the Khan had told Sandeman he wished to restore, was the result of his own past conduct, but 'by hearkening to Major Sandeman's counsels, and acting in conformity with his advice, your Highness... will relieve me from the necessity of taking further measures to secure the tranquillity of the British frontier and the protection of trade.'[26]

The Khan was no happier than Lytton about Sandeman's mission. It is very likely that the widespread rumour about its imminent recall had been reported by the Naib of Quetta and Sandeman's credentials were once more in question. The Khan seemed also to have a good knowledge of British policy discussions, probably from the same Jacobabad source as before. He asked Wylie what Munro's powers were and what Merewether retained. He enquired if Merewether would become Governor of Bombay (where Wodehouse was nearing the end of his term) and remarked that if Bombay lost Sind, together with Baroda (where Bombay's involvement was once more under consideration) it would really be too small to merit a Governor. He again complained that the British, having urged him to subdue the rebel sardars, then had dealt directly with them when he could not meet the impossible terms of Merewether's award. Instead of treating him as they had Amir Sher Ali, they had arrested his ministers and listened to the evil words against him of his former Wazir, Wali Muhammad.

Correspondance between Sandeman and Khudadad Khan continued throughout May 1876. Sandeman twice invited him to a meeting at Mastang, citing Nasir Khan II's meeting with Jacob there as the precedent to be followed. The Khan initially declined, saying that protocol required Sandeman to come to him, at Kalat, or somewhere near it. Rumours in the bazar suggested that the real reasons were that his ministers urged him to make difficulties so as to show that he was not desperate for a settlement. Other rumours were that he feared being arrested by the British or attacked by the dissident sardars who had joined the British camp. To allay this last fear, Sandeman told the Khan that he had sent the Brahuis away after hearing their petitions. Eventually, when Sandeman declared that he was about to leave Quetta for Mastang, Khudadad Khan gave way and arrived at Mastang on 31 May to a salute from the Jacobabad mountain guns.[27]

Meanwhile, no words of encouragement had arrived from the new Viceroy, whose first discussions in Council included the question of Sandeman's immediate recall. Davies, the Lieutenant-Governor of the Punjab, wrote later to Northbrook that Sandeman had eventually succeeded in his mission 'but not without my having to take some abnormal steps to support him'. Hobhouse, the senior Member of Council, told him that Lytton had wished to supersede the Kalat mission as soon as he reached India and would have done so, had he not been opposed.[28] When Munro reported the Khan's agreement to British mediation, Lepel Griffin (Thornton's successor as Secretary to the Punjab Government) asked the Government of India for a sign of clear support, so as to strengthen Sandeman's position in negotiations with the Khan and sardars and to remove their obvious doubts about his authority. Thornton replied with the viceroy's congratulations to Sandeman on achieving the agreement of all parties to mediation, and a warning not to commit the Government of India to any line of policy 'founded on statements apparently incompatible with recorded facts which were carefully examined into at the time of their occurrence', nor in any way to weaken the Khan's authority over his 'disaffected vassals'.[29]

The Mastung Conference, June–July 1876

At Mastang the conference went ahead after the usual ceremonial meetings, speeches of welcome and presentation of officials. The Khan's claims were that the British should pay the compensation due to the kafilas plundered in revenge for Nur al-Din Mingal; they should refund him the cost of the campaign in Las Bela, as it was undertaken on their advice; Las Bela should be annexed either by the British or Kalat, or else the Jam should be restored on condition of accepting the Khan's overlordship as formerly; ex-wazir Atta Muhammad, in asylum with rebel sardars, should be expelled from Kalat territory; the lakh of rupees awarded by Merewether's settlement, which he had had to spend on compensating the merchants robbed by the Brahuis, should be restored; the annual subsidy provided by the 1854 treaty should be renewed as, for his part, he had kept the customs tolls down to the agreed tariff; and the commandant and munshis still in British custody should be released. He offered to appoint Nawab Muhammad Khan as vakil to the mission, guarantee the Brahuis' share of the transit fees, restore their ancestral land-holdings and refer any future disagreement to the British Agent for arbitration; and finally, if the British approved all these terms and the Brahuis returned to their former alliegance, he would do his best to keep the passes open.[30] Discussions continued throughout June 1876, with these terms eventually being accepted by all parties as the basis for a settlement.

At the beginning of July, Sardar Ali Khan Jamot, the son of Jam Mir Ali of Las Bela, arrived at Mastung with the Jhalawan sardars. A committee of arbitration was formed, with three members (headed by Vakil Nawab Muhammad Khan) representing the Khan and three (Sandeman's two Baloch henchmen, Sardars Imam Baksh Mazari and Jamal Khan Laghari, and Sardar Mulla Muhammad Raisani) representing the Brahuis. Sandeman's head munshi, Hittu Ram, acted as secretary and Sandeman himself as final arbiter. The committee sat between 9 and 11 July 1876, after which, in return for the Khan's promise to settle their claims in accordance with the committee's awards, the sardars acknowledged his sovereignty and withdrew their demand for Nur al-Din Mingal's blood-money. The Khan then appointed Sardar Ala al-Din Kurd to guard the Bolan and arrange escorts for the caravans, with armed retainers stationed at intervals along the pass. Escort fees were to be paid to the tribal sardars and moderate customs duties to the Naibs of Dadhar and Quetta, as formerly. Sardar Mulla Muhammad was given supervision of this arrangement to prevent misappropriation of funds. All parties assembled in a grand darbar, attended by the British officers in the camp, and swore on the Koran to observe the agreed terms.[31]

'It is impossible to express a confident opinion on results of Major Sandeman's mission', Lytton telegraphed to Salisbury, 'but up to the present time they are, as represented by himself, to following effect. On 22 July a reconciliation had been effected between the Khan and his principal Sirdars who mutually swore on the Koran to fulfil the conditions agreed upon. We are not in possession of that agreement, nor judging by former ones of the same character do I place much dependance upon it.'[32] When the details reached him, Lyttton considered them unduly favourable to the sardars, but decided that, as the Khan seemed to have accepted them, they could be endorsed. The sardars would have no further excuse for rebellion and the Khan, finding that the British were willing to support his authority and 'place him in a better and safer position than he was before, or Sandeman's attitude could have led him to expect', might be counted on to become a grateful and faithful ally. In consequence, Lytton planned to renew the 1854 treaty as the basis for a strong British military and diplomatic presence in Balochistan; the Khan was to be persuaded to request a meeting with Lytton on his forthcoming tour of the frontier, at which the new treaty would be signed; to ask, as a personal favour, that the troops of Sandeman's escort should remain in his country (Lytton observing that it was fortunate they were there already); and finally, 'to assist in Caesar's triumph' he would be invited to the Imperial Assemblage at Delhi where Queen Victoria was to be declared Empress of India.[33]

At the same time, Salisbury was writing to Lytton that the establishment of a British Agent in Kalat could be given great prominence as an alternative to the proposed mission to Kabul, which Amir Sher Ali was proving reluctant to accept (as Northbrook and his Council had forecast would be the case). This Resident, he mused, based nominally at Kalat but working chiefly from Quetta, would not only advise the Khan and influence the sardars but also gather information from Kandahar, Herat, Kabul and Balkh. He would be able to contact agents of all kinds as they travelled through the Bolan, without exciting undue suspicion. Possibly he would be visited by discontented subjects of the Amir. 'English rupees would try conclusions with Russian roubles in the zenana and divan'. He therefore welcomed Lytton's proposals and wrote back that Kalat was 'the key of our position'. It was of secondary importance whether Sandeman was right or wrong, or whether the Khan or sardars should be supreme. The prime consideration was that Kalat should be as much under British control as Rajasthan or Kathiawar.[34]

The arrival of Colley

Sandeman accompanied Khudadad Khan back to Kalat, where, in the Khan's name, he drew up a set of rules for the settlement of disagreements between sardars and the Khan's naibs. These, for the first time, formally provided for the British involvement in the internal government of the country. In any revenue dispute, if a sardar disagreed with the naib's decision, the question was to be referred to the Khan. If the sardar was dissatisfied with the Khan's award, he could appeal to the British Agent. The rules for settling civil cases and debts did not mention British intervention, but in criminal cases, if ordered by the Khan to implement what he considered a wrongful decision, a sardar could appeal to the British Agent. Sardars were bound to support the Khan against rebels, but the Khan would obtain the approval of the British Agent before calling on them for such support. If any sardar considered the Khan's troops were acting oppressively, he could complain to the Khan and then, if still dissatisfied, appeal to the British Agent.[35]

Lytton, on receiving the report with these rules, refused to approve them. Such terms, he told Sandeman, would reduce the Khan to a status lower than the smallest feudatory prince in India, whereas British interests required a single strong central authority through which Kalat could be controlled without the need for constant interference in petty decisions. What, he asked, would be the effect on the Amir when he saw that, as the result of accepting a British mission, his neighbour the Khan was stripped of all power and reduced to a political nonentity? Frontier policy had to be governed by more than local factors. The Amir and the Khan were mere dummies or counters 'which would be of no importance to us, were it not for the costly stakes we put on them, in the great game for empire we are now playing with Russia'. Sandeman was ordered to have the rules allowing appeals to the British Agent withdrawn; arrange a meeting between the Khan and a representative of the Viceroy who would be bringing a draft new treaty to replace that of 1854; obtain the Khan's consent to its terms and induce him to ask for a meeting with Lytton, and to request that British troops should remain in his country.[36]

The Viceroy's representative was Colonel George Colley, his military secretary, selected as, of Lytton's two other special advisers, Burne could not be spared and Pelly would attract too much attention. In view of the intention to make military dispositions in Kalat, a serving soldier was in any case the preferred option. Colley reached Kalat with the draft new treaty on 14 October 1876 and reported back that there was a disposition among the Sind officers to see his arrival as a snub to Sandeman, whom he found 'nervously anxious about the position I should take up, and the Khan's vakil also waiting very carefully to see our relative position'. Sandeman immediately moved to recover lost ground by ingratiating himself with Colley, who reported back to Lytton that Sandeman really had done good service in a number of ways. 'He really appreciates your having written to him directly and fully as you did, and assured me many times that your letter and my visit, far from weakening, had strengthened his position with both Khan and Sirdars'.[37]

Colley's opinion of Khudadad Khan was that he was a rather incompetent tyrant, ready to obey the British government 'which he is shrewd enough to see has both the power and inclination to help him... The people certainly generally hate him, but I think it is rather on account of his want of kingly qualities than his actual oppression. I believe a good Kingly ruler like one of our Plantagenets might oppress them ten times as much and yet remain popular'. He also met Sardar Ala al-Din Kurd, 'a sort of fat Rob Roy, the plunderer *par excellence* of the pass, who admits that his happiest days were when he sat on the top of a rock with a long-range rifle, picking off the bullocks which were drawing the Khan's guns in the pass below' (he might equally well have referred to the Army of the Indus but, diplomatically, neither side mentioned this) 'and now with a leer says he is growing thin from anxiety and care for the protection of the pass—he would make four ordinary men now'.[38] The Khan agreed to most of the proposed terms and the draft treaty was accepted at a ceremony in the Khan's palace on 18 October 1876.

The next day, Colley left Kalat to go with Sandeman to Quetta. The troops were redeployed, ostensibly to fit in with the climate and the intended movements of Sandeman and the Khan, but actually to bring them to positions they were tasked to hold. Thus the Punjab infantry went to Quetta at the top of the Bolan, both cavalry squadrons to Dadhar at its foot, where the Kacchi plain was well suited to mounted operations, and the Bombay riflemen, with their mountain guns, remained at Kalat ready to go with the Khan to Mastang. After inspecting Quetta, Colley recommended to Lytton that it should be the principal British garrison in Kalat. 'With three companies in the Miri it would be unassailable except with artillery, and with a mountain gun or two added I believe all the armies of Central Asia could not take it, as it commands an absolutely flat and shelterless plain for miles around'.[39]

Writing to Northbrook in an attempt to reconcile him to the occupation of Quetta, which neither he nor any of his Council had intended when they sent Sandeman into Kalat, Colley dwelt on the way that the local inhabitants had crowded round to point out where the best water and camp-grounds were. 'Considering that their recollections of 1839–41 can hardly be pleasant, it is quite extraordinary how friendly they are to us. I never met an unfriendly look all the time I was in the country'. Sandeman, who by this time knew very well what Lytton's intentions were, was less than frank when he wrote to his old patron, 'It is true troops are still to be kept in Kelat, but only as a friendly aid to the Khan and his Sirdars, both sides accepting this as such'.[40]

The Occupation of Quetta

In London, the Council of India accepted the draft treaty without difficulty, but the occupation of Quetta proved far more controversial. Rawlinson, vice-president of the Council and long-term advocate of a forward policy, told Lytton that the move was strongly opposed by those who looked on the possibility of an advance beyond the passes 'with perfect terror'. Another Indian veteran, Major General Sir Henry Daly thought Quetta 'a dangerous move at the best, but its tenure by a few hundred natives is sheer madness'. Sir Robert Montgomery, a former lieutenant-governor of the Punjab, argued that the force at Quetta was in an exposed position and should be recalled, leaving the Agent under the Khan's protection, with just a small escort. Sandeman, he thought, should be replaced by an officer unconnected with the recent controversies. Colley, to whom Lytton seems to have referred these objections, answered that to recall Sandeman, whose personal influence seemed to have been a success, would benefit no-one. The Quetta force was strong enough to defend itself against the Khan and sardars combined and, as two of the Khan's naibs, to whom he had presumably given all the protection in his power, had been killed by rebels, a British Agent would need more than a small escort to be safe. (The possibility of such a danger had been behind the decision to withdraw Harrison from Kalat. Curiously, Lytton would make that very mistake in 1879, when Sir Lewis Cavagnari, the British Resident he installed at Kabul after invading Afghanistan, was murdered along with his own small escort).

In India, many senior figures had doubts about the new frontier policy, of which the advance to Quetta was the first demonstrable outcome. Hobhouse, the Law Member, told Northbrook that Lytton and Indian government officials all wished for a war with Russia 'and they go on repeating the old cantilena' (a word presumably familiar to Hobhouse from his interest in psalmody) 'about Russian aggression and perfidy, and Constantinople, and the road to India, and Central Asia, and "prestige", and British interests, as if they were gospel, and as if they had never misled us into folly or plunged us into disaster or made us contemptible to others'. General Sir Neville Chamberlain, a veteran of the Punjab frontier, and at that time Commander in Chief, Madras, wrote to Lawrence in London that he himself had always opposed the occupation of Quetta. 'We know the result of our interference in Afghan affairs in 1838–39, and we know what was the ending of our Political Agent, Loveday, in Baloochistan. The people of the ruling class of both countries are the same now as they were then—the same policy will bring about the same political results'.

To Salisbury, such views were those of men 'who in their youth have seen the Affghan ghost and never lost the impression' so that every move on the frontier brought on the cry that Auckland's policy was being renewed. 'In Parliament, in the press, in Cabinet, in this Office, the influence of this terror is felt'. As for Indian officials in general, his view, in contrast to that of Hobhouse, was that they all opposed the very idea of establishing a British Resident at Kabul; 'the iron of 1842 has entered into their soul'. The controversy continued long after the formal signing of the treaty, with Salisbury telling Lytton that 'The whole Indian world here is divided into Quettitites and anti-Quettitites, who hate each other with all the hatred of the Big Endians and Little Endians, and at present the Quettitites are much in the minority'.[41]

The Treaty of Jacobabad, December 1876

None of this prevented the new treaty being made as Lytton had intended. During November 1876 he moved with his suite from Simla on a tour of the frontier that brought him to Sukkur on the Indus. There they were joined by Merewether, still Commissioner in Sind and the head of local government, who, in the words of Thornton (who accompanied the tour as officiating Foreign Secretary) 'bore his trying position with dignity and throughout the subsequent proceedings displayed the best qualities of a loyal public servant'.[42] Thence they moved through the desert to Jacobabad, variously in wheeled carriages, on ill-tempered Baloch riding camels and cavalry horses borrowed from the Scinde Horse. They arrived at the crenellated Residency known locally as 'Jacob's Castle' on 7 December 1876, where Khudadad Khan and his retinue awaited them, along with the sardars of Sarawan, Jhalawan, Makran, Panjgur and the eastern Baloch tribes, including the Marris and Bugtis.

The Khan had objected to two articles proposed in the draft treaty. He could not afford the 1,000 rupees a month that it would cost him to keep an agent at the Viceroy's court so, unless the British were prepared to pay for this, preferred to have a vakil resident at Jacobabad as formerly. Nor could he enforce the abolition of slavery in his country, as any attempt to do so would provoke disturbances. Lytton accepted both these objections, as the idea of the Khan having an agent at Calcutta had only been put in as a gesture of reciprocity, and the anti-slavery proposal, a sop to progressive opinion in the United Kingdom, involved British intervention in internal affairs.

The provisions in the 1854 Treaty were reaffirmed, with the Khan accepting them on behalf of himself, his heirs, successors and sardars. This, the first time that the sardars had been mentioned in a treaty, was clear evidence of Sandeman's successful advocacy of their position. The British once more agreed to help the Khan against invasion (something he had several times requested with limited success) and maintain a just authority (something with which, like most rulers, he had always claimed to act). It was agreed that in any dispute between the Khan and his sardars, the British would offer advice to both parties and, in the last resort, impose binding arbitration. This was another unprecedented provision, recognising the sardars as the Khan's peers and effectively placing his relations with them in British hands.

In accordance with the terms of the previous treaty (invoked ostensibly at the Khan's request), British troops would be stationed in his country at locations selected by the British Government. Railways and telegraphs might be built anywhere, subject to the Khan's insistence on giving permission in each case (though officials from the Indian Public Works Department had already been detailed to survey the routes from Sukkur). As long as the Khan observed the treaty, he would receive an annual subsidy of one lakh of rupees (double the previous figure) and the British would spend another 20,500 rupees annually in the Khan's name, but only as they selected, for the employment of mail couriers and the like.[43]

The treaty was enacted with great ceremony (Lytton being convinced of the impact of such pageantry on the Oriental mind) on 8 December 1876. Lytton told the sardars, to whom Sandeman had already explained the treaty's terms, that, as they were mentioned in it, they were bound by it (not quite as accurate an interpretation as might have been expected from a professional diplomat, but one that allowed him to claim that the treaty had the agreement of all classes in Kalat). In another gesture of reconciation, the exiled Jam of Las Bela was freed from British supervision in return for agreeing to the terms accepted by his son at the recent Mastung arbitration, and for withdrawing his claim to the village of Kamal Khan, awarded to the Khan of Kalat by Harrison in 1869. Commandant Shakar Khan and Munshis Salah Muhammad and Gul Muhammad, arrested by Merewether during Khudadad Khan's meeting with Northbrook in November 1872, and held since then as State prisoners, were released and sent to Jacobabad to await their master's orders. To complete the settlement, the Khan was given a special grant of three lakhs of rupees to refill his treasury, drained by years of warfare.[44]

Lytton and the vice-regal entourage returned to Sukkur and thence journeyed by river to Karachi, by sea to Bombay, and by rail to Delhi, the ancient Mughal capital. There, on 1 January 1877, the Queen of England was declared Empress of India. The event was entirely a ceremonial one, as the Government of India had been under the British Crown since 1857, and people, including the Queen herself, had spoken freely of the British Indian Empire long before that. Many in the United Kingdom were opposed to the title, which to freeborn Britons seemed redolent of continental tyrannies, and typical of Disraeli's fanciful extravagances. On the other hand, the Queen herself welcomed the idea, especially with the King of Prussia having become German Emperor only six years earlier, and it was hoped that the new title, with the associated displays of pomp and power, would attach her Indian subjects, or at least their princes, more securely to the British Raj.

The Khan and sardars, escorted by Sandeman, attended this 'Imperial Assemblage', where they appeared exotic figures even by comparison with the richly-adorned Indian princes and their retinues. It was said that, by a too-literal translation of the makers' name "Pears", they mistook the scented soap provided in their tents as a sweetmeat, and ate it. The Khan himself was impressed by the heraldic banners presented to each prince as he declared his alliegance to the new Empress and asked why he had not been given one. Told that the banners were for vassals, not for allies, he replied "Give me a banner and I will be your vassal." Subsequent events were to prove that he had indeed become one, in practice if not in theory.[45]

The new order in Balochistan

The new arrangements for British relations with Kalat were introduced on 1 January 1877. The title of the Political Superindendant, Upper Sind Frontier, dating from Jacob's time, was changed to Superintendant, with all political duties being transferred to the new post of Agent to the Governor-General for Balochistan. Political relations with Kalat and its dependencies were transferred from Bombay to the Government of India in the Foreign Department, with which the new Agent would correspond directly. He was also given responsibility for dealing with the Baloch tribes inside as well as outside the British border. Colonel Munro was ordered to hand over to him all the local records relating to Balochistan (these having been with some difficulty unbound from the rest of those belonging to Sind). Reports from the Sind Frontier police, previously sent to the Political Superintendant at Jacobabad, were henceforth to go to the Agent to the Governor-General based at Quetta.

Unsuprisingly, the new appointment was bestowed on Sandeman, with the grade of Resident, 2nd Class, and a salary of 2,500 rupees each month. He was given three assistants (Political Agents, 2nd Class) each with a salary of 1,500 rupees. His former deputy in Dera Ghazi Khan, R. I. Bruce, was assigned to Quetta; Captain Wylie of the Punjab Cavalry to the Khan's court, and Captain E. S. Reynolds of the Scinde Horse to Jacobabad, with command of the Baluch Guides, now transferred from the Military to the Political Department. Surgeon Duke got the job of Residency Surgeon, with promotion to Civil Surgeon, 1st Class. Sandeman was made a Companion of the Order of the Star of India. The garrison of Quetta was initially fixed at one infantry battalion, one cavalry squadron and a mountain battery from the Punjab Frontier Force, and one regiment of cavalry, a wing (half-battalion) of infantry, and the Jacobabad mountain train from the Sind Frontier Force, part of the Bombay Army. For operational purposes, all were under the Commandant of the Sind Frontier Force at Jacobabad, where the Bombay troops were to return to their barracks for the hot weather.

The Letter from India announcing the terms of the treaty was prepared under the eye of Lytton himself. According to Thornton, who as Secretary in the Foreign Department would normally have drafted it, the document was 'so altered, added to, and re-written by him that much of it is in his own words, and to the best of the writer's recollection it was reprinted some seventeen times before it was finally approved'. The official line was that the new arrangements arose primarily from the internal affairs of Kalat. Both the Khan and the sardars had previously sought British mediation in their quarrels, but all attempts at such had only resulted in even greater confusion. Sandeman's second mission, supported with unusual pomp and publicity and an imposing military force, had secured the agreement of all sides to accept a British award. However, in the view of 'an officer exceptionally well-qualified to form an opinion on this subject' (Sandeman) 'and indeed of all parties in Khelat', mediation would be worthless without British supervision and enforcement, so that the Government of India could not avoid accepting a greater degree of involvement in the affairs of the country.

In Lytton's characteristic literary style, the Letter continued 'We could not decline the position thus decreed to us by a long course of antecedent circumstances without thereby incurring the grave responsibility of thereby plunging into renewed bloodshed and interminable anarchy, a neighbouring and friendly country which had urgently appealed to us for timely rescue from these evils'. At the same time, it claimed that the higher interests of the British Empire as a whole now demanded closer relations with Kalat, irrespective of previous disinclination to take this course. It spoke of the warlike nature of the frontier populations, of possible foreign intrigues in the area, and the consequent need to deal with problems with more important aims than merely the prevention of plundering, though even the latter required more energetic measures such as the ruler, chiefs and people now asked for.

Lytton had by this time completely changed his attitude towards Sandeman and made him one of his favourites, as he did with others who implemented his new policies against those long-supported by the British Indian establishment. He concluded the Letter by commending Sandeman's services and stressing the benefits of having British officers in contact with the tribes and people beyond the British border (a riposte to those who, in London and his own Council, opposed the idea of a Resident at Kalat as much as one at Kabul. 'It is by the everyday acts of earnest upright Englishman that lasting influence must be obtained'.

The treaty, accompanied by over 600 pages of the correspondence leading up to it, were sent to the India Office, where even those officials in favour of the forward policy jibbed at Lytton's enconiums. A.W. Moore, acting Secretary in the Political Department, commented that Sandeman's reports and his Kalat Diaries were 'full of insinuations against the Sind officials'. Sir William Merewether, translated to the Council of India on retiring to England after completing six years as Commissioner in Sind, minuted that Sandeman had acted 'neither openly nor straightforwardly' and the 'Papers submitted to the Government of India, but which I do not find here, will I am sure convince any unprejudiced mind that there was no obstruction from Col. Loch or any other officer on the Sind Frontier'.[46]

The proposed re-organisation of the North-West Frontier proved even more controversial than the occupation of Quetta. Northbrook's final despatch had recommended the transfer of Sind from Bombay to the Punjab but objected to giving the Central Provinces to Bombay as compensation. Salisbury, with the full support of the Council of India, rejected the Calcutta arguments that the Central Provinces were too far from Bombay and would be unsettled by the move and by the seditious nature of the Bombay native press. The India Office reply was that they were as near to Bombay as to Calcutta, and that neither their administration nor their public opinion would be affected by such a transfer, while their transfer to Bombay would provide scope for the officers of that presidency who would become available when it lost Sind. The question of frontier re-organisation, Salisbury ordered, was to be decided after the incoming Viceroy toured the area.[47] This decision later led Sir Henry Norman, the Military Member of the Viceroy's Council, to write to Northbrook in June 1876, 'I look with dread to Lord Lytton's visiting the frontier in the winter... when absent from the Council he might under inspiration from home do something we might bitterly regret. His advisers on such matters are only Burne and Pelly'.[48]

Lytton decided against the idea of simply adding Sind to the Punjab on the grounds that this would produce an area too great for one man to govern well. He therefore proposed unifying only the trans-Indus districts so as to form a new Frontier Government, under a Chief Commissioner and Agent to the Governor-General at Peshawar, to deal with Afghanistan and the Pathans (Pashtuns), with an assistant at Jacobabad to deal with Kalat and the Baloch. He also proposed amalgamating the two frontier forces of Sind and the Punjab and placing them under the Commander in Chief, India, instead of their respective local governments. The new province was to be under civil, not military, administration (contrary to Frere's recommendation that it should be based on the Sind system). Bombay should be compensated by the transfer of the Central Provinces (something about which Lytton had originally had reservations). Salisbury agreed with all these proposals, which reflected his own views on how the frontier should be re-organized.[49]

Frere, and anyone identified with Bombay was regarded with hostility by the Calcutta establishment. A letter to Northbrook from a former viceregal aide-de-camp reported 'Sir B Frere is giving much trouble by writing minutes drawing comparisons between Bombay and Bengal... Sir R Temple goes to Bombay: it is to be hoped that he will bring the people there to their bearings as they have got almost out of control. Lord Lytton when he came to Calcutta had an idea that much of the friction arose from Calcutta, that is to say Sir B Frere told him, but he was quickly undeceived'.[50] Frere's grandiose suggestion that the new Frontier Government should be a Presidency was rejected because it involved needless extra appointments and expenditure. In any case, both Lytton and Salisbury wished to simplify border administration, under a firm central control, rather than complicate it by introducing the level of constitutional independence associated with Presidential status. Mayo and Northbrook had both complained about the Bombay Government's defence of its (in their view, anachronistic) position. In March 1877 Salisbury told Lytton 'Wodehouse has been a thorn in our side ever since I have been at the Office... there is round him a band of irreconcilable Bombay partisans... Since I refused to reverse the action of the Supreme Government about Sandeman, I have never heard from him, and if he wants to communicate anything he writes to Sir L Mallet [the Permanent Under-Secretary]'.[51]

The Council of India's power of veto over expenditure, used by Salisbury to delay Nothbrook's attempted transfer of Sind to the Punjab, now operated against his own plan for rationalising frontier organisation. The Punjab Government, happy enough to add Sind to its territory, reacted with horror to the prospect of losing its frontier districts. If the new organisation came into effect, the Punjab, the show province of the Indian Empire, would no longer hold a monopoly of the stimulating and well-paid political duties offered by posts on the frontier. Such posts, the Government of the Punjab protested, were ones in which their most promising officers gained experience to fit them for high office in their later careers. Certainly the prestige and status of the Punjab service had brought many of its former officers to seats on the Council of India, where they now rallied to its defence. During July 1877 Salisbury had to tell Lytton that opposition to the idea of a Trans-Indus province was increasing by the day. 'It commits the sin of *lese-Punjab*', 'The Council is getting wilder and wilder about the North-West frontier question. They favour me with interviews on the subject and positively stamp about the room.'[52]

In August 1877 the first attempt to secure approval for the proposed new province failed, when Salisbury arrived at the Council's monthly meeting to find that Rawlinson, the leader of those in favour, had been thrown out of his waggonette, and Sir Barrow Ellis, a former Commissioner in Sind whose support he had counted on, was ill and could not come. 'Meanwhile all the enemies of change had, returning from all parts of Europe, gathered in great force'. The next month the situation was no better. 'I am rather at my wits' end, for although the Prime Minister is with us, a discussion we had in the Cabinet was not wholly satisfactory'. The Laurentians, as Salisbury dubbed them, opposed the scheme because they saw it as associated with the forward policy. Of the fifteen Members, only four (including Merewether and Sir Garnet Wolseley) were in favour and because Council approval was required for all major expenditure, such as the new scheme would involve, neither Salisbury nor Lytton had the power to bring it into effect.

A compromise proposal was sent to Lytton as an official despatch, dividing responsibility for the trans-Indus area between two Commissioners, both of whom would be under the Lieutenant-Governor of the Punjab for the internal administration of their charges. The senior, to be based at Peshawar, would correspond directly with the Viceroy on political matters, and command the amalgamated Frontier Forces. The junior would also be the Commissioner in Sind.[53] Discussions were still in progress in April 1878, when Salisbury left the India Office for the Foreign Office. His successor, Gathorne Hardy (Lord Cranbrook), imposed further delays and the outbreak of the 2nd Afghan War later that year turned the minds of statesmen to other, more urgent, questions.

Sind never became part of the Punjab or indeed of a new trans-Indus province. Lord Curzon would in 1901 carve a North-West Frontier Province out of the Punjab for much the same reasons as those advocated by Lytton, but this time planned in secret so that the Punjab's defenders had no time to muster an opposition. This province (renamed Khyber-Pakhtunkhwa in 2008) did not extend along the whole frontier but was, essentially the old Mughal province of Peshawar, possession of which had been so important a factor in the British invasion of Afghanistan in 1839. The creation of the Baluchistan Agency in 1876 meant that, for Sind, the Great Game was over. Its border guardians remained based at Jacobabad, but their outposts could now be advanced to Quetta, where Jacob had always said they needed to be.

12

THE COMPLETION OF BRITISH CONTROL, 1877–1893

Princes come, princes go,
An hour of pomp and show they know,
And over the sands,
The sands of time, they go.

'Kismet' (after *the Rubbaiyat of Omar Khayyam*)

Scarcely was the ink dry on the Treaty of Jacobabad when the tide of European politics once more began to run into the creeks and shallows of Central Asian diplomacy. The treaty of San Stefano (3 March 1878) that ended the Russo-Turkish War of 1877 established a large Bulgaria, free from Ottoman rule but under Russian dominance. Disraeli (ennobled in 1876 as Earl of Beaconsfield) responded by sending the British Mediterranean Fleet to the Turkish Straits and Indian troops to Malta. The threat of war between Russia and the United Kingdom only faded when Bismarck, Chancellor of the new German Empire, stood forth as 'the honest broker' and invited all the European Powers to the Congress of Berlin, to settle all outstanding international disputes. The consequent Treaty of Berlin (13 July 1878), among its other provisions, reduced Bulgaria to more acceptable limits and the tension eased. During this crisis, a Russian mission made its way across Central Asia to Kabul, arriving there on 22 July 1878, a week after the Treaty of Berlin was signed. It was recalled following the Anglo-Russian detente, but Lytton argued that, having accepted a Russian mission, Amir Sher Ali could no longer refuse a British one. When Afghan troops prevented this from crossing the border, Lytton demanded its admission and redress for the insult to British prestige. The British Cabinet reluctantly supported him and on 21 November 1877 British forces invaded Afghanistan.

The Opening of the Second Afghan War

In Kalat, the treaty of Jacobabad was not as universally welcomed as Lytton's official Letters indicated. The Khan initially refused to accept the three lakhs of rupees, on the grounds they were insufficient to reimburse him for the expenses he had incurred through following British advice. He was further alienated when, in a sign of things to come, Sandeman refused to aid him against Sardars Isa Khan Gichki in Panjgur and Azad Khan Nausherwani in Kharan without first investigating his complaints against them. At Quetta, two officers of Royal Engineers working on the new Agency building were killed by Pashtun religious extremists. Sandeman suspected that the Khan's ministers were to blame and used this incident to occupy the Miri, the Quetta citadel. In the run-up to the new Afghan War, the troops at Quetta were brought up to divisional strength under Major General Michael Biddulph. On the outbreak of hostilities, Biddulph and Sandeman marched into Pishin, the large Afghan border district extending north-eastwards from Quetta to southern Waziristan. At the same time, troops from Jacobabad occupied the Afghan enclave of Sibi.

While two British columns invaded Afghanistan from the Punjab, a third, led by Lieutenant General Sir Donald Stewart, moved up the Bolan to Quetta and thence to Kandahar. Sandeman, who already had been in correspondence with the Governor of Kandahar and other local Afghan notables, sought to go with it as chief political officer. He was told he was needed in Balochistan, and the appointment was given to Major Oliver Beauchamp St John of the Royal (originally Bengal) Engineers, whose experience of the country included the construction of the Indo-Iranian telegraph line through Makran and, following Goldsmid's Iranian boundary commission, investigating rival claims to Sistan. Sandeman's part in the campaign was to obtain the supplies needed by Stewart's army and secure the friendship of the tribes along its route. Khudadad Khan declared for the British and demonstrated his support by producing large numbers of transport camels and sending his eldest son, Mir Mahmud Khan, to join Stewart's headquarters. Not to be outdone, the Jam of Las Bela pledged his own troops to the British cause.

As in 1839, the first phase of the war went well for the British. Amir Sher Ali fled and was succeeded by his son, Yakub Khan. The peace treaty of Gandamak (8 May 1879) installed a British Resident at Kabul, with control over Afghan foreign policy. The British handed back all the territory occupied during the invasion except for the Kurram valley, Pishin and Sibi, which were assigned to British administration, the last two being placed under the Agent to the Governor-General for Baluchistan (Sandeman). Ayub Khan's uncle, Sardar Sher Ali Khan, was appointed the new governor of Kandahar. Honours were distributed on a lavish scale. Among the recipients were Sandeman, Colley and Burne (by this time back at the India Office), who became KCSIs, with an honorary knighthood for Khudadad Khan. Sandeman's two Baloch henchmen, Sardars Imam Baksh Mazari and Jamal Khan Laghari, were given the title Nawab, and his chief munshi, Hittu Ram, that of Rai, its Hindu equivalent.

Sandeman now fought a lively battle with the Punjab Government over dealings between his successor as Deputy Commissioner of Dera Ghazi Khan and the Khatrans, whose country lay to the east of his old district and extended as far north as Pishin. As Agent to the Governor-General for all Balochistan, Sandeman claimed that in dealing with the Khatrans, the Deputy Commissioner of Dera Ghazi Khan should come under his orders. R.E.Egerton, the new lieutenant-governor of the Punjab, saw no reason why his officers should not deal directly with their Khatran neighbours as previously. Quoting arguments that Sandeman himself had used during his turf war with the Sind officials, he insisted that as there were Khatran clans living on both sides of the Punjab border, Punjab frontier officials needed to be able to negotiate with the entire tribe.

The controversy reached Lytton who, with his scheme for a new Frontier Province at a standstill, was minded to support Sandeman's idea that Dera Ghazi Khan should be brought entirely under the Baluchistan Agency. Once again, the Punjab lobby proved victorious. A compromise placed relations with the Khatrans under Sandeman, but those with the other Baloch tribes on the Punjab frontier remained outside his remit. He was only given the right to be consulted by the Lieutenant-Governor of the Punjab or the Commissioner in Sind on any proposals likely to affect Kalat, to enter their Baloch frontier districts, and call on their local officials for information.[1]

The renewal of the Second Afghan War

On 3 September 1879 Sir Louis Cavagnari, the new Resident at Kabul, was killed along with his escort, in a rising of the Amir Yakub Khan's unpaid troops. A column under Sir Frederick Roberts was sent to Kabul, ostensibly to assist the Amir in restoring order. Yakub Khan, once popular, found that his people had turned against him, as a British puppet, and abdicated on 12 October. Roberts reached Kabul, where he was besieged until a relief force arrived on 24 December 1879. Lytton then decided that Afghanistan should be divided into three seperate states, Kabul, Kandahar and Herat. After many assurances that the British would never withdraw from Afghanistan, in May 1880 Sher Ali Barakzai, a nephew of Amir Dost Muhammad, agreed to become Wali (Ruler) of Kandahar. In a complete reversal of previous policy, Salisbury, now at the Foreign Office, proposed that, to secure his friendship against the Russians, Nasir al-Din Shah of Iran be informed that the British would raise no objection to his taking Herat. St John, the senior political officer at Kandahar, recommended that Kabul should be handed to Abdul Rahman, the late Amir Sher Ali's nephew, who was about to return from exile in Russian territory to claim the Afghan throne. Lytton welcomed this solution as 'a ram caught in a thicket' and ordered Lepel Griffin, late Secretary to the Punjab Government and now the political officer at Kabul, to open negotiations with Abdur Rahman accordingly.

As in 1841, a British general election brought a new government in London and a new policy towards Afghanistan. Beaconsfield gave place to Gladstone, who had denounced the British invasions of Afghanistan and Zululand (the latter launched by Frere, High Commissioner in South Africa since April 1877). Lord Hartington took over from Cranbrook at the India Office. Lytton resigned immediately and was succeeded by the Earl of Ripon. His dream of a quick, cheap campaign to secure British control over Afghanistan had turned into an expensive nightmare and he had already told Griffin, who had advocated making an ally of Abdul Rahman, merely to inform him that the British were going home. Only Kandahar, under Wali Sher Ali, would be left with a British garrison. Nasir al-Din Shah had hesitated over the British offer of Herat, as involving an expensive campaign with an uncertain outcome. When he re-opened the subject, he found the new British government was no longer interested, and the governor of Herat, Sardar Ayub Khan (a brother of the ex-Amir Yakub Khan) was claiming the Afghan throne for himself.[2]

Phayre and Sandeman re-united

Sandeman's old ally, Phayre, had returned to military employment after his unsuccessful foray into the political sphere. During the first part of the new Afghan war he commanded the lines of communication from Sind through the Bolan and worked in close co-operation with Sandeman (with whom he had remained in correspondence) to protect the construction of a light railway being made from Sukkur. This track, initially intended as a war-time measure, had been started in October 1879 and made good progress through the levels of Upper Sind and Kachhi to reach Sibi on 14 January 1880. In the autumn of 1879, with the treaty of Gandamak having made Afghanistan a British protectorate, Lytton despatched Sir Richard Temple, the Governor of Bombay, to plan a permanent broad-gauge line all the way to Kandahar. Advised by the military railway engineers, Temple recommended that, because of the gradients, the permanent line should not be laid through the Bolan but 40 miles to its east and thus run from Sibi, via Harnai, to Pishin and thence into Afghanistan through the Khojak Pass. A light railway would run through the Bolan from Sibi to Quetta, and rejoin the main line at Bostan, halfway between Quetta and Pishin.

This plan made it logical for Kandahar to be held by the Bombay rather than the Bengal Army, and Phayre arrived there with the first Bombay troops in March 1880. Lytton, on the grounds that Phayre's record showed him lacking in tact, good temper and sober judgement, decided not to give him command there, and instead appointed Major General Primrose, a British Army officer who had previously served with the Bombay Army. As Primrose had no experience of Afghan diplomatic affairs, St John was given full political control. Phayre was consoled with appointment as GOC Bombay Reserve Division, with his headquarters located alongside Sandeman at Quetta.

In June 1881 St John reported that Ayub Khan's army had left Herat and Wali Sher Ali had taken the field to oppose it. The Wali's men subsequently went over to Ayub Khan, whose forces included a contingent sent by Sardar Azad Khan Nausherwani of Kharan. A British brigade, despatched on St John's advice to support Wali Sher Ali, was routed at Maiwand, in the Helmund province (27 July 1881). The survivors retreated to Kandahar, which then came under siege. This defeat was as dramatic in its effect on British prestige as had been the destruction of the Kabul garrison forty years earlier, but Khudadad Khan used the new telegraph line to tell Sandeman, 'My head and my all belong to the British. I shall never draw back. Whatever grain or money is required by the British Government, I am ready to supply'. When Ayub Khan summoned him to join a holy war against the British with his regular troops and tribal contingents, he dismissed the messenger and sent the letter on to Sandeman, along with 400 camels to help British troop movements. The Brahui sardars also declared for the British, but the Marris, whom

Sandeman had long claimed to be able to control, attacked a British convoy near Harnai, on the uncompleted railway to Pishin town. They killed a dozen men and made off with two lakhs of rupees before making another raid in Sibi district a few weeks later. A 2,000 strong Pashtun war party from the Zhob valley, in the north-east of Pishin district, also menaced the intended railway and attacked British outposts guarding its stores and materials.

Immediately on hearing the news of Maiwand, Phayre and Sandeman agreed on the need to concentrate the forces at their disposal. The new posts in Sibi and Pishin districts were evacuated and the unfinished line to Quetta abandoned to the care of local headmen. Ripon telegraphed his approval and stressed the need to push reinforcements forward to Kandahar. Just as in 1842 there had been a race to Kabul between the Bombay troops under Nott and the Bengal troops under Pollock, now there was one to Kandahar between a Bengal flying column from Kabul, led by Roberts, and Phayre's Bombay division. Phayre was delayed by transport difficulties and the need to detach troops to Kalat, where a thousand of the Khan's mercenaries had deserted and gone to join Ayub Khan. Roberts, aided by Abdul Rahman, won the race and defeated Ayub Khan outside Kandahar (1 September 1881). Wali Sher Ali abdicated and went into comfortable exile in Karachi. After Maiwand, St John was blamed by the military for giving them faulty intelligence, based on his misjudgement of Ayub Khan's intentions. Sandeman, at Quetta, seems to have had a better appreciation of the danger and sent some kind of warning to the Foreign Department at Simla a week before the battle. The British handed over Kandahar to Abdul Rahman in April 1881. Ayub Khan returned from Herat and captured the city but was defeated there by Abdul Rahman in the following September. Herat fell to Abdul Rahman's troops and was reincorporated into the Afghan state. In a final echo of 1839, a British brigade on its way back from Kandahar marched through the Marri hills in retribution for raids on the Sibi railway and reached Kahan, where the Marris paid a fine of two lakhs of rupees and gave hostages for future good conduct.[3]

British Balochistan

During 1881 Sandeman returned to the United Kingdom on a long-delayed furlough. Most authorities on frontier affairs, Merewether and Rawlinson among them, were in favour of restoring Pishin and Sibi to Afghanistan, on the grounds that, without Kandahar, they would be untenable. Sandeman spent the next six months lobbying hard to retain his new domains, stressing their strategic importance and claiming that it would be morally wrong to abandon the local sardars who had co-operated with him during the previous three years. His arguments proved successful and, with his new bride, he made a triumphal journey back to Quetta at the end of 1882.

Following the withdrawal from Kandahar, the retention of Quetta itself had been in question, and the war-time railway had been abandoned, with its materials being hastily sold off to help pay the soaring costs of the campaign. During 1883, following further Russian moves in the Great Game, this policy was reversed. Sandeman was authorised to establish British administration over Harnai, thus securing the route of the proposed broad-gauge railway, and also over Thal and Chotiali, 60 miles to the east, thereby entirely surrounding the Marris by British-held territory. Further west, in 1883 Khudadad Khan was persuaded to grant the province of Quetta to the British on a perpetual lease for a rent of 80,000 rupees per annum. Work on the railways, halted on the British withdrawal from Kandahar in 1881, was renewed in 1883. Raids by local tribesmen on the railway during 1883–84 were countered by military expeditions and Sandeman's appointment of a pro-British sardar over the Kakar Pashtuns of the Zhob valley in 1886. The rail-head, overcoming vast technical challenges, reached Quetta in 1887.

In June 1887, Sandeman's appointment was up-graded to Resident, 1st Class. In the following November, the assigned districts of Sibi and Pishin were annexed to India under the title 'British Baluchistan' (something of a misnomer, as the population was predominantly Pashtun) with the Agent to the Governor-General for Baluchistan governing them as chief commissioner. Quetta and Pishin were combined into one district, and Sibi, Loralai, Zhob, Thal and Chotiali into another. A conventional administration was established, with deputy commissioners and district officers conforming to the pattern in the existing provinces of British India. On 1 January 1891, to deal with the increase in population and business, a Revenue Commissioner was appointed, charged with collecting the revenue and supervising the police, jails and public works on which most of it was expended. This post was awarded to Hugh Barnes, an Indian Civil Servant who had for several years been Sandeman's senior administrative assistant.

Extending British influence into southern Waziristan, Sandeman accompanied strong military expeditions to secure the Gomal Pass in both 1889 and 1890, the second one being sanctioned by the then governor-general, the 5th Marquess of Lansdowne, only because, as he told Sir James Lyall, lieutenant-governor of the Punjab (a younger brother of the former Indian Foreign Secretary), Sandeman was 'difficult and dangerous to thwart'. Lansdowne, an Irish peer who had been under-secretary of state for India under Gladstone, had proved a capable governor-general of Canada and, having joined the Conservative and Unionist party, was appointed viceroy by Salisbury in 1888. In an echo of the old turf wars between the Punjab and Sind, Lyall claimed control of the lower Gomal Pass, leading down into the Punjab border district of Dera Isamail Khan. Sandeman, by then at the peak of his prestige, argued that the entire pass and the tribal areas flanking it (which under Lyall's proposals would have been left unadministered, as in the Khyber), should be under his Agency. After various compromises, Lansdowne decided that the long-established Punjab policy of leaving the border tribes to administer themselves did not fit in with his policy for extending British control over this area. The Gomal River was made the boundary between British Balochistan and Waziristan. On the creation of the North-West Frontier Province in 1901, the Punjab Government ceased to be responsible for this area, but the new province and the Baluchistan Agency still retained their separate policies. In Zhob, an adminitrative centre named Fort Sandeman was established at Apozai.[4]

Kharan

In Kharan, Sardar Azad Khan Nausherwani defeated a rebellion by one of his sons who, himself in his seventies, had tired of waiting for the throne. The undutiful one and his adherents were bricked up in pillars to mark the routes across the desert to his capital, Azad Khan saying that thus they would be more useful after their deaths than they ever had been in their lives. In 1883, he sent his favourite son, Nauroz Khan, to collect the land revenue of jagirs he claimed in Panjgur. Fighting took place, in which Sardar Mir Gajian Gichki, the local chief and representative of the Khan of Kalat, was killed. To settle the dispute, Sandeman marched to Kharan, accompanied by an escort of Scinde Horse and two engineer officers who used the chance to survey large tracts that the British had never previously entered. Azad Khan agreed to acknowledge the Khan of Kalat as his nominal overlord, in return for Kharan being recognised as autonomous in all other respects. Sandeman described him at this period as 'unable to mount a horse without assistance, but once in the saddle, his endurance is greater than that of many a younger man. Possessed of unflinching resolution, impatient of wrong, generous to reward, stern and relentless in punishment, Sirdar Azad Khan... is never known to depart from his word, once given'. As Sandeman took his side against Khudadad Khan, the sardar thereafter adopted a pro-British policy. He died in 1886, being then aged 101 according to Muslim reckoning, and was succeeded by Nauroz Khan.

This prince, finding that the British would not aid him to regain lands that Azad Khan had claimed in Iranian territory, approached the Governor of Bampur for redress. This gave Sandeman an opportunity to persuade Khudadad Khan, with the agreement of the Makran sardars and Nauroz Khan himself, to ask for the administration of western Balochistan to be taken over by the British. Pending a decision from the Government of India, he toured Makran, Kech and Panjgur, conferred with the Jam of Las Bela, the Gichki sardars and Nauroz Khan, and installed his political assistants with instructions to collect the revenue at the usual rate. Early in 1891 he went on leave to England, and while there learned that the Government of India, alarmed by various disturbances such as revenue collection in this region commonly provoked, had decided to withdraw the officials he had left there, along with their military escort. Once more, Sandeman's lobbying in London succeeded in reversing a decision, at least to the extent that he was authorised to instal British officers in the Khan of Kalat's niabat of Nushki, north of Makran, where the boundary with Iranian Sistan and the upper Helmund valley had yet to be defined.

Las Bela

Jam Mir Ali of Las Bela, while in exile in India, had married a Delhi lady, with whom he had a son. After being restored, in response to her persuasion he nominated their infant son as his heir. In 1886 the Jam's eldest son, Sardar Ali Khan Jamot, who had fought so long and hard against Khudadad Khan over Las Bela, rose in defence of his own claims to the succession. He was defeated and exiled to Sibi, but escaped British supervision and remained in arms until eventually arrested on the orders of Oliver St John, acting as Agent to the Governor-General for Baluchistan during Sandeman's absence on furlough. St John recommended that, in view of Sardar Ali Khan Jamot's rebellious conduct, the son nominated by Jam Mir Ali should be recognised as the rightful heir.

When Jam Mir Ali died in January 1888, Sardar Ali Khan Jamot again pressed his claims to the throne. Sandeman placed Las Bela under Rai Bahadur Hittu Ram while the question of the succession was considered. He eventually decided in favour of Sardar Ali Khan Jamot, as a man of mature years and experience and the son of a Brahui princess (the sister of the late Sardar

Nur al-Din Mingal) whereas the younger son was a youth, and had no local supporters. In January 1889, therefore, Jam Ali Khan was placed on the throne of Las Bela, with (thanks to Hittu Ram) a full treasury containing 50,000 rupees in cash. In 1891 Jam Ali Khan's own eldest son, Mir Kamal Khan, rebelled and fled to Quetta. Sandeman had already planned to return to Makran during January 1892 in order to restore the administrative arrangements that had collapsed during his recent absence. He now decided to combine this tour with visit to Las Bela, hoping he could achieve a reconciliation between the Jam and Mir Kamal Khan. En route, he became ill and died at Las Bela on 29 January 1892, a month before his fifty-seventh birthday. He was interred outside the town, in a ceremony attended by his wife, his senior British and Indian staff, Jam Ali Khan and numerous local sardars. From Kalat, Khudadad Khan wrote a letter of condolence to Lady Sandeman, saying that Sandeman should be buried in his own native land or the Khan's dominions, and if the chief of Las Bela objected, he was ready to send his army to carry the body to Quetta by force.[5]

Sandeman's influence on Balochistan

Sandeman's role in the history of Balochistan had been as important as that of Jacob on the Sind frontier a generation earlier. Within nine years of the treaty of Jacobabad, he had turned Kalat into the 'Brahui confederacy' that had long been his interpretation of the state's constitution. The Khan still reigned as the nominal sovereign, but outside his crown lands he no longer governed the country. The real ruler was the Agent to the Governor-General, whom everyone knew had the Quetta garrison to enforce his decisions. By directly subsidizing the major sardars, Sandeman strengthened their position against both the Khan and their own tribesmen, thus turning them into the strongly pro-British group that he and Phayre had aimed to establish twenty years earlier. In areas under British administration, his 'Sandemanian' policy of employing para-military tribal contingents, recruited through the sardars, paid to keep the peace as an alternative to disturbing it, was much the same as Jacob's had been. Advocates of the old close-border policy dismissed it as an expensive form of blackmail and pointed to its lack of success among the Pashtun tribes of the misnamed 'British Balochistan'. His admirers (dubbed 'Sandemaniacs' by their opponents) claimed that, had he lived longer, his personal force of character would have enabled him to pacify the Pashtuns under his government just as he had the Baloch and Brahuis.

His distinctive contribution was the formalization of the long-existing institution of the *jirga* (council), through which local disputes were resolved by clan elders. Under Sandeman, jirgas were established at local, district and provincial level, composed of tribal chiefs and religious leaders, appointed in practice by British political officers who could take part in their deliberations and ensure their judgements were enforced. His personal career success was achieved mostly though a readiness to disregard his immediate superiors and appeal directly to higher authority. By exploiting the differences between the governments of Sind and the Punjab, he extended his area of responsibility from his own district over all Balochistan. He was lucky in that the crisis of his personal ambition coincided with the arrival of Lytton, who found him useful when a more ambitious policy of frontier re-organisation came to nothing.

Having used the prestigious Punjab government to achieve his advancement, Sandeman thereafter intrigued vigorously to maintain and extend his position. One of his last letters was to the Honourable George Curzon (with whom he had previously established an acquaintance as a rising member of the Conservative Party and its expert on Central Asian affairs), congratulating him on appointment as Under-Secretary of State for India, lauding his own achievements in Balochistan and denouncing Lansdowne's recent decision to withdraw from Makran. The completion in 1890 of the Trans-Caspian Railway had alarmed Curzon and Salisbury, as they feared it would allow Russia to occupy Mashshed, Herat and Balkh. Like Sandeman himself, they feared that Lansdowne's emphasis on settling the Afghan frontier was leading him to neglect that with Iran, where the anticipated demise of the ageing Nasir al-Din Shah was thought likely to open the way to Russian expansion.

Sandeman's successor

Sandeman's unexpected death posed a problem over his replacement. An obvious choice would have been Oliver St John, who had three times officiated as Agent to the Governor-General in Balochistan when Sandeman was on furlough. On the last occasion, however, having eagerly accepted Lansdowne's invitation to leave his Residency at Mysore, he had died of pneumonia at Quetta on 20 May 1891, two weeks after his arrival. In January 1892, after an interregnum of three months, Sandeman was succeeded by a fellow-Scotsman, the fifty-two-year-old Colonel (about to become Major General Sir) James Browne, an officer of the Royal (originally Bengal) Engineers. Powerfully built and standing over six feet high, he had spent much of his career on the Punjab frontier attached to the Indian Public Works Department, where he become a specialist in railway construction.

During 1877, following the new Treaty of Jacobabad, Browne was one of the officers employed in surveying the route for a line from Sukkur to Sibi, and received instructions directly from Lytton, the Governor-General. His views on frontier communications made him one of Lytton's favourites and he was added to the Governor-General's personal staff. From there he was assigned to the Foreign Department as a political officer, dealing with the Kakar Pashtuns, near whose country the Sibi railway would run. With instructions from Lytton to go in disguise if necessary, he travelled to his new area of responsibility via Dadhar, Kachhi, the Marri country, Kalat and Quetta, where he joined the engineers strengthening the defences of the citadel, the Miri. During the first phase of the Afghan War, Browne served as political officer in Stewart's column at Quetta, Kandahar and Kalat-i-Ghilzai, and with Biddulph's division when this returned to India through Thal and Chotiali in February 1879.

When the Afghan War was renewed, Browne was on furlough in the United Kingdom. He subsequently served with the Indian contingent in the British campaign in Egypt and fought at Tel-el-Kebir (13 September 1882). After returning to India in 1883 he was given charge of the construction of the Sibi-Harnai railway as a permanent line. This took three years and was achieved despite major engineering difficulties, floods, financial problems and outbreaks of disease among the Indian Pioneer units and locally-employed Ghilzais and Pashtuns who provided the labour force. The main line eventually reached the Afghan frontier at Chaman in 1892, with major works including the Khojak Pass tunnel, two and a half miles long and three years in the construction. Meanwhile, Browne was rewarded by appointment in 1889 as Quartermaster General (India), responsible for the plans, operations, logistics and fortifications of the Bengal Army. He made a special study of the defences of the North-West Frontier and the routes from Sistan, at a time when the Great Game was again assuming importance in international relations.

Browne himself had been the first engineer officer to hold the post of QMG (India), and hoped for a military command on completion of the normal period of office there. He was reluctant to accept the Balochistan Agency and urged that the post should be given to Hugh Barnes, the experienced Civil Servant who had been Revenue Commissioner for Baluchistan since 1890 and officiating Agent to the Governor General during the three months since Sandeman's death. Lansdowne seems to have decided that Browne's experience of the frontier tribes and his tough character (indicated by his nickname

'Buster') made him a better candidate. Writing to Viscount Cross, Secretary of State for India in Salisbury's second Cabinet, he said that he had been 'much exercised' to find a suitable successor for Sandeman and had selected Browne as someone who knew the country, the tribes and their language, and was the kind of strong man needed on the frontier at a time of increasing tension with Afghanistan. He would confront any difficulties 'with tact as well as courage'.[6]

What Lansdowne did not take into account was that Browne had no experience of dealing with princes, least of all one such as Khudadad Khan of Kalat. According to Browne's biographer, many officials in the Indian Foreign Department foresaw trouble and viewed the new Agent as someone 'anxious, in order to gratify his ambitious ends, to stir up a big row'.[7] Sandeman's biographer, referring to the misfortunes that were about to befall the Khan, wrote in 1895 that they were 'a sad termination of the career of one who, with all his faults, had proved himself a loyal friend and ally of the British Government'.[8]

The fall of Khudadad Khan

Certainly, the big row was not long in coming. By his own admission, within a short time of taking over the Baluchistan Agency, Browne decided that he disliked the tone adopted towards him by the Khan,[9] though in fact the nature of Khudadad Khan's correspondance with Sandeman and other British officers at his court had always been entirely diplomatically correct nor had there ever been any objection to its 'tone' even if there had been to its content. Browne also reported that he disliked the Khan's methods of government (notwithstanding that for at least fifteen years past the Khan had ruled in accordance with Sandeman's advice). Disappointed in his hopes of military advancement, Browne may well have hoped to use the Baluchistan Agency, a backwater given him in lieu of an Army command, to make his name in a new field, by showing everyone that Sandeman's era was past and a new broom had arrived. Sandeman himself, despite having originally seen Khudadad Khan as a tyrant whose rule was as pitch upon the faces of his subjects, had mellowed towards that prince once he achieved his own ambitions and, in one of his last letters to Curzon, wrote that, although the Khan was far from being all that could be desired, and could never forgive the sardars for their successful rebellion (success that in fact had owed much to Sandeman himself) under British paramountcy both sides could be kept as useful friends.

Browne's opportunity came late in 1892 when, as he later told Lansdowne, 'after a hard struggle with myself I resolved so decidedly against Sandeman's system of policy as to upset [here meaning *overturn*] the Khan'.[10] Following a report from the Naib of Bagh that money was missing from the local treasury, the Khan ordered an investigation which established that 8,500 rupees had been stolen and that the culprits were eight of the Khan's own slaves. Khudadad Khan then had the five women 'killed with the sword' (probably beheaded, though Browne interpreted it as having their throats cut), one man stoned to death and two castrated. Browne returned from leave in December 1892 and decided to make an issue of these punishments, as being excessively severe for theft from an inadequately guarded treasury. Khudadad Khan eventually stated that they were not actually for theft but for adultery and therefor sanctioned by Holy Law (which would certainly fit with the penalties of stoning and beheading) but that, as the case concerned females, it could not be reported as such without dishonour to Muslims. Browne chose to disbelieve him, arguing that the Khan had not offered this justification when first challenged, but only subsequently.

On 26 December 1892 Browne raised the subject of the recent punishments with the Khan's wazir, Mustaufi (accountant) Fakir Muhammad. The wazir said that he supposed the Khan thought he had a right to do as he pleased in his own country. More cogently, he said that he feared for his own life, as the Khan was planning to kill him and sieze his very considerable wealth. Some time later, Major H. M. Temple, the Political Agent at Kalat, reported to Browne that the wazir was following British advice to serve the Khan loyally, that the number of complaints about tyranny by the Khan had fallen, and several fugitives from British justice had been handed over. On 17 February Browne ordered the two castrated men to be sent to Temple for medical examination because proof was needed to support an expression of British disapproval. On 25 March the wazir demonstrated his attachment to the British by aiding the arrest of a suspected Russian agent in Bagh, while at the same time again expressing fears for his own life.

On 28 March, Temple telegraphed to Browne at Quetta that the wazir and his family had been arrested. Browne immediately sent orders for the Khan to hand over the prisoners, unharmed, to Temple while their offence was investigated. The Khan telegraphed back to say that the wazir had entered his personal quarters and tried to murder him with a pistol, but had been disarmed by the Khan's younger son, Mir Muhammad Azim. The wazir, along with his son, father and one of his servants, had therefore been arrested and put to death for treason. Temple's agents reported that the Khan had ordered these deaths partly out of pique, because the wazir had advised him to rule less tyrannically and had handed over the castrated men and the suspected Russian agent to the British, but mostly to gain possession of the wazir's money and jewels. This accounted for the killing of the wazir's two closest heirs, one an elderly cripple and the other a young man aged about nineteen, and his servant, Havaldar Sher Dad, a British subject who, as the wazir's factotum, knew about his wealth. Browne refused to believe the Khan's story and ordered him to return all valuables taken from the late wazir's household. The Khan replied on 9 April denying that any valuables had been taken, and stating that he sent his servants to the wazir's house to prevent looting. He then offered to visit Browne to explain in person what had taken place.

Browne chose to ignore this offer and ordered the Khan (who was at that time in Bagh) to attend on him at Quetta, threatening that, if he did not come, British troops would be sent to compel him, with the cost deducted from the Khan's subsidy. Khudadad Khan prevaricated but eventually agreed that, despite the lack of water along the road, he would go to Belpat, the railway station about 10 miles east of Bagh, where a special train had been ordered. The gradient and lack of haulage power meant there was only space on the train for two companies of Bombay Infantry (who happened to be passing on relief from Upper Sind to Quetta), thus giving Browne a pretext for detaching the Khan from his own guards.

Browne's telegram to the Khan on 13 April 1893 makes clear his determination to force an incident. Instead of addressing him in the third person and as 'Your Highness', he wrote baldly 'You can send any followers you like by the mail train that leaves Bellpat tonight or tomorrow night but I will not allow you to bring in the special train a single man more than the number permitted by Major Temple. You have evaded my orders much too often and put my troops to inconvenience and trouble far too often for your convenience in a manner I will tolerate no longer. I therefore order you to comply with Major Temple's wishes whatever they may be'. The Indian Foreign Department, to whom the correspondence was being copied by Browne, immediately ordered him not to make any troop movements without its authority, and told him it saw no need to send reinforcements to Quetta, as he had requested. Browne, on his own initiative, had already despatched a cavalry regiment from Jacobabad to the Kalat border. He was, however, given authority to send troops to secure the Khan's treasury at Kalat, where the only British soldiers were seventeen Bombay infantrymen, and where it was reported that, with large numbers of Ghilzais and Pashtuns arriving daily, the Khan's regulars were talking of plundering the treasury and deserting.

Browne mobilised two columns. One, composed of a battalion of the Middlesex Regiment, a regiment of the Scinde Horse, Jacob's Rifles and a mountain battery, occupied Kalat and removed most of the treasury, leaving only 10 lakhs of rupees for day-to-day government business. When the remaing 44 lakhs reached Quetta, the finance department had no room for them, and they had to be placed in the armoury of the local European Volunteer Rifles. The second column, consisting of the 7th Bombay Cavalry and the 4th Bombay Infantry, with two mountain guns, went to Belpat. When Khudadad Khan arrived, he found Browne with the military drawn up on three sides of a hollow square, facing outwards, and the special train on the fourth. No compliments were paid and after the Khan entered the square as if it were a guard of honour, the troops were turned about and he was carried off to Quetta as a prisoner of state.[11] Browne reported that he had taken this action in response to petitions from the sardars of Kalat for the Khan's deposition.

The Indian Foreign Department, headed since 1884 by Sir Henry Mortimer Durand (son of the Sir Henry Durand who had been killed in 1871 when lieutenant-governor of the Punjab), was increasingly alarmed at Browne's proceedings. On 13 April it telegraphed him 'Viceroy desires if Khan comes voluntarily to Bellpat or Quetta he should be reassured against arrest' and, after reports that the Khan had been tricked into surrendering, telegraphed on 28 April 'Can you arrest him without breach of faith? The Government of India must be assured that he has no grounds for complaints of entrapment. Can you show, beyond all reasonable doubt, Khan is guilty of wanton murder? He has power of life and death and interference is only justified in case of gross abuse'. Browne was asked to name the sardars whom he claimed were begging for Khudadad Khan's deposition. Was their request based on the alleged murders and was Mir Mahmud (Khudadad Khan's oldest eligible son, generally recognised as his heir) fit to take over?

After a delay of some weeks, Brown replied on 2 June 1893. He denied any breach of faith, arguing that he had not acknowledged the letter in which Khudadad Khan had proposed a meeting; the Khan had never been promised safe conduct; and that he had not come to Belpat voluntarily but under compulsion. The sardars who had complained were mostly from Sarawan, being those nearest to Quetta. Their complaints were about misgovernment in general. Mir Mahmud was a steady character, who had expressed disapproved of the killings. Khudadad Khan had now declared his abdication in favour of Mir Mahmud, saying he wished to retire from the throne and devote the rest of his life to religious studies.

Browne was promptly told to keep this secret until the Government of India had reached its own decision on the succession, but as the agreement between the two princes had already been made public, he was able to disregard this instruction. Pressed by Durand for his full report on these proceedings, he said that he was unable to submit it without understanding the wishes of the Government. He was answered on 8 June 1893 'You need not be afraid of increasing the difficulties of the Government of India by not sending in your report. The delay in receiving it is very inconvenient and the Government cannot decide the case without seeing any evidence'. He responded, after another twenty-one days, that the delay was regrettable but inevitable, involving an enormous amount of labour on a mass of vernacular papers and that he was sparing neither himself nor his officers, being well aware of the evils arising from needless delay.

Lansdowne told the Earl of Kimberley (Cross's successor as Secretary for State for India following the defeat of Salisbury by Gladstone in August 1892) that the Khan's resignation would be the best solution, as he did not wish to depose him and had cautioned Browne not to proceed too fast. Kimberley answered 'Sir J Browne does not seem to me a very suitable person to be entrusted with the management of one of our most difficult agencies. I am glad you are keeping a tight rein on him.'[12] Browne finally reported on 15 July 1893, with over 900 pages of manuscript containing his own observations and statements by some forty witnesses. 'I cannot help thinking', Lansdowne told Kimberley, 'that Browne wished to pay us out for having told him he must take all the evidence against the Khan with great care and confront His Highness with the hostile witnesses... but we shall I hope be able to arrive at a decision before long.'[13]

Browne argued that Khudadad Khan had never accepted there were limits beyond which the British would not tolerate his misgovernment. Writing much as Phayre and Sandeman had done twenty years earlier, he declared that the history of the thirty-six years of Khudadad Khan's reign was one of brutality, oppression, broken oaths and violated agreements, and that his own countrymen now wanted him gone. The recent castrations, stoning, and cutting women's throats were merely the latest examples of his cruelty. His sardars were petitioning for the curtailment of such powers and, seeing the prosperity of British Baluchistan, desired a similar administration in Kalat state. The Khan answered allegations that he had used threats of castration to extort large sums of money by saying that these cases were those of criminals sentenced according to law. Cash fines were imposed as alternatives and he always allowed time for the sums to be collected. He had castrated men twice before, once in Harrison's time, and once in Sandeman's. He estimated he had imposed about a hundred death sentences in each year of his reign, a figure Browne expressed as a total of 3,600.

Taken overall, the evidence, presented to Browne's enquiry during the first week of May 1893, showed that the wazir's son, Ghulam Farukh, had intended to take service with the British. The Khan had summoned him, together with the wazir, the wazir's aged father Abdul Aziz (a former naib of Bagh who had been wounded in the Khan's service) and Havaldar Sher Dad to the palace and then had them seized and bound, accusing them of treason, kicking them and asking where 'Baran (Browne) Sahib' and their British friends were now? He sentenced them to be beheaded and cut to pieces and then retired for four hours, during which Malvi Abdul Ghafur, the highly respected Qazi of Bagh, attempted unsuccessfully to intercede for them. The Khan then returned and ordered their execution after their faces, soiled from being on the ground, had been washed. Mir Muhammad Azim refused to allow them to say their prayers and struck the first blow himself, followed by a crowd of swordsmen from the Khan's guards and servants.

The Khan's defence was that he had committed no crime against the British and the men were his slaves whose lives were in his hands. Against this it was stated that the wazir and his family were free men, originally from Iran, and the havaldar was a British subject. A small American-made Derringer pistol was produced to support the Khan's story. The manufacturers, in Hartford, Connecticut, were contacted, but stated they kept no records of who purchased this type of pistol. It was judged likely to have reached Kalat through Iran. Witnesses disagreed on which pocket the pistol came from, whether it was fired, or even whether it had been seen at all. No-one could say why the wazir would have attempted to commit murder with such a small piece, especially with the Khan's guards outside the door and no means of escape. Evidence was given that the Khan had sent his cavalry to block the roads to prevent news of the planned executions reaching British officials. The wazir's ladies gave evidence that the Khan had sent men to find the wazir's infant son, and on being told the child had recently died, dug up the grave to verify the wazir had no male heirs living. Much was made of the disappearance of a valuable jewel that the wazir had obtained at a good price from an Iranian dealer. The ladies appealed to Browne for the return of their late husbands' property to maintain their households. Browne convened a jirga of sardars to hear the complaints against the Khan. Unsurprisingly, as many of them had fought against him for years and all knew what Browne, who controlled their allowances, expected them to say, they decided that Khudadad Khan was guilty of tyranny and oppression and should be deposed.

Browne himself seems to have been anxious about his own position at this time. He wrote privately to Lansdowne on 21 July 1893 to express his unease about the reception his Kalat report would have from the Foreign Department and appealed for support if he had 'got into any pitfalls' from lack of experience. Any shortcomings should be attributed to his limited experience in political work, as in his thirty years in India he had never had to deal with such a case, and his methods therefore might not have been up to Durand's standards.

Durand, after wading through Browne's report, came to the conclusion that, though in Browne's place he would have recommended a less public way of enquiry and punishment, as the case had been dealt with in the way that it had, there was no way by which the Khan, after being proven guilty of murder and cruel barbarities, could be left in power. This decision, in effect, meant that Kalat had imperceptibly changed in British eyes from being an ally, subordinate only in respect of its foreign policy in accordance with the Treaty of Jacobabad, into a vassal state no different from the other protected principalities of the Indian Empire. Durand was expressing the view dating as far back as the days of Sir John Malcolm, that if the British supported a native prince, they became morally responsible for the good government of his state, because if he became an oppressor, their support denied his subjects their only means of redress, deposing him by rebellion or welcoming an invader. What Durand failed to see was that in Kalat, the British subsidy was not paid to the Khan so that he could retain power, but as compensation for the loss of revenue cause by his reduction of transit fees on the kafilas. At the same time, Durand expressed reservations about Browne's apparent desire for greater interference in the internal affairs of Kalat. When the papers reached the India Office, the view taken was that they showed the Khan was a ruffian 'even by Oriental standards'. Browne's old chief, Sir Donald Stewart, on the Council of India, wrote to him stating that the Government of India would be left to do as it wished as long as there was no question of annexation and the existing ruling family was left on the throne.[14]

Concerned at his own position, Browne also wrote to Lansdowne about Hugh Barnes, who had been summoned to Simla to discuss his joining Durand's proposed mission to Kabul. Barnes, he said, had a wide circle of native friends, who all knew that he considered that Khudadad Khan's oppressive behaviour had been quite consistent with the customs of the country, as the only way that an Oriental ruler had of squeezing out of his subordinates monies they had embezzled. Consequently, he had taken what Browne saw as a lenient view of the episode, and was widely considered the Khan's champion. His going to Simla would be widely interpreted as evidence that the Government of India accepted his opinions, thereby weakening Browne's position. Personally, Browne said, he was on good terms with Barnes and did not wish to stand in his way, but asked to accompany him to Simla so as not to give encouragement to the Khan's party.[15] Durand admitted the force of this and decided that Barnes should not leave Baluchistan while the Khan's future remained unsettled.

Despite having agreed to resign in favour of Mir Mahmud, Khudadad Khan had still not given up hope of recovering his throne. His sister, Bibi Fatah Khatun, (avoiding attempts by Browne and Mir Mahmud to prevent her) went to Simla, hoping to plead his case with Lansdowne, though ultimately to no effect. She also acted as the Khan's intermediary with Sardar Gauhar Khan Zahri, a former chief of the Jhalawans who had been arrested several times by Sandeman, but released when his fellow sardars pleaded that he was insane. Another sardar had been appointed in his place, but he was now preaching holy war and had gathered 2,000 men to fight for the restoration of Khudadad Khan. The Khan, though his government funds were now all under British control, still had ample personal wealth at his disposal and was suspected by Browne of spending lavishly to gain popular support, including that from Gauhar Khan and his followers.

At the end of August 1893 Browne asked for regular troops to suppress Gauhar Khan and restore order in the Jhalawan country, thus protecting both the Bolan and Makran, from where the troops left behind by Sandeman had been recalled by Lansdowne despite Browne's objections. He had to admit that the Mingals, Bizenjaus and other major Jhalawan tribes were not supporting Gauhar Khan, but asked for them to be given service in the same way as Sandeman had done with the Sarawans. Sandeman, he added, had never gone into Jhalawan country without a strong escort and, as they had nothing to lose, they were outside British control.[16] He was allowed to arrange employment as long as it was paid for out of Kalat rather than British funds. His plans for a large British force were scaled down by the Government of India to Temple and his escort accompanying Mir Mahmud's army (a combination of Sarawan contingents and the Khan's regulars), to give moral support. In September 1893 these defeated the insurgents, but Gauhar Khan himself escaped to continue resistance from Makran, while Mir Mahmud was reluctant to continue operations until his own position was recognized by the Government of India. Browne's request to be present when the jewelled turban ornament of chieftainship was presented to Mir Mahmud was refused, and he was told that the ceremony was to be regarded as a family affair, not one of state.

After further exchanges of correspondence between London and India, and for want of any viable alternative, Mir Mahmud was recognized as Mahmud Khan II on 10 November 1893, in the presence of the assembled sardars of Balochistan. The extent to which his state had become subject to the British is clear from his installation ceremony being held not at his capital, Kalat, but at Quetta, no longer under the Khan's rule, but the headquarters of British administration in Balochistan and the site of the second largest garrison in the Indian Empire. Browne addressed the gathering at length, calling on the new Khan to govern for the good of his subjects and on the sardars to be reconciled to him, with all parties recognizing the rights of the others.

Neither side paid more attention than they had to. Khudadad Khan himself was exiled first to Harnai and then Loralai, where he outlived Browne, his near contemporary, by some years. Browne died at Quetta, after a sudden illness, on 13 April 1896, still in disagreement with Hugh Barnes, the newly-created Judicial Commissioner for Baluchistan, who succeeded him as Agent to the Governor-General. Mahmud Khan II reigned until his death in 1931. His successor, Azam Jan Khan, came to the throne at an advanced age, and was himself succeeded in 1933 by his second son, the then twenty-nine year-old Ahmad Yar Khan, under whom Kalat acceded to Pakistan on the achievement of Independence in 1947.

With the installation of Mahmud Khan II, British authority over Baluchistan, first attempted by Alexander Burnes fifty-four years earlier, was virtually complete. Nushki was taken over on permanent lease in 1896, following the final demarcation of the Iranian, Afghan and Kalat borders by the Goldsmid and Durand Lines, and administered as part of British Balochistan. The railway from Chaman reached Nushki in 1905 and was extended into Sistan between 1917 and 1922, but by then the Great Game, at least as played between the Russian and British Empires, was over.

With the rise of Imperial Germany, both these old empires needed to patch up their differences in Asia to meet their new rival in Europe. The assassination of Nasir al-Din Shah in May 1896 had, as generally forecast, been followed by a breakdown of authority in Iran, but neither Russia nor the United Kingdom could allow the other to take advantage of it. At the beginning of the twentieth century, both had suffered military humiliation, the British temporarily at the hands of Boer farmers and the Russians decisively at the hands of an emergent Japan. In December 1905 Balfour's Conservative ministry was replaced by Campbell-Bannerman's Liberals. The new Cabinet was horrified by estimates from the Commander in Chief, India, Lord Kitchener, the first soldier of the Empire, that to fight the Russians in Central Asia he would need reinforcements of 160,000 British soldiers at once and another 300,000 in the second year of such a war. His demands, coupled with the needs of domestic reforms, helped the ministers decide on an entente with Russia, similar to that recently concluded with France. The Anglo-Russian Convention of 31 August 1907 settled differences between the two states over Tibet, Afghanistan and Iran. The latter was divided into two spheres of influence with a neutral zone between them, all still under Iranian sovereignty. The agreement, aiming to end the rivalry that dated back to Napoleonic times, was criticized both in St Petersburg and London by statesmen who thought it too favourable to their old rivals, but it served its purpose. In the coming crisis of the First World War, Balochistan was the target not of Russian but German agents and though the Great Game was still being played over a century later, the original players had long retired from the board.

As for the border guardians, in 1902 Kitchener decided that his reconstructed Indian Army no longer needed special frontier forces. First-line defence against armed robbers and bandits was handed over to a variety of para-military bodies, mostly recruited from the inhabitants of the areas to be protected, lightly-armed and commanded by British officers on temporary assignments. All units of the Indian Army were thenceforth to take their turn in frontier garrison duties. Those previously localised became liable for general service anywhere they were needed. The former Scinde Irregular Horse, Jacob's 'Ironsides of India', became two regular cavalry regiments, later amalgamated into one, with the slogan 'Man dies, but the Regiment lives'. Its lineal successor forms part of the present-day Indian Armoured Corps as the 14th Horse (Scinde Horse).

APPENDIX A

TREATY OF KALAT, 28 MARCH 1839, BETWEEN THE BRITISH GOVERNMENT AND MAHRAB KHAN II

Whereas a Treaty of lasting friendship has been concluded between the British Government and His Majesty Shah Shuja-ul-Mulk, and Mehrab Khan, the chief of Kalat, as well as his predecessors, has always paid homage to the Royal House of the Sadozais, therefore, with the advice and consent of the Shah, the undermentioned Articles have been agreed upon by Mehrab Khan and his descendants from generation to generation. As long as the Khan performs good service, the following Articles will be fulfilled and preserved.

Article I

As Nasir Khan and his descendants, as well as his tribe and sons, held possession of Kalat, Kachhi, Kohistan, Makran, Kech, Bela and the port of Sonmiani in the time of the lamented Ahmad Shah Durrani, they will in future be the masters of their country in the same manner.

Article II

The English Government will never interfere between the Khan, his dependants, and subjects, particularly lend no assistance to the Muhabatzai branch of the family, but will always exert itself to the utmost to put away evil from his house. In case of His Majesty the Shah's displeasure with the Khan of Kalat, the English Government will exert itself to the utmost to remove the same, in a manner which may be agreeable to the Shah and according to the rights of the Khan.

Article III

As long as the British army continues in the country of Kohistan, the British Government agrees to pay to Mehrab Khan the sum of one and a half lakhs of the Company's rupees from the date of this engagement by half-yearly instalments.

Article IV

In return for this sum, the Khan, while he pays homage to the Shah and continues in friendship with the British nation, agrees to use his best endeavours to procure supplies, carriages and guards to protect provisions and stores coming and going to Shikarpur by the route of Rozan, Dadar, the Pass of Bolan, through Shal to Kuchlak from one frontier to another.

Article V

All provisions and carriage which may be obtained through the means of the Khan, the price of the same is to be paid without hesitation.

Article VI

As much as Mehrab Khan shows his friendship to the British Government by service and fidelity to the Saddozai family, so much the friendship will be increased between him and the British government; and in this he should have the fullest reliance and confidence.

This agreement having been concluded, signed, and sealed by Lieutenant-Colonel Sir Alexander Burnes, Kt., Envoy on the part of the Right Honorable George, Lord Auckland, GCB, Governor-General of India, and Mehrab Khan, of Kalat, on the part of himself, the same shall be duly ratified by the Right Honorable the Governor-General.

Done at Kalat, the 28th day of March, AD 1839, corresponding with the 12th day of Muharram, AH 1255.

APPENDIX B

TREATY OF KALAT, 6 OCTOBER 1841, BETWEEN THE BRITISH GOVERNMENT AND NASIR KHAN II

Whereas Meer Nasseer Khan, son of Mehrab Khan, deceased, having tendered his allegiance and submission, the British Government and His Majesty Shah Suja-ool-Moolk recognise him, the said Nusseer Khan, and his descendants as Chief of the principality of Khelat-i-Nusseer on the following terms-

Article I

Meer Nusseer Khan acknowledges himself and his descendants the vassals of the King of Cabool, in like manner as his ancestors were formerly the vassals of His Majesty's ancestors.

Article II

Of the tracts of country resumed on the death of Meer Mehrab Khan, namely Cutchee, Moostung, and Shawl, the first two will be restored to Meer Nusseer Khan and his descendants through the kindness of His Majesty Shah Suja-ool-Moolk.

Article III

Should it be necessary to station troops, whether belonging to the Honourable [East India] Company or Shah Suja-ool-Moolk, in any part of the territory of Khelat, they shall occupy such positions as may be thought advisable.

Article IV

Meer Nuseer Khan, his heirs and successors will always be guided by the advice of the British officer residing at his court.

Article V

The passage of merchants and others into Afghanistan from the river Indus on the one side, and from the sea-port of Sonmeeanee on the other, shall be protected by Meer Nusseer Khan as far as possible, nor will any aggression be practised on such persons, or undue exactions made beyond an equitable toll to be fixed by the British Government and Meer Nusseer Khan.

Article VI

Meer Nusseer Khan binds himself, his heirs and successors, not to hold any political communication or enter into any communication with foreign powers without the consent of the British Government and His Majesty Shah Suja-ool-Moolk, and in all cases to act in subordinate co-operation with the governments of British India and the Shah; but the usual amicable correspondence with neighbours to continue as before.

Article VI

In case of an attack on Meer Nusseer Khan by an open enemy, or of any difference arising between him and any foreign power, the British Government will afford him assistance or good offices, as it may judge to be necessary or proper for the maintenance of his rights.

Article VII

Meer Nusseer Khan will make provision for the support of Shah Nawaz Khan, either by pension to be paid through the British Government on condition of that Chief residing in British territory or by grant of estates within the Khelat possessions, as may hereafter be decided by the British Government.

Negotiated by Major James Outram and sealed by Nasir Khan II, 6 October 1841.

Ratified by George, Lord Auckland, Governor-General of India.

APPENDIX C

TREATY OF MASTUNG, 14 MAY 1854, BETWEEN THE BRITISH GOVERNMENT AND NASIR KHAN II

Whereas the course of events has made it expedient that a new agreement should be concluded between the British Government and Meer Nasseer Khan, Chief of Khelat, the following articles have been agreed upon between the said government and his Highness.

Article I

The treaty concluded between the British Government and Meer Nusseer Khan, Chief of Khelat, on the 6th October 1841, is hereby annulled.

Article II

There shall be perpetual friendship between the British Government and Meer Nusseer Khan, Chief of Kalat, his heirs and successors.

Article III

Meer Nusseer Kahn binds himself, his heirs and successors, to oppose to the utmost all the enemies of the British Government, in all cases to act in subordinate co-operation with that Government, and to enter into no negotiation with other States without its consent, the usual friendly correspondence being continued as before.

Article IV

Should it be deemed necessary to station British troops in any part of the territory of Khelat, they shall occupy such positions as may be thought advisable by the British authorities.

Article V

Meer Nusseer Khan binds himself, his heirs and successors, to prevent all plundering or other outrage by his subjects within or near British territory; to protect the passage of merchants to and fro between the British dominions and Afghanistan, whether by way of Sindh or by the seaport of Sonmeeanee or other seaport of Makran, and to permit no exactions to be made beyond an equitable duty to be fixed by the British Government and Meer Nusseer Khan, and the amount to be shown in the Schedule annexed to this Treaty.

Article VI

To aid Meer Nusseer Khan, his heirs and successors, in the fulfilment of these obligations, and on condition of a faithful performance of them year by year, the British Governnment binds itself to pay to Meer Nusseer Khan, his heirs and successors, the annual subsidy of fifty thousand (50,000) Company's Rupees.

Article VII

If during any year the conditions above shall not faithfully be performed by the said Meer Nusseer Khan, his heirs and successors, then the annual subsidy of fifity thousand (50,000) Company's Rupees will not be paid by the British Government.

Signed by Major John Jacob, Political Superintendant and Commandant on the Frontier of Upper Sind and sealed by Mir Nasir Khan II, Khan of Kalat, 14 May 1854.

Ratified by James, Marquis of Dalhousie, Governor-General of India.

APPENDIX D

TREATY OF JACOBABAD, 8 DECEMBER 1876, BETWEEN THE BRITISH GOVERNMENT AND KHUDADAD KHAN

Whereas it has become expedient to renew the treaty of 1854 between the British Government and Nusseer Khan, Khan of Khelat, the following articles are agreed upon... on behalf of the British Government on the one hand and His Highness Meer Khodadad Khan, Khan of Khelat, on the other.

Article I

The treaty concluded between the British Government and Meer Nusseer Khan, Khan of Khelat, on the 14th of May 1854 is hereby renewed and reaffirmed.

Article II

There shall be perpetual friendship between the British Government and Meer Khodadad Khan, Khan of Khelat, his heirs and successors.

Article III

Whilst on his part Meer Khodadad Khan, Khan of Khelat, binds himself, his heirs and successors, and Sirdars to observe faithfully the provisions of Article Three of the Treaty of 1854, the British Government on its part engages to respect the independence of Khelat, and to aid the Khan in case of need, in the maintenance of a just authority and the protection of his territories from external attack, by such means as the British Government at the moment deems expedient.

Article IV

For the further consolidation of the friendship herewith renewed and reaffirmed between the two Governments, it is agreed that the British Agents and suitable escorts shall be duly accredited by the British Governments to reside permanently at the Court of the Khan and elsewhere in the Khan's dominions and, on the other hand, that a suitable representative shall be duly accredited by his Highness to the Government of India.

Article V

It is hereby agreed that should any dispute, calculated to disturb the peace of the country, arise hereafter between the Khan and the Sirdars of Khelat, the British Agent at the Court of his Highness shall in the first place use his good offices to effect by friendly advice and amicable settlement between them, failing which the Khan will, with the consent of the British Government, submit such dispute to its arbitration, and accept and faithfully execute its award.

Article VI

Whereas the Khan of Khelat has expressed a desire on the part of himself and his Sirdars for the presence in his country of a detachment of British troops, the British Government, in accordance with the provisions of Article Four of the Treaty of 1854, and in recognition of the intimate relations existing between the two countries, hereby assents to the request of his Highness, on condition that troops shall be stationed in such positions as the British Government may deem expedient, and be withdrawn at the pleasure of that Government.

Article VII

It is also agreed that such lines of telegraph or railway as may be beneficial to the interests of the two Governments shall be from time to time be constructed by the British Government in the territories of the Khan, provided that the conditions of such construction be a matter of previous arrangement between that Government and the Government of his Highness.

Article VIII

There shall be entire freedom of trade between the State of Khelat and the territories of the British Government, subject to such conditions as the British

Government may, at any time, in concert with the Khan of Khelat, deem necessary for the protection of fiscal interests.

Article IX

To aid Meer Khodadad Khan, his heirs and successors, in the efficient fulfilment of the obligations contracted by them under the Treaty of 1854, the British Government hereby undertakes to pay to the said Khan, his heirs and successors, an annual subsidy of one lakh of rupees, so long as they shall faithfully adhere to the engagements heretofore and hereby contracted.

Article X

The British Government further undertakes to contribute Rupees 20,500 annually towards the establishment of posts and development of traffic along the trade routes in his Highness's territories, provided such money is expended by the Khan in the manner approved of by the British Government.

Sealed by Khodadad Khan, Khan of Kalat.

Signed by Edward Bulwer Lytton, Baron Lytton of Knebworth etc, Viceroy and Governor-General of India.

LIST OF INTERNATIONAL TREATIES
REFERRED TO IN THE TEXT

(NB, except for rulers of Kalat, Ranjit Singh and Shah Suja-ul-Mulk, contracting parties are expressed as nations or states)

Tehran 4 January 1801; British and Iran

Tilsit 25 June 1807; France and Russia

Finkenstein 10 May 1807; France and Iran

Tehran 15 March 1809; British and Iran

Tehran 23 August 1809; British and Iran

Treaty of Friendship and Mutual Defence 17 June 1809; British, Iran and Afghanistan (Shah Suja ul-Mulk)

Tehran 17 March 1812; British and Iran

Gulistan 12 October 1813; Russia and Iran

Hyderabad August 1809; British and Sind

Turkmenchai 22 February 1828; Russia and Iran

Hyderabad 20 April 1832; British and Sind

Hyderabad 20 April 1838; British and Sind

Simla 25 June 1838; British, Ranjit Singh of Lahore, and Shah Suja ul-Mulk

Hyderabad 6 Feb 1839; British and Sind

Kalat 28 March 1839; British and Mahrab Khan II of Kalat

Kalat 6 October 1841; British and Nasir Khan II of Kalat

Hyderabad 12 February 1843; British and Sind

Lahore 9 March 1846; British and Punjab

Mastung 14 May 1854; British and Nasir Khan II of Kalat

Paris 30 March 1856; British, France, Piedmont, and Russia

Paris 4 Mar 1857; British and Iran

Jacobabad 8 December 1876; British and Khudadad Khan of Kalat

San Stefano 3 March 1878; Russia and Iran

Berlin 13 July 1878; British, Austria-Hungary, France, Germany, Italy, Ottoman Empire and Russia

Gandamak 8 May 1879; British and Afghanistan

Convention of St Petersburg 31 August 1907; British and Russia

NOTES

1. BALOCHISTAN BACKGROUND: THE COUNTRY, THE PEOPLE AND THE PRINCES

1. Times Books, *The Times Comprehensive Atlas of the World 2000*, 1999.
2. Baluchistan District Gazetteers, 14 vols, Government of Bombay Press, Bombay, 1906–08.
3. Baluch, Mir Ahmad Yar Khan, *Inside Baluchistan. A Political autobiography of H H Baiglar Baigi Khan-e-Azam XIII, ex-ruler of Kalat State*, Royal Book Company, Karachi, 1975.
4. Dames, E. Longworth, *The Baluch Race*, London, 1904.
5. Baluch, Mir Ahmad Yar Khan, op. cit.
6. ibid.
7. Baluchistan District Gazetteers.
8. Avery, P., Hambly, G. and Melville, C., *Cambridge History of Iran, Vol. 7, From Nadir Shah to the Islamic Republic*, Cambridge University Press, Cambridge, 1991.
9. Heathcote, T. A., *The Afghan Wars 1839–1919*, 2nd edn., Spellmount, Staplehurst, 2003, chap. 1.
10. Pottinger, Henry, *Travels in Beloochistan and Sinde: accompanied by a geographical and historical account of those countries*, Hurst, Rees, Orme and Brown, London, 1816, Part II, chaps 1–3 et seq.
11. Masson, Charles, *Narrative of Various Journeys in Balochistan, Afghanistan, the Panjab and Kalat*, Vol. IV, Richard Bentley, London, 1844, p. 149, ibid., pp. 150–52.
12. ibid., pp. 150–52.

2. THE OPENING OF THE GREAT GAME: BRITISH INDIA, RUSSIA, IRAN AND AFGHANISTAN, 1798–1838

1. Hunter, William Wilson, *The Indian Empire: Its people, history and products*, 3rd edn., Smith, Elder & Co., London, 1893, chapter XVI.

2. Avery, P., Hambley, G. and Melville, C. *The Cambridge History of Iran, Vol. 7: From Nadir Shah to the Islamic Republic*, Cambridge: Cambridge University Press, 1991.

3. Yapp, M.E., *Strategies of British India: Britain, Iran and Afghanistan 1793–1850*, Oxford: Oxford University Press, 1980. See also *Copies of letters and enclosures from British representatives at the Court of Persia to the Secret Committee of the East India Company*, India Office Political and Secret Dept. Records (British Library IO Collection), L/P&S/9/67–78.

4. Pottinger, Henry, *Travels in Beloochistan and Sinde: accompanied by a geographical and historical account of those countries*, Hurst, Rees, Orme and Brown, London, 1816, Part II, chapters 1–3.

5. Pottinger, op. cit.

6. Avery, P, op. cit.

7. Lambrick, H.T., *Sir Charles Napier and Sind*, Pt I, chapter 2, Clarendon Press, Oxford, 1952.

8. Lambrick, H.T., op. cit.

3. THE BRITISH ARMY IN KALAT, 1839

1. Cadell, Patrick, *History of the Bombay Army*, London: Longmans, London: Green & Co., 1938, p. 173.

2. Masson, Charles, *Narrative of Various Journeys in Balochistan, Afghanistan, the Panjab and Kalat*, chapter 3, Richard Bentley, London, 1844.

3. Masson, Charles, op. cit.

4. Aitchison, C.U., *A Collection of Treaties etc., relating to India and Neighbouring Countries*, Govt. of India, Calcutta, 1893.

5. Masson, Charles, op. cit.

6. Dowdell. H.H, *Cambridge History of India, Vol.V, 1497–1858*, Cambridge University Press, 1929, p. 500.

7. *Cambridge History of India, Vol V*, Chapter XXVII, pp. 485–533.

8. Goldsmid, F.J., *James Outram. A Biography*, Vol. 1, Chapter VI, Smith, Elder & Co., London, 1880.

9. Masson, Charles, op. cit.

10. Intelligence Branch India, *Frontier and Overseas Expeditions from India, Vol.III, Baluchistan and the First Afghan War*, (reprint) Chapter 3, Sussex: Naval and Military Press, Uckfield, 2006.

11. Goldsmid, F. J., *James Outram: A Biography, Volume 1*, Smith, Elder, & Co., London, 1880, p. 196.

12. Davis, John, *The History of the Second, Queen's Royal Regiment of Foot, Vol. V from 1837 to 1905*, Eyre and Spottiswoode, London, 1906.

13. Ibid.

14. Davis, John, op. cit.

15. Webb, E.A.H., *A History of the 17th (The Leicestershire) Regiment*, 2nd Edn., Vacher and Sons, Ltd., London, 1912.
16. cit.in. Trotter, Lionel J., *The Bayard of India; A Life of General Sir James Outram* p. 79.

4. THE THREAT FROM THE BALOCH HILLS, 1839–40

1. Lambrick, H.T., *John Jacob of Jacobabad*, Cassell, London, 1960, pp. 34–36.
2. Lambrick, H.T., op. cit.
3. [Jacob, John,] *Memoir of the First Campaign in the Hills North of Cutchee, under Major Billamore, in 1839–40 by one of his Surviving Subalterns*, W.H.Allen and Co., London, 1852, p. 14.
4. From the report of Captain Lewis Brown, cit. in Williams, Charles Reynolds, *The Defence of Kahan*, W.H.Allen & Co, London, 1886.
5. Jacob, John, op. cit.
6. Lambrick, op. cit., pp. 46–47.
7. Jacob, op. cit.
8. Capt Lewis Brown's report, loc.cit.
9. Capt Lewis Brown's report, loc.cit.
10. Cadell, Patrick, *History of the Bombay Army*, Longmans, Green & Co., London, 1938. pp. 175–76.
11. Capt Lewis Brown's report, loc.cit.
12. Ibid.
13. Intelligence Branch, India, *Frontier and Overseas Expeditions from India, Vol.III, Baluchistan and the First Afghan War*, (reprint), Naval and Military Press, Uckfield, 2006, p. 86.

5. INSURGENCY IN KALAT, 1840–41

1. Masson, Charles, *Narrative of Various Journeys in Balochistan, Afghanistan, the Panjab And Kalat*, Vol. IV, Richard Bentley: London, Chapter 3.
2. Masson, Charles, Chapter 4.
3. Masson, Charles, Chapter 6.
4. cit in. Beveridge, Henry, *A Comprehensive History of India*, Blackie and Son, London, Vol. 3, Book VIII, p. 376.
5. Beveridge, Henry, op. cit.
6. Intelligence Branch, India, *Frontier and Overseas Expeditions from India, Vol.III, Baluchistan and the First Afghan War*, (reprint), Naval and Military Press, Uckfield, 2006, Chapter 3, p. 45.
7. Intelligence Branch, India, p. 45.
8. Goldsmid, F.J., *James Outram. A Biography*, Smith, Elder & Co., London, 1880, Volume I, pp. 229–30.

9. Stacy's report, cit. in Goldsmid, op. cit. p. 230.
10. Trotter, Lionel J., *The Bayard of India; Life of General Sir James Outram, Bart.*, William Blackwood and Sons, Edinburgh and London, 1903, pp. 91–92.
11. Aitchison, C.U., *A Collection of Treaties, Engagements and Sunnuds relating to India and the Neighbouring Countries*, Govt. of India, Calcutta, 1893.
12. Outram to Colvin, 7 Oct. 1841, cit.in.Goldsmid, op. cit., p. 231.
13. Lambrick, H.T., *John Jacob of Jacobabad*, Cassell, London, 1960, p. 55.
14. Lambrick, H.T., op. cit.

6. THE FIRST NORTH-WEST FRONTIER, 1842–46

1. Numerous accounts of the 1ˢᵗ Afghan War are in existence. The account relied on in this chapter is Sir John Kaye's exhaustive 3-volume *History of the War in Afghanistan*, which is generally listed among the sources for other scholarly works.
2. cit. in Goldsmid, F.J., *James Outram. A Biography*, 2 Volumes., Smith, Elde & Co., London, 1880, p. 273.
3. Trotter, Lionel J., *The Bayard of India; A Life of General Sir James Outram*, Bart., William Blackwood and Sons, Edinburgh and London, p. 103.
4. Goldsmid, op. cit.p. 275.
5. Goldsmid, op. cit. p. 275.
6. Goldsmid, op. cit. p. 275
7. Lambrick, H.T., *Sir Charles Napier and Sind*, Clarendon Press, Oxford, 1952, Pt. 2, Chapters 1–4, passim.
8. Goldsmid, op. cit., Vol. 1, Book I, Chapter 10.
9. Cadell, Patrick, *History of the Bombay Army*, Longmans, Green & Co.,London, 1938, pp. 181–87.
10. Lambrick, op. cit.,chap. 6. This work, written in 1959 by a former Commissioner in Sind under British rule, is the main source for the following narrative of the Upper Sind frontier and Hill campaigns during Napier's governorship of Sind.
11. Everett, Henry, *The History of the Somerset Light Infantry (Prince Albert's Own) 1695–1914*, Methuen and Co., 1901, pp. 215. et seq.
12. Lambrick, H.T., *John Jacob of Jacobabad*, Cassell, London, 1960, p. 127.

7. THE PALADINS OF THE UPPER SIND BORDER, 1847–54

1. Summary of Arrangements made on the North-west Frontier of Sind. Cit.in Pelly, Lewis, ed., *The Views and Opinions of Brigadier-General John Jacob*, Smith, Elder and Co., London 1858, reprint by General Books, Berkeley, Ca., p. 176.
2. Lambrick, H.T., *John Jacob of Jacobabad*, Cassell, London, 1960, p. 135.
3. Pelly, op. cit., reprint p. 167.
4. Lambrick, op. cit., p. 137.
5. Merewether's report, 2 Octobr 1847, cit. in Pelly, op. cit., reprint, pp. 160–162.

6. Merewether's report, 2 Octobr 1847, cit. in Pelly, op. cit., reprint, pp. 160–162.

7. Lambrick, op. cit., p 147.

8. Maunsel, E.B., *Prince of Wales's Own; The Scinde Horse*, pub. privately, 1926, p. 15.

9. Pelly, op. cit., p. 166.

10. Merewether to Van Courtland, no. 47, 22 Feb. 1852; Jacob to Frere, no. 44, 23 Feb. 1852; Frere to Melvill, Sec. to Board of Admin, Punjab, No. 499, 1852; Melvill to Frere, No. 179, 14 April 1854, enc.9 in Secret Letter from India, No. 9, 8 Feb. 1855. IOC/BL Secret Letters from India, Vol. 141.

11. Jacob to Frere, No. 36, 27 Feb. 1854, enc.3 in Secret Letter from India, no. 9, 8 Feb. 1855.

12. Minute by Dalhousie, 22 April 1854. ibid. enc.4.

13. Bruce to Melvill, Sec. to Govt. of the Punjab, 19 Jun. 1854. ibid. enc.14.

14. Melvill to F.G.Edmonstone, Sec. to Govt. of India in the Foreign Dept., no. 431, 23 May 1854, ibid., enc.13.

15. Edmonstone to H.Anderson, Sec. to Govt. of Bombay, No. 13, 26 Jan. 1855, ibid., Enc.9.

16. Martineau, John, *The life and Correspondance of the Right Hon.Sir Bartle Frere*, vol. 1, pp. 164–65. Lambrick, op. cit., p. 170, Pelly, op cit., p. 166.

8. THE GREAT GAME RENEWED: INDIA, IRAN AND BALOCHISTAN, 1854–58

1. Sketch of States and Tribes on the Sind Frontier, by Major J Jacob, Published Selections from the Records, Bombay Govt., New Series, Vol. 17.

2. Jacob to Ellis, Nov. 1853, cit. in Shand, A. Innes, *General John Jacob*, Seeley and Co., London, 1900.

3. Govt. of Bombay to Govt. of India in the Foreign Dept., No. 159 of 24 Nov. 1853, enc.4 in Govt. of Bombay to Court of Directors, No. 10 of 28 Jan. 1854. Secret Letters from Bombay, Vol. 118.

4. cit. in Trotter, Lionel J., *The Bayard of India; A Life of General Sir James Outram, Bart.*, William Blackwood and Sons, Edinburgh and London, 1903, p. 164.

5. cit. in Trotter, op. cit, p. 164.

6. Dalhousie to Outram (pte) 7 Dec. 1853, Dalhousie Papers, Scottish Record Office, vol. 84 (Misc Letters in India) *also in* Outram Papers, National Army Museum, bundle 61.

7. Outram to Dalhousie, (pte), memo 8 Dec. 1853, Outram Papers, loc.cit.

8. Govt. of India to Pol. C'tee No. 6 of 19 Jan. 1854. Pol. Letters to India 1854.

9. Pol. C'tee to Board of Control for India, precom 8721. Drafts & Precoms, 1854, vol. 3.

10. Wood to Dalhousie (pte), 24 Dec. 1853. India Board Letter Books, vol. 4, Halifax Papers, British Library, India Office Collections.

11. Wood to Dalhousie (pte), 4 Jan. 1854, loc.cit.

12. enc. in Gov-Gen. to Sec. C'tee, no. 15 of 8 June 1842, in Afghan Blue Book No. 226.

13. Jacob to Frere, no. 290 of 2 Dec. 1853, enc. 3 in Secret Letter from Govt. of Bombay to Ct. of Directors, Secret C'tee, no. 1 of 14 Jan. 1854, Enc. to Secret Letters from Bombay, vol. 118.

14. Frere to Elphinstone (Govr. of Bombay), no. 62 of 27 Feb. 1854, enc. 3 in Bombay to Pol. C'tee, no. 22 of 14 Apr. 1854. Enc. to Secret Letters from Bombay, vol. 118.

15. Dalhousie to Jacob, pte. and confidential, 11 April 1854. Dalhousie Papers, Sec.6, vol. 85 (Misc Letters in India), Scottish Record Office.

16. Wood to Elphinstone (pte) 8 Jun. 1854. Wood Papers, India Board Letter Book vol. 5, p. 80.

17. Wood to Dalhousie (pte) 8 Jun. 1854, ibid.

18. Jacob to Frere, 14 May 1854.

19. Dalhousie to Wood (pte) 30 May 1854, Wood Papers, bundle 18a.

20. Wood to Dalhousie (pte) 24 July 1854, Dalhousie Papers, Sec.6, vol. 57, Wood Papers Indian Board Letter book vol. 5.

21. Dalhousie to Sir George Couper (pte), 9 Sep. 1854.

22. Pol. C'tee, Ct. of Directors, to Gov-Gen. in Council, No. 49 of 8 Nov. 1854, Pol. Letters to India 1854.

23. Frere to Dalhousie (pte. and conf.) 9 Sep. 1854, Dalhousie Papers Sec. 6, vol. 163.

24. Dalhousie to Frere (pte) 7 Oct. 1854, ibid vol. 86.

25. Lambrick op. cit., chap. xvii

26. Officiating Commr. in Sind to Govt. of Bombay, 4 Jul. 1856, enc. to Sec. Letter from India, No. 31 of 30 Jul. 1856, Encs. to Sec. Letters from India, vol. 147, pp. 91 et seq.

27. Minute by Canning, enc. to Sec. Letter from India, No. 31 of 30 Jul. 1856, loc. cit.

28. Govt. of India in the Foreign Dept to officiating Commr. in Sind (sec), 23 Jul. 1856, ibid.

29. Trans of letter from Babar Shah Khan to HH the Khan of Kalat, undated, forwarded by Merewether to Jacob, 28 Jul. 1856, enc. in Sec. Letter from India, no. 37 of 8 Sep. 1856, Sec. Letters from India, vol. 147, p. 463.

30. Minute by Canning, 27 Aug. 1856, ibid.

31. Trans of letter from Babar Shah Khan to HH the Khan of Kalat, undated, forwarded by Jacob to Govt. of India, no. 101 dated 17 Aug. 1856, enc. in Sec. Letter from India, no. 37.

32. Merewether to Jacob, no. 338 of 21 Oct. 1856, Papers relating to the Bigari Canal, Selections from the Records of the Bombay Govt, New Series, no. XLII, 1857.

33. Lambrick, op. cit., p. 311.

34. Trotter, op. cit., chap.xiv

35. English, Barbara, *John Company's Last War* passim.
36. Avery, Hambly and Melville, *Cambridge History of Iran, Vol 7*, pp. 394–96.
37. Merewether to Asst. Commr. in Sind, June 1857; Frere to Elphinstone 13 Jun. 1857; Resolution of Bombay Govt., 19 June 1857. Encs. to Secret Letters from Bombay to Pol. Committee, Vol. 131.
38. Commr. in Sind to Govt. of Bombay, No. 64 of 19 Feb. 1858.
39. Govt. of Bombay in the Military Dept to Cmmr in Sind, no. 7274 of 21 Dec. 1857.
40. Jacob to Frere, no. 126 of 16 Mar. 1858, enc. in Letters from India, vol. 13, July 1872, p. 1227.
41. Jam of Las Bela to Commr in Sind, 25 Zilkaid 1274 (7 Jul. 1858) enc. 3 in Sec. Letter from Govt. of Bombay to Sec. of State for India, no. 102 of 18 Aug. 1858. Sec. Letters from Bombay, vol. 136.
42. Jam of Las Bela's ambassadors to Frere, 20 July 1858. ibid.

9. CIVIL WARS, 1858–1872

1. Cranborne to Lawrence (pte) 27 Aug. 1866; Lawrence to Cranborne (pte) 4 Oct. 1866; Cranborne to Lawrence (pte) 19 Nov. and 10 Dec. 1866, John Lawrence Papers. Memo by Green, 16 Aug. 1866; minute by Frere, 26 Nov. 1866; minute by Mansfield, 31 Jan. 1867; Gov-Gen.in Council to Sec. of State for India, 8 Feb. 1867, cit. in Return to an Address of the House of Commons, 20 Feb. 1879, calling for copies of despatches on Quetta.
2. Thornton, Thomas Henry, *Colonel Sir Robert Sandeman. His Life and Work on our Indian Frontier.* John Murray, London 1895, reprinted with an introduction by Sir Ronald Wingate, Oxford University Press, Karachi, 1979, pp. 30–31.
3. Green to Owen Tudor Burne, Secy. to Pol. C'tee, Council of India, 27 Feb. 1875. Pol. and Sec. Letters and Enclosures to India, Vol. 1, 1875, p. 328.
4. Green to Sandeman, Jan. 1867, 6 Feb. 1867; Sandeman to Green, 2 Mar. 1867; Green to Sandeman, 8 Mar. 1867, cit. in Depty Commr, Dera Ghazi Khan, to Commr in Sind, no. 543 of 1 Jul. 1872. Secret Letters and Encs from India, vol. 13, p. 1297.
5. Trans of letters, Pol. Procs of Govt. of India in the Foreign Dept, March 1868, no. 339; Sec. Letters from India Vol. 4, 1868, p. 513.
6. Phayre to Merewether, no. 703 of 27 April 1869; Merewether to Phayre, no. 226 of 1 May 1869; Phayre to Merewther, nos. 1725 of 6 Dec. 1869 and 1839 of 31 Dec. 1869, cit. in Proceedings of Govt. of India in the Foreign Dept, vol. 759, May 1871, nos. 196–206.
7. Sandeman to Graham, no. 482 of 14 Dec. 1869. Proceedings of Govt. of India in the Foreign Dept, vol. 759, May 1871, no. 196.
8. T. H. Thornton, Secy. to Punjab Govt, to C. U. Aitcheson,Secy. to Govt. of India in the Foreign Dept, no. 57/170 of 7 Feb. 1870, ibid.

9. Merewether to Phayre, no. 825 of 15 Dec. 1869, ibid.
10. Merewether to Phayre, 28 Aug. 1870, India Foreign Proceedings Nov. 1871, no. 107.
11. Mayo to Argyll (pte) 16 Mar. 1869; vol. 43, no. 201; memo by Mayo, 27 Mar. 1870, bundle 3 (Central Asia); Mayo Papers, University of Cambridge Library.
12. Phayre to Harrison, no. 1110 of 21 July 1870. India Foreign Proceedings, vol. 761, Nov. 1871, no. 46.
13. Commr in Sind to Govr of Bombay, no. 528 of 25 Aug. 1870, ibid., no. 41.
14. Memo by Charles Girdlestone, Asst. Secy. to Govt. of India in the Foreign Dept, Sep. 1870. Mayo Papers, bundle 3.
15. Gov-Gen.in Council to Secy. of State for India in Council no. 158 of 31 Oct. 1871, Secret Letters from India, vol. 10, p. 263.
16. enc. in Kalat Diaries (weekly rpts from Pol. Agent, Kalat), Oct-Nov. 1871.
17. Vakil Nawab Muhammad Khan to H H the Khan of Kalat, enc. in Khan to Harrison 24 Dec. 1871, enc. 22 in Sec. Letters from India no. 44 of 24 June 1872, vol. 12, 1872.
18. Kalat Diary for w/e 15 Dec. 1871.
19. Aitchison to Merewether, no. 48P of 6 Jan. 1872, enc. 54 in Sec. Letters from India no. 5 of 1872, vol. 12, p. 232.
20. Fitzgerald to Merewether (copy to Viceroy) tel.12 Jan. 1872. Enc. 66 in Sec. Letters from India, vol. 11 of 1872, p. 238.
21. Aitchison to Wedderburn (Sec. to Govt. of Bombay in the Pol. Dept), loc. cit.
22. Miles to Merewether, no. 4 of 7 Jan. 1872, enc. in Sec. Letters from India, vol. 12 of 1872, p. 605.
23. Faujdar (military commander) of Las Bela to Merewether, 12 Dec. 1871, ibid p. 601.
24. Merewether to Fitzgerald, no. 66 of 22 Jan. 1872, ibid p. 623.
25. Bellew, Henry, *From the Indus to the Tigris, a narrative of a journey through the countries of Baluchistan, Afghanistan, Khorassan, and Iran in 1872, together with a synoptical grammar and vocabulary of the Brahoe language*, Trubner & Co., London, 1874.
26. Gov-Gen.of India in Council to Sec. of State for India in Council, no. 13 of 1 Mar. 1872. Secret Letters from India, vol. 11, 1872, p. 445.
27. Memo by Mayo, 29 Dec. 1871, enc. in Sec. Letter from India, 19 Jan. 1872, ibid, p. 77.
28. MSS note by Merewether on Sandeman to Phayre of 23 Feb. 1872, enc. 89 in Sec. Letters from India, vol. 12, p. 711.
29. Phayre to Merewether no. 452 of 23 Feb. 1872, ibid.
30. Memo by Merewether no. 265 of 16 March 1872, ibid.
31. Phayre to Merewether no. 477 of 27 Feb. 1872, enc. 69 in Sec. Letters from India, vol. 12.

32. Fitzgerald to acting Viceroy (Napier), telegram 27 Feb. 1872, enc. 43 in above.

33. Aitchison to Wedderburn, Secy. to Bombay Govt, and Thornton, Secy. to Punjab Govt, telegrams 469P and 470P of 29 Feb. 1872, enc. 44 in above.

34. Fitzgerald to Napier, telegram of 4 Mar. 1872, enc. 69 in above.

35. trans of letter from Shahgasi Wali Muhammad, wazir to H H the Khan of Kalat, to Major Harrison, Pol. Agent, Kalat, 14 Muharram AH 1289 = 12 Mar. 1872.

36. attached to Fitzgerald to Napier, telegram of 18 March 1872, enc. 70 in above.

37. Napier to Fitzgerald, telegram no. 665P of 18 March 1872, enc. 71 in above.

38. Thornton, op. cit., pp. 58–59.

10. THE KAFILAS AND THE COLLAPSE OF BRITISH CONTROL, 1872–76

1. Commissioner in Sind's statement in durbar, Jacobabad, 28 Mar. 1872.

2. Merewether to Fitzgerald no. 340 of 5 Apr. 1872.

3. Kalat Diaries nos. 11 and 14 for w/e 25 May 1872; Thornton, T H, *Colonel Sir Robert Sandeman, his life and work on our Indian Frontier,* John Murray, London. 1895, reprinted with an introduction by Sir Ronald Wingate, Oxford University Press, Karachi, 1979. p. 81, n.

4. Northbrook to Salisbury (pte) 27 Mar. 1874, Northbrook Papers, vol. 9, xvii.

5. Aitchison to Merewether (pte) 21 Mar. 1874, ibid., vol. 15.

6. Mallet to Northbrook (pte) 5 Jun. 1874, ibid., vol. 22, p. 121.

7. Salisbury to Northbrook (pte), 6 and 27 Mar, 22 May 1874. ibid, vols. 9 and 11.

8. Northbrook to Salisbury (pte), 16 Jun. 1874, Northbrook to Mallet (pte), 7 Jun. 1874, ibid, vols. 9 and 22.

9. Salisbury to Northbrook (pte), 3,10 and 17 Jul. 1874, ibid, vol. 9, pp. 36–39.

10. Northbrook to Merewether (pte), 18 Aug. 1874; Merewether to Northbrook (pte), 24 Sep. 1874, ibid, vol. 16, xxxi, p. 81.

11. Foreign Dept to Commr in Sind, no. 2214P of 9 Oct. 1874; Northbrook to Merewether (pte), 6 Oct. 1874.

12. Merewether to Northbrook (pte), 8 Oct. 1874; Thornton (Sec. to Punjab Govt) to Aitchison, no. 2078 of 14 Dec. 1874; Aitchison to Merewether, no. 16P of 5 Jan. 1875.

13. India Office Lists 1874–75; notes by Burne and Salisbury on Pol. Letter from India, no. 13 of 22 Jan. 1875. Pol. and Sec. Letters from India and Encs, vol. 1, Jan. 1875, pp. 330 et seq; Northbrook to Salisbury (pte) 6 Jan. 1875. Northbrook Papers, vol. 17, p.viii.

14. Green to Burne, 18 and 27 Feb. 1872, ibid, pp. 328.

15. Memo by G.Vesey Fitzgerald, 16 Mar. 1875, ibid. p. 327.

16. Note by Burne on above.

17. Frere to Northbrook (pte), 26 Feb. 1875; Northbrook to Frere (pte), 1 Apr. 1875,

18. Salisbury to Northbrook, pte, 16 Apr. 1875; Northbrook to Salisbury (pte) 13 May 1875. Northbrook Papers, Vol. 12.
19. Resolution of Govt. of India in the Foreign Dept, no. 2819 of 16 Oct. 1875, enc. in Pol. and Sec. Letters from India, vol. 7, Jan-Feb. 1876.
20. Salisbury to Northbrook (pte) 5 Nov. 1875. Northbrook Papers, 1875, vols. 12, 23.
21. Merewether to Sandeman, No. 918 of 21 Nov. 1875, enc. in Letter from Govt. of India in the Foreign Dept to Sec. of State for India, no. 64 of 17 Mar. 1876. Pol. and Sec. Letters from India, vol. 8, Mar-May 1876.
22. Commr in Sind to Foreign Sec, Govt. of India, 13 Dec. 1875, enc. 6 in above. Foreign Sec. to Commr in Sind, 16 Dec. 1875, enc. 7 in above.
23. Sandeman to Loch, No. 171 of 22 Dec. 1875, appendix A to enc. 5 in above.
24. cit. in Sandeman's Report to Munro, no. 8 of 5 Feb. 1876, Proceedings of the Govt. of India in the Foreign Dept, no. 429, Mar. 1876, vol. 1031.
25. telegrams between Commr in Sind and Foreign Dept, 20 and 22 Dec. 1875, encs 6 and 12 in above.
26. Sandeman to Foreign Sec, Calcutta, 1 Jan. 1876, enc. 18 in above.
27. Aitchison to Merewether, telegram no. 143P of 13 January 1876, enc. 30 in above.
28. Sir P Wodehouse, Govr of Bombay, to Lord Lytton (Gov-Gen.desig), 13 June 1876, Lytton Papers, Letters from India 1876.
29. Northbrook to Merewether (pte), 6 and 24 Jan. 1876, Merewether to Northbrook (pte), 13 and 15 Jan. 1876, Northbrook to Salisbury (pte), 7,14 and 28 Jan. 1876, Salisbury to Northbrook 11 Feb. 1876. Northbrook Papers, vols. 12/II, pp. 18–19.
30. Lytton to Salisbury (pte), 14 Apr. 1876, Lytton Papers, vol. 518/1, p. 80.

11. QUETTA AND THE SETTLEMENT OF KALAT, 1876–78

1. Govt. of India in the Mil Dept to Govt. of Bombay, telegram, 1 April 1876.
2. Bombay to Govt. of India in the Foreign Dept, no. 2120 of 8 April 1876.
3. cit in T A Heathcote, *The Afghan Wars 1839–1919, 2ⁿᵈ edn., Spellmount, Staplehurst, 2003*, pp. 89–91.
4. Sec. of State to Gov-Gen. in Council (Pol) no. 15 of 3 Feb. 1876. Sec. & Pol. Despatches to India, vol. 2, 1876, no. 489.
5. Gov-Gen.in Council to Sec. of State, no. 85 of 7 April 1876.
6. Resolution of the Govt. of India in the Foreign Dept, no. 671(a)P of 14 March 1876.
7. Telegrams, Viceroy to Sec. of State, 672P of 14 Mar. 1876; Sec. of State to Viceroy, 17 Mar. 1876, Pol. & Sec. Letters from India 1876, vol. 8, p. 579.
8. Northbrook to Salisbury (pte), 17 Mar. 1876. Northbrook Papers, vol. 12, no. 13.
9. Northbrook to Salisbury (pte), 31 Mar. 1876. Northbrook Papers, vol. 12, no. 15.
10. Govt. of Bombay to Sec. of State for India, no. 20 (Pol) of 3 April 1876. Letters from Bombay 1876, vol. 4.

11. Lytton to Rawlinson,(pte) 5 Aug. 1876. Lytton Papers,518/1. Letters despatched 1876.
12. Heathcote, op. cit., pp. 92–93.
13. Sec. Instrs to Gov-Gen.from Sec. of State for India, 28 Feb. 1876. Sec. & Pol. Despatches to India, Feb. 1876; Lytton to Hobhouse (Law Member of Council), pte, Jul. 1876. Lytton Papers, 518/1, Letters despatched, 1876, p. 363.
14. Resolution of the Govt. of India in the Foreign Dept, no. 671(a)P of 14 Mar. 1876.
15. Lytton to Salisbury (pte) 1 Apr. 1876. Lytton Papers 518/1, p. 57.
16. Lytton to Northbrook (pte) 6 Apr. 1876, ibid, p. 69.
17. Lytton to Northbrook (pte) 10 Apr. 1876, ibid, p. 74.
18. Munro to Sandeman, no. 117 of 3 April 1876, Thornton, op. cit., p. 74.
19. H.H. the Khan of Kalat to Munro (trans), AH 2 Safar 1293 = AD 23 Mar. 1876.
20. Lytton to Morley (pte) 27 Mar. 1876. Lytton Papers, vol. 518.
21. Lytton to Frere (pte), 3 July 1876, ibid.
22. Lytton to Pelly (pte), 19 Aug. 1876, ibid 518/1 p. 74.
23. Lytton to Salisbury (pte), 14 Apr. 1876, ibid, p. 94.
24. Foreign Sec, Govt. of India, to Munro, telegram no. 965(a)P of 20 Apr. 1876, enc. 35.
25. Kalat Diary for w/e 26 May 1876, enc. 52 in above.
26. Viceroy and Gov-Gen.of India to H.H. the Khan of Kalat, 20 Mar. 1876, enc.11 in above.
27. Sandeman to Munro, no. 122 of 14 June 1876, enc. 69 in above.
28. Davies to Northbrook (pte), 17 April 1877; Hobhouse to Northbrook (pte), 2 Feb. 1877, Northbrook Papers, vol. 18 II, pp. 150, 123. See also Thornton, op cit., p. 78.
29. Griffin to Thornton, tel.no. 10K of 10 June 1876; Thornton to Munro, telegram no. 1426P of 13 June 1876, enc. 58 in Govt. of India to Sec. of State, Pol, no. 50 of 23 Mar. 1877, Pol. & Sec. Letters and Encs from India, vol. 13.
30. H.H. the Khan of Kalat to Sandeman (trans), 6 June 1878, ibid, enc. 69.
31. Munro to Thornton, no. 257 of 14 July 1876, ibid, enc. 81.
32. Viceroy to Sec. of State, telegram no. 1745P of 31 Jul. 1876, ibid, enc. 88.
33. Lytton to Salisbury (pte), 22 Jul, 20 Aug. 1876, Lytton Papers 518/1, Letters despatched, pp. 305, 408.
34. Salisbury to Lytton (pte), 22 Aug. 1876, Lytton Papers 516/1, no. 42, and 18 Sep. 1876, no. 50.
35. Appendix A4 of Sandeman to Munro, no. 167 of 31 Jul. 1876.
36. Lytton to Sandeman (pte), 29 Sep. 1876. Lytton Papers, letters dispatched 1876, 518/1, p. 507.
37. Colley to Lytton (pte), 28 Oct. 1876, cit in Butler, W.F., *Life and Correspondance of Sir George Pomeroy Colley*, London, 1899, p. 167.
38. Colley to Lytton (pte), 28 Oct. 1876, cit in Butler, W.F., *Life and Correspondance of Sir George Pomeroy Colley*, London, 1899, p. 167.

39. Treaty between H. H. the Khan of Kalat and the Govt. of India, 8 Dec. 1876, enc. 135 in Govt. of India to Sec. of State, Pol, no. 50 of 23 Mar. 1877, Pol. & Sec. Letters and Encs from India, vol. 13.

40. Colley to Northbrook (pte), 8 Nov. 1876, Northbrook Papers, vol. 18, ii; Colley to Lytton (pte), 28 Oct. 1876, Butler, op cit, p. 167; Sandeman to Northbrook (pte), Northbrook Papers, vol. 18, ii, p. 131.

41. Rawlinson to Lytton (pte), 10 Nov. 1876, Lytton Papers 516/1; Daly to Northbrook (pte), 6 Sep. 1877, Northbrook Papers, vol. 18 ii; Montgomery to Salisbury (pte), 9 Nov. 1876, Colley to Lytton (pte), 10 Dec. 1876, Lytton Papers 516/1, no. 60; Hobhouse to Northbrook (pte), 2 Feb. 1877, Northbrook Papers, vol. 18 ii, p. 123. Chamberlain to Lawrence (pte), 26 Jan. 1878, Northbrook Papers, vol. 19; Salisbury to Lytton (pte), 4 Sep. 1876, Salisbury Papers, microreel 811, letterbook 3.

42. Thornton, Thomas Henry, *Colonel Sir Robert Sandeman, his life and work on our Indian Frontier*, John Murray, London, 1895, reprinted with an introduction by Sir Ronald Wingate, Oxford University Press, Karachi, op cit., p. 91.

43. vide Appendix D.

44. Conv. between Khan and Gov-Gen, and Execution of the Treaty, 8 Dec. 1867; Res. of Govt. of India, no. 57P of 12 Dec. 1876; Thornton to Gonne, telegram no. 50P of 17 Jan. 1877; Res. of Govt. of India, no. 620P of 12 Dec. 1876; Memo by Commr in Sind, no. 9 of 8 Jan. 1877. Encs 133, 134, 137, 138, 141 and 144 in Govt. of India to Sec. of State, Pol, no. 50 of 23 Mar. 1877, Pol. & Sec. Letters and Encs from India, vol. 13.

45. Thornton, op. cit., p. 94. A letter by Lytton referring to the anecdote of the soap is exhibited in the Indian Gallery at Knebworth House, Herts.

46. Letter from Gov-Gen. in Council to Sec. of State, Political, no. 50 of 23 Mar. 1877, with 215 encs, Pol. & Sec. Letters from India, vol. 13, pp. 235–603; minutes by Moore and Merewether on above, Pol. & Sec. Despatches to India, vol. 3, 1877, pp. 603, 618.

47. Sec. of State to Gov-Gen, Pol. Despatch no. 72 of 13 July 1876, Sec. & Pol. Despatches to India, vol. 2, no. 830.

48. Norman to Northbrook (pte), 18 Jun. 1876, Northbrook Papers, vol. 18, ii, pp. 115.

49. Minute by Lytton, 22 Apr. 1877, enc. in Letter from Gov-Gen. to Sec. of State, no. 86 of 17 May 1877, Pol. & Sec. Letters from India 1877, vol. 14; Salisbury to Lytton (pte), 19 May 1876, Lytton Papers, 516/1, p. 21.

50. Capt. Biddulph to Northbrook (pte), 22 Nov. 1876, Northbrook Papers, vol. 18, p. 91.

51. Salisbury to Lytton (pte), 2 Mar. 1877, Salisbury Papers, microreel 811, Letterbook 2.

52. Salisbury to Lytton (pte), 6 & 13 July 1877, Lytton Papers, 516/2.

53. Salisbury to Lytton (pte), 10 Aug. 1877, 21 Sep. 1877, ibid; Sec. of State to Gov-Gen, no. 119 of 29 Nov. 1877, Sec. & Pol. Despatches to India, 1877, vol. 3, p. 1363.

12. THE COMPLETION OF BRITISH CONTROL, 1877–1893

1. Thornton, Thomas Henry, *Colonel Sir Rober Sandeman, his life and work on our Indian Frontier*, John Murray, London, 1895, reprinted with an introduction by Sir Ronald Wingate, Oxford University Press, Karachi, op. cit., chaps 13–16.
2. Heathcote, T.A., *The Afghan Wars 1839–1919*, 2nd edn., Spellmount, Staplehurst, 2003, op cit, chaps 7–9.
3. Robertson, Brian, *The Road to Kabul. The Second Afghan War, 1878–1881*, Arms and Armour Press, London, 1986.
4. Thornton, op. cit., chaps 21–25.
5. Ibid.
6. Lansdowne to Cross (pte) 17 Jun. 1893. Lansdowne Papers, Correspondance with S of S for India, Vol. 5. India Office Collection, Mss Eur D 558.
7. Innes, J. J. McLeod, *Life and Times of General Sir James Browne, Buster Browne*, John Murray, London, 1905, p. 305.
8. Thornton, ibid, p. 327.
9. AGG Baluchistan to Govt. of India, Foreign Dept, 6 Apr. 1893, enc. in Report to Foreign Dept, 15 Jul. 1893. Political and Secret Letters from India, 1893, India Office Records, L/PS/7/71.
10. Browne to Lansdowne (pte) 13 Aug. 1893, Lansdowne Papers.
11. Intelligence Branch, India, *Frontier and Overseas Expeditions from India, Vol.III, Baluchistan and the First Afghan War*, (reprint), Naval and Military Press, Uckfield, 2006, pp. 158–59.
12. Lansdowne to Kimberley (pte,) 23 May 1893. Kimberley to Lansdowne (pte), 17 June 1893.
13. Lansdowne to Kimberley (pte), 25 July 1895.
14. Browne to Lansdowne (pte), 21 Jul. 1893. Durand to Lansdowne (pte), 6 Aug. 1893.
15. Browne to Lansdowne (pte), 30 Jul. 1893.
16. Browne to Lansdowne (pte), 13 Aug. 1893.

SELECT BIBLIOGRAPHY

Aitchison, C.U., *A Collection of Treaties, Engagements and Sunnuds relating to India and the Neighbouring Countries*, Govt. of India, Calcutta, 1893.

Avery, P., Hambly, G. and Melville, C., *Cambridge History of Iran, Vol. 7, From Nadir Shah to the Islamic Republic*, Cambridge University Press, Cambridge, 1991.

Axmann, Martin, *Back to the Future. The Khanate of Kalat and the Genesis of Baloch Nationalism 1915–1955*, Oxford University Press, 2008.

Baluch, Mir Ahmad Yar Khan, *Inside Baluchistan. A Political autobiography of H H Baiglar Baigi Khan-e-Azam XIII, ex-ruler of Kalat State*, Royal Book Company, Karachi, 1975.

Bellew, Henry, *From the Indus to the Tigris, a narrative of a journey through the countries of Baluchistan, Afghanistan, Khorassan, and Iran in 1872, together with a synoptical grammar and vocabulary of the Brahoe language*, Trubner & Co., London, 1874.

Beveridge, Henry, *A Comprehensive History of India*, 3 vols., Blackie and Son, London,1865.

Butler, William Francis, *Life and Correspondence of Sir George Pomeroy Colley*, J. Murray, London, 1899.

Cadell, Patrick, *History of the Bombay Army*, Longmans, Green & Co., London, 1938.

Dames, E. Longworth, *The Baluch Race*, London, 1904.

Davies, C.C., *The Problem of the North-West Frontier 1890–1908, with a survey of policy since 1849*, Cambridge University Press, 1932.

Davis, John, *The History of the Second, Queen's Royal Regiment of Foot, Vol. V, from 1837 to 1905*, Eyre and Spottiswoode, London, 1906.

Dodwell.H.H., *Cambridge History of India, Vol. V, 1492–1858*, Cambridge University Press, 1929.

Dutta, Simanta, *Imperial Mappings in Savage Spaces: Baluchistan and British India*, B.R.Publishing Corporation, Delhi, 2002.

English, Barbara, *John Company's Last War*, Collins, London, 1971.

SELECT BIBLIOGRAPHY

Everett, Henry, *The History of the Somerset Light Infantry (Prince Albert's Own) 1695–1914*, Methuen & Co., London, 1934.

Goldsmid, F.J., *James Outram. A Biography*, 2 vols., Smith, Elder, & Co., London, 1880.

Heathcote, T.A., *The Afghan Wars 1839–1919*, 2nd edn., Spellmount, Staplehurst, 2003.

Holditch, Thomas Hungerford, *The Indian Borderland 1880–1900*, Methuen and Co., 1901.

Hopkins, B.D., *The Making of Modern Afghanistan*, 2nd edn., Palgrave Macmillan, Basingstoke, 2012.

Hunter, William Wilson, *The Indian Empire: its peoples, history and products*, 3rd edn., Smith, Elder, & Co., London, 1893.

Ingram, Edward, *The Beginning of the Great Game in Asia*, Clarendon Press, Oxford, 1979.

——— *Britain's Persian Connection 1798–1828*, Clarendon Press, Oxford, 1984.

Innes, J.J.McLeod, *Life and Times of General Sir James Browne, Buster Browne*, John Murray, London, 1905.

Intelligence Branch, India, *Frontier and Overseas Expeditions from India, Vol. III, Baluchistan and the First Afghan War*, (reprint), Naval and Military Press, Uckfield, 2006.

[Jacob, John,] *Memoir of the First Campaign in the Hills North of Cutchee, under Major Billamore, in 1839–40 by one of his Surviving Subalterns*, W.H. Allen and Co., London, 1852.

Lambrick, H.T., *Sir Charles Napier and Sind*, Clarendon Press, Oxford, 1952.

Lambrick, H.T., *John Jacob of Jacobabad*, Cassell, London, 1960.

Martineau, John, *The life and Correspondence of the Right Hon. Sir Bartle Frere*, 2 vols., John Murray, London, 2nd edn., 1895.

Masson, Charles, *Narrative of Various Journeys in Balochistan, Afghanistan, the Panjab and Kalat*, Vol. IV, Richard Bentley, London, 1844.

Maunsel, E.B., *Prince of Wales's Own; The Scinde Horse*, pub. privately, 1926.

Napier, Priscilla, *Raven Castle; Charles Napier in India 1844–51*, Michael Russell, Salisbury, 1991.

Napier, William, *The History of General Sir Charles Napier's Conquest of Sindhe*, 2nd edn., Charles Westerton, London, 1857.

——— *The History of General Sir Charles Napier's Administration of Sindh*, Charles Westerton, London, 1854.

Outram, James, *Rough Notes on the campaign in Sinde and Afghanistan*, J.M. Richardson, London, 1840.

Pottinger, Henry, *Travels in Beloochistan and Sinde: accompanied by a geographical and historical account of those countries*, Hurst, Rees, Orme and Brown, London, 1816.

Robertson, Brian, *The Road to Kabul. The Second Afghan War, 1878–1881*, Arms and Armour Press, London, 1986.

Roe, Andrew M., *Waging War in Waziristan*, University Press of Kansas, Kansas City, 2010.

Shand, Alexander Innes, *General John Jacob*, Seeley and Co., London, 1900.

Spear, Percival, ed., *Oxford History of India*, Clarendon Press, Oxford, 1958.

Spring, F.W.H., *The Bombay Artillery List of Officers*, William Clowes & Sons, Ltd., London, 1902.

Thornton, Thomas Henry, *Colonel Sir Robert Sandeman, his life and work on our Indian Frontier*, John Murray, London, 1895, reprinted with an introduction by Sir Ronald Wingate, Oxford University Press, Karachi, 1979.

Trotter, Lionel J., *The Bayard of India; A Life of General Sir James Outram, Bart.*, William Blackwood and Sons, Edinburgh and London, 1903.

Tucker, A.L.P., *Sir Robert G. Sandeman, K.S.I.E., Peaceful Conqueror of Baluchistan*, Society for Promoting Christian Knowledge, London, 1921.

Ure, John, *Shooting Leave. Spying on Central Asia in the Great Game*, Constable, London, 2009.

Webb, E.A.H., *A History of the 17th (The Leicestershire) Regiment*, 2nd Edn., Vacher and Sons, Ltd., London, 1912.

Whitteridge, Gordon, *Charles Masson of Afghanistan. Explorer, Archaeologist, and Intelligence Agent*. Orchid Press, Bangkok, 2002.

Williams, Charles Reynolds, *The Defence of Kahan*, W.H.Allen & Co, London, 1886.

Yapp, Malcolm E., *Strategies of British India: Britain, Iran and Afghanistan 1793–1850*. Clarendon Press, Oxford, 1980.

—— "*The Legend of the Great Game*", Proceedings of the British Academy, No. 111, London, 2000.

Yorke, Edmund, *Playing the Great Game. Britain, War and Politics in Afghanistan since 1839*. Robert Hale, London, 2012.

Private Papers and Correspondance

Thomas George Baring, 1st Earl of Northbrook (IOC,BL).

Richard Southwell Bourke, 6th Earl of Mayo (Cambridge University Library).

George Douglas Campbell, 8th Duke of Argyll (India Office Collections, British Library).

Robert Arthur Talbot Gascoyne Cecil, 3rd Marquess of Salisbury (Christ Church Library, University of Oxford *and, in microfilm*, (IOC,BL).

John Jacob and Henry Bartle Frere (SOAS, University of London).

Sir John Lawrence, 1st Baron Lawrence (IOC,BL).

Edward Robert Bulwer Lytton, 1st Earl of Lytton (IOL,BL).

Sir James Outram (National Army Museum).

Henry Petty-Fitzmaurice, 5th Marquess of Lansdowne (IOC,BL).

James Andrew Brown Ramsay, 1st Marquess Dalhousie (Scottish Record Office).

Sir Charles Wood, 1st Viscount Halifax (IOC, BL).

SELECT BIBLIOGRAPHY

Official Papers and Correspondance, India Office Records (IOC, BL)

India Foreign and Political Proceedings, Range 203–204.

India Foreign Proceedings Range, 437–438 (1867–70).

India Foreign Proceedings, Vols 758–1036 (1871–77).

Secret Letters from Bengal and India, Vols 39–42 (1854–59).

Enclosures to Secret Letters received from India, Vols 137–176 (1854–65).

Secret Letters and enclosures received from India, Vols 1–19 (1866–74).

Political and Secret Letters and Enclosures received from India, Vols 1–14 (1875–77).

Political Letters received from India, Vols 23–34 (1854–58).

Political and Secret Letters from India, No. 7/71 (1893).

Drafts and Precoms, Vols 149–170 (1854–58).

Political Letters sent to India, Vols 19–25 (1854–58).

Political Despatches to India, Vols 1–17 (1858–74).

Political and Secret Despatches to India, Vols 1–3 (1874–77).

Bombay Political Proceedings, Range 394–441 (1854–70).

Bombay Political Proceedings, Vols 478–1128 (1871–77).

Political Letters received from Bombay, Vols 1–10 (1859–74).

Political and Secret Letters and Enclosures received from Bombay, Vols 1–7 (1875–77).

Political Letters sent to Bombay, Vols 16–20 (1858–74).

Political Despatches to Bombay, Vols 1–14 (1858–74).

Political and Secret Despatches to Bombay, Vols 1 & 2 (1875–78).

INDEX

INDEX